CONSTITUTIONAL ACTORS IN THE UK CONSTITUTION

This book brings together leading experts on the United Kingdom's constitutional arrangements to show how the constitution works, the role played by actors, and the scope for reform.

The experts are practitioners from the fields of law and politics, and include former judges, ministers and law officers, parliamentarians, a law commissioner, barristers, a former clerk of the House of Commons, Lord Speaker, First Minister of Wales, and the Prime Minster of New Zealand. Each contributor has been, or is, a constitutional actor and their chapter draws upon this unique first-hand experience.

In addition to contributions on the UK Constitution, there are three comparative chapters that explore constitutional reform in Jamaica, and the constitutions of Denmark and New Zealand. The chapters explore issues and themes such as devolution, protecting standards in public life, breaches of political trust and the role of the law, House of Lords reform, the role of the law officers, the role of the Law Commission, the Supreme Court as a Constitutional Court, and the experiences of those working in Parliament. Constitutional Actors in the UK Constitution will be of interest to those working in politics, the law or the civil service, academics who teach and research in politics or law, postgraduate and undergraduate students, and members of the public looking to learn more about the constitution.

Constitutional Actors in the UK Constitution

Edited by Chris Monaghan

•HART•
OXFORD • LONDON • NEW YORK • NEW DELHI • SYDNEY

HART PUBLISHING
Bloomsbury Publishing Plc
Kemp House, Chawley Park, Cumnor Hill, Oxford, OX2 9PH, UK
1385 Broadway, New York, NY 10018, USA
Bloomsbury Publishing Ireland Limited, 29 Earlsfort Terrace, Dublin 2, D02 AY28, Ireland

HART PUBLISHING, the Hart/Stag logo, BLOOMSBURY and the Diana logo are trademarks of
Bloomsbury Publishing Plc
First published in Great Britain 2026

1

A catalogue record for this book is available from the British Library.

A catalogue record for this book is available from the Library of Congress.

Library of Congress Control Number: 2026030540

ISBN: HB: 978-1-5099-8876-1
ePDF: 978-1-5099-8878-5
ePub: 978-1-5099-8877-8

Typeset by Lumina Datamatics Ltd

For product safety related questions contact productsafety@bloomsbury.com

To find out more about our authors and books visit www.hartpublishing.co.uk.
Here you will find extracts, author information, details of forthcoming events and
the option to sign up for our newsletters.

FOREWORD

This book is a notable collection of essays by experts in the often tendentious discussions about the indefinable relationship between those who rule and those who are ruled. Of course, that sentence in itself is problematic, as with no exception those who run the country and decide upon the making and interpretation of laws are themselves ruled in some ways. That this applies even to the Royal Family has been shown starkly in early 2026.

Without a documented constitution we work with an unwritten living instrument, in the opinion of many a settlement more suited to a fast-changing world in which rights come and go at a pace not experienced in the past: this is clearly illustrated by the breathtakingly urgent discussions about artificial intelligence, and also about access for the young to certain internet spaces.

The contributions to this book are provided by experts who have spent their lives in their named sub-specialties. They provide remarkable insights – for example, into the role of civil servants, the process of criminal courts and inquiries, the holding of parliamentarians to account for actual or perceived impropriety and misdeeds, and the form and purposes of the House of Lords. As a barrister, former MP and a current cross-bench peer, I recognise the difficulty of providing such insights without raising yet more questions. How do we reconcile the undemocratic composition of the House of Lords with the undoubted fact that it is a more effective scrutineer of draft legislation than the elected 'other place'? On all the issues discussed, how far can apparently fair and successful pragmatism be a substitute for more logical conceptual thinking?

I have enjoyed the privilege of reading the essays before publication. The first chapter is a fascinating introduction by the book's editor, Dr Chris Monaghan. He sets out the historical and legal context, and in doing so rightly denies any oblique cause behind the volume other than to inform readers on key and fascinating legal policy issues of our time.

One of those issues is the role of the media in relation to criminal trials – about which Sir John Saunders' chapter is a profound and provocative exploration of one of the dark parts of the trial process.

Another challenge, and very fundamental, is whether now substantial statutory law or the common law has done more than pay lip service to clearly defining equality. As Karon Monaghan KC argues in the book's fascinating and persuasive final chapter, so far as case law is concerned there is little sign of even the barest principle of equality. Such principle as can be found of equal treatment falls far short of being a building block in the development of a common law principle of substantive.

The book should be required reading at all levels, from cabinet ministers and senior civil servants to students and interested members of the public. The careful combination of accurate factual information and well-expressed opinions will benefit all readers.

Alex Carlile
Lord Carlile of Berriew CBE KC LLD(Hon)

ACKNOWLEDGEMENTS

An edited book relies upon a lot of goodwill. The contributors to this volume all kindly agreed to contribute a chapter notwithstanding their already substantial work commitments. What arises as a result of the contributions is a variety of different views about the roles of constitutional actors and the UK's constitution. The book was intended to be eclectic in the sense that it is not a textbook on the workings of the UK's constitution, and the contributors would be given the intellectual freedom to develop their perspectives on constitutional actors and the constitution. I would like to thank the contributors for their support. Editing this book from the initial conception of the idea right through to the final edits has been an enjoyable experience mainly because of the generosity and good humour of the contributors.

A massive thank you must go to the team at Hart Publishing. Kate Whetter, the senior commissioning editor, has been nothing but supportive throughout the entire process. Likewise, I would like to thank Verity Stuart, Sasha Jawed, Vicki Hillyard, Linda Goss and the rest of the team at Hart Publishing.

I would like to thank my colleagues at the University of Worcester for their support. Finally, I would like to thank my family for their support and encouragement whilst I worked on this project.

This book is dedicated to Katherine and Rebecca.

Chris Monaghan
Worcester
January 2026

CONTENTS

PART III
THE EXECUTIVE

PART IV
JUDGES, LAW REFORMERS AND LAWYERS

PART V
DESIGNING CONSTITUTIONS

PART VI
COMPARATIVE PERSPECTIVES

LIST OF CONTRIBUTORS

Richard Albert is the Hines H Baker and Thelma Kelley Baker Chair in Law, Professor of Government, and Director of Constitutional Studies at the University of Texas at Austin.

Jack Simson Caird is Deputy Counsel for Justice and Constitutional Affairs in the House of Commons.

Sir Ross Cranston is Professor of Law at the London School of Economics and Political Science, and was formerly a judge of the High Court, Queen's Bench Division, a Member of Parliament, and served as the Solicitor-General for England and Wales.

Daniel Greenberg CB is the Parliamentary Commissioner for Standards, House of Commons, UK Parliament.

Robert Hazell is Professor of Government and the Constitution in the Department of Political Science and School of Public Policy at University College London. He was the founding Director of the Constitution Unit.

Jeremy Horder is Professor of Criminal Law at the London School of Economics and Political Science and was formerly a Law Commissioner for England and Wales.

Sir Malcolm Jack was formerly the Clerk of the House of Commons.

The Rt Hon the Lord Jones of Penybont was formerly the First Minister of Wales and is a Professor in Law at Aberystwyth University.

Matthew Lloyd is a political science academic at the School of Politics and International Relations, Queen Mary University of London.

Chris Monaghan is a Principal Lecturer in Law at the University of Worcester.

Karon Monaghan KC is a member of Matrix Chambers, London.

Aidan O'Neill KC is a member of Matrix Chambers, London.

Rt Hon Sir Geoffrey Palmer KC, KCMG, AC, PC is a Distinguished Fellow, Te Herenga Waka, at the Faculty of Law and Centre for Public Law, Victoria University of Wellington. He was formerly the Prime Minister of New Zealand.

Gillian Peele is an Emeritus Fellow Lady Margaret Hall, Oxford and a member of the Committee on Standards in Public Life.

Sir John Saunders was formerly a judge of the High Court, King's Bench Division.

Henrik Skovgaard-Petersen is Head of the Legal Department, Prime Minister's Office, Denmark and was formerly the Head of the Constitutional and Human Rights Law Division at the Danish Ministry of Justice.

The Rt Hon the Baroness D'Souza CMG was formerly the Speaker of the House of Lords.

Gisela Stuart (The Rt Hon the Baroness Stuart of Edgbaston) is the First Civil Service Commissioner and was formerly a Member of Parliament and Parliamentary Under-Secretary at the Department of Health.

Alison Young is a member of the Law Commission for England and Wales and is the Law Commissioner for Public Law and the Law in Wales, Sir David Williams Professor of Public Law, University of Cambridge and a Fellow of Robinson College, Cambridge.

TABLE OF CASES

England and Wales/Scotland/Northern Ireland/United Kingdom

Privy Council

Court of Justice of the European Union

European Court of Human Rights

International Court of Justice

New Zealand

United States

TABLE OF LEGISLATION

United Kingdom

Scotland

Wales

Council of Europe

Australia

Denmark

New Zealand

1

Giving a Voice to Constitutional Actors and the UK's Constitution

CHRIS MONAGHAN

1.1 Introduction

The UK's constitution is very much a strange beast. Depending on your view as to what is required and the definition that you employ, the UK either seemingly lacks a constitution and thus is masquerading as having one (relying on a mixture of history, convention, prerogatives, and the common law to justify the existence of a constitution), or it does in fact have a constitution and to argue otherwise is pedantic and misses the point.[1] As FF Ridley, who held the former view, observed in the late 1980s:

> Though there is broad agreement on the contents of such books on constitutional law, in the last resort it depends on what academic lawyers consider relevant—and a quick survey of standard textbooks will show that at the margins there are significant variations in what is brought into the orbit of the British "constitution". In the absence of legal criteria that distinguish constitutional law from other laws, the definition become so broad that it defines nothing at all. In the context of the British legal system, the term constitutional law is thus literally meaningless.[2]

A similar view was articulated by the English-born radical and supporter of the American War of Independence, Thomas Paine in *The Rights of Man*. Paine's book was intended as a critique of Edmund Burke, the Whig parliamentarian, philosopher, and the man responsible for the impeachment of Warren Hastings, the former Governor-General of Bengal in 1787 (with the impeachment trial lasting from 1788 to 1795). Burke was an early critic of the French Revolution and this forced him to break his friendship and political partnership with the leader of the Foxite Whigs in Parliament, Charles James Fox MP.

[1] See the different views of two former Presidents of the UK Supreme Court: Lord Neuberger, 'UK Supreme Court decisions on private and commercial law: The role of public policy and public interest', Centre for Commercial Law Studies Conference 2015 (4 December 2015) and Lady Hale, 'The United Kingdom Constitution on the move' The Canadian Institute for Advanced Legal Studies' Cambridge Lecture 2017 (7 July 2017).

[2] FF Ridley, 'There is no British Constitution: A Dangerous Case of the Emperor's Clothes' (1988) 41 *Parliamentary Affairs* 340, 341.

Thomas Paine denied that Britain had a constitution and called upon Edmund Burke to prove him wrong:

> But it will be first necessary to define what is meant by a Constitution. It is not sufficient that we adopt the word; we must fix also a standard signification to it. A constitution is not a thing in name only, but in fact. It has not an ideal, but a real existence; and wherever it cannot be produced in a visible form, there is none… Can, then, Mr. Burke produce the English Constitution? If he cannot, we may fairly conclude that though it has been so much talked about, no such thing as a constitution exists, or ever did exist, and consequently that the people have yet a constitution to form.'[3]

The caricaturist James Gillray parodied the dispute between Paine and Burke in his caricature, 'The Rights of Man; -or- Tommy Paine, the little American taylor, taking the measure of the crown, for a new pair of Revolution-breeches', published in May 1791.[4] Gillray who himself was a critic of the French Revolution and would later be paid to create caricatures hostile to the Revolution in the *Anti-Jacobin Magazine*, depicts Paine dressed in rags sizing up the Crown with a tape measure, saying inter alia, 'I would soon stitch up the mouth of that Barnacled Edmund from making of any more Reflections upon the Flints - & so Flints & Liberty for ever & damn the Dungs.'

The existence and status of the British constitution was in dispute. Burke in his critique of the French Revolution, *Reflections on the Revolution in France*, had argued that England had a constitution that had been defended through the revolution of 1688. The constitution was an inheritance that was the product of hard-fought liberties:

> The Revolution was made to preserve our *ancient* indisputable laws and liberties, and that *ancient* constitution of government which is our only security for law and liberty… You will observe, that, from Magna Charta to the Declaration of Right, it has been the uniform policy of our Constitution to claim and assert our liberties as an *entailed inheritance* derived to us from our forefathers, and to be transmitted to our posterity,— as an estate specially belonging to the people of this kingdom, without any reference whatever to any other more general or prior right. By this means our Constitution preserves an unity in so great a diversity of its parts. We have an inheritable crown, an inheritable peerage, and a House of Commons and a people inheriting privileges, franchises, and liberties from a long line of ancestors.[5]

Such an argument would still have credence today, with much of the constitution dependent on the settlement of 1688–89.

Even if it is accepted that the UK does in fact have a constitution, then critics will often make the case for reform, codification, or that the existing constitution has been proved to be unsatisfactory due to the challenges of Brexit and in

[3] *The Rights of Man, The Writings of Thomas Paine*, Vol 2 (1779–92).
[4] Published by Hannah Humphrey, 23 May 1791, 18 Old Bold Street, London.
[5] Edmund Burke, *Reflections on the Revolution in France* (first published 1790).

particular the Johnson Government.[6] Examples include Andrew Blick's *Stretching the Constitution: The Brexit Shock in Historic Perspective*[7] and Catherine Haddon's critique that, 'the process of Brexit has done lasting damage to the constitution'.[8] In their report for the Constitution Society, 'Brexit and the Melting of the British Constitution', Andrew Blick and Peter Hennessy observed that, 'The British constitution seems to be in a more molten condition now than at any other point in anyone's lived lifetime.'[9] Likewise Lisa James makes the point that the premiership of Boris Johnson (2019–22) was detrimental to the Executive's respect for constitutional checks and balances.[10] Hannah White's assessment of the Johnson administration has demonstrated the vulnerability of the UK's constitution.[11]

1.2 The Scope of the Book

This book is *not* concerned with these arguments. What it is concerned with is how the constitution of the UK actually operates on a day-to-day basis and first-hand perspectives on what works well, where reform may be required, and the role played by key individuals and institutions. In the absence of a written constitution, and the emphasis on the need for 'good chaps',[12] self-restraint, a 'dash of principle',[13] and the necessity to accept the existing constitutional norms, the role of the individual becomes increasingly significant. This book seeks to offer an account of the individual's relationship and understanding of the constitution, their role within

[6] See the argument for constitutional reform by R Gordon, *Repairing British Politics: A Blueprint for Constitutional Reform*, 2nd edn (Hart Publishing, 2025); R Blackburn, 'Enacting a Written Constitution for the United Kingdom' (2015) 36 *Statute Law Reform* 1. See also Aileen McHarg, 'Reforming the United Kingdom constitution: Law, convention, soft law' (2008) 71 *Modern Law Review* 853; JE Khushal Murkens, 'A written constitution: a case not made' (2021) 41 *Oxford Journal of Legal Studies* 965; A Kavanagh, *The Collaborative Constitution* (Cambridge University Press, 2023); and C Monaghan, 'Muddling-Through Constitutionalism: The Importance of the Relationship Between the Monarch and the Prime Minister' in M De Visser et al (eds), *European Yearbook of Constitutional Law 2024: Varieties of Constitutionalism* (Springer, 2025).

[7] Hart Publishing, 2019.

[8] C Haddon, 'The Brexit battle is fundamentally changing the constitution' (Institute for Government, 2 September 2019), www.instituteforgovernment.org.uk/article/comment/brexit-battle-fundamentally-changing-constitution.

[9] A Blick and P Hennessy, 'Brexit and the Melting of the British Constitution' (The Constitution Society), https://consoc.org.uk/wp-content/uploads/2019/07/Blick-and-Hennessy-Brexit-and-the-Melting-of-the-British-Constitution.pdf. See also A Blick, 'The constitutional consequences of Mr. Johnson' (The Constitution Society, 7 July 2022), https://consoc.org.uk/the-consequences-of-johnson.

[10] L James, 'The Johnson legacy: the UK constitution' (UK in a Changing Europe, 1 September 2022), https://ukandeu.ac.uk/the-johnson-legacy-the-uk-constitution.

[11] H White, 'What Boris Johnson taught us about the UK constitution' *Prospect* (17 August 2022), www.prospectmagazine.co.uk/politics/38876/what-boris-johnson-taught-us-about-the-uk-constitution.

[12] See A Blick and P Hennessy, 'Good Chaps No More? Safeguarding the Constitution in Stressful Times' (The Constitution Society, 18 November 2019), https://consoc.org.uk/publications/good-chaps-no-more-safeguarding-the-constitution-in-stressful-times-by-andrew-blick-and-peter-hennessy.

[13] See D Woodhouse, 'Individual Ministerial Responsibility and a "Dash of Principle"' in D Butler, V Bogdanor and R Summers (eds), *The Law, Politics, and the Constitution: Essays in Honour of Geoffrey Marshall* (Oxford University Press, 1999) 102–30.

it, the challenges that they encountered, and at times a critical assessment of the workability of institutions as constitutional actors. The contributors are (or have been) constitutional actors or have worked for (or worked with) a constitutional actor and are drawn from a range of disciplines and professions. Some contributors have previously been elected by voters; however, most were not and were either appointed, or in the case of academics and lawyers, have developed a reputation that allows them to be included within the managing, or rather the regulation of the constitution.

These actors represent politicians, ministers, civil servants, academics who have served on the Law Commission of England and Wales, lawyers who regularly appear before the Supreme Court, those engaged in constitutional reform or scrutiny, as well as those who have held the highest office in government.

Many of the contributors have held a number of roles, for example Sir Ross Cranston was a Member of Parliament, served as Solicitor-General (1998–2001) and upon his retirement from politics was appointed as a High Court judge in 2007. Traditionally, such appointments had been standard practice, as the Attorney-General could be expected to be appointed as Lord Chief Justice of England upon standing down, if a vacancy arose. As James Hand notes, 'the nineteenth-century tradition was that the Attorney-General would have a judicial rather than a ministerial career, with 60% going on to hold high judicial office – or 70% if including the Lord Chancellorship.'[14] The last Attorney-General to become a judge was Sir Donald Sommervell in 1946.[15] Hand notes that a similar trend can be seen with Solicitor-Generals, with just three former Solicitor-Generals being appointed as a judge since 1951.[16] Cranston's appointment to the High Court was significant in the fact that today it is difficult (although not impossible) to see this repeated, in light of the toxicity of the Brexit years.[17] Other contributors too have held a variety of different roles, with Sir Geoffrey Palmer KC serving in a variety of positions such as New Zealand's Attorney-General, Minister of Justice, Minister of the Environment, and finally Prime Minister. The current UK Prime Minister, Sir Keir Starmer KC MP (himself not a contributor to this book), had worked as a civil servant in his role as the Director of Public Prosecutions.

It can often be tempting to think of institutions and the big events when addressing the workings of the UK's constitution. The public may have their attention drawn to constitutional matters only when something has gone wrong, or is proving to be politically controversial, which makes for a good headline in the press. One such example of this is the media coverage of *R (on the application of Miller) v Secretary of State for Exiting the European Union (Miller No 1)*,[18] which is known as the 'Article 50' case, as

[14] J Hand, 'The Attorney-General, politics and logistics – a fork in the road?' (2022) 42 *Legal Studies* 425, 430.

[15] ibid.

[16] ibid, fn 32.

[17] See for example J Rozenberg, 'Judges need help to counter the dark arts' *The Law Society Gazette* (9 September 2025), www.lawgazette.co.uk/commentary-and-opinion/judges-need-help-to-counter-the-dark-arts/5124395.article.

[18] [2016] EWHC 2768 (Admin).

it concerned the question of whether the Prime Minister, Theresa May, could use the royal prerogative to trigger Article 50 of the Treaty on the Functioning of the European Union. The High Court[19] and Supreme Court[20] held that this was not the case. Whilst the *Daily Mail's* 'Enemies of the People' headline from 4 November 2016[21] stoked controversy and within 12 days saw the Independent Press Standards Organisation receive over 1,000 complaints,[22] other headlines were similarly aggressive in tone, such as *The Telegraph's* 'The judges versus the people',[23] and the *Daily Express*, which declared, 'Three judges yesterday blocked Brexit, now your country really does need you… We Must Get Out of the EU'.[24] These headlines all related to the High Court's decision: the press coverage of the subsequent Supreme Court decision was more restrained.[25]

In terms of the 'big events' – such as Brexit, the devolution settlement, the referendum on Scottish independence in 2014, and the prorogation of Parliament – these events will garner considerable media coverage, and the press will bring in experts to help explain the constitutional dimension or to ignite debate between different studio guests. It is questionable just how many people (outside of Parliament and government) had heard of prorogation (or had given it much thought) before 2019, or understood how this differed from the dissolution of Parliament.

Alongside these political 'big events', in recent years the family drama of the House of Windsor has played out and received considerable attention – this in terms of the constitution rather the dynamics of one family, touches upon who should be a Counsellor of State,[26] the revocation of a royal title (and how this can be achieved),[27] and the status of the King's wife.[28]

[19] ibid.

[20] *R (on the application of Miller) v Secretary of State for Exiting the European Union (Miller No 1)* [2017] UKSC 5.

[21] 4 November 2016.

[22] R Pells, 'Daily Mail's "Enemies of the People" front page receives more than 1,000 complaints to IPSO' *Independent* (10 November 2016), www.independent.co.uk/news/media/daily-mail-nazi-propaganda-front-page-ipso-complaints-brexit-eu-enemies-of-the-people-a7409836.html.

[23] P Dominiczak, C Hope and K McCann, 'Judges vs the people: Government ministers resigned to losing appeal against High Court ruling' *The Telegraph* (3 November 2016), www.telegraph.co.uk/news/2016/11/03/the-plot-to-stop-brexit-the-judges-versus-the-people.

[24] 'After judges' Brexit block now your country really needs you: We MUST get out of the EU' *Express* (4 November 2016), www.express.co.uk/comment/expresscomment/728602/Brexit-judges-block-leave-EU-referendum-High-Court.

[25] R Greenslade, 'How the press reacted to the article 50 verdict' *The Guardian* (24 January 2017), www.theguardian.com/politics/2017/jan/24/article-50-how-press-front-page-supreme-court-verdict.

[26] See the Counsellors of State Act 2022 which was enacted to prevent the possibility that Andrew Mountbatten-Windsor (formerly Prince Andrew, the Duke of York) or Prince Harry, the Duke of Sussex would be required to act as a Counsellor of State on behalf of the King. The Counsellors of State Act 2022 provides for Prince Edward, the Duke of Edinburgh, and Princess Anne, the Princess Royal to be Counsellors of State.

[27] In 2025 there were demands from the public and politicians that Andrew Mountbatten-Windsor have both his Dukedom of York and title of Prince removed. There was debate over how this could be achieved, and whether this would require legislation (such as the Titles Deprivation Act 1917). The title of Prince was removed by the King using his prerogative in the form of Letters Patent. The Dukedom of York was removed by the King using a Royal Warrant. See D Torrance, 'The removal of titles and honours' Research Briefing (The House of Commons Library, 17 November 2025), available at: https://commonslibrary.parliament.uk/research-briefings/cbp-10370.

[28] C Davies, 'King Charles's coronation invitation confirms use of title of "Queen Camilla" *The Guardian* (4 April 2023).

Despite this attention, much of the constitution, those who play key roles within it, and its workings are shrouded (to some degree) in mystery.

1.3 Constitutional Actors

This book is focused not on the institutions or the big event that ignites public attention and a media circus, but rather on the individual actors. It is the constitutional actor that takes centre stage in this volume, rather than purely academic perspectives on the constitution. But the question is how to define those who are constitutional actors? As Stephanie Reynolds has argued:

> The term 'constitutional actor' is not explicitly defined in the constitutional literature. This is surprising given how commonly it is used and the constitutional implications that accompany the label, including its links to the assumption of a constitutional role and the accompanying expectation of constitutional safeguards in relation to the exercise of constitutional functions.[29]

The phrase 'constitutional actor' is indeed frequently used, typically when discussing the role of constitutional conventions and the role of constitutional actors in observing the convention or ensuring its compliance.[30] It is typically taken to be those with an active role within the constitution – as epitomised by the key players (ministers, parliamentarians and judges). It is hardly surprising that individuals might feel awkward wearing the label 'constitutional actor' given the somewhat grandiose nature of the term. Slightly overlapping with constitutional actors is the idea of constitutional guardians, which are individuals and institutions that are required to 'oversee, monitor and uphold different parts of the constitution and collectively protect the democratic integrity of the governance of the UK'.[31] These guardians can be distinguished between those who are core guardians, auxiliary guardians, and tertiary guardians.[32] As Dawn Oliver has observed, the lack of a codified constitution 'presents something of a puzzle for those seeking authoritative sources for the meaning of "constitutional" and thus for constitutional guardianship'.[33] This point applies as much to 'constitutional actors' as it does 'constitutional guardians'.

For the purposes of this volume a constitutional actor is someone who plays an active role in the UK's constitutional arrangements (or the constitutional

[29] S Reynolds, 'The high-profile private individual as constitutional actor' (2025) 36 *King's Law Journal* 104, 109.

[30] See for example A Perry and A Tucker, 'Top-Down Constitutional Conventions' (2018) 81 *Modern Law Review* 765.

[31] M Thimont Jack and Jack Pannell, 'Constitutional Guardians', Bennett Institute for Public Policy and the Institute for Government (November 2022) 4, www.instituteforgovernment.org.uk/sites/default/files/publications/constitutional-guardians.pdf.

[32] ibid.

[33] D Oliver, 'Constitutional Guardians: The House of Lords' (The Constitution Society, 2015) 8, https://consoc.org.uk/wp-content/uploads/2015/12/COSJ3942_Constitutional_guardians_WEB.pdf.

arrangement of another country, in the case of three of the contributors to this volume). Thus, they play a part in the workings of the constitution. Theirs is an active role, which regardless of size, scope, or public recognition of their job, renders them a constitutional actor. This is quite a broad definition and is deliberately so. It is a top-down and bottom-up approach. A senior civil servant advising a government minister is as much a constitutional actor as the minister, irrespective of how much power each has or the autonomy to make decisions that have constitutional implications.

The question is how to define a constitutional actor beyond a description as an individual who plays an active role in the UK's constitutional arrangements. Their roles are linked to the constitution and the operation of the state. Using power as a starting point, we have individuals concerned with the three classic powers: the executive; the legislative; and the judiciary. In terms of the executive power, this includes the political actors: the Prime Minister, cabinet ministers, junior ministers, the government's law officers, and political advisors, as well as the monarch in their ceremonial role and exercise of their three rights as outlined by Walter Bagehot in *The English Constitution*.[34] For the devolved nations the political actors include the First Ministers and those holding ministerial office and equivalent. Beneath the political actors are those individuals that advise or ensure the effective running of the executive. These are the civil service, that is often unfairly dismissed as the 'blob',[35] which, crucially since the Northcote-Trevelyan Report of 1854 and the reforms that it introduced, is non-political.[36]

In terms of the legislative power, this incudes parliamentarians from both Houses of Parliament, members of the Senedd Cymru, the Scottish Parliament, and the Northern Ireland Assembly. In addition to the political actors[37] who are concerned with lawmaking, scrutiny, and in some cases constituency work, there are individuals who are constitutional actors and serve inter alia as clerks, parliamentary officials, those appointed to scrutinise the conduct of members, legal advisors to select committees and those that draft legislation. Their role is to ensure the effective operation of the legislative function. There are also individuals appointed to institutions created by Parliament, such as Law Commissioners and Ombudsman. Finally, in terms of the judicial power, there are the judiciary

[34] 'The sovereign has, under a constitutional monarchy such as ours, three rights— the right to be consulted, the right to encourage, the right to warn': W Bagehot, *The English Constitution* (Chapman and Hall, 1867) 103.

[35] See P Seddon, 'Calling us the Blob is insulting, says top civil servant' BBC News (12 July 2023), www.bbc.co.uk/news/uk-politics-66174373.

[36] See for example J Heywood (Sir), 'Timeless values in an age of change' Civil Service Blog (24 May 2015), https://civilservice.blog.gov.uk/2015/05/24/timeless values - -in-an-age-of-change. The then Head of the Civil Service observed that 'the report, and the Commission that followed, was a vital catalyst for a permanent, meritocratic Civil Service, based on the guiding principles of integrity, honesty, objectivity and political impartiality that we still adhere to today'. See also 'The Northcote-Trevelyan Report' (1954) 32 *Public Administration* 1 (this is a reprint of the report).

[37] Although it is important to note the Church of England's representation in the House of Lords and those members of the House of Lords who are crossbenchers.

and members of tribunals. Lawyers too are constitutional actors, as they play an important role in facilitating the administration of justice and, especially in the case of counsel, can via their submissions have an impact on the constitution. This is by no means exhaustive nor is it intended to be. For instance, legal academics and journalists could perhaps be regarded as constitutional actors depending on their role and impact.[38] Equally, there is the potential for a private individual to be a constitutional actor, such as Marcus Rashford, the Manchester United football player.[39] The classic examples are the journalist Walter Bagehot or the academic AV Dicey.

In public discourse, these constitutional actors have always been important and have had varying degree of name recognition. If we were to make the analogy between constitutional actors and actors (the everyday use of the word), then actors range from Hollywood film stars, right through to those who are a steady fixture on the terrestrial primetime or steaming series dramas, and finally to those large number of individuals whose face we might at times recognise but cannot put a name to. Such an analogy may appear to be somewhat of a stretch, but much of our enjoyment of, and the feasibility of, television, films, and plays is owed to these varied individuals. Yes, some will require no introduction, and others may prompt the viewer to reach for their mobile phone to do a quick internet search in order to ascertain a particular actor's identity.

In terms of fame or infamy, the Prime Minister is the most obvious example of a constitutional actor who most of the public know by name.[40] Even prime ministers who have left office several decades ago are still remembered, even if they eventually, bar a few political and cultural giants, fade into obscurity and the remit of scholarship and the history book. Other senior frontline politicians are well known, often caricatured by satirists, cartoonists, and the press, as are other politicians who may lack office, but who have developed notoriety through their work or media engagement. Most politicians will be relatively unknown. According to the Hansard Society in 2013, only 22 per cent of those interviewed were able to name the Member of Parliament for their constituency.[41]

[38] For example see N Barber, T Hickman and J King, 'Pulling the Article 50 "Trigger": Parliament's Indispensable Role' (UK Constitutional Law Association, 27 June 2016), https://ukconstitutionallaw.org/2016/06/27/nick-barber-tom-hickman-and-jeff-king-pulling-the-article-50-trigger-parliaments-indispensable-role. See also L Lazarus, 'Constitutional Scholars as Constitutional Actors' (2020) 48 *Federal Law Review* 483. As Lazarus observes at 484, 'While formal constitutional recognition of constitutional scholars may be a step too far, the purpose of this article is to explore the idea of constitutional scholars as analogous to integrity institutions. The analogy is made because of the facilitative role of the constitutional academy to "well-functioning constitutionalism" and because of its constitutive role in shaping constitutions and constitutional doctrine.'

[39] See S Reynolds, 'The high-profile private individual as constitutional actor' (2025) 36 *King's Law Journal* 104-145.

[40] For example, in a 2002 survey, all but 11% of respondents could name a then world leader, with 83% naming Tony Blair. See 'Britons "fail to name key figures"' BBC News (22 October 2002), http://news.bbc.co.uk/1/hi/uk/2345355.stm.

[41] 'Three quarters of people "cannot name their local MP"', BBC News (16 May 2013), www.bbc.co.uk/news/uk-politics-22555659.

If we can presume that ordinary Members of Parliament do not enjoy ready name recognition, even within their own constituency, then there is a cohort of politicians who enjoy a strong degree of public recognition. For example, many readers will remember Martin Bell in his white suit, a choice which carried instant recognition as the white suit had been worn since Bell worked for the BBC as a war correspondent.[42] Or indeed George Galloway, the outspoken critic of the Labour Government, Betty Boothroyd as the Speaker of the House of Commons, and Diane Abbott perhaps through watching *This Week* where she appeared as a regular commentator alongside Michael Portillo. As has been observed, the acquisition of celebrity is useful in furthering a political career:

> Celebrity, then, can be seen as important for democracy as aesthetic 'likeness' is a central part of any 'representative' democratic system. Moreover, in an age of anti-politics, politicians are more likely to reach out to disaffected voters via what Turner (2004: 94) calls 'democratainment' as 'the consumption of celebrity has become a part of everyday life in the twenty-first century.[43]

The vast majority of constitutional actors are however unknown to most people as individuals, yet in public discourse we have the judiciary (with its myths and stereotypes, which Penny Darbyshire has sought to address through her research),[44] the civil services (stereotyped unflatteringly as the blob,[45] or for older members of the public by the television shows *Yes Minister/Yes Prime Minister*). In recent years the Brexit, Scottish independence and COVID-19 dramas have made Brenda Hale,[46] John Bercow,[47] Sue Gray, Ruth Davidson, Nicola Sturgeon, Matt Hancock,[48] and Chris Whitty to some extent household names. It is not just the public that might be skewed towards having more awareness of the big players and big events. Brian Christopher Jones highlights the obsession of legal academics with the big events: 'Just as the masses continue to queue at cinemas worldwide for epic superhero battles of good versus evil, legal scholarship remains obsessed with classic battles

[42] See for example, A Barnett, 'Sleaze, scandal and the man in the white suit' *The Guardian* (16 May 2004), www.theguardian.com/politics/2004/may/16/uk.eu. Few followers of current affairs in 2004 would not have known that the article concerned Martin Bell and his political reputation for taking on political sleaze. Indeed, Bell's famous white suit was auctioned for charity in 2013; see 'A Frontline home for Bell's iconic white suite' *The Standard* (25 January 2013), www.standard.co.uk/news/londoners-diary/a-frontline-home-for-bell-s-iconic-white-suit-8467541.html.

[43] M Wood, J Corbett and M Flinders, 'Just like us: Everyday celebrity politicians and the pursuit of popularity in an age of anti-politics' (2016) 18 *The British Journal of Politics and International Relations* 581, 594.

[44] P Darbyshire, *Sitting in Judgment: The Working Lives of Judges* (Hart Publishing, 2011).

[45] Seddon (n 34).

[46] See for example L Cochrane and M Belam, 'Say it with a brooch: what message was Lady Hale's spider sending?' *The Guardian* (24 September 2019), www.theguardian.com/fashion/2019/sep/24/say-it-with-a-brooch-how-a-fashion-item-became-a-political-statement; and A Sampson, 'Why everyone is talking about Baroness Hale's bejewelled giant spider brooch' *Tatler* (24 September 2019), www.tatler.com/article/baroness-hale-spider-brooch-supreme-court.

[47] The former Speaker of the House of Commons appeared in Season Two of *The Traitors US* in 2024.

[48] The former Health Secretary has appeared in two reality TV shows, *I'm a Celebrity... Get Me Out of Here!* and *Celebrity SAS: Who Dares Wins*.

of constitutional authority: the legislature versus the judiciary, or the judiciary versus the executive.'[49] Jones is critical of legal scholars and argues that 'Just as the film critic can bring a relatively unknown movie to our attention, so should legal scholars be searching beyond legal blockbusters.'[50] He highlights the '"forgotten" constitutional actors' (here the Office of Parliamentary Counsel and Parliamentary Clerks) who are both actors and constitutional guardians.[51]

Yet the reality is that these constitutional actors carry on their work in the large part without much public awareness or recognition as to what their role entails. They keep the constitution and the state functioning and do so in the background of the public consciousness. This is not intended to be a critique of the general public or the actors themselves in how they have communicated their role; rather it is a recognition that we often do not know much about something or someone unless we have the occasion to find out more. In a forum removed from academia, we have television programmes informing us about how goods are made inside factories, the intricacies of repairing antiques or other old items, what happens in hotels, and the realities of being a schoolteacher. Often, we have some idea about certain jobs or processes, but what these programmes do is to shed light on how things work and the importance of the individual or groups of people. There have been to some extent similar documentaries on topics such as the Supreme Court and the role of the Justices. The point is that individuals working within the constitution play an important role and have perspectives that may not be readily apparent.

1.4 The Contributors

The book is intended to be deliberately eclectic in the sense that what it is not, is a primer to understanding the workings of the constitution as a whole, with discrete chapters describing the work of each branch to serve as textbook. Neither is the book intended to be a volume focused on the case for and against constitutional reform. Engagement with reform is something that is inevitability addressed by some contributors, such as the former Lord Speaker reflecting on the arguments for reforming the House of Lords, and where they believe reform should be focused. Rather the focus is on the experiences and viewpoints of the contributors and their unique perspectives. Each contributor has chosen to place their emphasis on either the need for reform (based upon their experiences), the workability of the current arrangements, the importance of the body that they work for as a constitutional actor (in the case of the Justice Committee or the Law Commission), or the challenges that they encountered whilst in their role (such as the Clerk of

[49] BC Jones, 'Our Forgotten Constitutional Guardians: Preserving Respect for the Law' (2021) 42 *Statute Law Review* 1, 2.
[50] ibid.
[51] ibid.

the House of Commons or the Solicitor-General). Each contributor has been given the intellectual freedom to reflect on the theme of a constitutional actor and what it means. This freedom is essential as it has allowed contributors to focus on what matters to them.

The contributors offer a broad range of experiences and involvement as constitutional actors within their own right, working or advising constitutional actors (such as serving on the Constitutional Reform Committee of Jamaica), or rather as commentators who are best placed to assess the performance of constitutional actors and propose reforms (such as a former Law Commissioner on using the criminal law to prosecute politicians, the former Director of the UCL Constitution Unit on the challenges facing the monarchy, or a leading barrister on the Supreme Court). The genesis of the book was in the value of these first-hand perspectives, and how these powerfully augment academic commentary on the themes raised within the book. The volume deliberately takes a broad view as to the definition of a constitutional actor, as this acknowledges the large number of individuals and institutions that work within (or with authority comment on) the constitution. Given the limitations of undertaking this project as one volume, it is had the consequence of resulting in omissions. Examples include representation from the devolved government and legislature in Scotland and from the Northern Ireland Assembly. Other examples would be the inclusion of more civil servants. Whilst the focus of the book is on the UK, I wanted to include two chapters that would offer comparative perspectives. New Zealand provided an interesting comparator, given the UK and New Zealand both have uncodified constitutions, but also that there are significant political and constitutional differences. Likewise, Denmark, being a liberal democracy and a member of the Council of Europe, which is facing many similar challenges to the UK, provided a useful comparator.

The book is divided into six parts. Part one of the volume address the real concerns that exist about declining public confidence in politicians and the institutions. This declining trust owes a lot to a series of scandals, including the parliamentary expenses scandal from 2009 and the media's reporting of the failings of individual politicians. They each offer a unique perspective from their authors. In chapter two Daniel Greenberg, the Parliamentary Commissioner for Standards, addresses the problem with declining public trust in politicians. Greenberg observes that 'trust between parliamentarians and the public appears to be at an alarmingly low level'. Coupled with this declining level of trust, he highlights the decrease in the number of people willing to vote in elections. Greenberg cites the failure of certain politicians and people in public office to abide by the law during the COVID-19 pandemic and the Post Office Horizon scandal as further causes for the declining in the public's trust of politicians. Greenberg observes that 'Speaking theoretically about trust is both relatively easy and relatively unhelpful' and he explores standards and conduct arrangements in the House of Commons. As he notes, 'This is a very important feature of an ethical regulatory system designed to build trust.' Greenberg argues that arrangements within the House of Commons work and questions why, then, is public trust and confidence so low? Greenberg's answer is twofold: firstly, media attention and thus the public's attention will be drawn to instances of individual misconduct; and secondly, there is scope to improve public trust in politicians by 'helping the public to understand the standards system and how it works'. The latter requires increased public education to counter the media's narrative, which focuses on instances of individual misconduct, as opposed to how the system as a whole works. Greenberg's case is one not of the need to reform the way that the House of Commons is regulated, but rather to seek to improve the standard of education that we offer and to invest in outreach opportunities.

In chapter three Gillian Peele, a member of the Committee on Standards in Public Life, addresses the role of the Committee as a constitutional actor since it was established in 1994. Peele too warns about the dangers of declining public trust and confidence in politicians and institutions. Peele observes that, 'The whole integrity system is still heavily dependent for its efficiency on the compliance of those working the system, on conventions and the values of those who work in the public sector.' She explores the role of the Committee on Standards in Public Life in reforming the way that the House of Commons is regulated in terms of ethics, and the role of the Committee in the creation of the Independent Parliamentary Standards Authority. The Committee plays an important role in trying to improve public confidence which, as Peele observes, was one of the reasons that the Committee recommended that its membership should include lay members to, 'avoid public suspicion that the regulatory procedures are not genuinely independent'. Similarly, the Committee on Standards in Public Life has been instrumental in providing for the regulation of public appointments, with its recommendations leading to the creation of the Commission for Public Appointments. Peele emphasises how the Committee seeks to promote reform, such as its criticism of the current powers of the Independent Advisor on Ministers' Interests in the wake of Sir Alex Allan's resignation. The chapter captures the ebbs and flows of ministerial willingness to improve the ethical regulation of the House of Commons, with Peele noting that controversy surrounding Owen Paterson and the then government's partizan tactics to protect Paterson.

Finally in chapter four, Jeremy Horder, a former Law Commissioner for England and Wales, whose proposals for reform as a Law Commissioner of the law relating to bribery resulted in the Bribery Act 2010, explores how the criminal law can be used to control political wrongdoing. This, unlike the two previous chapters, is concerned with the consequences when there have been serious failings by individual politicians, and not the broader efficacy of the regulation and governance that have been established to regulate ethics in politics. Horder's chapter addresses the suitability of using the criminal law to prosecute politicians. He argues that there is a legitimate place for the criminal law to be used in these circumstances, arguing that 'the application of the criminal law to public decision-making at the highest level should not be barred purely on the grounds that public law remedies seem (from a bureaucratic-administrative point of view) more appropriate'. The main concern of the chapter is the offence of misconduct in public office and how it applies to elected officials. Horder draws upon the US Supreme Court's decision in *US v Trump*[52] and the UK Supreme Court's decision in *R v Chaytor*.[53] He asks when politicians should enjoy immunity from misconduct charges, and draws upon three different classifications of wrongdoing: personal corruption; political corruption; and improper exercises of power.

The chapters in part two are written by individuals who have first-hand experience of working in legislatures. In chapter five Sir Malcolm Jack, the former Clerk of the House of Commons, offers a reflection on the role in the constitution, and draws upon his own first-hand experience. As Jack notes, the role is significant, as the Clerk of the House is 'the principal adviser on procedure and practice to the Speaker of the House and to all MPs'. Former Clerks of the House include John Hatsell and Sir Thomas Erskine May, whose legacy is *Erskine May*, the authoritative rules for parliamentary practice. Jack addresses a number of important areas of parliamentary practice, such as parliamentary privilege. As Jack observes, freedom of speech and debate is 'the most widely acknowledged of Parliament's rights'. He considers the Supreme Court's decision in *R v Chaytor* and why it was significant that the Speaker did not make an intervention. Jack explores how the Parliamentary Standards Bill in 2009 presented a threat to parliamentary privilege and his own contribution in warning that from a constitutional perspective this had worrying implications for parliamentary privilege. To conclude he offers his own view on whether reform is needed.

In chapter six Baroness D'Souza, the former Lord Speaker, considers the thorny issue of House of Lords reform from the perspective on an insider. D'Souza observes that there are arguments against the current composition of the House of Lords, in that it 'is an unelected body – a factor of great contention, provoking calls for a democratically elected second chamber'. However, D'Souza emphasises where the House of Lords can claim to have legitimacy, which is how it engages in the scrutiny and revision of proposed legislation. As D'Souza states, 'Bills leave the Lords in a far better shape than when they arrived!' For her part, D'Souza argues that reform of the House of Lords is needed in order to reform how new members are nominated and to reduce the overall membership of the House of Lords. However, she is in favour of retaining the House of Lords as a second chamber. She states: 'It could be argued that in the absence of a second chamber, something very similar would have to be invented.'

Lord Jones of Penybont, the former First Minister of Wales, offers his perspectives on the Welsh devolution journey from 2011 to 2017. Lord Jones, the former First Minister of Wales, in chapter seven provides a history of devolution in Wales. Looking at the situation before 2011, Lord Jones argues that whilst 'The Government of Wales Act 2006 was undoubtedly a major piece of legislation, creating the path for the later establishment of a fully-fledged legislature although it did not go far enough for many of us at the time.' He then explains the significance of the 2011 referendum whereby Welsh voters were given the choice of

[52] 603 US 593 (2024).
[53] [2010] UKSC 52.

extending the Assembly's powers. The practicalities of holding a referendum are explored, with Lord Jones noting that the choice of 3 March (which he supported) did give him some concerns, with Jones stating, that 'I have always thought that holding a vote at a time of year when it gets dark early depresses turnout.' He then explains the significance of the Wales Act 2014 and the role of the Supreme Court in helping to clarify ambiguities about the legal competencies of the Assembly. Finally, there is consideration of the Wales Act 2017 and why it is 'significant in that it introduced for the first time the reserved powers model for Wales.' However, as Jones observes, there were some anomalies, such as the decision not to include Milford Haven waterway in the list of ports that were to be devolved to Wales, for which he offers an interesting insight into the UK Government's reasoning.

In chapter eight Jack Simson Caird reflects on the work of the Justice Committee during the 2019 Parliament. Caird's perspective is informed by his role as part of the Office of Speaker's Counsel since 2020, which requires him to offer select committees legal advice. Caird makes the case for the Justice Committee being 'an important constitutional actor within the House of Commons'. It crucially offers a 'check on the government's approach to justice policy and monitoring the operation of the justice system'. His chapter explores the composition of the Justice Committee, and the reasons for the choice of chair being so significant. Caird offers the example of Sir Bob Neill, who became chair of the Justice Committee in 2015, demonstrating how Neill's experience was important in determining the scope of the Justice Committee's work. He then considers the powers and working methods of the Committee. In terms of the non-inquiry work conducted by the Justice Committee, Caird observes that the Lord or Lady Chief Justice's annual evidence session before the Committee 'served a vital accountability function, enabling the Committee to hold the Government to account for the issues raised by the head of the judiciary and the Crown Prosecution Service'. The chapter outlines the inquiry work conducted by the Justice Committee and then the importance of the work that the Committee does with the judiciary. Caird notes that, 'Arguably the most high-profile judicial evidence session in the Parliament was Baroness Carr of Walton-on-the-Hill's first appearance as Lady Chief Justice on 16 January 2024.' This provided the Lady Chief Justice with the opportunity, of which she readily availed herself, 'to set out the judiciary's position on matters of live political debate where the judiciary had been implicated'.

In part three the chapters have as their mutual theme different aspects of the executive. In chapter nine Sir Ross Cranston, the former Solicitor-General and retired High Court judge, offers his first-hand perspectives on the role of the law officers. As Cranston observes, 'The law officers are a critical part of the UK's constitutional arrangements' and 'are at the forefront of ensuring adherence to the rule of law'. His analysis of the role of the law officers within the constitution focuses on the different functions that law officers are required to carry out, including inter alia advising the government or having regard to the public interest. Cranston's account draws upon his experience as Solicitor-General. He considers the law officers' relationship with the courts, noting the times that the Attorney-General (during Cranston's tenure) would appear on behalf of the government before the court, an appearance that would depend on 'the pressure of other business, the experience of the law officers, and their own inclination'. As to his own court appearances as Solicitor-General, Cranston reflects that his choice of when to appear was due to mixed motives, including the importance of the case and the need to 'retain the trust of the courts', and notes that on 'a personal level, however, I found the work to be a challenge and one of the most intellectually stimulating aspects of being an MP and member of the government'.

Given the importance of the monarchy, the monarch as a constitutional actor is addressed by Robert Hazell in chapter ten. Hazell examines the role of the monarchy and is keen to place emphasis on just how tightly regulated the monarchy is by law. He rejects the notion that the monarch enjoys 'some agency' which would allow him to have an influence on the key constitutional issues facing the country. The monarch 'has relatively little autonomy', and Hazell advises those that would criticise the monarchy for 'its cost, its pomp and pageantry, or its ties to the Anglican church' to instead look to 'government and Parliament for setting the legal and financial framework within which the monarchy operates'. As a constitutional actor, Hazell argues that the monarch's powers may appear to be significant, but tight regulation refuses any monarchical choice as to how these powers should be exercised. The chapter then considers what discretion the monarch actually enjoys, in light of the tight regulation, and gives, as two examples of discretion, the ability of the monarch to develop their own 'style' and 'programme' as a ceremonial head of the nation, and the ability to choose royal patronages. Finally, the chapter ends with an assessment of the future challenges facing the monarch. One such challenge is the possibility of Scottish independence and what it means to the monarch, even if he were to remain as head of state in a newly independent Scotland.

Part four considers the role of judges, law reformers and lawyers. In chapter eleven Sir John Saunders draws upon his experience as a judge to reflect on the effect of pre-hearing publicity on criminal trials. Saunders has been the trial judge in some very significant and high-profile cases, such as the trial of parliamentarians in connection to the parliamentary expenses scandal (*R v Chaytor*) and the trial of Andy Coulson and Rebekah Brooks. His chapter addresses the problems of pre-hearing publicity on criminal trials and the implications for trial by jury. He questions whether the complacency of judges who maintain that jurors always follow the judge's instruction to ignore prejudicial material can be accepted: 'The Judges who say that juries are very conscientious no doubt believe it, but that belief cannot be objectively verified.'

In chapter twelve, Alison Young, the current Law Commissioner for England and Wales for Public Law and the Law of Wales explores the constitutional role of the Law Commissions across the UK. Young notes that 'it may seem odd to regard the Law Commission… playing a role in the UK constitution', as it is an advisory body and cannot initiate new law or implement reform. However, Young argues that the Law Commission does indeed play such a role, due to 'being uniquely placed to reform the law'. Young examines the role of the Law Commissions, their influence on the rule of law, through law reform which makes 'the law clearer and more accessible', and democracy, through the use of the consultation process, which 'provides a means of enhancing democratic law-making'. She then addresses the challenges facing the Law Commissions. Importantly, Young stresses the importance of balancing the Law Commissions' independence, 'whilst being able to effectively work with governments and legislatures to ensure their proposals are implemented'. This balancing act needs to be effective to allow the Law Commission 'to continue to fulfil their constitutional role'.

Karon Monaghan KC in chapter thirteen explores Reimagining the Rule of Law: Substantive Equality, Feminism and Critical Race Theory. Monaghan considers why the common law does not recognise a substantive principle of equality. She argues that reimagining the rule of law to contain some substantive equality content, would help to redeem the rule of law from the criticisms levelled against the rule of law by feminist and critical race theory scholars in particular.

The Supreme Court is the focus of Aidan O'Neill KC in chapter fourteen. He addresses trust in the UK Supreme Court after Brexit. His perspective comes from his considerable experience of appearing before the Supreme Court in high-profile constitutionally important cases, such as *Cherry & others v Advocate General for Scotland*[54] and *For Women Scotland v Scottish Ministers (No.2)*.[55] O'Neill draws upon the work of the late Conor Gearty, to whom his chapter is in memoriam. The key issue in the chapter is that of trust post-Brexit. As part of this O'Neill engages with the view that Lord Reed, the President of the Supreme Court (after Lady Hale's tenure came to an end), is 'the prime and decisive mover behind the changes' that Conor Gearty and other academics have identified in the Supreme Court post-Brexit. The chapter asks inter alia, 'Can we properly talk of a *Reed* Supreme court?' It also questions the ability of the President to nominate individuals to join the Court (as chair of the Selection Commission), given that he is the only member of the Court involved in the appointment of new Justices. The chapter emphasises the importance of the individual in shaping the constitutional jurisprudence of the UK, and the potential for how influence can be exercised. O'Neill also addresses the levels of representation within the Supreme Court, noting that it has gone from a high of three females Justices, to now just two, despite the opportunity to appoint more female Justices as others have taken retirement in recent years.

Part five is concerned with drafting constitutions. Chapter fifteen by Gisela Stuart (Baroness Stuart of Edgbaston) and Matthew Lloyd examines the pitfalls of constitution writing. In particular Stuart's perspectives are informed by her experience in government as Parliamentary Under-Secretary of State for Health between 1999 and 2001, 20 years as a Member of Parliament, and now a crossbench peer in the House of Lords and the First Civil Service Commissioner. Stuart has first-hand

[54] [2019] CSOH 20, [2019] CSIH 49, [2019] UKSC 41.
[55] [2022] CSOH 90, [2023] CSIH 37, [2025] UKSC 16.

experience of such pitfalls, having been a member of Presidium of the European Convention on the Future of Europe, which set out to create a draft Treaty, which, if it had been ratified by Member States, would have given the EU a constitution. Stuart and Lloyd are critical of the process, observing that 'Those who drafted the document were more concerned with institutional self-interest than democratic accountability.' The problem was that the focus was ill-placed. The chapter then considers the UK's constitution and reflects on whether the current arrangements work and where initiatives for future reform could come from. Finally, Stuart and Lloyd offer advice on how to avoid the pitfalls of constitution writing. They note that 'Constitutional reform is most likely to succeed when it is grounded in popular demand, rather than serving the interests of institutions or political elites.' Where this is not the case, attempts to reform in the UK 'have often backfired, leading to adverse unintended consequences.' Stuart and Lloyd conclude, that 'Constitution writing, like politics, is an art and not a science and, if in doubt, it should always err in favour of the people!'

In chapter sixteen Richard Albert, a member of the 15-person Constitutional Reform Committee of Jamaica, looks at the use of the poison pill in Commonwealth Caribbean constitutions, which are designed to make it extremely difficult for states to remove the British monarch as their head of state. Albert notes that should Canada seek to become a republic, under the Canadian constitution the 'the unanimous approval of Parliament in addition to approval resolutions from each of the provincial assemblies' would be required. This form of amendment procedure is the 'most onerous' and would be difficult to achieve. He then looks at the role of poison pills in the constitutions of those Caribbean countries where the British monarch is head of state. As Albert notes, all but one of the eight countries have within their constitutions a poison pill, which makes it more onerous than the default process to amend the constitution to become a republic. Finally, the chapter considers Jamaica and the steps taken for it to become a republic. The poison pill has previously thwarted its attempts to become a republic in the past, 'the poison pill in its constitution [having] been a pivotal factor' in why each attempt failed. Albert then looks at the most recent attempt, in which he has first-hand experience as a member of the Constitutional Reform Committee of Jamaica.

Finally, part six provides an important comparative perspective into the role of constitutional actors. In chapter seventeen Sir Geoffrey Palmer KC addresses the constitution from a New Zealand perspective. Having held the highest political office in New Zealand, serving as Prime Minister, and having played a leading role in developing what became the New Zealand Bill of Rights Act 1990, he offers a first-hand perspective of how New Zealand is governed and its constitutional arrangements. His chapter explores the constitutional history of New Zealand from its original status as a Crown Colony in 1841, the importance of the Treaty of Waitangi (te Tiriti o Waitangi), and the current constitutional and political landscape. The chapter explores the use of constitutional conventions, the introduction of the Cabinet Manual, the Constitution Act 1986, and the operation of the New Zealand Bill of Rights Act 1990. Palmer notes that New Zealand and the

UK both have an uncodified constitution, but he observes that 'the political culture is quite different'. In New Zealand the unicameral system has resulted in 'executive domination and diminished accountability'. However, as Palmer writes, there is a lack of support for introducing a written constitution. Finally, in chapter eighteen Henrik Skovgaard-Petersen explores the role of Danish civil servants as constitutional actors. Skovgaard-Petersen draws upon his experience as head of the Constitutional and Human Rights Law Division at the Danish Ministry of Justice (2019–23), before then working for the Prime Minister. The chapter explores 'how the Danish civil service – generally considered a well-functioning impartial civil service – grapples with some of these balancing exercises as actors in the constitutional landscape'. He outlines the core duties of civil servants under Code VII (Medarbejder- og Kompetencestyrelsen) before looking at the challenges facing civil servants. As Skovgaard-Petersen notes, civil servants play an important role and serve a vital function in assisting the legislative and the executive, despite being, 'almost completely absent from the written constitution'.

PART I

Promoting Public Confidence in Politics

2

Government by Consent – The Requirement of Trust

DANIEL GREENBERG CB*

2.1 Introduction

Since I took up my appointment as Parliamentary Commissioner for Standards at the beginning of 2023, I have been reminding Members of Parliament (MPs) of the bleak fact that trust between parliamentarians and the public appears to be at an alarmingly low level.

It seems that politicians have traditionally been treated with a certain amount of suspicion.[1] Certainly, general trends of literature have long been drawn along the lines of cynical or satirical portrayals of politicians as self-serving and untrustworthy. One need only remind oneself of the contemptuous treatment by Gregsbury MP of the deputation of his constituents led by the discomforted Pugstyles in *Nicholas Nickleby* to recall that the representation of politicians as actuated more by their own immediate interest than by desire to deliver on promises made during election times is hardly a modern concern.

Perhaps comparisons between one century and another are largely pointless, but it is nevertheless an incontrovertible fact that whether this is a modern phenomenon or a continuation of an eternal reality, the present state of trust between the public and parliamentarians as a class is dispiritingly low.[2]

In general, I have found that politicians appear to accept this as a fact, but I have not always felt that it is a fact that is treated with the urgency and gravity that it deserves. It almost appears sometimes as though some politicians – although

* Views expressed in this chapter are personal to the author.

[1] Some commentators have even suggested that this is a positive, or at least an inevitable, aspect of the relationship between governing and governed: 'There is one safeguard known generally to the wise, which is an advantage and security to all, but especially to democracies as against despots. What is it? Distrust.': *Demosthenes, Philippic 2 (Dem 6 24)*; see also J Philpot Curran on the election of the Lord Mayor of Dublin in 1790: 'The condition upon which God hath given liberty to man is eternal vigilance'; see also W Phillips, to the Massachusetts Anti-Slavery Society in 1852: 'Eternal vigilance is the price of liberty'.

[2] For a particularly thorough and revealing analysis of the lack of trust between the public and politicians see A Renwick, B Lauderdale, M Russell and J Cleaver, *Public Preferences for Integrity and Accountability in Politics – Results of a Second Survey of the UK Population – Third Report of the Democracy in the UK after Brexit Project* (The Constitution Unit, University College London, March 2023).

by no means all – regard trust as a dispensable luxury – something that might be a desirable bond between them and the electorate – but the absence of which need not unduly disturb the smooth and self-congratulatory atmosphere of Westminster.

Signs from those who stand outside the Westminster bubble, however, appear to suggest that the present situation is increasingly urgent. Although data is necessarily hard to establish, one could certainly note that the turnout at the last general election was alarmingly low[3] and part of a trend of apparently decreasing electoral interest and engagement. More graphically, perhaps, when large sections of the public appear to believe that sitting down in roads is a more effective method of changing public policy on environmental or other matters than seeking to influence, or become, politicians, there is a sign of danger. As I regularly put it when addressing MPs, just as the opposite of love is not hate but indifference, the opposite of trust is not suspicion but disengagement; and there are increasing signs of disengagement that all bespeak a lack of trust.

2.2 The Constitutional Role of Trust

Democratic societies rest on an electoral contract supported by the rule of law. Individuals consent to be governed based on their trust of the system, even if they dislike particular actions of the executive, legislative and judicial branches of the state. If that trust is removed, consent is vitiated, and the system loses legitimacy.[4]

It is tempting to suggest that there is a critical distinction to be drawn between trust in individual personalities and trust in the over-arching system. Members of

[3] 'Turnout at the 2024 general election was 59.7%, which was the lowest at a general election since 2001. Turnout was 7.6 percentage points lower than in 2019.This represented the largest drop in turnout between elections since between 1997 and 2001. The chart [*not shown*] shows turnout at general elections since 1918, during which time it has varied between 57.2% (1918) and 83.5% (1950). Since the drop in 2001, turnout has never fully returned to the levels between the 1922 and 1997. … Turnout differed widely across the UK at the 2024 general election, with the highest turnout (64.9%) in the South West of England and the lowest turnout (55.7%) in Yorkshire and the Humber. Turnout was lower in all parts of the UK compared with the notional results for the same boundaries in 2019.': https://commonslibrary.parliament.uk/general-election-2024-turnout.

[4] 'If all power is in the people, if there is no higher law than their will, and if by counting their votes, their will may be ascertained—then the people may entrust all their power to anyone, and the power of the pretender and the usurper is then legitimate. It is not to be challenged since it came originally from the sovereign people.': W Lippmann, *The Essential Lippmann: A Political Philosophy for Liberal Democracy* (Harvard University Press, 1982); see also 'Surely anyone who has ever been elected to public office understands that one commodity above all others, namely the trust and confidence of the people, is fundamental in maintaining a free and open political system.': HH Humphrey, Former Vice President of the United States, Address at Georgetown University Law Center Commencement, 3 June 1973 (transcript in Minnesota Historical Society archives); see also 'Government is a trust, and the officers of the government are trustees. And both the trust and the trustees are created for the benefit of the people.': R Seager (ed), *The Papers of Henry Clay: Candidate, Compromiser, Whig, 5 March 1829 – 31 December 1836*, Vol 8 (University Press of Kentucky, 1984) 42.

the public are undoubtedly able to differentiate between a feeling that certain individual politicians are not to be trusted and a consequent lack of trust in the rule of law system as a whole. A number of recent occurrences have, however, tended to damage trust both at individual and systemic levels.

Perhaps the most compelling and penetrative example is the legal measures taken to respond to the COVID-19 pandemic in 2020–22. There were a number of widely reported instances of politicians and others in public office declining to comply with the rules that they had put in place for others, and there can be no doubt that this exacerbated a lack of trust in individual policy-makers. But at a systemic level too, the irrationality of some of the health measures enacted into law has been seen to have had the potential for diminishing respect for the criminal law, which could contribute to the more general erosion of trust in the political system as a whole.[5]

There have been a number of other issues that threaten to damage public trust, both in individual public servants and in rule of law systems as a whole. In particular, the Infected Blood Scandal, and the wrongful treatment of sub-postmasters and sub-postmistresses in connection with the Horizon scandal, may have contributed to an erosion of trust at both individual and systemic levels.

Ultimately, all political and governmental systems are necessarily composed of individuals, and while it may be true that a given number of individual actors can be considered untrustworthy without the overall fabric of society losing that degree of trust that is necessary to maintain it, it is equally ineluctable that each

[5] See, in particular, the following extract from the Joint Committee on Statutory Instruments First Special Report of Session 2021–22, Rule of Law Themes from COVID-19 Regulations (HL 57; HC 600), 23 July 2021 (the author was Commons Counsel to the Committee at that time): '**Irrationality** 34. In a different category of cases, restrictions underpinned by criminal offences have been defined with sufficient precision to provide certainty, but in terms that make it difficult to identify any rational purpose behind the precision. For example, it is difficult for businesses and customers to have respect for a law that prohibits off-licences from selling alcohol at certain times, but expressly permits them to remain open for the purposes of delivery and collection of orders placed remotely, without specifying any kind of minimum delay between order and collection. The enacting Department publicly admitted that it would be entirely lawful for an off-licence to remain open, for customers to go in, browse and select the alcohol they wish to purchase, to leave the shop, to telephone to the counter from immediately outside the door and place an order, and to re-enter the shop and buy the alcohol. It is the apparent irrationality of such precise provisions that make them dangerous in rule of law terms, particularly in contexts where a breach of the regulations is a criminal offence, as they inevitably tend to diminish respect for the criminal law. 35. Another obvious avoidance opportunity was in Regulations which introduced requirements for operators of commercial transport services to ensure that passengers travelling to England from outside the common travel area completed a Passenger Locator Form and possessed notification of a negative test result. An operator who failed to ensure that a passenger had completed a Passenger Locator Form committed an offence. It was a defence for an operator to show that it had recorded a unique passenger reference number for the relevant passenger before that passenger boarded the relevant service. A unique passenger reference number is a number received by the passenger from the Home Office on completion of the Passenger Locator Form. The Department recognised that falsification of this number in the correct format was possible as there was no requirement to verify the reference number. It is difficult to understand the logic of creating an offence that can be committed by the operator subject to a defence that a passenger gave them a number, if that number can be a complete fabrication. This kind of obvious avoidance opportunity has significant potential for diminishing respect for the law.'

individual component has the power to strengthen or weaken that trust, and that each must therefore accept the risk that their individual behaviour may affect aspects of trust that go beyond their own actions.

This is recognised explicitly in the House of Commons Code of Conduct for Members of Parliament[6] which declares that it 'does not seek to regulate what Members do in their purely private and personal lives', but which expressly imposes a rule (Rule 11) that: 'Members shall never undertake any action which would cause significant damage to the reputation and integrity of the House of Commons as a whole, or of its Members generally.' The Code thereby draws an express distinction between individual behaviour which redounds to individual reputation alone and individual behaviour which diminishes the reputation of the broader body politic.[7] Overall, the purpose of the Code is to identify and articulate standards of behaviour that are likely to encourage trust between the institutions of Parliament and the public that they serve.

2.3 The Seven Principles of Standards in Public Life

Speaking theoretically about trust is both relatively easy and relatively unhelpful. One of the purposes of this chapter is to use the standards and conduct arrangements for the House of Commons in the UK as a model, to illustrate ways in which trust in public contexts can be required, provided, measured and demonstrated.

The Code of Conduct for Members of the House of Commons is constructed on a foundation of the Seven Principles of Public Life: honesty; integrity; openness; accountability; selflessness; objectivity; and leadership.[8] Those are the founding principles of the rules of conduct, but they are not rules in themselves. In particular, the Code expressly prevents the Parliamentary Commissioner for Standards from investigating allegations of breaches of the principles themselves, while requiring the Commissioner to take them into account when investigating allegations of breaches of specific rules.

This is a very important feature of an ethical regulatory system designed to build trust. A series of random and unconnected rules cannot expect to

[6] 2023 Version, HC 1083, 10 February 2023.

[7] For example, in my Report to the Committee on Standards about the behaviour of Margaret Ferrier MP I observed 'Conduct amounting to a criminal offence is conduct that would cause significant damage to the reputation and integrity of the House of Commons as a whole, or of its Members generally, there being an inevitable risk of a damaging perception on the part of members of the public that MPs consider themselves not obliged to keep the rules that they make for others.' See House of Commons, Committee on Standards – Ninth Report of Session 2022–23 – *Margaret Ferrier* (HC 1276; 30 March 2023), Appendix 1: Parliamentary Commissioner for Standards Memorandum.

[8] The 'Nolan Principles', named after the document in which they were first articulated in their modern form, the First Report of the Committee on Standards in Public Life, chaired by Lord Nolan, published on 1 May 1995.

command respect in the same way as rules that clearly and expressly emanate from and give expression to a consistent and coherent overarching policy. That policy in itself, however, is insufficient to build trust, primarily because it is not capable of being benchmarked and enforced without specific rules to underpin it.

The rules themselves focus on four principal components: registration of interests; declaration of interests; prohibition of paid lobbying; and limits on outside interests; alongside an additional and overarching rule prohibiting any action that seriously damages the reputation of the House as a whole. Taken together, those rules are designed to deliver the core principles in an enforceable and measurable way.

2.4 Openness

The foundation stone of the parliamentary standards system is undoubtedly registration, embodying the Nolan principle of openness.

While none of the principles is more important than any of the others, openness is a practical prerequisite for the operation of parliamentary standards as a whole. It is through the registration, in a publicly accessible register, of financial and other interests that MPs are able to demonstrate that they seek to carry out their wide-ranging functions in accordance with the Nolan principles generally. Without a requirement for the registration of interests, it would be difficult or impossible for the public at large to have confidence in the system of declarations of interests or in the efficacy of the prohibition on paid lobbying, each of which is required to implement the separate principles of accountability, objectivity and selflessness.

It is for this reason that the rules on registration are necessarily relatively complicated and technical: while principles-based regulation is undoubtedly desirable in the context of parliamentary standards for a range of reasons, when it comes to registration there must be an element of certainty and clarity, for the benefit of MPs and the public alike. In the present Code of Conduct, out of a satisfyingly concise 39 pages overall, nearly half are occupied by the specific rules of registration, divided into 10 categories, most of which have specific thresholds and other rules. Those categories of registrable interest range from obvious matters, including political donations and support, through gifts and hospitality, to a range of miscellaneous interests, including, broadly, any formal roles in an organisation that might reasonably be thought to influence an MP's political activities.

Under the 'Safe Harbour' provision, MPs are able to seek advice on registrability from the Registrar of Members' Financial Interests, and to rely on that advice should a question about registration be raised at a later date.

2.5 Accountability

Although transparency is the foundation stone of trust, by itself it can achieve nothing unless it leads to and facilitates a process of accountability.[9]

Accountability is again an easy requirement to assert, but rather more difficult to define in all its necessary attributes. In particular, accountability has to mean more, and be more nuanced, than simply providing for punitive consequences in cases of failures in transparency or other breaches of standards.

Extreme sanctions are certainly necessary for extreme cases, but by themselves they will not engender trust in the effectiveness of the system. Indeed, the danger is that much-publicised impositions of extreme sanctions serve mostly to accentuate the severity, and mask the infrequency, of non-compliance with the rules, rather than demonstrating widespread compliance and implementation.

For this reason, in the House of Commons standards system accountability takes a wide range of forms, some emphasising compliance and some identifying and addressing non-compliance, again in a variety of ways.

The most regular form of accountability arises where an MP in speaking in parliamentary proceedings makes an express declaration of an interest of some kind. In Chapter 2 of the Guide to the Rules relating to the Conduct of Members, the process for declaration is expressed to extend beyond the set of interests that are registrable in the Register of Members' Financial Interests under Chapter 1.

For declarations there is a wide, but potent and effective, test: the test of relevance. Paragraph 6 of Chapter 2 of the Guide requires MPs to consider whether an interest 'might reasonably be thought by others to influence his or her actions or words as a Member'. Although this is a wide, and even in some senses vague, concept, in practice it appears to work very well and is honoured far more in the observance than in the breach. Declarations are required to be concise and informative, and a simple reference to an MP's registered interests is not sufficient to comply with the rules. By making an effective declaration drawing attention to a specific interest that might be thought relevant to the proceedings at hand, an MP is in effect making themselves accountable to their fellow MPs and to the listening or later-reading public, by having potentially influential interests taken into formal account.

Ultimate accountability under any regulatory system, of course, requires a mechanism for permitting complaints of non-compliance to be made and for

[9] 'At the establishment of our constitutions, the judiciary bodies were supposed to be the most helpless and harmless members of the government. Experience, however, soon showed in what way they were to become the most dangerous; that the insufficiency of the means provided for their removal gave them a freehold and irresponsibility in office; that their decisions, seeming to concern individual suitors only, pass silent and unheeded by the public at large; that these decisions, nevertheless, become law by precedent, sapping, by little and little, the foundations of the constitution, and working its change by construction, before any one has perceived that that invisible and helpless worm has been busily employed in consuming its substance. In truth, man is not made to be trusted for life, if secured against all liability to account.': T Jefferson, Letter to Monsieur A Coray, 1823.

those complaints to be investigated effectively and, where relevant, punished appropriately.

In the House of Commons, transparent and thorough provision for the investigation of complaints of failure to comply with the Code of Conduct is provided for in the Procedural Protocol relating to the Code of Conduct.[10] Paragraph 21 provides for investigations to be initiated in a number of ways, most notably including public complaints, self-referral by the MP concerned, and the own initiative of the Commissioner.

My Annual Reports record the number of complaints that I receive each year,[11] and each complaint is scrutinised by a triage team and responded to with a target response of five working days, which is presently being met in 99 per cent of cases. Again, this is designed to ensure a degree of confidence in the operation of the system and to support trust between parliament as an institution and the public.

Perhaps unsurprisingly, the vast majority of complaints received from the public relate to matters which I cannot directly investigate. Recurrent among these are failures by MPs to respond to constituency concerns satisfactorily or at all, and the choice of language by MPs in their parliamentary and public discourse. These are both matters which the Procedural Protocol quite properly prevents me from investigating, as they are quintessentially matters for each MP's own judgement. Members of the public are therefore routinely informed that I am unable to investigate these particular matters. As explained in my team's individual responses to correspondents, however, all complaints, including those which I am not able to investigate directly, are taken carefully into account and used to inform MPs in my Annual Report and in other ways. Members of the public are therefore hopefully assured that their diligence in raising concerns is not wasted and can be expected to have a degree of impact on parliamentary behaviour overall.

The Standing Orders additionally give me powers to express concern to MPs in relation to matters that do not appear to engage a rule of conduct, and to give confidential words of advice in relation to matters that may breach a rule but in respect of which an investigation, for one reason or another, is not justified or proportionate. I make relatively extensive use of those powers and my feeling, based on interactions with MPs generally, is that they have a significant influence on MPs' behaviour and attitudes.

Where I launch a formal investigation, the fact that I have done so is immediately published on my parliamentary webpage, alongside identification of the MP concerned and the relevant rule or rules whose breach I am investigating. The entirety of every formal investigation, including all correspondence and transcripts of all interviews, is published on the parliamentary website at the end of

[10] Procedural Protocol in respect of the Code of Conduct, HC 1084, 24 February 2023.

[11] The Parliamentary Commissioner for Standards Annual Report 2023–24 (HC 252, 6 November 2024) records the following numbers of complaints received: 2021–22 = 1,434; 2022–23 = 5,672; 2023–24 = 2,350.

the investigation,[12] irrespective of its result. Most commonly, I determine the complaint through a process of rectification, a consensual process in accordance with which the MP concerned apologises to the House through me and undertakes any other corrective measures, or measures designed to prevent recurrence, agreed with me. In a small number of cases, I determine that a breach has occurred and that it requires the imposition of a sanction, in which case I report the matter to the Select Committee on Standards, which makes a finding and then recommends a sanction, which may be a requirement for an apology, but in more serious cases may involve suspension from the House for a number of days, and the House takes the final decision on the imposition of the sanction recommended.[13] An MP dissatisfied with a report of the Committee on Standards has the right to appeal to the Independent Expert Panel, a body provided for this purpose and chaired by a former Court of Appeal judge. The entire process is therefore composed of a number of checks and balances designed to ensure accountability and to deliver it in a spirit of transparency.

2.6 Selflessness and Objectivity

Transparency and accountability together are still insufficient to engender trust unless the overall perception of public servants is that they are primarily motivated by a wish to exercise their functions in the public good.

In the case of MPs, now that membership of the House has been a paid profession for over a century,[14] there is nothing wrong with MPs being seen to be 'in it for themselves' in the same sense that the personal motivation of every professional is to be paid and to achieve success in their chosen profession. It was decided long ago that confining membership of the elected House to those who could afford to undertake it as an unpaid hobby was fundamentally undemocratic and was likely to lead to those elected to be trusted less by the public in general than if MPs were paid a salary.[15]

The requirements of selflessness do not, therefore, mean that MPs should undertake their profession without expectation of reward, and the Independent Parliamentary Standards Authority has statutory responsibilities under the Parliamentary Standards Act 2009 to set the pay of MPs at a level thought likely to attract an appropriate quality of candidate with the requisite skills and experience.

[12] With redactions where appropriate to protect identities or private personal details.

[13] Suspension involves loss of pay; and an MP who is suspended for 10 days or more faces the possibility of a by-election for their seat under the procedure set out in the Recall of MPs Act 2015.

[14] Previous arrangements for maintenance and allowances of various kinds were formalised into a simple salary for MPs without other paid political appointment by Resolution of the House of Commons in 1911.

[15] See, for example, the debate on the Chancellor of the Exchequer's Motion on Payment Of Members on Thursday 10 August 1911, https://hansard.parliament.uk/commons/1911-08-10/debates/36a91ce4-2902-4282-90c2-1720ac40077f/PaymentOfMembers.

What the joint requirements of selflessness and objectivity do require, however, is that having accepted that salary MPs should exercise their parliamentary functions, each in accordance with their own understanding of how best to perform the role of a constituency MP, motivated solely by the desire to further the public interest, both in relation to constituency casework and in relation to public policy and other matters dealt with in the Chamber and in Committee.

The Code of Conduct summarises this in Rule 2 as a requirement that 'Members must base their conduct on a consideration of the public interest, avoid conflict between personal interest and the public interest and resolve any conflict between the two, at once, and in favour of the public interest.'

That requirement is supplemented by a prohibition on the taking of bribes set out in Rule 3 of the Code, and rules restricting paid lobbying set out in Rule 4 of the Code and Chapter 3 of the Guide. Taken together with restrictions on accepting outside remunerated positions set out in Chapter 4 of the Guide,[16] the overall intent is to ensure that MPs treat their position with selfless professionalism, and do not seek to advance their own personal enrichment by the way in which they perform their functions as parliamentarians.

2.7 Leadership

As to the final Nolan principle of leadership, the general tenor of the Code of Conduct is to require MPs to behave in such a way as to 'protect and enhance the reputation of the House of Commons, in order that the public can have justifiable confidence in it'.[17]

Rule 1 of the Code requires 'Members to treat staff, visitors and colleagues in Parliament with dignity, courtesy and respect';[18] and Rule 11 requires them 'not to undertake any action which would cause significant damage to the reputation and integrity of the House of Commons as a whole, or of its Members generally'.

Overall, there is a hope and expectation that by compliance with the requirements of the Code and Guide and their associated rules and policies MPs will show in their public activities an example which qualifies them to be considered as trustworthy leaders.

[16] As at the time of writing, Chapter 4 prohibits only the provision of paid parliamentary advice or agreeing to undertake services as a parliamentary strategist, adviser or consultant; but the incoming Labour Government, following the general election in 2024, reflected a manifesto commitment to consider further restrictions on outside paid employment by arranging for the Modernisation Select Committee and the Committee on Standards to consider the matter and make proposals to that effect to the House.

[17] Code of Conduct, Section A(c).

[18] This supplements the general *Behaviour Code* for Parliament, underpinned by a policy dealing with bullying and harassment and a policy dealing with sexual misconduct, which is enforced through the Independent Complaints and Grievance Scheme established for that purpose by the two Houses together; in the case of complaints of breach brought against Members of Parliament, the Parliamentary Commissioner for Standards is decision-maker, with a right of appeal to the Independent Expert Panel.

2.8 Conclusion

If the fundamental components of the House of Commons standards system are as serviceable as shown, the question arises why the trust levels between the UK public and politicians as a class are as dangerously low as I described them at the outset of this chapter.

I believe the answer to this consists of two parts.

First, it is undoubtedly true that even if only a very small minority of MPs flagrantly breach the Code of Conduct it is to them and their misbehaviour that the public attention will be drawn by media, social media and others, and it is not unreasonable that this should be so. To that extent, the burden of leadership is such that failures on the part of individual leaders can be expected to do more harm than silent compliance by the majority can do good.

In relation to the requirements of openness, for example, predictably and not unreasonably, the press in general focus on the relatively rare failures of registration – in the sense of occasions on which an MP fails to register an interest in accordance with the rules – and the overall impression of some members of the public is not surprisingly formed by having their attention drawn to occasional breaches, rather than to widespread compliance. (I have discussed the systemic impact of individual non-compliance with standards systems above in the context of the constitutional role of trust.)

Secondly, however, it is arguable that the degree of confidence in the generality of UK politicians, at least in the House of Commons, deserves to be significantly higher than it is, and that it can be increased by helping the public to understand the standards system and how it works.

In my Parliamentary outreach engagement with students and others, I draw attention to scandals relating to non-registration or other matters, based on which they have generally formed their unfavourable impression of politics and politicians, not as evidence of the failure of the system as a whole, but on the contrary as evidence that the system works well and that the public would be entitled to have confidence in it. In particular, the facts that there is a published register of MPs' interests, that it is relatively rare for investigative journalists or others to uncover evidence of failure to comply, and that systems exist to investigate and sanction non-compliance in the ways I have adumbrated above, can be seen as evidence of a healthy regulatory system, compliance with which is very much the natural order of events.

For me, again, while the emergence of occasional scandals is only to be expected, the test of the system is how it responds to those scandals in terms of accountability. In the case of the UK Parliamentary system, each time in the last 30 years that there has been a significant scandal involving impropriety that will have reduced public trust, our response has been to strengthen the system in a way that by rights should have restored or enhanced it. In particular: the office of Parliamentary Commissioner for Standards was created as a response to the 'Cash for Questions' scandal in the 1990s; the Independent Parliamentary Standards Authority which controls MPs' pay and expenses was created in response to the expenses scandal in 2009; and the Independent Complaints and Grievance Scheme was created in 2018 in response to an investigation into bullying and harassment and sexual misconduct in the parliamentary community.

Overall, an institution that experiences occasional scandals and responds to them with regulatory enhancement is an ethically healthy institution. An institution that experiences no scandals as a result of publishing little or no information about its internal workings may be ethically sound or rotten to the core, but as there is no way of telling which there is no reason to expect public confidence.

Looked at in the round, the present Code and its attendant rules appear to be fit for the purpose of maintaining a significant degree of confidence in the system overall. Undoubtedly, as is the case for any system, it is possible to improve, and the Select Committee on Standards is under a duty under Standing Orders to conduct a periodic review of the operation of the Code of Conduct in relation to registration and other matters, and to consider whether it is working appropriately and to make recommendations to the House for changes.

So why does the system fail to produce the level of trust that it deserves? My experience suggests that a significant part of the answer lies in traditional parliamentary institutional failures to do as much as we should to draw to the attention of the public the nature of the standards system, the way in which it works and the reasons why people can reasonably trust in it.

As Parliamentary Commissioner for Standards I regularly undertake outreach and engagement work in universities, schools and elsewhere, and I have invariably met with an initial frank and honest lack of confidence in the political class, followed by a fair and open-minded reception to my outlining the standards systems, resulting in a general agreement that the audience is less disposed to general mistrust of politicians as a class than they were before they had explained to them the mechanisms that exist for the maintenance of standards of ethics and propriety.

Some politicians are individually reluctant to draw attention to their own compliance with the standard systems, and generally grateful if they can simply avoid allegations of non-compliance with the ensuing negative publicity. That is not unreasonable: MPs protesting the effectiveness of the standards system and their own commitment to compliance are likely to be met with a degree of scepticism. Accordingly, one of the core functions of the permanent service of any parliamentary system is, in my view, to support the vast majority of those who comply with the rules, by demonstrating to the public what good looks like, and to what extent they are justified in placing trust in it.

Overall, therefore, my view is that in the interests of the stability of our political institutions we need to invest in educational exercises designed not to conceal or understate any actions of politicians that render them unworthy of trust, but to ensure that, as a balance to the media's representations of wrongdoing, the public also hear fair and dispassionate accounts of the different ways in which the standards systems work to ensure that the overwhelming behaviour of politicians deserves a sufficient degree of trust to underpin and justify the continuance of the social contract on which the rule of law is based.

Given the positive reception generally given by schools and universities, in particular, to suggestions of events along these lines, I am confident that a concerted campaign to strengthen and support educational exercises would meet with significant success in enabling a measure of reasoned trust in the underlying strengths of our parliamentary institutions, to the benefit of the nation as a whole.

3

The Committee on Standards in Public Life and the Integrity System

GILLIAN PEELE*

3.1 Introduction

This chapter examines the role of the Committee on Standards in Public Life (CSPL) as a constitutional actor in the British system of government. Its establishment by John Major's Government in 1994 makes it a relatively new addition to the constitutional firmament. Yet, as I shall argue, the CSPL has already made significant contributions to the quality and working of the British governmental system. It has achieved its impact through the elucidation of the values which should govern public life, through its work on the creation of new regulatory bodies across a range of key governmental institutions and by the way it has addressed a changing agenda of standards issues. The subjects tackled by the CSPL range from ones which regularly confront modern democracies, such as party funding, lobbying, transparency and the revolving door to newer problems generated by social, cultural and technological developments. The CSPL has necessarily devoted a significant amount of attention to such newer developments including the intimidation of election candidates, the spread of disinformation in elections and how best to secure accountability for the use of artificial intelligence (AI) in the public sector. These three dimensions of the CSPL's work – clarifying the norms that should govern the public sector, building an effective integrity system for a complex administrative structure and trying to resolve the range of ethical problems which challenge the political system in a rapidly changing society – are essential to maintaining public confidence in its governmental system. The relationship between public opinion and standards issues is clearly a crucial element in the evaluation of any integrity system. Unfortunately, as polls have increasingly demonstrated, the current period is one which has seen a marked decline in the British public's confidence in its politicians and its institutions.[1]

* The views expressed here are personal opinions.

[1] See for example the most recent National Centre for Social Research, 'Damaged Politics? The Impact of the 2019 -2024 Parliament on Political Trust and Confidence' (June 2024).

While the period since the CSPL's founding in 1994 has seen an extensive development of the mechanisms of ethical regulation in the public sector, the system is one which for many critics still lacks coherence and continues to display significant weaknesses. In this chapter I shall look at the various dimensions of the CSPL's work referring where relevant to reports of the CSPL and related standards bodies.[2] I do not intend, however, to provide a comprehensive history of the changing standards landscape since that is available in other writing and the CSPL's own publications[3] as well as that of other bodies such as the Public Administration and Constitutional Affairs Committee of the House of Commons, which has recently launched an inquiry into the standards landscape.[4]

Rather, I want to concentrate on some general themes affecting the handling of integrity issues in the British political system. These themes have shaped the approach of the CSPL and will be likely to continue to shape the constitutional impact of the CSPL's successor body, the Ethics and Integrity Commission (EIC). The transformation of the CSPL into the EIC, as well a number of other changes, occurred in mid-2025 as a result of the 2024 Starmer Government's commitments to strengthen Britain's integrity arrangements. The changes were deemed necessary because of widespread concern about the 'downward spiral' of public standards, especially during the premiership of Boris Johnson (2019–22).[5] Apart from offering an obvious target for the Labour opposition from 2019, this 'downward spiral' generated a good deal of think tank and academic activity focused on the reform of the regulatory bodies responsible for the country's patchwork quilt of probity watchdogs.[6]

Although Labour had committed itself in opposition to a series of standards-related reforms, including the creation of an Ethics and Integrity Commission, the detail of these reforms was left vague. Once in power in 2024 Labour encountered criticism for its slow action in making good its commitments, although some changes such a revision of the Ministerial Code and a strengthening of the role of the Independent Adviser on Ministerial Standards were made in the first months of the new administration. Labour was also embarrassed by scandals of its own early in the new administration as it was revealed that the Prime Minister and his wife had accepted 'freebies', including gifts of clothing and spectacles, from a wealthy Labour donor, the peer Waheed Alli. A series of ministers had

[2] For a complete list of CSPL and EIC reports see https://eic.independent-commission.uk/the-standards-landscape.

[3] See for example D Hine and G Peele, *The Regulation of Standards in British Public Life: Doing the Right Thing?* (Manchester University Press, 2016).

[4] Hine and Peele (n 3).

[5] See House of Commons Public Administration and Constitutional Affairs Committee, Inquiry into propriety and ethics (June 2025) and J Bowers, *Downward Spiral: Collapsing Public Standards and What We Can Do About It* (Manchester University Press, 2014; paperback revised edition, 2026).

[6] On this see O Gay and P Leopold (ed), Conduct Unbecoming: *The Regulation of Parliamentary Behaviour* (Politico's, 2004).

to resign including the Government's anti-corruption champion Tulip Siddiq.[7] Other damaging allegations related to lobbying, consultancy and procurement and to the acceptance by various ministers of 'freebies'. These allegations underlined the continuing vulnerability of governments of all parties to accusations of improper behaviour.

There had been much speculation about how any new body established by Labour would relate to the existing machinery. In the period before the 2024 general election there had been some voices calling for a single powerful new body which could amalgamate many of the functions of the existing regulators. This mega-body did not materialise. The EIC was established in October 2025 and replaced the CSPL. However, for the most part, that change took the existing CSPL role, machinery and personnel and continued them with a new name (I have used the nomenclatures CSPL and CSPL/EIC as appropriate in this chapter).

There were, though, some significant alterations to the CSPL's workings in a bid to strengthen it. First the EIC was given a formal responsibility for coordinating the other ethical watchdogs exercising specific regulatory functions. These watchdogs included the Electoral Commission, the former Advisory Committee on Business Appointments (ACOBA), the Civil Service Commission and the House of Lords Appointments Commission (HOLAC). Until this point the coordination had largely been done informally by meetings between the chair of the CSPL and the chairs of each of the other bodies who also had occasional meetings with the full Committee on Standards in Public Life. It is envisaged that, although such informal cooperation will continue, there will in addition be more formalised and regular meetings. Secondly, the EIC is now expected to submit an annual report to the Prime Minister on the overall health of the standards system, a move which should provide for a regular focus on standards issues. Thirdly, the reform included a commitment by the government to reply to any report from the EIC in a timely manner following the unsatisfactory experience of delayed responses to the CSPL's work under the previous government.

In addition to the establishment of the EIC significant changes were made to the machinery governing politicians and civil servants taking appointments in the private sector on retirement. The much-criticised ACOBA was abolished and its work split between the Independent Adviser on Ministerial Standards and the Civil Service Commission, although the rules on business appointments have not as yet been changed. It is worth noting that ACOBA is only the visible part of a much wider system. ACOBA provided independent advice for senior civil servants and ex-ministers, while departments themselves considered all other cases. Given the turnover of civil servants below the most senior levels (with about 40 per cent of civil servants leaving annually) there was a major gap in scrutiny at this level, a point which, as Lord Pickles has emphasised, was a real vulnerability in the system.

[7] See R Booth, 'Read Tulip Siddiq's letter in full as Treasury minister resigns' *Independent* (14 January 2025).

3.2 The Role of the CSPL

The decision by John Major to set up the CSPL was prompted by a series of scandals in the 1990s when it was revealed that a number of Members of Parliament (MPs) had been taking money to put down parliamentary questions in return for payment. These revelations of parliamentary 'sleaze', a word which entered the political vocabulary in the 1990s, highlighted a series of seedy relationships between MPs, private business interests and the burgeoning ranks of lobbyists. They also drew attention to the absence of effective rules governing MPs' conduct. Traditionally MPs were self-regulating and set their own rules, a system they had jealously defended since the seventeenth century. But such rules were imprecise and weakly enforced. Major's initiative was occasioned by the hope that the new CSPL would be enough to quell the widespread public outrage and prompt Parliament to produce a robust and effective disciplinary system. Whether the CSPL was expected to be permanent is a moot point. While some critics later questioned the continuing need for such a body, it was clearly intended by those who established the CSPL that it would be on hand to operate in the case of future episodes of misconduct in public life. John Major himself in a foreword to the 2021 *Standards Matter* Report of the CSPL declared that the Committee would never be redundant, a judgement which seems entirely justified by the continuing eruption of ethical controversies in British public life.[8]

The CSPL as established by John Major was not intended itself to be a regulator or to investigate individual cases. Nor does it comment on individual cases. Rather its role was to create new regulatory machinery and to keep it under review. The membership of the CSPL was small – four independent members, recruited by open competition, and a chairman selected for a non- renewable period of five years. In addition, although as far as possible the Committee sought consensual remedies for problems and would approach issues in an objective manner, it had to ensure that it kept in touch with the realities of party concerns and government. Accordingly, the largest parties in the House of Commons were asked to provide a member of the CSPL for a five-year term.

The CSPL has since its inception been served by a secretariat provided by the Cabinet Office, which is its sponsor. The CSPL was thus a non-statutory advisory body which reported directly to the Prime Minister. As its role was advisory it had no formal power to ensure compliance. As noted earlier, one problem increasingly encountered by the CSPL in recent years has been the failure of the Government to respond quickly to reports even if it is going to reject recommendations. From the Government's perspective many of the CSPL reports such as the wide-ranging 'Upholding Standards in Public Life': the *Standards Matter* 2 report of 2021 could be challenging because they required complicated adjustments to existing

[8] Committee on Standards in Public Life, *Upholding Standards in Public Life: Final Report of Standards Matter 2 Review* (November 2021).

arrangements and presented drafting difficulties as well as demanding legislative time. Inevitably, too, other issues may tend to crowd out standards-related ones. However, for critics the tactic of delaying any response to a report suggested a deliberate reluctance to address key standards issues especially if they required action which would go against the Government's interests. Other weaknesses in the British integrity machinery have appeared over time. There has been a slowness in the process in making new appointments to the CSPL and in filling vacancies in other watchdogs such as ACOBA, although the problem may in part have reflected overload on the Cabinet Office's internal processes.

It was noted when the CSPL was created that it had no statutory basis and that its existence was not even underpinned by Orders in Council. Its functions and operation were governed by terms of reference set by the Cabinet Office. It could therefore have been abolished at any time and, although the CSPL survived to celebrate its 30th anniversary, there were times when abolition seemed a real possibility. The CSPL incurred hostility from some MPs who found the rules it recommended irritating and burdensome, and in some political and media circles which questioned the right of a regulatory body to challenge the judgment of elected officials.[9]

The remit of the Committee has not been static. Tony Blair's 1997–2001 Government added political funding to its responsibilities in the Political Parties, Elections and Representation Act 2000. A new Electoral Commission was set up to enforce the rules on political donations and keep election law generally under review. There were other changes to the remit of the CSPL. The advent of devolution prompted the removal from the CSPL of jurisdiction in Scotland, Wales and Northern Ireland as it was anticipated that the devolved bodies in those areas would establish their own standards machinery. And it was made clear that the remit of the CSPL applied to private sector bodies if they had responsibility for delivering public services or functions.[10]

The effectiveness of the CSPL's work has also of course been affected by the resources available to it. Following a triennial review of the CSPL in 2013, which recommended a larger secretariat funded by the loss of the CSPL's own research programme, the Government accepted the cut to the research budget but did not enhance the CSPL's secretariat resources. In 2025 when the Government proposed that the CSPL should be transformed into the new EIC with additional functions it was recognised that this change would need to be supported by additional resources to facilitate the enhanced workload.

Mention has already been made of the changing agenda of the CSPL. In theory the CSPL has had a completely free choice in relation to the topics it will investigate.

[9] See for example comment on the difficulties encountered by Andrew McDonald, the first chief executive of IPSA, in E Owen, 'Andrew McDonald: Obituary' *The Guardian* (5 November 2021). A good example of some media hostility to efforts to restrict political autonomy can be found in A Heath, 'The Blob is taking back control and destroying Boris Johnson's premiership' *Sunday Telegraph* (24 November 2021).

[10] See CSPL, *Ethical Standards for Providers of Public Services* (2014).

The selection of a topic has been shaped by an awareness of which issues needed attention and were not being investigated by other bodies. There have also been occasions when the government has asked the CSPL to investigate a problem as Theresa May did in 2017 when there was grave concern about an increase in the intimidation of MPs and candidates for public office.[11]

3.3 The Nolan Principles

One of the earliest actions of the CSPL under its first chairman, Lord Nolan, was to articulate a set of values which should govern all those in public life. These values expressed as general principles (the Seven Principles of Public Life, or Nolan Principles) have provided the underpinning of much of the subsequent work of the Committee as specific sectors have developed their own codes and rules to adapt the Principles. The CSPL has informed debate about standards issues not just in the public sector, narrowly defined, but across the range of public services including in education, the police and the health service. The private sector also has widely adapted the Nolan Principles.

The seven Nolan Principles are selflessness, integrity, objectivity, openness, accountability, honesty and leadership. It has sometimes been argued that these principles may not automatically resonate with the public so that attention needs to be paid to the extent to which they might require to be amended to reflect a changing social context. To ensure that the Nolan Principles retain relevance the CSPL has been careful to monitor the understanding of the Principles over time and especially to be sensitive to any generational differences which may emerge in the evaluation of these values. In fact, support for the Principles has remained solid and the Nolan Principles have become iconic. Thus far the only major changes that have been made have been to the descriptors – the explanatory statements attached to the Principles. Here, rising concern with bullying and harassment on the parliamentary estate caused the CSPL in 2021 to refine the descriptor of leadership to include the notion of respect. The descriptor of leadership therefore now states that 'holders of public office should exhibit these principles in their own behaviour and treat others with respect. They should actively promote and robustly support the principles and challenge poor behaviour wherever it occurs.'[12] In Scotland Nolan's original seven Principles have been extended to nine principles. The eighth principle in Scotland emphasises the obligation of public office-holders to act in the interests of the public body of which they are a Board member and to act in accordance with the core tasks of the body to promote the public interest. The ninth states that holders of public office must respect fellow

[11] Committee on Standards in Public Life, *Intimidation in Public Life* (December 2017).

[12] CSPL, *Upholding Standards in Public Life: Final Report of Standards Matter 2 Review* 1.45 (November 2021).

members of their public body and employees of the body and the role they play, treating them with courtesy at all times.[13]

The Nolan Principles are not formal rules but provide an ethical framework for all those in the public sector. As Mark Philp has written, the principles are designed to emphasise the priority to be accorded to the public interest over personal, individual or even organisational and reputational interests.[14]

In order to give effect to this framework of values the CSPL has promoted a tripartite structure of codes of conduct, independent institutional scrutiny, and education. The CSPL has always been very aware that attaining high standards within any organisation depends not just on the process of enforcing rules but on building a supportive ethical culture within that organization to keep the Nolan Principles at the forefront of decision-making at all levels.

This emphasis on developing a robust ethical culture inside government has shaped much of the recent work of the CSPL. Thus, two recent major reports have analysed the importance of leadership in building an ethical culture inside an organisation. The 2023 Report *Leading in Practice* explored how leaders can best ensure that the Nolan values are embedded in practice in their organisations at every level, not just the most senior.[15] A 2025 report explored how public sector organisations can avoid major blunders by responding to early warning signals.[16] This report was especially apposite given a series of highly damaging episodes of organisational failure and cover-ups across the public sector including the Hillsborough stadium tragedy, the Grenfell Tower fire and the Post Office Horizon IT scandal. To achieve cultural awareness of the Nolan Principles the CSPL has urged a commitment to regular induction and training for public sector organisation staff and the encouragement of all members of an organisation to speak up (as well as formal whistleblower protections) when there is any sense of unease about the organisation or its processes. There has thus been a strong emphasis on the need for all individuals with public sector roles to take personal responsibility for the character of decision-making and behaviour in their organisations.

The process of developing codes of conduct incorporating the needs of particular sectors formed the early agenda of the CSPL as it addressed major institutions first at the national level but later taking in local government and such topics as party finance. The process was not always entirely straightforward. Introducing new rules and machinery was often greeted with suspicion and hostility by those affected, and in some areas such as the regulation of parliamentary conduct encountered irritation, resentment and some outright resistance. The spur to establishing the CSPL had been the 'cash for questions' affair which pointed to the need for a much more rigorous approach to MPs' conduct, so it was hardly

[13] For a statement of the Principles of Public Life in Scotland see www.qmu.ac.uk/media/8d891e-c38791ae1/appendix-08-the-nine-principles-of-public-life-in-scotland.pdf.

[14] M Philip, 'The Nolan Principles: Keeping the Public Front of Mind', https://cspl.blog.gov.uk/2024/10/24/the-nolan-principles-keeping-the-public-front-of-mind.

[15] CSPL, *Leading in Practice* (2023).

[16] CSPL, *Recognising and Responding to Early Warning Signs in Public Sector Bodies* (March 2025).

surprising that the House of Commons should be one of the first institutions to be subject to critical appraisal. Reform of the House of Lords came about much more slowly with a report in 2000 and subsequent major changes.[17] The CSPL in its First Report recommended the creation of a new code of conduct for MPs which could be regularly reviewed and the creation of a new office for adjudicating breaches of the rules – a Commissioner for Parliamentary Standards. The Privileges and Standards Committee (PSC) was given the role of considering disciplinary issues and overseeing the work of the Parliamentary Commissioner for Standards. In 2012 the House divided the work of the PSC and set up a new body committee – the Standards Committee – to focus on the disciplinary matters and the role of the PSC.

Although the thrust of the CSPL proposals contained in the CSPL's First Report was accepted and the House of Commons put in place a new Code of Conduct and acquired a new officer – the Parliamentary Standards Commissioner – to investigate allegations of breaches of the Code, the new system was not universally accepted immediately. In theory this new office of the Commissioner should have been independent, but the Commissioner has had to negotiate the sensitive relationship between his office and MPs. Some MPs who had hitherto been used to a less rigorous regime resented the new arrangements and at least two holders of the office – Elizabeth Filkin and Kathryn Stone – experienced personal opposition from MPs. In Filkin's case there was intense public controversy when her appointment was not renewed following claims from some MPs that she had been too proactive. In Stone's case her role in relation to a number of high-profile cases, including that of Owen Paterson, led to efforts to discredit the whole standards machinery.

It should be noted that several aspects of the House of Commons regulatory machinery have changed since the early 1990s, sometimes as part of a review by the Commons itself or by the CSPL and sometimes as a result of episodes of misconduct.[18] The 2009 scandal surrounding MPs' expenses signalled new demands for stricter scrutiny of MPs. It prompted a CSPL inquiry and further new machinery in the form of the Independent Parliamentary Standards Authority (IPSA) which itself experienced difficult relationships with MPs in its early days.[19] As a result of a CSPL recommendation, the Committee on Standards now includes lay members to avoid public suspicion that the regulatory procedures are not genuinely independent. Allegations of sexual and other harassment within the parliamentary estate prompted the creation of new machinery the Independent Complaints and Grievance Scheme. Of course, problems about parliamentary conduct remain. One major issue which has yet to be resolved is whether and to what extent MPs should be allowed to hold second jobs in addition to their parliamentary responsibilities.

[17] CSPL, *Standards of Conduct in the House of Lords* (2000).

[18] See for example the CSPL Eighth Report, *Standards of Conduct in the House of Commons* (2002), which reviewed the working of the reformed system.

[19] See Hine and Peele (n 4) ch 5.

While there has been some agreement that not all outside employment should be prohibited, defining an agreed yardstick for how much outside employment should be permitted is however likely to prove difficult.[20]

3.4 Public Appointments

There were other early changes to the machinery of government. As a result of the CSPL's first report a new office – the Commissioner for Public Appointments (CPA) – was established to strike a balance between ministerial patronage and merit in relation to a range of public appointments where the minister would have the final say but the process would be regulated until that point. The role of the Commissioner was to ensure that the process for making these appointments was transparent and likely to encourage applications from a diversity of candidates who would see that their credentials would be fairly assessed on merit. Although the final decision would be for the relevant minister, the new process was designed to provide safeguards to protect the quality of appointments through a system of what Sir Peter Riddell has called 'constrained patronage'. On one level this balance could be seen as operating to limit cronyism and ensure the principle of merit operated in government appointments. On another level, however, it could be seen by critics as limiting ministerial control of policy. Increasing demand for more ministerial control inevitably meant a retreat from the early balance established by the CPA. The Grimstone review of 2016 strengthened the role of ministers in the appointments process. It removed the Code setting out how appointments should be made from the Commissioner, where it had been before 2016, and transferred it to the Government.[21] This shift was to some extent countered by new procedures introduced by Sir Peter Riddell as CPA; but in the eyes of many critics the period after 2016 saw a retreat from the principles initially enunciated by the CSPL. Critics also noted the use of underhand tactics to skew some appointments as well as the growth in the number of appointments that were not regulated.

The dilution of the appointments system established in the early years of Nolan in many ways appeared part of a more general trend of subordinating ethical concerns to party or governmental self-interest. A series of controversies arose during the Parliament of 2019–24, especially during Boris Johnson's premiership, and these episodes created widespread public concern and intensified the debate about standards. Much of this concern reflected the failure of Johnson to provide strong ethical leadership in government as well perhaps as the complacency of a government with a large majority in Parliament. One of the problems which has

[20] For initial background on this, see House of Commons Research Brief, https://commonslibrary.parliament.uk/research-briefings/cbp-10055/#:~:text=MPs%20are%20currently%20allowed%20to%20take%20second%20jo.

[21] For a trenchant overview of the public appointments system see Bowers (n 5) ch 5 and The Grimstone Review, 'Better Public Appointments: A Review of the Public Appointments Process' (March 2016).

always beset the standards regime has been the clash between the legitimacy of those who can claim a mandate from the electorate, whether as MPs or in government, and those charged with administering the procedural rules that provide safeguards against misconduct in public office.

3.5 The Ministerial Code and the Management of the Executive

This clash of legitimacies emerged very strongly during the Parliament of 2019–24, especially under the Johnson administration, where a series of episodes including 'Partygate' contributed to a sense of public anger about the behaviour of politicians. In 'Partygate' it emerged that ministers and staff had been holding social gatherings in Downing Street contrary to the lockdown regulations imposed to combat COVID-19. Cumulatively these episodes led to Johnson's resignation as Prime Minister.

Maintaining high standards of probity within the Executive for ministers and civil servants is central to ensuring the probity of the governmental system as a whole. The rules governing ministerial conduct are set out in the Ministerial Code, which is normally issued afresh with each administration and which has increasingly become the yardstick by which the behaviour of ministers is publicly evaluated. Ultimately it is the Prime Minister who has responsibility for the enforcement of public ethics at the highest level and who sets the tone for the Government as a whole. Ministers and civil servants are expected to adhere to the Nolan Principles to ensure their actions are governed by public not private concerns, and they must operate within the law. In the case of alleged breaches of the Ministerial Code it is the Prime Minister who decides whether an allegation should be upheld and what if any sanctions should be applied. In such instances there is a difficult political trade-off for the Prime Minister between being seen to impose appropriate standards on a minister and the risk of losing a valuable colleague as well as conceding ground to the opposition. Prior to 2006 there was also the difficulty that the initial fact-finding process was also likely to be suspect since even if handed over to a senior civil servant such as the Cabinet Secretary to manage, that official might find it hard to question the word of a minister.

In order to overcome this difficulty a new office – the Independent Advisor on Ministers' Interests – was set up in 2006 with a double role. First the Advisor was given responsibility for advising ministers about the management of private interests to minimise the risk that there was any conflict between the private interests of a minister and his or her public responsibilities. Secondly he was given power to investigate alleged breaches of the Code and make recommendations to the Prime Minister. Such a role obviously could prove to be highly controversial, and so it turned out dramatically under Boris Johnson where one of his cabinet ministers (Priti Patel, the Home Secretary) was accused of bullying her civil servants sometimes by swearing and shouting. Bullying is specifically prohibited by the Ministerial Code. Although the Independent Advisor Sir Alex Allan found that there was evidence of bullying and hence a breach of Ministerial Code had occurred, Boris Johnson rejected that finding. Patel was allowed to remain in her post without sanctions. Sir Alex Allan accordingly resigned. The controversy highlighted weaknesses in the role of the Independent Advisor and the CSPL was not alone in calling for a strengthening of the office.[22]

The Patel case had exposed significant weaknesses in the office of the Independent Advisor. These weaknesses became even more apparent during the tenure of Sir Alex's replacement, Lord Geidt. Lord Geidt resigned a year into the office following a series of issues surrounding the Prime Minister's own conduct in relation to the refurbishment of No 11 Downing Street, in relation to 'Partygate', and in relation to a possible breach of international law.[23] Unsurprisingly there were widespread calls for a strengthening of the office and powers of the Independent Adviser including from the CSPL. In December 2022 Sir Laurie Magnus was appointed to the role (renamed as the Independent Advisor on Ministerial Standards) and continues to hold the post at the time of writing.

The Patel case and the outrage about Boris Johnson's apparent toleration of the parties illegally held in Downing Street were far from the only integrity issues where Johnson blatantly defied the rules or flouted ethical convention. Other matters where Johnson's handling occasioned condemnation were the award of peerages, the rules governing business appointments, and the disciplining of his own backbenchers. On a number of occasions when controversy arose he appeared to be less than candid about the facts of the situation or careless about complying with convention.

3.6 ACOBA and the Revolving Doors

The system for protecting the integrity of government when former ministers and senior civil servants leave public office, and the role of ACOBA, have been increasingly criticised as 'toothless'. ACOBA's former chairman Lord Pickles among others described the system as massively in need of reform.[24] ACOBA was established in 1975 to provide independent advice to Permanent Secretaries to regulate movement between public and private appointments. Following the First Report of the CSPL, a major change occurred in 1995 when ministers were brought within its remit, and it was renamed the Advisory Committee on Business

[22] See for example the work of the Constitution Unit, especially R Hazell, M Boo and Z Pullar, 'Parliament's Watchdogs: Independence and Accountability in Five Constitutional Watchdogs' (Constitution Unit, July 2022).

[23] Lord Geidt had been asked by Johnson to advise on placing tariffs on steel, which would have been contrary to World Trade Organization rules.

[24] See Lord Pickles evidence to the Public Administration and Constitutional Affairs Committee (PACAC) on the role of PACAC, https://committees.parliament.uk/oralevidence/16069/pdf.

Appointments. In theory the committee at the same time became more transparent. However, it remained an advisory committee and there was no way of enforcing its recommendations.

Inevitably it was the incidence of non-compliance which gained attention. The 2021 Report of the CSPL recommended putting the committee on a statutory basis and strengthening its powers of enforcement by incorporating compliance with the rules of ACOBA into contracts and proposing new sanctions for failure to comply with the rules. These sanctions could have included such financial penalties as the docking of severance pay or pensions of former employees. Although there was a mounting case for reform nothing was done in the 2019–24 Parliament.

3.7 The Owen Paterson Affair

The scepticism and even contempt for many aspects of the regulatory system emerged in Parliament in the bitterly fought row about the suspension of Owen Paterson. Paterson was a former minister under David Cameron who after leaving government used his backbench position to lobby on behalf of companies for whom he acted. He was found to have broken advocacy rules for his approaches to the Food Standards Agency and the Department for International Development as a paid consultant in what the Parliamentary Standards Commissioner said was an exceptionally serious breach of the rules.[25] Paterson claimed the disciplinary process he had been subjected to by the House of Commons was unfair and did not comply with the principles of natural justice. Although a motion to enforce the Committee on Standards decision was moved, an amendment to it was put forward by a Conservative backbencher to investigate the disciplinary process by setting up a new committee to review the procedure – a move which threatened to overthrow the whole system for regulating MPs' conduct.

The Government initially appeared to side with Paterson by putting on the whip to secure a vote for this wrecking amendment. The amendment passed but with a significant body of Conservative MPs abstaining or being absent. There was intense criticism of the Government's partisan manoeuvre, including from the then chair of the CSPL, Lord Evans; and Labour refused to participate in any effort to review existing procedures via a new committee. The Government then backtracked, and Paterson resigned triggering a by-election in his safe Conservative seat, which was lost to the Liberal Democrats. Paterson took his claim against the House of Commons disciplinary procedure to the European Court of Human Rights, but the claim was rejected by the Court.[26]

[25] Parliamentary Commissioner for Standards: Mr Owen Paterson MP (26 October 2021), https://committees.parliament.uk/committee/290/committee-on-standards/news/158246/committee-on-standards-publish-report-on-the-conduct-of-rt-hon-owen-paterson-mp.

[26] *Paterson v United Kingdom* (App no 23570/22).

3.8 Reviewing the Landscape: the CSPL 2021 Report

The period following the Brexit referendum and the 2019 election thus saw a series of incidents which suggested neglect of, if not contempt for, the ideals represented by the Nolan Principles. A former chair of the CSPL, Lord Evans, captured this change of mood in his 2020 lecture, 'Are We Living in a Post Nolan Age?'[27] In 2021 the CSPL issued a report surveying the standards landscape in which the Committee urged the need for more independence for key regulatory institutions and more enforcement powers, including for ACOBA and HOLAC, which regulated appointments to the House of Lords.

The 2021 Report had thus been conducted against a backdrop of major controversies within the Johnson Government and a growing sense that his premiership had manifestly failed to provide the ethical leadership which was required to retain public trust. In addition to the episodes already mentioned there had also emerged a series of public sector scandals which raised major questions about the aspects of the administrative system. This litany of public disasters was compounded by efforts at a cover-up of the wrongdoing and a failure to provide compensation to those damaged by the episodes. It was then hardly surprising therefore that Labour in opposition took up the theme of standards and making restoring trust in public life a key part of its agenda.

3.9 Labour and the Demand for Standards Reform

In office, Labour took some initiatives relatively quickly even if its creation of the EIC did not occur immediately. The Government produced a new Ministerial Code in 2024 and moved to strengthen the power of the Independent Adviser on Ministerial Standards by giving him the power to initiate investigations without the consent of the Prime Minister. The handling of the case of Angela Rayner in 2025 was widely seen as enhancing the authority of the Independent Adviser process. The 2024 version of the Ministerial Code reinstated the Nolan Principles at the beginning of the text. And, as detailed earlier, it created an expanded version of the CSPL renamed as the EIC, and abolished the ACOBA, although the much-criticised rules remained the same. There was, however, much the Government did not do, at least in this early period. It did not, for example, take any action to enact most of the recommendations of the CSPL's 21st Report by strengthening the independence of regulatory bodies. Indeed, in relation to the Election Commission it replicated earlier action by the Johnson Conservative Government of 2019–22 by allowing the Government to set priorities for the Electoral Commission. The Starmer Government did, however, implement some of the CSPL's recommendations from

[27] Lord Evans of Weardale, 'Are We in a Post Nolan Age?' Hugh Kay Lecture to the Institute of Business Ethics (12 November 2020).

its 2021 Report, Regulating Election Finance.[28] And, it did in September 2025, after some much-criticised delay, introduce the Public Office Accountability Bill, or Hillsborough Law, to fulfil it manifesto promise to impose a duty of candour on public authorities, and expanded legal aid provision for those in dispute with public authorities over official wrongdoing and disasters, such as Hillsborough, the Post Office Horizon IT scandal and the infected blood scandal.

3.10 Conclusions

The integrity machinery of the UK developed extensively under the aegis of the CSPL. Although the machinery is now wide-ranging and a variety of bodies cover most of the public sector, whether these bodies with disparate powers and functions constitute a 'system' is debatable. Some critics have pointed to the extent to which the variety of regulators may confuse the public and the need for a 'one-stop shop' to channel complaints to the right body. Weaknesses and gaps in the watchdogs persist. It is too early to say how the new system of the EIC works in practice. Much will depend on how seriously the Government takes the pledge to respond quickly to reports and presumably to the annual reports on the state of public standards. It is also unclear how the new system for governing the revolving door will work. This reform did not secure cross-party consensus and encountered criticism from the Conservatives for including special advisors in the remit of the Civil Service Commission. The whole integrity system is still heavily dependent for its efficiency on the compliance of those working the system, on conventions, and the values of those who work in the public sector. The remedy may be more formal rules and compliance powers, as suggested in the 2021 CSPL Report. Labour's current initiatives suggest that for the moment at least the Government retains faith in a blend of the existing institutional framework with some more formal measures. This incremental approach may still be able to work, but it will require constant attention to ensure standards issues are not sidelined to the pressure of the Government's immediate political agenda. It remains to be seen whether ethics and standards can command that centrality from the Government and the wider political community.

[28] www.gov.uk/government/publications/restoring-trust-in-our-democracy-our-strategy-for-modern-and-secure-elections/restoring-trust-in-our-democracy-our-strategy-for-modern-and-secure-elections.

4

Controlling Political Wrongdoing: The Role of the Criminal Law

JEREMY HORDER

4.1 Introduction

Does the criminal law have a role to play in holding high-level government officials to account for wrongdoing in public office? In a democracy, legal governance is not to be equated with the one-way projection of claimed authority, even if governance may remain perfectly legal when it lacks substantive merit. The process by which public decisions are made need not (and should not) always be left purely as a matter of trust placed in in a public authority, however trustworthy that authority may be in general. Accordingly, a flourishing democracy will provide readily accessible means to challenge the validity of many kinds of public decisions, on the grounds that they were (for example) outside the scope of the decision-maker's powers, or were irrational.[1] In that respect, it might be argued that the modern ability to challenge public decisions through judicial review makes the accountability of public decision-makers in criminal law of marginal relevance to the process of ensuring the legality of public decision-making; and rightly so. Nullifying or reversing invalid or inappropriate public decision-making, so that the decision may be made afresh, seems obviously to be far more important than punishing the decision-maker whilst leaving the decision unchallenged. However, just as the power of private criminal prosecution remains a symbol of the public's right to challenge official hegemony over determinations of wrongdoing fit for subjection to the criminal process, so the application of the criminal law to public decision-making at the highest level should not be barred purely on the grounds that public law remedies seem (from a bureaucratic-administrative point of view) more appropriate.

The criminal law is concerned, after the event, with the role of an individual or corporate person in bringing about or risking some instance of wrongdoing. It is concerned with the formal merits of that person's conduct, as a manifestation of legal governance, only in so far as that issue bears on the person's role in the

[1] See eg A Tomkins, 'The Role of the Courts in the Political Constitution' (2010) 60 *University of Toronto Law Journal* 1.

(risk of) wrongdoing. For example, suppose that a Supreme Court judge (D) sides with the appellants in an appeal, because he knows that they will reward him handsomely for so doing. As it turns out, all the other (impartial) members of the court independently also find for the appellants. The criminal law of bribery will be concerned with the judge's conduct as a possible instance of wrongdoing prohibited by section 2 of the Bribery Act 2010,[2] irrespective of its impact on the Supreme Court's decision. By contrast, the question of whether or not D's corrupt conduct – when discovered – is regarded as invalidating the entire decision is a question of public law.[3] In some respects, thus, the ex post facto responsibility and blame-focused role of the criminal law, in relation to public decision-making, seems closer to the aspects of an after-the-event public enquiry that are focused on who was responsible and to blame for harm done or threatened, than the more *ex ante*, validity-focused dimensions of judicial review. There is, thus, the potential for abuse of the criminal law, in relation to public decision-making, through instances in which a prosecution is employed solely or mainly to vent political grievances about someone's role in bringing about a controversial change.[4]

The Supreme Court judge example just given might give the impression that, although both have an application to high-level decision-making, the criminal law and the process of judicial review lead separate, parallel lives, with the former having no significant independent role as a means of impugning a public decision as such; but this is not so when it comes to the juridification of issues of public trust. First, there are some instances in which the character of a betrayal of trust is such that it is not amenable to judicial review. An important example is the acceptance by Members of Parliament (MPs) of bribes in exchange for asking questions in the Houses of Parliament or for engaging in other parliamentary activity.[5] In such cases, there may be no 'decision' to be declared null and void or retaken, and yet – particularly where such activities have been engaged in systematically – dealing with the matter merely as a breach of the rules of Parliament seems inadequate. Even so, prosecuting MPs for bribery in such circumstances runs up against a formidable objection. That is the clear terms of Article 9 of the Bill of Rights, which says that 'freedom of speech and debates or proceedings in Parliament ought not to be impeached or questioned in any court or place out of Parliament'. Considering the issue of 'freedom of speech and debates', Article 9 clearly exempted MPs from prosecution for criminal defamation (before the abolition of the offence in 2008[6]), but what about taking bribes to ask questions on the floor of the House?[7] In its review of the Bribery Act 2010 in 2019, the

[2] Improperly engaging in conduct in order to obtain an advantage.

[3] See, for an analogous case, *In Re Pinochet* [1999] UKHL 52.

[4] See, for example, the discussion of the private prosecution of Boris Johnson MP, respecting his role in the campaign for the UK to leave the EU, in J Horder, 'Criminal Law at the Limit: Countering False Claims in Elections and Referendums' (2021) 84 *Modern Law Review* 429.

[5] https://publications.parliament.uk/pa/cm199798/cmselect/cmstnprv/030ii/sp0157.htm.

[6] Criminal Justice and Immigration Act 2008.

[7] House of Lords Select Committee on the Bribery Act 2010, Report of Session 2017–2019, *The Bribery Act 2010: Post-Legislative Scrutiny* (HL Paper 303, 2019).

House of Lords Select Committee (post-legislative scrutiny) suggested that whilst it was clear that the 2010 Act applied to MPs, there was still no 'demarcation line' in relation to parliamentary privilege.[8]

Secondly, most democracies will have an offence of misconduct in public office, according to which – to give the English law definition – it is an offence when a public officer acting as such wilfully neglects to perform their duty or wilfully misconducts themselves to such a degree as to amount to an abuse of the public's trust in the office holder.[9] The broad definition of the misconduct offence – misconducting oneself 'to such a degree as to amount to an abuse of the public's trust in the office holder' – gives it a potential relevance to betrayals of public trust in the integrity of political decision-making that are not captured by more discrete criminal offences. The broad definition also means that this is an offence in which the personal involvement of the offender in wrongdoing, and the legal status of their conduct as a public decision, may be inextricably interlinked.[10] Moreover, it is a defence to a charge of misconduct that there was a justification or excuse for the action,[11] potentially bringing into play not only the formal but also the substantive merits of the conduct in question. Whilst misconduct offences are normally understood as having a 'top-down' manner of operation, applying mainly to officials lower in the hierarchy than parliamentarians at the democratic summit, there is commonly no legal barrier preventing the use of the offence in a 'bottom-up' manner, to hold parliamentarians (or judges) to account. In that regard, even though the monarch himself may be all-but immune from criminal liability,[12] the servants of the Crown – be they never so high and mighty – are not.[13] So, for example, it would have been perfectly possible to prosecute former Prime Minister Tony Blair for misconduct in public office, in relation to alleged serious failings that led to the UK Parliament's decision to send troops to Iraq.[14]

My main concern will be with the application of the offence of misconduct in a public office to elected officials. Here is an example for discussion:

[8] ibid, para 26.

[9] *Attorney General's Reference No 3 of 2003* [2004] EWCA Crim 868.

[10] An example might be where a police officer arrests a man (X) on suspicion of domestic violence against X's wife (V), in circumstances in which the evidence comes from private information given to the officer by V when she was having an affair with the officer: see www.standard.co.uk/news/crime/met-police-officer-sex-domestic-abuse-victim-misconduct-b1123590.html.

[11] *Attorney General's Reference No 3 of 2003* [2004] EWCA Crim 868.

[12] See the discussion in M Sunkin, 'Crown Immunity from Criminal Liability in English Law' [2003] *Public Law* 716.

[13] *M v Home Office* [1993] 3 All ER 537, 551 (Lord Woolf). See, also, the decision of South Korean prosecutors to charge the President with insurrection, following his unsuccessful attempt to impose martial law: J Mackenzie and R Comerford, 'Impeached S Korean president charged with insurrection' BBC News (26 January 2025), www.bbc.co.uk/news/articles/cr53r1d0jz4o. Clause 5 of the Danish Ministerial Responsibility Act says that 'A minister is liable to punishment if he wilfully or by gross negligence disregards the duties which fall on him under the Constitution or under other laws, or due to the nature of his office.'

[14] J Rozenberg, 'The Iraq war Inquiry has left the door open for Tony Blair to be prosecuted *The Guardian* (6 July 2016), www.theguardian.com/commentisfree/2016/jul/06/iraq-war-inquiry-chilcot-tony-blair-prosecute.

> Private DNA testing reveals to the Prime Minister that one of his MPs (X), at risk of losing her seat at the impending General Election, is in fact a close relative. Without revealing the result of the test publicly, he secures the elevation of X to the House of Lords. The secret comes out following X's death two years later.

Nepotism at the highest level of government commonly goes unchecked worldwide. Many people in the UK and elsewhere find it extraordinary that, for example, a US President is free to use powers of pardon respecting his own relatives,[15] when there might be hundreds of thousands of other far more deserving cases.[16] Clearly, on the facts of my example, judicial review – even were that remedy to extend to Prime Ministerial recommendations for membership of the House of Lords – is of no assistance in calling to account the Prime Minster himself for such inexcusable nepotism in the exercise of a prerogative power. Even so, a question arises over whether the Prime Minister could in theory be prosecuted for misconduct in a public office, on the grounds that he wilfully misconducted himself to such a degree as to amount to an abuse of the public's trust in the office holder.

Two key questions arise. First, are there any species of official conduct engaged in by elected officials, however egregiously wrong, that should be entirely exempt from the criminal process? Secondly, even if a species of official conduct is not entirely exempt from the criminal process, what considerations ought to determine the applicability of that process? The issues have been given contemporary significance by the decision of the US Supreme Court in *Trump v US*.[17] This case broke new ground by creating actual or potential presidential immunity in relation to a range of 'official' acts taken by a US President acting in that capacity, even when those violate otherwise generally applicable (criminal) laws. The decision was not concerned with a misconduct in public office offence – Trump was charged with conspiring to commit election offences[18] – but the issues raised are of general significance to legal systems around the world. The approach of the US Supreme Court can usefully be compared with the decision of the UK Supreme Court in *R v Chaytor & Others*.[19] This was the case in which it was unsuccessfully argued by Chaytor and others that parliamentary privilege (and hence immunity from prosecution) covered their conduct in dishonestly over-claiming parliamentary expenses.[20]

[15] See the discussion of the President Biden case, below.

[16] Article II, Section 2 of the Constitution of the United States empowers the President with executive clemency, the power to grant reprieves and pardons. The power to pardon is in US law regarded as outside the scope of judicial review: *Connecticut Board of Pardons v Dumschat* 452 US 458 (1981). See the authoritative discussion in FO Bowman III, 'Presidential Pardons and the Problem of Immunity' (2021) 23 *Legislation and Public Policy* 425. The concept of a mercy prerogative exercised by the King was formally established by Parliament as a right exclusive to the Crown during King Henry VIII's reign by 1535.

[17] *Trump v United States* 603 US 593 (2024).

[18] Conspiracy to defraud the US in violation of 18 USC §371, (2) conspiracy to obstruct an official proceeding in violation of §1512(k), (3) obstruction of and attempt to obstruct an official proceeding in violation of §1512(c)(2), §2, and (4) conspiracy against rights in violation of §241.

[19] [2010] UKSC 52.

[20] For detailed discussion, see J Horder, *Misconduct in Public Office: Law and Politics* (Oxford University Press, 2018).

What is significant in this context is that in *Trump v US*, the US Supreme Court was clear that if an *ex hypothesi* criminal act fell within the scope of official acts attracting presidential immunity, then the immunity would apply even if the act was committed with an improper motive. Article II of the US Constitution provides that 'The executive Power shall be vested in a President of the United States of America.' Speaking for the majority, Justice Roberts said:

> We conclude that under our constitutional structure of separated powers, the nature of Presidential power requires that a former President have some immunity from criminal prosecution for official acts during his tenure in office. At least with respect to the President's exercise of his core constitutional powers, this immunity must be absolute.[21]

The analogy with *Chaytor* is the implicit proposition in that case that, even if individual expense abusers could be held to account for defrauding a bona fide parliamentary scheme, if the scheme itself was corruptly devised and agreed by parliamentarians to benefit themselves (whether or not the scheme was then abused by individual MPs), this agreement would be covered by parliamentary privilege and immune from suit.

These court decisions are significant. A fundamental presupposition of public-decision-making is that decisions are justified by public reason, and are not attributable (say) to personal or self-serving reasons.[22] In this respect, thus, the criminal law – along with public and private law – has been rendered powerless to deter and punish some species of important breaches of political trust involved when one or more public officials at the highest level engage in wrongdoing for self-serving reasons.

4.2 When should Politicians be Immune from Misconduct Charges?

As Hegel acknowledged, there can be no official response to crime until the advent of civil society, with the establishment of state institutions in which the principles governing criminal law and its enforcement are embedded;[23] and the establishment of those institutions may involve imposing limits to the reach of those legal principles. To give a simple example, the political value of maintaining the supreme legislative authority of Parliament itself may take precedence over the protection of rights and duties by other bodies such as criminal courts, bodies that are themselves subject to Parliament's authority concerning their jurisdiction. Accordingly, if (say) a government legalises and then employs bribery to win contracts overseas, it ought not to be possible to seek to impugn such

[21] *Trump v United States* 603 US 593 (2024), 606.
[22] Horder (n 20) 149–54.
[23] GWF Hegel, *Outlines of The Philosophy of Right*, TM Knox, trans (Oxford University Press, 2008) 220.

actions – however reprehensible – through a prosecution for misconduct in public office. The use of bribery in such circumstances manifests a 'proceeding in Parliament' (authorisation through the supreme legislative process), and is for that reason legitimate, involving, in law, no 'misconduct' in public office. How far should such an immunity from suit extend?

In *Trump v US*, the US Supreme Court rejected the view that safeguards against vexatious prosecution (such as a test, in English law, of whether a prosecution is in the public interest) were sufficient to justify taking a relaxed view about the scope for criminal proceedings against presidential action.[24] To begin with, regarding matters within the President's 'conclusive and preclusive' authority, authority not derived from or shared with Congress, there can be no form of legal challenge.[25] Included within the scope of 'core constitutional powers' are the power to pardon convicted offenders, the power to remove – and thus supervise – those who wield executive power on the President's behalf, and the power to control recognition determinations of foreign countries. In the court's view, thus, an act falling within the scope of such core constitutional powers could not be subject to prosecution, even if it fell squarely within the definition of a (serious) criminal offence. That might seem controversial, but it is submitted that it seems so only because of the privileged position given by the US Constitution to one person – the President – in relation to the use of powers respecting which there is no requirement to be accountable to law during tenure.[26] In effect, the court in *US v Trump* turned core presidential powers into powers akin to those involved in the prerogative powers reserved for the monarch, the very kind of powers from which the founders of the US Constitution sought to escape.

So far as official acts involving authority derived from or shared with Congress are concerned, a different test applies:

> [T]he President must therefore be immune from prosecution for an official act unless the Government can show that applying a criminal prohibition to that act would pose 'no dangers of intrusion on the authority and functions of the Executive Branch'.[27]

The justification given by the Supreme Court for the application of the presumption of immunity was that, to expose the President to prosecution for official acts might entail 'that the President would be chilled from taking the "bold and unhesitating action" required of an independent Executive'.[28] One may, perhaps, marvel at the idea that what requires shielding from criminal prosecution or civil action, when – for example – a President attempts to influence the Vice President's oversight of the

[24] *Trump v United States* 603 US 593 (2024), 615.

[25] *Trump v United States* 603 US 593 (2024), 607 and 609.

[26] 'The only person who alone composes a branch of government': *Trump v Mazars USA*, 591 US 848, 868 (2020). I put on one side here the possibility that a President can be impeached, which is as much a political as it is a legal process.

[27] *Trump v United States* 603 US 593 (2024), 611, citing *Nixon v Fitzgerald* 457 US 731, 754.

[28] *Trump v United States* 603 US 593 (2024), 670 (Justice Roberts). The Supreme Court added that there could be no immunity for 'unofficial' actions engaged in by the President.

certification proceeding in his capacity as President of the Senate,[29] is the possibility of 'bold and unhesitating action', as if the use of such corrupt presidential influence is to be equated with the position of doctor who must take a series of rapid emergency treatment decisions after coming upon the scene of an accident with many people seriously injured.

Putting such points on one side, the constitutional position of a US President is, of course, very different from that of any executive official in the UK. Even so, it is not wrong to side with the US Supreme Court in thinking that there might be different levels or stages of immunity from criminal (or civil) action. For example, in the UK context, one might follow the US Supreme Court's basic line of analysis as follows:

(a) *Complete immunity from prosecution*: Debates and legislative decisions in Parliament; prerogative powers reserved to the monarch.
(b) *Presumptive immunity from prosecution*: Parliamentary conduct or activity other than debates or legislative decisions; executive actions including use of prerogative powers, such as appointments to office and pardons.
(c) *No immunity from prosecution*: Conduct outside the scope of official duties or powers.

Which decisions fall into which of these categories? I will not dwell on (c). A US example is the sexual harassment case involving Paula Jones and Bill Clinton.[30] In this case, the Supreme Court held that a sitting President was not immune from civil suit, respecting allegations involving unofficial conduct prior to becoming President; and the same was held to be true of criminal allegations arising in similar circumstances in *US v Trump*.[31] In the UK, it has long been the understanding that criminal conduct falling outside the scope of official duties may be subject to prosecution, even if in some sense it is the performance of the official duties that provides the explanation for the conduct: an example would be an assault committed following heated debate in the House of Commons.[32]

Included in category (a) are the prerogative powers reserved to the monarch, including the power to appoint the Prime Minister, the power to summon and dissolve Parliament, and the power to prorogue and recall Parliament.[33] Also covered, as suggested at the beginning of this section, will be the adoption of

[29] See the discussion of this example in *Trump v United States* 603 US (2024), 622.
[30] *Clinton v Jones* 520 US 681 (1997).
[31] 603 US 593 (2024), 615.
[32] In recent times, there have been brawls in Parliaments, or violence used or threatened, around the world, including in Italy, Israel, Japan, Australia, Hong Kong, Serbia, Turkey, South Africa and Jordan. A serious incident in the Greek Parliament led to criminal charges being preferred: www.politico.eu/article/greece-parliament-brawl-konstantinos-floros-vassilis-grammenos.
[33] See the discussion in R Hazell and C Sayers-Carter, *Reforming the Prerogative* (UCL Constitution Unit, 2022), www.ucl.ac.uk/constitution-unit/sites/constitution_unit/files/198_reforming_the_prerogative.pdf.

substantive legislative measures, changes to procedures for debates and the processing of legislation, along with immunity from the laws of libel as it might otherwise apply to debate in Parliament.

Why should such decisions be completely immune from prosecution or challenge? The difficulty with opening such decisions to prosecution, when they are taken in bad faith, is this. To say that accountability in criminal law for wrongdoing in breach of political trust must remain a legal possibility, no matter the nature of the political decision or the status of decision-maker, grants an ultimate discretion in the matter of remedy for breach of political trust to (unelected) prosecution authorities. That is no less controversial than saying that deterrence and 'punishment' for such wrongdoing must sometimes come only in the form of (fear of) internal Parliamentary sanctions, public disgrace or ejection from office. In the political sphere, what may matter as much as the nature of the person or body that has engaged in an alleged wrong, is the nature of the person or body in whose hands it is proposed to place the power to remedy that wrong. What, though, about the example of 'cash for questions' mentioned earlier? If complete immunity is conferred on debates in Parliament, then the asking of Parliamentary questions in exchange for (hoped for) reward, cannot in itself give rise to criminal liability for bribery or attempted bribery. However, that leaves open the possibility that related actions outside of Parliament – such as prior meetings to agree terms of reward for the asking of questions, or the subsequent acceptance of rewards – would not be protected by immunity.

That brings us to the implicit decision in *Chaytor*[34] that immunity would extend to the collective Parliamentary decision to adopt an *ex hypothesi* corrupt scheme to lavishly over-compensate MPs for expenses incurred. Did that decision involve a 'parliamentary proceeding', meaning that it should be covered by absolute immunity ((a) above)? It can be argued that the notion of a 'proceeding in Parliament' should not be extended to cover 'housekeeping' matters purely ancillary to the democratic or legislative process itself, such as expense allowance schemes, or (say) financial allocations to refurbish Parliament.[35] So, in principle, MPs who corruptly agree an 'expenses' scheme designed to enrich themselves rather than simply to cover costs, should be in no better a position than individual MPs who dishonestly abuse a legitimate scheme.

These matters should properly fall into (b) above, meaning that they are covered by immunity – following the categorisation in *US v Trump* – only if, to deny such immunity would acceptably intrude on the executive function in question. In considering whether immunity applies to issues arising within category (b), the courts should have regard (i) to the high public interest in avoiding public sector corruption: a particular risk in the devising and use of MPs' expense schemes, if not – at least not to the same extent – in the making of decisions about the refurbishment of Parliamentary buildings, but also (ii) to

[34] See text at n 18 above.

[35] For further discussion of these issues, see Horder (n 20).

the importance of ensuring that challenges are not permitted to such decisions unless – to use a test from a different context – the decisions to be challenged are 'manifestly without reasonable foundation':[36] Parliament has a wide margin of appreciation for action in relation to such matters. Even so, in relation to point (ii), as Lord Neuberger put it in *R (RJM) v Secretary of State for Work and Pensions*, there may 'come a point where the justification for a policy is so weak, or the line has been drawn in such an arbitrary position, that, even with the broad margin of appreciation accorded to the state, the court will conclude that the policy is unjustifiable'.[37]

The expenses policy example is one falling within category (b) where prosecutors and the courts should be confident in acting on their judgments about whether or not a policy is 'manifestly without reasonable foundation'. That is because this example is one in which the political system is being used in a financially self-serving way. The example thus involves what I have called 'personal' corruption, a form of corruption widely condemned as wrong in countries across the world.[38] Personal corruption involves the use of a political or otherwise public position or system (and in cases involving fiduciaries, a business position or system) to advance the personal interests of oneself or one's family and friends. Imagine that the Home Secretary granted a pardon in exchange for a secret bribe, or gave passports to wealthy friends overseas. In such cases, a prosecution respectively for bribery, or for misconduct in public office, ought to be a legal possibility.

The case of the President Biden pardoning his own son is also an example that should be treated very differently under UK law, as is the incident in which Boris Johnson used his position as Prime Minister to nominate his brother for membership of the House of Lords.[39] As a matter of law under the US Constitution, President Biden is entitled to benefit from complete immunity respecting such an instance of personal corruption; but under the UK Constitution, notwithstanding the possibility that the law might in some such instances be used inappropriately for partisan reasons,[40] prosecutors should in general not hesitate to use the criminal law to punish and deter egregious instances of such high-level personal corruption in executive actions. It will then be for the allegedly corrupt office

[36] *R (on the application of SC, CB and 8 children) v Secretary of State for Work and Pensions and others* [2021] UKSC 26 [97] (Lord Reed).

[37] *R (RJM) v Secretary of State for Work and Pensions* [2008] UKHL 63 [57].

[38] For a discussion of personal and political corruption, see Horder (n 20) ch 5.

[39] H Gye, 'Boris Johnson in cronyism row after appointing his brother Jo Johnson and political allies to the House of Lords', *The i Paper* (31 July 20200, https://inews.co.uk/news/politics/boris-johnson-cronyism-row-house-of-lords-jo-johnson-ian-botham-56880.

[40] The Boris Johnson example is not entirely straightforward because it is an example of an appointment concerned with the exigencies of political government, and hence too easily exploited by litigants intent only on hampering the process of government, or on embarrassing a political opponent, for their own partisan reasons. On the problems that this issue poses for the courts, see *R (on the application of SC, CB and 8 children) v Secretary of State for Work and Pensions* [2021] UKSC 26 [162] (Lord Reed).

holder to show that, if such is the case, they had sufficient justification or excuse for their action.[41]

In determining whether a presumption of immunity should be considered rebutted, it may assist to prove a three-fold classification of the grounds on which this could be done:

(i) 'personal' corruption (benefiting oneself, family and friends, as in *Chaytor*, or the prime minister example);
(ii) 'political' corruption (involving a partisan motivation benefiting a particular party, religious or other similar group, whether or not one benefits oneself);
(iii) poorly judged or otherwise improper exercises of entrusted power (the Tony Blair case is an example of this).

Some examples of political decision-making within category (b) above may be challenged because they are alleged to have involved involve a different and more contentious type of corruption described in (ii) above. This is what I have called 'political' corruption, corruption in the form of partisan bias, that may not involve any personal (eg financial) benefit to the official displaying such bias.[42] An example, leading to a conviction at first instance, was the alleged misuse by Marine Le Pen of more than €4 million ($4.3 million) in European Parliament funds to cover domestic party expenses between 2004 and 2016.[43] In such cases, prosecutors should tread far more warily when considering whether not the public interest criteria for launching a prosecution have been met, not least because whether or not wrongdoing has occurred – or if it has occurred, whether it was justifiable or excusable to engage in it – may be a highly contested matter.

In many cases involving political decision-making falling within category (b), it is not wrong – or only contentiously so – to display political corruption (partisan bias) in taking a decision. That is because whereas the avoidance of personal corruption operates as a non-negotiable side constraint on activity in the public sphere, whether or not political corruption – involving partisan bias – should be avoided depends entirely on the decision-making context. For example, falling within category (b) will be uses of certain prerogative powers such as the power to make public appointments, the power to recognise foreign states or governments, declaring war, the power to sign international treatises, and the power to (re)organise the civil service.[44] In most normal cases, decision-making in relation

[41] For example, in the case of Boris Johnson's proposal of his brother for elevation to a peerage, Mr Johnson might argue that his brother could justifiably have been nominated by a disinterested party.

[42] See Horder (n 20) ch 5.

[43] www.politico.eu/article/marine-le-pen-guilty-verdict-national-rally-viktor-orban-giorgia-meloni-kremlin-donald-trump-elon-musk-reactions.

[44] See the discussion in Hazell and Sayers-Carter (n 33). For the view that such powers are in fact powers delegated by Parliament, see RD Kershaw, 'Revolutionary Amnesia and the Nature of Prerogative Power' (2022) 20 *International Journal of Constitutional Law* 1071.

to such matters will rightly be treated as in practice immune from challenge on the merits. One reason for that is that it seems tolerably clear that a bona fide decision concerning whether or not (say) to recognise a foreign state should not be influenced by the possibility that such a decision will be challenged by 'die-hard' political opponents of recognition; still less, that a prosecution for misconduct in public office may follow. More fundamentally, though, when it occurs, corruption in these decision-making spheres is likely to be political rather than personal in nature.

For example, a decision may be taken to recognise the government of a foreign state, in part because the government is currently politically aligned with (of the same political hue as) the UK Government. Another example might be a decision to send British troops to assist in a conflict overseas, where amongst reasons to do this features the partisan intention to bolster the Government's popularity at home. Decisions of this type are generally regarded as outside the scope of review and (a fortiori) prosecution for misconduct in public office, even if they do manifest partisan bias: political corruption. That is because governments enjoy a wide latitude to act on a range of reasons in such cases, meaning that acting for partisan reasons may permissibly feature in support of a decision – even if, perhaps, not as the sole reason for the decision. The same point could be made about decisions falling within category (iii), decisions that, although falling outside categories (i) and (ii), still involve an improper or poorly judged use of public power.

Quite simply, politicians have a very wide (criminal law) remit to get things wrong and take poor decisions. In the case of Tony Blair's advocacy in favour of military intervention in Iraq, the former Director of Public Prosecutions said that, 'without seeking any advice whatsoever, or calling for any evidence to determine whether this critical condition was met, Mr Blair simply expressed "the unequivocal view" that such further breaches [of Security Council Resolution 1441] had indeed occurred'.[45] Whatever one makes of a decision-making process, it seems strongly arguable that to expose the political decision-maker to criminal prosecution simply because of deficiencies (however egregious) in that process carries with an unacceptable risk of politicising the prosecution process and undermining its integrity.

So, where there is great latitude for ('wrong') decision-making within categories (ii) or (ii) above, there is a significant risk of the credibility of the prosecution services or the judiciary as impartial bodies being undermined, if they intervene:

> Judicial [or prosecutorial] independence is accepted only if the judiciary [or prosecution service] refrains from interfering with political processes. If the judicial [or prosecutorial] power is to be independent, the judicial [or prosecutorial] and political spheres have to remain separated.[46]

[45] C Coleman, 'Could Tony Blair face legal action over Iraq War' BBC News (7 July 2016), www.bbc.co.uk/news/uk-36738086.

[46] *R (on the application of SC, CB and 8 children) v Secretary of State for Work and Pensions* [2021] UKSC 26 [162] (Lord Reed).

In other cases, the case against prosecutorial intervention will be that there are some benefits to partisan bias in decision-making, rather than simply that such bias is unobjectionable when it forms part of a range of otherwise permissible reasons for political action. For example, someone might be appointed to ministerial office in part because they are a member of the Prime Minister's own party, even though it would have been in the national interest to appoint someone else. In such a case, the Prime Minister manifests partisan bias, but this kind of bias is tolerated in the UK political system, and might be justified to some extent if it means that ministerial political loyalty is more likely to be secured.[47]

However, with other kinds of public appointment powers in the hands of ministers, such as the appointment of the Chair of the BBC,[48] there is an implicit constitutional understanding – as a matter of public trust – that those powers will not be used corruptly: either in the form or personal or political corruption. In the UK, that implicit constitutional understanding has its roots in the reforms of public office-holding in the late eighteenth and early nineteenth centuries.[49] It can be inferred from the range of bodies set up to guide the use of powers of patronage and high-level discretion by public office-holders,[50] and from the development of general principles – such as the Nolan Principles and the Ministerial Handbook – to govern all forms and levels of public decision-making. The existence of that implicit constitutional understanding means that, albeit in exceptional circumstances, the offence of misconduct in a public office (like corruption offences) can in theory be applied to grossly improper decision-making in relation to some public appointments. That is because the applicability of such offences is triggered by the extension of norms of public integrity into that high-level political domain.

In that regard, it is disappointing that the US Supreme Court's saw fit to find that, when scrutinising the exercise of presidential powers conferred by or exercised jointly with Congress, prosecutors must take no account of the President's motive for acting.[51] It is a criminal law commonplace that the intentions with which actions are performed can change their normative significance, and can hence turn a seemingly 'official' act into an unofficial one. One hopes that the UK Supreme Court, considering a misconduct in public office case such as the

[47] As indicated above, it would be a different matter in a case of personal corruption. So, for example, an incoming Prime Minister should not necessarily be immune from prosecution for misconduct in public office, if their method of appointing people to ministerial positions is to offer them to the highest bidder.

[48] See Hazell and Sayers-Carter (n 33), and www.gov.uk/government/publications/bbc-charter-and-framework-agreement/bbc-charter.

[49] See, for example, the discussion in B Buchan and L Hill, *An Intellectual History of Political Corruption* (McMillan, 2014), conclusion.

[50] See eg the discussion in Hazell and Sayers-Carter (n 33).

[51] *Trump v United States* 603 US 593 (2024), 619 (per Justice Roberts), citing *Harlow v Fitzgerald* 457 US 800 (1982), 817–18, 'bare allegations of malice should not suffice to subject government officials either to the costs of trial or to the burdens of broad-reaching discovery'.

example of the nepotistic appointment to the House of Lords, given above, would not adopt a similar line of argument. Of course, allegations that improper motives influenced the taking of a controversial political decision, or the performance of a difficult official duty, are commonplace, and frequently just an unnecessary distraction; but that kind of worry needs to be met not with the granting of immunity, but simply with a high bar for evidential sufficiency, and a stringent test of public interest in prosecution.

PART II

Working in Parliament and the Senedd Cymru (Welsh Parliament)

5

Reflections on the Constitution: A Clerkly View of Privilege

SIR MALCOLM JACK

5.1 Role of the Clerk of the House

The Clerk of the House of Commons is the principal adviser on procedure and practice to the Speaker of the House and to all Members of Parliament (MPs). In that role the Clerk is at the centre of the British mix of Executive and Legislature which characterises its constitution. Members of the House of Commons (and of course the House of Lords) include Government ministers. As well as advising MPs who are not part of the Government about how to achieve their goals through the procedural rules and mechanisms of the House, the Clerk will be consulted by members of the Government, particularly the Whips, about how business is conducted. This consultation is made easier by the fact that the government bench is next to the Table of the House where the Clerk sits during sessions. Through other offices of the Clerk's department, clerks will be consulted by parliamentary counsel on the passage of legislation and in select committees, by civil servants in the department on which a particular committee is focused. All these connections are links between the Executive and the Legislature.

The role is an ancient one dating back to 1363 when Roger de Melton was appointed the first Clerk. The two Clerks who have played the most prominent role in the history of constitutional affairs are John Hatsell (1733–1820) and Sir Thomas Erskine May (1815–86).

Hatsell's tenure of the Clerkship of the House is the longest recorded. Beginning in 1768, it continued until his death in 1820 despite the fact that he had retired to live in the country for his last 20 years of his life. His retirement was cushioned by an extremely generous financial settlement. That arrangement and the conditions of tenure of the Clerkship were changed after his death. His abiding contribution to constitutional history was his *Precedents of Proceedings in the House of Commons*[1] which, according to one distinguished historian, 'is deservingly regarded as an

[1] Precedents of Proceedings in the House of Commons (J Dodsley, 1781).

authority upon all matters which it treats'.[2] It was, in fact, the first comprehensive guide to the procedures of the House current in his time, dealing with such matters as prorogation and adjournment of the House, the stages of bills, impeachment and the work of committees. Hatsell acknowledged his debt in preparing his work to the heavily annotated *Precedent Book* of Speaker Arthur Onslow from earlier in the century.

Hatsell's legacy has been overshadowed by the work of Sir Thomas Erskine May. May was Clerk of the House from 1871 to his death in 1886. Deeply involved in the day-to-day business of the House, May also produced the first nine editions of *Parliamentary Practice* which has subsequently become the bible of parliamentary practice and procedure, reaching a twenty-fifth edition in 2019.[3] Starting with a detailed description of the constitution and organisation of Parliament, May, as it is colloquially known, covers the subjects of elections, membership of the House and its officers, the rules governing conduct of MPs, relations with the Crown, legislation and Select Committees and, most significantly, with the privileges of Parliament.

5.2 Parliamentary Privilege

Parliamentary privilege – those rights and immunities enjoyed by Parliament collectively and by Members of each House individually – is a complex subject with a long history. The House of Commons has asserted certain privileges since the Middle Ages. The broad context of the early history of privilege is the House's stand against executive interference in the person of the monarch; the later context is broadly that of Parliament's struggle with the courts over jurisdiction in this area of *privata lex* (the law of Parliament).

The Resolution of the House of Commons of 1675 stated that purpose in the clearest possible terms when it said that privilege exists so that Members might freely attend the public affairs of the House, without disturbance or interruption.

The second important matter to understand is that the most widely acknowledged of Parliament's rights – free speech – is already codified in Article IX of the Bill of Rights 1689. Freedom of speech is famously asserted in Article IX of the Bill itself which provides that: 'The freedom of speech and debate or proceedings in Parliament ought not to be impeached or questioned in any court or place out of Parliament.'[4] Whatever the nuances of the words of Article IX, the principle of freedom of speech underpins it. That core principle enables a Member of either House to say whatever he or she thinks fit in debate. However offensive or injurious

[2] OC Williams, The Clerical Organisation of the House of Commons 1661–1850 (Clarendon Press, 1954) 82.

[3] T Erskine May, A *Treatise Upon the Law, Privileges, Proceedings and Usage of Parliament* (Charles Knight & Co, 1844).

[4] Bill of Rights, 1869, Art IX.

those remarks might be to a named individual, that individual will have, as matters currently stand, no obvious recourse to the courts – at least to the British courts – since they will, amongst other things, not be able to take out any action for defamation. Within the House of Commons itself certain rules and conventions about decorum and the proper way of addressing MPs themselves are enforced by the Chair. Nevertheless, as Enoch Powell reminded the House, the absolute nature of privilege protects an individual MP even when he or she is expressing opinions abhorrent to all of his or her colleagues.[5]

Nevertheless, throughout the modern period of the history of privilege, the courts have not hesitated to interpret provisions of that statute. Parliament eventually accepted that the parameters of privilege are indeed defined by the courts while the courts accepted that the internal working of Parliament (exclusive cognisance) was an area into which they would not venture.

The boundary line between what is a matter for Parliament and what is a matter for the courts is set out in a pronouncement made by the then Attorney-General in 2009. The most significant principle enunciated in that Memorandum is the Attorney-General's statement that: 'it is clear that the determination of whether material is inadmissible in a criminal trial by virtue of Article IX is a matter for the court.'[6] This would not prevent Parliament from intervening in any proceedings to assert the privileges of the House, something that has happened on a number of occasions. That could include the House arguing that reliance on particular material in court proceedings could contravene Article IX, though the court is not bound by views of the House, as has been shown in the case of *Pepper v Hart*.[7] In 1992 as a result of the decision in that case, of the courts now feel freer to refer to Parliamentary material where legislation is considered to be ambiguous or obscure, or leads to absurdity. In such cases, Parliamentary material can be used to elucidate the meaning of statute.

Although it is true that the ruling in *Pepper v Hart* has been applied with some caution in subsequent case law, that decision and the examination which the courts now give to parliamentary materials to determine the proportionality of a measure in terms of its compliance with fundamental rights imperatives mean that the courts are becoming increasingly familiar with looking at statements made in Parliament and with the parliamentary process more generally.

Any attempt by the House to determine any questions of law relating to parliamentary privilege would risk upsetting the comity that exists between the two organs of the constitution. In a more general sense, for Parliament to justify privilege in the twenty-first century it is necessary to convince the public that it is a vital element in the functioning of a democratic Parliament. That objective can only be

[5] *Hansard* HC Deb Vol 949, cols 43–44 (2 May 1978).

[6] Memorandum submitted by the Attorney-General, Committee on the Issue of Privilege (Session 2009–10) HC 62 Appendix IV.

[7] [1993] AC 593. See M Hutton et al (eds), *Erskine May Parliamentary Practice*, 25th edn (LexisNexis, 2019) 340.

achieved if there is clarity about what parliamentary privilege is and how it enables Members of both Houses to fulfil the mandate given to them, in the case of the Commons by those who have elected them. The Houses also retain certain powers collectively. Among these is, at least in theory, the power to punish contempts. These powers derive from the historic nature of Parliament as a High Court; in modern times they are exercised extremely sparingly and only so that Parliament can function effectively and so that those who serve it (including those who come as witnesses before Parliamentary committees) can do so with impunity. These powers are an expression of the unique authority that Parliament as a whole exercises and they place Parliament in a special category.

When the rights or immunities of Parliament are attacked, a breach of privilege has occurred: in the House of Commons there are various ways in which Members can raise alleged breaches of privilege, the most regular being a written submission to the Speaker, who rules on whether a debate is in order on the question of referring the matter to the Committee of Privileges. While the Speaker's role is critical in deciding whether there appears to have been a prima facie breach, the substantive matter is settled by an inquiry by the Committee of Privileges. Each House retains the right to punish contempts – that is, actions that thwart the Houses in their business, which may go wider than a breach of one of the defined privileges. Free speech remains an essential part of the effective functioning of Parliament. However, the historical context of its provenance in the clash between the Commons and the monarch no longer applies. In modern day Britain the threat, real or imagined, is seen as coming from an increasingly powerful senior judiciary.

5.3 Other Privileges – Freedom from Arrest, Favourable Construction

Other earlier privileges were also historically important. Freedom from arrest was another part of the protection the Commons sought from action by the monarch against those who displeased it. As with other privileges it is based upon the absolute priority of Members to attend and to participate in the business of Parliament. But it is important to note that it has never been extended to protect Members from arrest on criminal charges (except in the Chamber when the House is actually sitting), a principle clearly upheld by the courts in the case of *R v Chaytor*[8] in which, significantly, the Speaker did not intervene on behalf of the House. The privilege of freedom from arrest, in modern times, is very limited and there are a number of statutory provisions of detention which apply to Members notwithstanding any privilege; other ancient privileges, such as asking the sovereign to place a 'favourable construction' on the House of Commons' proceedings, have fallen into desuetude.

[8] Hutton et al (n 7) 351. *R v Chaytor* [2010] UKSC 52.

5.4 Parliamentary Standards Bill 2009

One of the most threatening challenges to parliamentary privilege arose with the introduction of the Parliamentary Standards Bill in 2009. The Bill was introduced by the Government of the day following the so-called expenses scandal which had involved, as it later emerged, a small number of excessive claims for expenses by MPs. The Bill established a body corporate, to supervise the provision of salaries and allowances to members of the House of Commons with a commissioner who would investigate any matters connected with their payment.

In a memorandum to the Justice Select Committee, I, as the Clerk of the House of Commons, stressed that my concern was with the constitutional implications for parliamentary privilege (including the right of free speech) and the extent to which the courts are likely to come into conflict with Parliament thereby.[9] The first provision in the Bill addressed in my memorandum was in Clause 6, which required the House of Commons to maintain a code of conduct incorporating the Nolan Principles of public life. But the incorporation of such a provision in statute would make it possible for its interpretation to become a justiciable issue in the courts interfering with the principle of exclusive cognisance, the most important protection of parliamentary privilege.

Other provisions in the Bill also threatened the freedom guaranteed to Parliament under the Bill of Rights. One clause dealt with the reasonableness of the Commissioner's request opening up the possibility of the courts reviewing the exercise of disciplinary powers by the House.

A clause of enforcement in which the new authority could make recommendations about disciplinary powers to the Standards Committee could also open up a new area for action in the courts. One of the widest qualifications of the Bill of Rights was a provision to allow evidence of proceedings for offences to be admissible in court proceedings. In the last proposed clause there was a suggestion that actions of the Speaker in the House could be the subject of judicial review.

After considerable public airing and support from expert witness of the Clerk's criticism, much of the offending provisions were withdrawn in a newly drafted Bill.

5.5 Conclusion: Should Privilege be Codified?

While certain aspects of parliamentary privilege have arisen from common law practice, some recent attention has focused on whether ambiguities in the statutory provision, the Bill of Rights 1689, should be clarified by a modern statute.[10]

[9] See Justice Committee Constitutional Reform and Renewal Written Evidence of Dr Malcolm Jack, Clerk and Chief Executive of the House of Commons HC 791-I, 25 June 2009.

[10] See R Gordon and M Jack, *Parliamentary Privilege: Evolution or Codification?* (The Constitution Society, 2013).

A number of these difficulties were identified in the report of the Joint Committee, 1999. They include the exact meaning of the phrase 'proceedings in Parliament' and what is meant by the words 'impeached or questioned in any court or place out of Parliament'.[11]

Greater clarity, it is argued, would mean there was less need for recourse to the courts to determine the meaning of particular phrases. Clearer drafting would circumscribe further judicial intervention in defining the scope of parliamentary privilege.

There is also the question of penalties for those in contempt of Parliament. At present there is little that can be done by the House of Commons in cases where potential witnesses to select committees refuse to attend or in any other way impede the work of the committees.

Australian Parliamentary Privilege Act 1987

A Commonwealth precedent exists in Australia where the Australian Parliamentary Privileges Act 1987 redefines the ambit of privilege in modern, unequivocal language. The Australian Act is the principal comparative model for codification in the UK since it is in place in a Commonwealth country with a similar common law tradition.

The Australian Act begins with definitions (as envisaged by the Joint Committee on Parliamentary Privilege in their recommendation) but it does so in a broad way to maintain maximum flexibility. Thus contempt or offences against the Houses are not defined in terms, but rather the principle is stated and a threshold set. The Act states that conduct does not constitute an offence against the Houses:

> [U]nless it amounts, or is intended to amount to an improper interference with the free exercise by a House or committee of its authority or functions, or with the free performance of a member of a member's duties as a member.[12]

The Act sets out penalties for committing contempts in the presence of the Houses or their committees. Fines range from A$5,000 for individuals to A$25,000. There is also provision for imprisonment (and the release of anyone so imprisoned) by order of resolution of either House.

Other provisions of the Act deal with the reporting of proceedings with the defence of 'fair and accurate'[13] reporting in actions for defamation against those reporting; protection of witnesses from 'fraud, intimidation, force or threat'; unauthorised disclosure of evidence; and certain immunities from arrest and court attendance by Members.[14]

[11] Report of the Joint Committee on Parliamentary Privilege HL 43; HC 214 (Session 1998–99) para 37.

[12] Australian Parliamentary Privileges Act 1987 (as amended) s 4.

[13] ibid, s 10.

[14] ibid, s 12.

However, the application of federal law in the precincts is reasserted in case of doubt. Members are not protected from criminal prosecution by parliamentary privilege. One of the most important sections of the Australian Act deals with parliamentary privilege in the context of court proceedings. The section begins with a declaration that the provisions of Article IX of the Bill of Rights apply to Parliament. The next subsection defines 'proceedings in Parliament' as 'all words spoken or acts done in the course of, or for the purposes of or incidental to, the transacting of the business of the House or of a committee' and, 'without limiting the generality of the foregoing', includes:

(a) the giving of evidence before a House or a committee, and evidence so given;
(b) the presentation or submission of a document to the House or a committee;
(c) the preparation of a document for purposes of or incidental to the transacting of any such business; and
(d) the formulation, making or publication of a document, including a report, by or pursuant to an order of the House or a committee and the document so formulated, made or published.[15]

Further subsections prohibit the production of evidence, questions, statements, submissions or comments made in Parliament to be used in court or tribunal proceedings which either question proceedings or attempt to draw conclusions from them. Exceptions are provided for the use of such evidence so far as they relate to Section 57 of the Constitution (Disagreement between the Houses) as well as to the interpretation of an Act, following the principles established in *Pepper v Hart*.

The Australian precedent provides a form of codification which should be considered as a model for a necessary change in the UK.

[15] ibid, s 16(2).

6

House of Lords Reform

THE RT HON THE BARONESS D'SOUZA CMG

6.1 Introduction

So much has been written about House of Lords Constitutional Reform in the last century, one wonders what more there is to say. However, a brief survey of those incremental reforms that have been implemented might serve as an agenda for bolder reforms in the immediate future. Why should the Upper Chamber be reformed? Alright, it is not perfect but it does its job, does it not? My concern about the urgent need for reform of the House of Lords arises from my over 20 years as a Crossbench peer, and for nine of those years as the Convenor of the Crossbenches and then the Speaker of the House of Lords. It became obvious that reform, with particular focus on reducing the numbers of peers *and* updating the procedures for nominating new peers, was deeply desired not only by the public but by the Lords themselves. Each and every one of us is acutely aware that the present arrangement of an ever-growing Upper Chamber together with some dubious nominations was bringing the Second Chamber into disrepute, a status it does not deserve.

The questions to consider include the following: what does the Lords actually do? How well is it performing? Is it adequately equipped for its task? And what might make for a better chamber, or even a better system altogether? Above all, what is its constitutional position, and how far does this limit abrupt or radical changes?

The House of Lords is an unelected body – a factor of great contention, provoking calls for a democratically elected Second Chamber. I will return to this, but insofar as the Upper Chamber has legitimacy, it arises from its minute scrutiny and revision work. Large and complicated Bills pass from the Commons to the Lords, inadequately scrutinised. This occurs because of the conventions of a guillotine or programme motion in the Commons whereby only a certain amount of time is allocated to a given Bill, often resulting in whole sections of new legislation that have not even been looked at, let alone scrutinised. This can happen particularly at the start of a new government – which wishes to assert its power and desire for change with a virtual avalanche of new Bills.

The Lords, on the other hand, does not have severe time limits and therefore undertakes more thorough scrutiny, resulting in revision amendments. There is no doubt that due to this careful attention, Bills leave the Lords in a far better shape than when they arrived!

6.2 Constitutional History from the Tenth to Nineteenth Centuries

These functions of the House of Lords have a long history as part of the constitutional settlement of the UK.

Let us go back in history to appreciate how the Lords' composition and functions have changed by means of gradual evolution. It was William the Conqueror who began to consult his barons in council in 1066.[1] The first recognisable parliamentary system of nobles, clergymen and commoners was convened in 1295, eventually splitting into two bodies: nobles and clergymen[2] (Lords); and elected representatives (Commons). There followed some 400 years of relatively minor adjustments to the form and functions of the Upper Chamber, such as Acts of Union integrating Scottish and Irish representatives in the Upper Chamber. It was not until the Civil War of 1649 that the Lords,[3] as well as the King, were abolished only to be restored in 1660, with the return of the monarchy.

Profound Reform Acts were introduced in the nineteenth and early twentieth centuries, some 400 years later, and broadly defined what the House of Lords is today: a non-elected advisory chamber lacking the power of veto and with reduced delaying powers.

6.3 Constitutional History in the Twentieth and Twenty-First Centuries

The Parliament Acts 1911 and 1949 were seminal in the constitutional settlement of the Lords. In response to the 1910 Lloyd George's Peoples' Budget,[4] the nobles of the land were precluded from voting down money bills, and their delaying powers on other legislation were limited to two years; the 1949 Act reduced this delaying power to one year.[5] Furthermore, it was agreed that the House of Lords did not have the power to bring down a legitimately elected government, nor was it allowed to initiate financial legislation. The questions about the composition of the House as well as its size also began to be part of the discourse.[6]

But the debates following from the Parliament Act 1911 centred around aspects we continue to wrestle with today. The governments of the earlier part

[1] The UK has a largely unwritten constitution and proceeds, in the words of Bagehot, on the basis of habit, usage and convention. W Bagehot, *The English Constitution* (Chapman and Hall, 1867).

[2] The bishops survived Henry VIII's Dissolution of the Monasteries (1536–41) and 26, a number agreed in 1847, continue to sit in the House of Lords today.

[3] Described as 'useless and dangerous'.

[4] Aptly named 'the people's budget'.

[5] Use of the Parliament Act to override Lords objections is extremely rare, it has only been used seven times in the post-war years – the last time it was invoked was the Hunting Act 2004.

[6] The Parliament Act 1911 includes reference to the House of Lords being constituted on a 'popular and not on a hereditary basis'.

of the twentieth century constantly remarked on the difficulties of reforming the House of Lords. The Duke of Sutherland in a debate in 1925 said that reform of the House of Lords 'bristles with difficulties and has proved itself to be one of the most complicated and difficult questions of our modern times', adding that many who had considered it had given up in despair.[7]

There there has since been a slew of reform legislation and statutory instruments that have further altered the shape and powers of the Upper Chamber,[8] including the Life Peerages Act 1958 enabling women and commoners to be appointed to the House; and the Peerages Act 1963 allowing hereditary peers to renounce their titles and thus be eligible for election to the House of Commons.[9]

Since the Life Peerages Act 1958, allowing appointment on merit, reforms have, relatively speaking, arrived thick and fast![10] Three further significant modern Acts have defined the House of today and the House of Lords (Hereditary Peers) Act 2026 has altered radically its constitutional position. In 1999, under a Labour Government, the House of Lords Act mandated the removal of the greater majority of hereditary peers, the introduction of so-called 'peoples' peers',[11] and the establishment of an Independent House of Lords Appointments Commission (HOLAC),[12] the function of which is to nominate independent, Crossbench peers and to vet other nominees from the parties as to their 'propriety'.[13] It is important to remember that this Act was only intended to create an interim arrangement by retaining some 92 hereditary peers[14] until more radical reform could be agreed.

In 2005 the Constitutional Reform Act, among other major changes, created the Supreme Court and achieved a separation of powers between the legislature and the judiciary. In 2014 the House of Lords Reform Act introduced mechanisms for peers

[7] See M Purvis, 'Reforming the House of Lords in the Shadow of the Parliament Act', The House of Lords Library (23 April 2025), https://lordslibrary.parliament.uk/reforming-the-house-of-lords-in-the-shadow-of-the-parliament-act.

[8] For example, the Salisbury-Addison Convention, adopted in 1945, prevented the Lords from voting down any Bill presented in an election manifesto.

[9] As did Tony Benn, formerly Lord Stansgate, and later, the Earl of Home, who became Prime Minister Alec Douglas Home in 1963.

[10] No fewer than five Private Members Bills on Lords reforms have been tabled (some several times) between 2000 and 2024. In addition, two significant reports have been published: 'Report of the Speaker's Committee on the size of the House' (31 October 2017) (The Burns Report), www.parliament.uk/globalassets/documents/lords-committees/size-of-house/size-of-house-report.pdf; and 'A New Britain: Renewing our Democracy and Rebuilding our Economy: Report of the Commission on the UK's Future' (2022) (The Brown Report), https://labour.org.uk/wp-content/uploads/2022/12/Commission-on-the-UKs-Future.pdf.

[11] This allowed the appointment of non-party affiliated, or independent, peers usually based on having achieved excellence in their chosen profession.

[12] It is important to note that the establishment of HOLAC was not included in the Bill and thus it is not a statutory body.

[13] The term 'propriety' is contentious; essentially it means ensuring that party nominees are domiciled in the UK and are solvent. The call these days is to expand the term to include suitability and willingness to contribute to the work of the House. This is, in part, an attempt to rule out those who offer little expertise other than substantial donations to the party of their choice.

[14] By means of the Weatherill Agreement 1999.

to retire and to be removed following persistent non-attendance or the commission of serious crimes. Finally, in 2015, the House of Lords (Expulsion and Suspension) Act enabled permanent removal of peers following serious misdemeanours.

Meanwhile two Private Members Bills[15] were introduced by the Lords Grocott and Norton, which illustrates the eagerness within the House itself to hasten its own reform.

Lord Grocott, over many years and in different parliaments, introduced a Private Member's Bill which aimed to convert all existing hereditary peers to life peerages by ending the by-elections for their replacement, and thus finally terminated the hereditary principle implicit in the House of Lords Act 1999. This truly sensible Bill which would have rid Parliament of the principle but not the people, was, for unfathomable reasons, repeatedly dismissed by the governments of the day. Had it been enacted, the current Bill on dismissing *all* hereditary peers, causing much dissent, would have been redundant.

The constitutional expert, Lord Norton, who has long concerned himself with House of Lords reform, similarly introduced a Private Members Bill in 2025[16] – a Bill which again included sensible and much-desired reforms, such as putting HOLAC on a statutory footing and introducing merit-based criteria for nominees.

In 2017 Lord Burns published the results of a committee on Lords Reform[17] in which it was recommended that membership be capped at 600, that a 'two out, one in' procedure be adopted, and that there be a 15-year term limit for all new peers.

The Brown Report (2022)[18] sought to abolish the House of Lords and replace it with a smaller, democratically elected second chamber called the Assembly of the Nations and Regions. Although respected, the recommendations have, so far, not been seriously considered.

In 2024, the new Labour Government introduced a House of Lords (Hereditary Peers) Bill to complete the 1999 Act and remove remaining hereditary peers. It is anticipated that this Bill will be enacted within the current year, despite strong opposition.

6.4 The Urgent Need for Further Reform

Now this may seem an awful lot of reform Bills and Acts, but as the constitutional expert Meg Russell has pointed out, major reform legislation, averaged over the centuries, only comes roughly every 50–55 years.[19] Some have argued that this

[15] Private Members Bills do not usually make their way onto the statute book since they rely entirely on the gift of Parliamentary time granted by the Government of the day, which is sparingly given.

[16] House of Lords (Peerage Nominations) Bill 2025.

[17] The Report of the Lord Speaker's Committee on the Size of the House 2017.

[18] The Brown Report (n 10).

[19] M Russell, *The Contemporary House of Lords* (Oxford University Press, 2013); and M Russell, 'A Stronger Second Chamber; Assessing the Impact of House of Lords Reform in 1999 and the Lessons for Bicameralism' (2010) 58 *Political Studies* 866.

slow pace is a safeguard – the UK, as we know, has a largely unwritten constitution and the intricate connections between legislative procedures are delicate and in danger of having major unintended consequences if abruptly removed.[20] The clamour for an elected upper chamber does not address potential constitutional dilemmas; for example, what mechanisms would there be to resolve major disagreements between the Lords and the Commons; and who would elect the valuable contingent of independent or Crossbench peers? How would the balance of power between MPs and peers within individual constituencies be managed? Would a newly elected House of Lords require a retinue of staff, offices and researchers at the taxpayer's cost? And would the current elected chamber, the House of Commons, feel easy about possible curbs to its powers from a competing chamber?

Another area of considerable media and parliamentary concern are the mechanisms by which peers are appointed to the House of Lords. The current system allows the Prime Minister of the day to exercise his or her privilege at any time during tenure, but usually at the end of each Parliament and/or upon the resignation of a Prime Minister.[21] This powerful gift has often resulted in the appointment of batches of peers whose suitability as legislators has been questioned. Briefly, a Prime Minister will wish to reward those who have given exceptional service to a given party, or even donated significant amounts to the party concerned. Sometimes party leaders will wish to create a vacancy in a safe seat, by elevating an MP to the House of Lords, to bring in potential ministers. All political groupings need to refresh their benches, bringing in new expertise, younger members and representatives of ethnic and religious groups. However, it is felt that this Prime Ministerial privilege has been unduly stretched to admit those whom HOLAC has ruled unsuitable on the grounds of propriety.

Independent or Crossbench peers are appointed by HOLAC, which follows selection criteria such as genuine political impartiality, a commitment to attend and participate in the work of the House, and to have relevant experience and distinguished achievement. HOLAC also vets all appointments as to evidence of domicile in the UK as a taxpayer and the absence of a criminal record.

There has been much debate within and outside Parliament on the role of HOLAC. It is widely felt that it should have statutory powers to withstand pressure from leaders to favour party-donors or those who are unsuitable or unwilling to commit to working as a legislator.[22]

[20] It has been suggested a statute encompassing the UK's structural constitutional principles to include the commitment to the rule of law and other civil liberties and human rights be agreed. Commission on Political Power: Options Paper: Executive Reform 2024

[21] Liz Truss, who was Prime Minister for a total of 49 days, was nevertheless granted, by convention, a resignation list of three peers. It is notable that both Gordon Brown and Theresa May exercised restraint in appointing peers at the end of their terms of office.

[22] The pending Private Members Bill, House of Lords (Peerage Nominations) Bill 2025, introduced by Lord Norton, specifies new criteria including 'suitability and willingness to work'.

The appointment of new peers is linked to the numbers dilemma. The House of Lords, as is well documented, is far more numerous than needed to fulfil its duties and cover all the Lords Committees. Ideally, it is believed that the Lords should never be larger than the Commons, and preferably much smaller than its present number of approximately 740 peers.[23] It is widely agreed amongst peers themselves that a House of 600 or less would be acceptable. However, by capping numbers, this would limit the power and privilege of the Prime Minister, something that most leaders would not easily accept! That said, the pressure for a reduction in numbers is reaching a point where some new constitutional arrangement will have to be reached if the – already dented – reputation of the Lords is to be preserved.

6.5 The House of Lords in Action

Few people really appreciate the limited but important revising and scrutinising tasks that the House of Lords undertakes; the Lords undoubtedly helps to shape legislation, although revisions are often rejected by the elected chamber, the House of Commons. To properly perform its function, the House of Lords, ideally, should be peopled by those who have genuine expertise and experience in a particular area and who are committed to scrutinising draft legislation – almost line by line. Additionally, it is preferable that those who do the detailed work of scrutiny are relatively independent in the sense of examining complicated Bills on their merits and not on a party-political basis. The goal is to achieve Bills that do not contradict existing legislation, are clear, especially for the courts to be able to interpret, do what they intend, and comply with democratic procedures and international treaties on human rights.

The question is to what extent does the patient work done by the Lords actually change legislation – in other words, how far does the government of the day accept the amendments from an unelected House? The short answer is more often than is supposed, although the mechanisms can at times be somewhat obscure. Let us take a few examples where the Lords has dug in its heels over legislative clauses; it will be noted from these examples that the predominant concerns expressed by the Lord refer to civil liberties and constitutional propriety including trial by jury, identity cards and Legal Aid.

In 2008 a Labour Government introduced a Counter-Terrorism Bill in which it was proposed to extend pre-charge detention of those suspected of terrorist acts from 28 to 42 days.[24] The Lords objected, in large numbers (309 to 118) to this curtailment of liberty, arguing that should there be a need for longer pre-charge detention to gather evidence, there was always the opportunity to provide relevant evidence for the courts to decide. A blanket period of 42 days would rapidly

[23] The much-repeated statistic here is that the world's only larger upper chamber is China's National Congress. This is also a cost since each individual attendance costs the taxpayer allowances of up to £371 per diem.

[24] Pre-charge detention for those suspected of terrorist acts was extended from 7 days to 14 days in 2003 and to 28 days in 2006.

become the norm and as such was a severe threat to individual liberty. The to-ing and fro-ing from the Lords to the Commons resulted in an unprecedented *38-hour* continuous sitting of Parliament, during which the amendment was passed and repassed from the Lords to the Commons several times. While this particular clause was finally omitted from the Act, other controversial clauses were resolved by a compromise whereby the legislation would be reviewed on an annual basis by means of a sunset clause.[25]

In 2012 the Welfare Reform Bill proposed, among other measures, to limit benefits to children and cancer patients, and to confer penalties on social housing tenants with a spare room. These measures were again defeated in the Lords and accepted by the Government.

In 2022–23 a Conservative Public Order Bill contained several clauses threatening to limit public protest, introducing new criminal offences, and giving the Secretary of State powers to bring civil proceedings against those causing serious disruption, including 'suspicion based' and 'suspicion-less' stop and search powers. The Bill also included many executive orders or secondary legislation conferring considerable powers on the Minister in the absence of the rigorous scrutiny given to primary legislation.[26]

The Bill was given Royal Assent in 2023 but remains highly controversial, occasioning debate and action on conflicting needs for public order *and* the right to freedom of expression, including public demonstrations. The High Court in *R (on the application of the National Council for Civil Liberties) v Secretary of State for the Home Department*[27] ruled that certain extension of powers within the Act were unlawful, citing concerns over Human Rights. It was argued that suppression of legitimate protest activities transgressed a fundamental pillar of democracy, namely the right to freedom of assembly and protest.

At the time of writing, the House of Lords is once again at odds with the Government in objecting to a clause in the the Data (Use and Access) Bill 2025 that enables artificial intelligence (AI) companies to use information from the creative arts for building training models, but crucially without attribution.[28]

A careful analysis of the period 1999–2013[29] shows that the governments suffered 181 defeats in the Lords and the amending clauses were accepted by the Commons. This, despite the lack of a veto and the lack of a 'democratic mandate', is certainly evidence of legislative influence.

Various factors persuade governments to accept Lords' amendments. A major factor is the number of votes cast and, in particular, how many backbench rebels

[25] This has been supplanted by new anti-terrorist legislation, but is still subject to an annual sunset clause.

[26] Secondary legislation, or Executive Orders, enables the Government of the day to issue, sometimes significant legislation by Order. These are not usually subject to normal parliamentary scrutiny, nor can they be altered by means of amendments. For example, Serious Disruption Prevention Orders.

[27] [2024] EWHC 1181 (Admin).

[28] This, it is argued, negates copyright, and severely penalises the creative arts.

[29] See Russell (2010) (n 10).

there are. Governments make shrewd judgements as to proper use of limited parliamentary time, public opinion and, of course, the importance of the policy under review. The Lords in turn takes account of other factors – the degree of cross-party support, public interest, and constitutional principles. For example, Manifesto Bills, according to a convention,[30] are always passed, although initial efforts to indicate disagreement may result in some exchanges between the two chambers. The House of Lords is mindful that it is a non-elected, advisory body – there to ask the Government of the day to think again, not to thwart government policies.

Another important factor that has assumed constitutional relevance is the expertise which the Lords has nurtured. In a debate[31] concerning the retention of the cultivation of 14-day-old embryos for laboratory research – a highly ethical and moral issue – those arguing passionately in its favour were themselves world-renowned research specialists on regenerative medicine and treatment of genetically based disabilities. Undoubtedly this persuaded many who did not necessarily fully comprehend the technical aspects. The argument was won, allowing the UK to remain as a world leader in such research. This reliance on specialist expertise becomes especially relevant when dealing with increasingly technical issues, such as climate change and AI. Apart from draft legislation, the House of Lords also debates issues of public concern such as assisted dying for the terminally ill. This Bill will be debated and voted in the House of Lords in the spirit of genuine enquiry into its strengths and weaknesses. Again, the tenor of the debates is not about gaining party political points, but more a thorough discussion on the moral, ethical and legal aspects of such contentious Bills. Expert, and disinterested, scientific and technical argument confers a degree of democratic legitimacy on the Lords' proceedings.

Of course, the Lords loses debates and amendments, often on important issues. A recent example of a Lords defeat relates to the Rwanda Bill. The 2023 Safety of Rwanda (Asylum and Immigration) Bill, passed without murmur in the Commons, allowed the Government to deport to Rwanda *all* illegal migrants arriving in the UK. On the face of it this seemed like a sensible solution to the increasing number of illegal migrants arriving in the UK by very dangerous routes. In fact, the Bill transgressed a number of obligations held by the UK under International Treaties[32] and failed in protecting human rights by not guaranteeing safety in Rwanda itself. The issue of *refoulement* was central to the Supreme Court's finding[33] that it would be unsafe to deport refugees to Rwanda. This notwithstanding, the Bill received

[30] The Salisbury-Addison Convention 1945, by which it is customary for such Bills to be passed. Coventions are not legally, but politically, binding and support constitutional stability in the largely uncodified Constitution enjoyed in the UK where formal rules may be absent.

[31] This was debated many times between December 1989 and February 1990 in the context of the Human Fertilisation and Embryology Bill, later The Human Fertilisation and Embryology Act 1990; the issue of extending the limit to 28 days has re-emerged in 2024.

[32] Notably the 1951 UN Refugee Convention ratified by the UK.

[33] *R (on the application of AAA) v Secretary of State for the Home Department* [2023] UKSC 42.

Royal Assent in April 2024. A few months later with advent of a new administration, the Act was dropped.[34]

This Bill was a clear example of the tensions between principle and political expediency that all governments have to confront. It was eventually lost due to legal challenges and ethical considerations, but most of all by a change in government at the 2024 general election.

6.6 What Constitutional Reforms would Improve the House of Lords?

Again, this is an area of research and comment that is difficult to summarise, so voluminous is the literature. That said, the issues that come up for discussion time and time again include the following.

6.6.1 The Size and Composition of the House including Political Balance

This is undoubtedly a pressing issue, as has been emphasised. The elimination of hereditary peers would reduce numbers by approximately 80. However, this would be unevenly distributed between the different groupings. The Conservatives and the Crossbenches stand to lose 37 and 32 hereditary peers respectively; whereas Labour would lose six and the Liberal Democrats would lose five. However, there is now serious consideration being given to reappointing those dismissed hereditary peers, many of whom perform an invaluable service, to life peerages.

Calculating the optimal size of the Upper Chamber is a tricky business if only because there should be more than lip service paid to the political balance in the House and on what measure it should be based. For some years there has been an imbalance of a larger Tory contingent; although this has never amounted to an overall majority due to the significant presence of groupings other than the two main parties.[35] The current Labour Government is addressing this imbalance by appointing several new peers in the first few months of its administration.

Perhaps even more pressing is streamlining the membership by barring those peers who either do not attend regularly or those, even regular attenders, who rarely if ever contribute to the work of the Lords. There has been an understandable reluctance on the part of whips to promote voluntary retirement and a firm reluctance of some peers to heed this pressure.[36] There is also a question of reviewing

[34] It is estimated that the total cost of this effort to deport refugees to Rwanda cost approximately £700 million; only four migrants, on a voluntary basis, actually went to Rwanda.

[35] That is the Liberal Democrats, the Crossbenchers, the Greens, the DUP and UUP and unaffiliated peers.

[36] There are cases where non-attenders have repeatedly been asked to step down – without results.

those on 'leave of absence', a convention that is often abused.[37] Some argue that the retirement provisions of the 2014 Act, although effective, could be made more so if there were to be a more permissive attitude to the retention of House of Lords-issued computers and telephones which have, after all, usually reached their end of life!

6.6.2 The Arrangements for Appointments to the House

This remains an area of discontent. As has been said, HOLAC has no statutory power[38] and its decisions have, on occasion, been subject to disagreement on the part of the Prime Minister of the day and adverse media comment. The hope is that in time a Convention would emerge in which the Prime Minister of the day would exercise considerable restraint in nominating peers and act always on the advice of the Independent Commission. This body, in turn, should have more detailed, more relevant,[39] and, possibly stricter, terms of reference for its nominations criteria.

Given the firm belief that the House of Lords is, and remains, an advisory chamber, the debate on its powers is muted. Some would wish it to have more powers over budgetary matters, or money Bills, but few would insist that its legislative revisions *must* be taken into account by the elected House of Commons.

6.6.3 Whether the Lords should be a Wholly or Partly Elected Chamber

This is an ongoing dilemma. The permutations are many; a fully elected Upper Chamber; partly elected, partly appointed – to preserve the Crossbenches; a wholly appointed house; a House composed of functional constituencies.[40]

The resolution of this dilemma in its essence is the 'democratic' argument. Certainly, a fully elected Upper Chamber would fulfil the democratic purpose but, as outlined above, it introduces some almost insurmountable difficulties such as cost, competition with the House of Commons, powers, and mediation between the two chambers. A compromise of some elected and some appointed would create two classes of peers, raising questions as to who would have precedence in legislative decisions. One outcome might be to rely mainly on appointed peers together with vastly improved recruitment procedures, but which would retain the

[37] In at least a few cases, peers have requested and been given, leave of absence for many years, although there are rules guiding this procedure.

[38] Were it to be made a statutory body, as many would wish, its decisions would be subject to judicial review and this might open a whole new area of challenges!

[39] Such as filling gaps in current expertise, with an emphasis on technological experience.

[40] In this permutation, the professions (medical, academic, legal, etc) would nominate one of their own to represent their interests.

all-important quality of a relatively non-party political membership in which draft legislation is considered on its merits.[41]

6.7 Conclusions

The UK's constitutional framework is based on parliamentary sovereignty, separation of powers and constitutional conventions.

The many efforts to reform the House of Lords have shown a gradual trend from a chamber dominated by hereditary peers towards one of appointed peers, reflecting a degree of meritocracy, expertise and geographic representation. It could be argued that in the absence of a second chamber, something very similar would have to be invented. This results from the traditions of the House of Commons which severely limit the degree of scrutiny legislation afforded – due as always to time pressures. Given that form should follow function, and given the advisory role of the House of Lords, the *complementarity* between the two chambers of Parliament is an important constitutional principle that must not be overridden lightly!

Even a cursory survey of the House of Lords as it was 100 years ago and today shows a radically altered Chamber. But the reforms have been largely incremental; sweeping suggestions such as abolishing the current Lords altogether in favour of a wholly elected chamber have not found, even public, favour.

The twenty-first century has seen steady pressure for reforms focusing on legitimacy, accountability, size and efficacy, and the modernisation of its powers and ethics.[42] The trend in the structure and work of the House of Lords has been towards more assertiveness accompanied by a degree of confidence, perhaps even a sense of legitimacy. It has also developed into a chamber in which over 30 per cent of its members are women. This gradual process will no doubt continue, despite the urgent need for reform. The House of Lords' role as a revising and scrutinising chamber remains constitutionally significant and provides a valuable check on government powers.

[41] Interestingly, in a survey carried out by *The Times* in 2006, 72% of the participants agreed that the Lords should be a partly elected legislature; when asked, in the same survey, if it should remain mainly appointed, 75% agreed in order to 'maintain a degree of independence'. The survey results are available at https://yonderconsulting.com/poll-archive/political-attitudes-27.pdf.

[42] For example, the House of Lords now has a Standards Commissioner and a Conduct Committee.

7

The Welsh Devolution Journey 2011–17

THE RT HON THE LORD JONES OF PENYBONT

When I was asked to write this contribution, I considered how I should approach it. Should I do it as an academic or as someone who was, to slightly misquote the musical *Hamilton*, in the room where it happened? I hope I have managed to do both. In section 7.1 I will firstly describe the history of devolution before 2011. In section 7.2 I will then look at the step change that took place in 2011 and developments through legislation and Supreme Court judgments since. Finally, in section 7.3 I will look at the issues that remain unresolved.

7.1 Devolution 1997–2011

On 18 September 1997 the Welsh people voted to establish a body that would be known as the National Assembly for Wales. Just over half the electorate voted, and, of those, just over half voted in favour. The new body was, in effect, to take over the executive functions of the then Welsh Office, which had acquired a steady stream of responsibilities since its establishment in 1964. The subsequent Government of Wales Act 1998 set up a body corporate[1] with no distinction between Executive and legislature, which perhaps is unsurprising given the fact that it had no primary legislative functions. It was to be made up of 60 members elected via a mixed system, where 40 were elected from individual constituencies and a further 20 members elected from five regions using the d'Hondt system.[2] This meant that a party that was more successful in electing constituency members would be far less so in terms of those in the regional list, a system designed, perhaps optimistically, to promote more consensual politics. The new body was to be funded entirely via block grant from Westminster[3] and had no powers to raise any income of itself. Its structure was more akin to a local council of the time rather than a parliament. Elections were to take place every four years. Despite being a corporate body, it would have a First Secretary and individual Secretaries holding a specific portfolio ('the Executive Committee')[4] and without

[1] Government of Wales Act 1998, s 1(2).
[2] ibid, Sch 1.
[3] ibid, s 80.
[4] ibid, s 56.

powers except those specifically delegated to them by the Assembly. This led to strange anomalies where, for example, I was a voting member of the committee that was responsible for scrutinising me.

The original Bill, before its amendment in Parliament, had proposed that instead of a cabinet there would be an Executive Committee made up of the chairs of the different subject committees. As an executive body, the early years of the Assembly was marked by a lack of serious business that could be taken. It was able to take important decisions such as the introduction of the bus pass for the over 60s, but much of the time was taken up in debating Statutory Instruments that were uncontroversial. So it was that the Potatoes Originating in Egypt Order and the Undersized Whiting Order found themselves the subjects of debate in the Assembly Chamber when they would simply have been made in one of the Whitehall government departments by a Secretary of State in England. The Assembly's powers at this stage were based on the conferred powers model. Those powers were found in the National Assembly for Wales (Transfer of Functions) Order 1999.[5]

The model was designed to be flexible so that further powers could be added without the need for primary legislation, an example of such a transfer being the devolution of responsibility for foot and mouth disease. As the minister responsible for agriculture at the time of the 2001 outbreak, I became acutely aware of the then status quo where animal health was devolved, with the exception of foot-and-mouth disease. This might have created problems if there had not been goodwill between the administrations in Cardiff and Whitehall. Despite having responsibility for the disease in Wales, the Ministry of Agriculture, Fisheries and Food (MAFF), as it was then, did not have any civil servants in Wales except for a small team of vets. An agreement was made that Assembly civil servants would be made available to MAFF to help with the fight against the disease. The Assembly's permission was also needed to dispose of infected carcasses, and the split in responsibilities could have caused major problems in Wales had there been a disagreement between the administrations. This led to the devolution of foot and mouth powers to Wales and the appointment of a Chief Veterinary Officer for Wales for the first time in the aftermath of the outbreak.[6]

Despite its flexibility, the basis of devolution in Wales was via the conferred powers model, meaning that unless a power was specifically transferred to Wales it was assumed to remain at Westminster, the opposite of the situation in Scotland.[7]

The absence of a difference between the Assembly and the Cabinet led in the early 2000s to the use of the term 'Welsh Assembly Government' by the then First Secretary, Rhodri Morgan, to describe the Assembly Cabinet. This also led a change of name for office-holders: the First Secretary became First Minister, in line

[5] www.legislation.gov.uk/uksi/1999/672/contents/made?lang-eng.

[6] 'Wales gains foot and mouth powers' BBC News (14 October 2004), news.bbc.co.uk/1/hi/wales/3744084.stm.

[7] Scotland Act 1998, Sch 5.

with Scotland and Northern Ireland; and secretaries became ministers.[8] Although of no legal effect as the Assembly still remained a corporate body, it created a de facto separation between the Executive and legislature to mirror the structure of the Scottish and Northern Irish devolution models.

However, the main debate in the middle of that decade revolved around whether the Assembly should gain primary legislative powers. At this stage in its development the Assembly was obliged to finance, for example, health, education and local government, but had little power to change their structures. That would require primary legislation, and this obliged the Assembly to bid for legislative time at Westminster in the same way as a UK government department. There was no doubt that such a step would be a major change in the Assembly's legislative competence, and it was the subject of a major political debate.

There were also internal challenges for those framing legislation. The old Welsh Office had sometimes shown some autonomy in creating secondary legislation, but in the main had followed English models when drafting Welsh secondary legislation. The Assembly's executive autonomy had meant that new, Wales-only legislation had to be drafted, but this had been done with skills that already existed in the civil service. Unlike Scotland, however, the Welsh Office had not been called on to draft standalone primary legislation from scratch and so there was a need to develop those skills for the future. What followed was a compromise piece of legislation which set the scene for the development of devolution over the next few years.

The Government of Wales Act 2006 was undoubtedly a major piece of legislation, creating the path for the later establishment of a fully fledged legislature, although it did not go far enough for many of us at the time. For the first time, primary legislative powers would be devolved and Acts of the Assembly would be created.[9] The Assembly's competence to legislate was found in Schedule 7 of the Act. Crucially, however, this competence would only come into being *after* a referendum on the issue.[10] This did not mean, however, that the Assembly's legislative powers remained where they were in 1999 because the Act also introduced a 'halfway' house where the Assembly could acquire primary powers, but only on a case-by-case basis.

To explain in detail the process that was created would take an entirely separate chapter, given how complicated it was, so instead I will try to summarise it. Schedule 5 of the Act created 20 *fields* of responsibility where the Assembly could acquire primary powers; these were largely based on the existing executive powers of the institution. However, when the Act came into force those fields were empty. How then to populate those fields? There were two ways in which powers to pass primary legislation could be obtained: firstly, through a provision in an Act of the UK Parliament; and secondly, through a process that became known as the

[8] www.senedd.wales/mediaiqoprscx/qg07-0056-english.pdf.
[9] Government of Wales Act 2006, s 107 unamended.
[10] ibid, s 103.

Legislative Consent process. The latter involved the Assembly making a request to Parliament to gain primary powers which, if successful, would insert a *matter* into one of the fields indefinitely. Thus, once a power was devolved, it remained so. The Assembly could not, however, gain a power which would populate a field in its entirety, so it was not open to the Assembly to request that the powers to legislate in a field should be devolved *en bloc*.[11]

What tended to happen was that the request was focused on a particular matter such as provision for the Welsh language in a specific context. The process involved the Assembly making a request to the UK Parliament for a matter to be devolved. This then went to Westminster for full consideration by both Houses of Parliament. If successful, a Legislative Consent Order would be made which gave the Assembly de facto primary powers regarding that matter. The Assembly could then then use its new legislative process to pass a*n Assembly Measure*, the first of which was the NHS Redress Measure 2008. A Measure would then require Royal approval. In reality, a Measure was an Act of Parliament in all but name and the process was criticised for its complexity. It did however give the Assembly the opportunity to acquire the skills to draft primary legislation but could not be a long-term solution to the question of primary powers.

Three other noteworthy changes were made by this Act. First, a Welsh Seal was commissioned for the first time. Created at the Royal Mint in Llantrisant, this metal disc is used to make the imprint on the seal of an Act, done manually by the First Minister using a peculiar yet effective machine.[12] Secondly, there was the creation of the post of Counsel General as a member of the Welsh Government, and as its chief legal advisor.[13] Although such a post had existed before, the title had been given to the head of the Assembly's legal department, a civil servant. Although not a law officer in the strictest sense given that there is not a Welsh jurisdiction (of which more below) it nevertheless created a post that is as close as Wales gets to an Attorney-General. Thirdly, the monarch was to formally appoint Welsh ministers[14] and would grant royal assent to future Assembly bills.[15] Finally, the Executive and legislature were separated, with 'Welsh Assembly Government' being recognised as the formal name for the Executive.[16]

7.2 Devolution Post-2011

In 2011 the opportunity came to hold a referendum on the full devolution of primary powers within the areas of competence listed in Schedule 7 of the Act. Together with Ieuan Wyn Jones, the Deputy First Minister, we set a date for

[11] ibid, ss 94–95.
[12] ibid, s 116.
[13] ibid, s 49.
[14] ibid, s 48.
[15] ibid, s 115.
[16] ibid, s 45.

3 March, with some reservations on my part. I have always thought that holding a vote at a time of year when it gets dark early depresses turnout but, once agreed, we were ready to go. Unlike in 1997, the 'Yes' campaign attracted support from Conservative politicians, and the then leader of the Opposition joined all the party leaders at the launch of the campaign at the University of South Wales. Crucially, the referendum was agreed by David Cameron, the then Prime Minister, otherwise it could not have taken place. The referendum question was not simple. It tried to explain the status quo and what would happen if there was a 'Yes' or 'No' vote. I was concerned that people would not understand what the question was about, so while campaigning I distilled the question down to 'Do you think all the laws that only affect Wales should be made in Wales?' The result was a resounding 'Yes', over 63 per cent voting in favour, and of the 22 Welsh counties, only Monmouthshire (just) voted against.[17]

Although the 2011 referendum extended the Assembly's powers significantly it remained the case that it was still dependent on the block grant it was able to draw down from the UK Government. Unlike the Scots, the Welsh Government (the 'Assembly' in the title having been dropped informally by me after the 2011 Assembly election), still had no powers to raise any form of taxation. This was to change with the Wales Act 2014, legislation introduced jointly by Chief Secretary of the Treasury, Danny Alexander, under then Secretary of State for Wales, David Jones.[18] Although a relatively short bill, it contained significant additions to the powers of the Assembly. For the first time some taxes were to be devolved, in particular stamp duty (now known in Wales as land transaction tax)[19] and landfill tax.[20]

For the first time, then, the Assembly acquired revenue-raising powers albeit in a limited form. There was also a further provision allowing for further tax devolution with the approval of the UK Parliament and the Assembly.[21] This was an important change to the principles that had previously governed the way Welsh devolution had operated, namely that lawmaking powers had been progressively devolved, but any taxation powers withheld. That taxation was not devolved was strictly observed by UK governments, and it had caused ambiguity in the way in which section 106 of the Town and Country Planning Act 1990 operated. This is the section that enables local authorities to require developers to pay a sum of money as part of the planning application. Was it devolved entirely to the Assembly as a planning matter, or was it a taxation matter that was not devolved? The matter was never tested in the courts.

The Wales Act 2014 also made provision for the future devolution in part of income tax[22] with fluctuations in revenue managed by new, limited borrowing

[17] www.senedd.wales/media/gclkwa5f/11-017-english.pdf.
[18] UK Government, 'Impact Assessment: The Wales Bill' (20 March 2014), www.gov.uk/government/publications/wales-bill.
[19] Wales Act 2014, ss 15–17.
[20] ibid, ss 18–19.
[21] ibid, s 116C.
[22] ibid, ss 8–11.

powers for Welsh ministers[23] and the power devolved to set a Welsh income tax.[24] Importantly, however, this was only to be devolved after a referendum,[25] which many in all parties thought was doomed to fail. There was no desire on the part of the Welsh Government to see income tax devolved and any referendum ran the danger of the public seeing it as a mechanism to increase taxes. Certainly, the assumption was at that time that these powers would not be devolved in the near future, if at all. Borrowing, however, remained a problem. And unlike governments in England and Northern Ireland, the Welsh Government could not borrow, which meant that projects that would move forward through borrowing in those two countries would not happen in Wales.

Other significant changes in the 2014 Act were a ban on holding a dual mandate as an Member of Parliament and Assembly Member;[26] the extension of an Assembly term to five years;[27] removing the prohibition on candidates being on both the constituency and regional election lists,[28] a restriction previously introduced in the 2006 Act; and the formal name change of the Welsh Assembly Government to the Welsh Government.[29]

However, there were still ambiguities regarding the Assembly's legal competence. The Government of Wales Act 2006 had sought to define the parameters of competence but three important cases before the Supreme Court were to have a lasting effect on the way Welsh devolution operated. Where there was a question as to the competence of an Act of the Assembly, the 2006 Act provided a process where the Supreme Court's view could be sought through a reference by either the Counsel General for Wales or the Attorney-General for England and Wales.[30]

It was, however, a Scottish case that was the first to test the way in which the Supreme Court's approach to the justiciability of the decision-making process in the devolved bodies. This was *AXA General Insurance & ors v The Lord Advocate & ors*.[31] The case revolved around the question of whether under a 2009 Act of the Scottish Parliament, pleural plaques (a medical condition) constituted personal injury under Scots law. This was challenged by the appellants on two grounds: first, that it was incompatible with Article 1 of the European Convention on Human Rights and therefore outside the competence of the Scottish Parliament;[32] and secondly, that the legislation was open to judicial review as to an unreasonable, irrational and arbitrary exercise of the legislative authority of the Scottish Parliament.[33] The second ground was perhaps the more interesting. Parliamentary

[23] ibid, s 20.
[24] ibid, s 8.
[25] ibid, s 12.
[26] ibid, s 3.
[27] ibid, s 1.
[28] ibid, s 2.
[29] ibid, s 4.
[30] Government of Wales Act 2006, Sch 9.
[31] [2011] UKSC 46.
[32] Scotland Act 1998, s 29(2)(d).
[33] *AXA General Insurance& ors v The Lord Advocate & ors* (n 31) [17].

sovereignty has of course long been accepted by the courts, but what of Acts of devolved bodies? Were they subject to judicial review in the same way as a local authority or UK government department? The Court found for the respondents on the first ground, but what was more striking is what was decided on the second ground, which had an effect on all devolved bodies. The Court held that acts of the Scottish Parliament (and by extension the National Assembly for Wales) were subject to judicial review (otherwise this would have closed off questions of whether the Court could decide issues of competence), but only on issues of competence.[34] It further held that it would be wrong for judges to substitute their views as to what is rational or reasonable for the considered judgment of the democratically elected legislature.[35] In the words of Hope SCJ: 'Acts of the Scottish Parliament are not subject to judicial review at common law on the grounds of irrationality, unreasonableness or arbitrariness.'[36]

This places the devolved bodies somewhere between local authorities with their liability for judicial review on all grounds, and the UK Parliament with its full immunity from the courts. This was a new concept to UK constitutional law: a doctrine of limited sovereignty, perhaps one quite different from the Brezhnev doctrine of limited sovereignty known to international lawyers!

The second case of interest involved the very first Act of the Assembly. In *Local Government Byelaws (Wales) Bill 2012-Reference by the Attorney General for England and Wales*,[37] the Court was asked to consider whether it was lawful for Assembly legislation to remove a role held by the Secretary of State for Wales regarding the process of making local byelaws, not perhaps the most controversial issue to refer to the Supreme Court. The facts of the case were that via the Bill, Welsh ministers and the Secretary of State would lose their concurrent powers to confirm local government byelaws in specific circumstances (the Court called these the 'scheduled enactments'), originally found in the Wales (Transfer of Functions) Order 1999. Sections 6 and 9 of the Bill were the subject of the reference. The Court looked at whether both sections went beyond the Assembly's legislative competence unless the provisions were incidental to, or consequential on, another provision contained in the Bill, which would bring them within competence. The Court held that the removal of the Secretary of State's confirmatory powers in relation to the scheduled enactments would be incidental to, and consequential on, the primary purpose, which was to remove the same power from Welsh ministers.[38]

The Court also provided a definition of 'concurrent', holding that in this instance it meant that a function could be exercised by *either* Welsh ministers or the Secretary of State, or both acting together. Indeed, the Court said that it would be up to either party to use their 'good sense' to decide who should exercise a

[34] ibid [47].
[35] ibid [49].
[36] ibid [52].
[37] [2012] UKSC 53.
[38] ibid [52] and [53].

particular function in a particular case,[39] a forlorn hope perhaps in the world of politics. The case was important in the way that it looked to define the Assembly's powers in removing functions from Westminster ministers. The Court also invoked section 154(2) of the 2006 Act, which provided for a provision of a Bill to be read as narrowly as possible as is required for it to be within competence.[40] In retrospect, this was an unlikely issue on which to fight a battle on the part of the UK Government, especially as it seemed trivial.

The third, and most significant, case to reach the Supreme Court concerned the Agricultural Sector Wales Bill. The Agricultural Wages Act 1948 had regulated wages in the sector through an Agricultural Advisory Board for Wales, which was to be abolished by the UK Parliament under section 72 of the Enterprise and Regulatory Reform Act 2013.[41] This was strongly opposed by the Welsh Government and we took a decision to retain the system as it applied in Wales via a bill brought before the Assembly. Before the Bill received Royal Assent the Attorney-General intervened, referring the matter of whether the Bill was within the competence of the Assembly under section 112(1) of the 2006 Act. The argument of the Welsh Government was that it was entitled to legislate in an area that 'related to' a devolved area as contained in Schedule7 of the 2006 Act (having been brought into force following the 2011 referendum). Within the schedule the Assembly had been conferred competence over agriculture, bringing the Bill within competence in the view of the Welsh Government. In contrast, the UK Government argued that, in reality, the Bill dealt with a matter not devolved, ie employment and industrial relations. It was certainly arguable both ways.

The judgment itself proved to be a landmark in interpreting the devolution settlement as it then was. The Court outlined three principles that governed its approach. First, it reiterated that its approach would be governed by section 108 and Schedule 7 of the 2006 statute. Secondly, it declined to classify the Government of Wales Act as a special kind of statute, holding that all statutes are subject to the same approach. Thirdly, it looked at the purpose of the 2006 Act, namely to achieve a constitutional settlement.[42]

The Court acknowledged that a narrow approach could define 'agriculture' as only the physical activity of cultivating land or animal husbandry. However, it took the view that the purpose of the Bill was to protect and promote agricultural activity and, given that it was seeking to reintroduce a regime previously established by an Act that had 'Agriculture' in its title, it saw no difficulty in finding that the Bill related to a devolved competence. It was the second limb of the judgment that changed the way the then settlement operated by resolving the question of what was to happen when a Welsh bill could be related to both a devolved and a non-devolved matter. The Court held that the only question for it to consider

[39] ibid [41].
[40] ibid [64].
[41] www.legislation.gov.uk/ukpga/2013/24/section/72.
[42] ibid [5]–[6].

was whether the Bill related to 'agriculture' and did not consider any other issue.[43] The legislation (the Government of Wales Act 2006) did not then require that a provision should *only* (my italics) be capable of being characterised as relating to a devolved subject.

It is fair to say that this changed the boundaries of devolution profoundly, offering possibilities for the exercise of devolved powers in ways not foreseen by the Government of Wales Act 2006. Having received the judgment, we were of course keen to drive a coach and horses through the door that had been opened to us. The main example of this was the Trade Unions (Wales) Act 2017. This made certain regulations regarding workers in the devolved public sector which, for example, banned the use of agency workers in that sector.[44] It clearly related to a devolved area (public services) and to a non-devolved area (employment law) but, given the Court's stance in 2013, was clearly within competence. On this issue at least we were in the luxurious position of having greater powers than Scotland.

It was not surprising, then, that Wales's devolved powers would be re-examined after the 2015 general election. The Conservative Party had been re-elected on a manifesto to introduce a bill that would ostensibly strengthen devolution. There was no doubt in my mind that it wanted to redraw the boundaries of competence following the 2013 ruling, but we also had an interest in seeing further devolution and so the scene was set for a negotiation that ended with the Wales Act 2017, the most current legislation on Welsh devolution.

During those discussions it became clear that there were elements in Whitehall who were not keen on further devolution and indeed questioned in its current form. One of the issues I heard raised many times was the unified legal system of England and Wales, and the need to ensure that there was a limit to how different Welsh law could be. Our response was that the people of Wales decided to have primary powers in devolved areas in 2011 and cared little for jurisdictional issues. In a way, though, these objections had some weight. How can a single jurisdiction have many different laws that apply in different parts of that jurisdiction? England and Wales is the only jurisdiction in the common law world where two parliaments exist within it. It stands out as an abnormality. In other countries it is the norm that a parliament has its own jurisdiction, except for Wales. More on that below.

The 2017 Act is significant in that it introduced for the first time the reserved powers model for Wales. In summary, whatever is not specifically reserved to Westminster is assumed to be devolved to Wales. This reflected the Scottish settlement and, in part, that of Northern Ireland. The original conferred powers model had been established in the days before a primary lawmaking body had been established and so the 2017 Act updated the situation.[45] It would be incorrect to say that the Welsh Government welcomed the Act in its entirety, but it was a step in the right direction. There were still anomalies, such as with the devolution of ports

[43] ibid [46].
[44] Trade Unions (Wales) Act 2017, s 2.
[45] Government of Wales Act 2006, Sch 7A as amended by Wales Act 2017, Sch 1.

where the Milford Haven waterway was not devolved but all other ports were. I am being serious when I write that a civil servant at Whitehall suggested that it was in case the Welsh Government decided to cut the flow of liquified natural gas from the two terminals in the waterway to the rest of the UK. I have to say that it was not the first time that a malign intent had been ascribed to a request for a devolved power. I remember in the discussion about reorganising flood defence committees in 2004 that a fear was expressed that we would 'do something to the Severn to cause Gloucester to flood'. I did point out that we were not actually at war.

The Act also re-emphasised the 'permanence of the Assembly and Welsh Government',[46] a questionable statement in the context of parliamentary sovereignty. It also mentioned the Sewel Convention (where the UK Parliament will 'not normally' legislate in a devolved area without the consent of the devolved institution).[47] There is, however, no legal remedy if this is ignored by the UK Parliament, given the existence of (UK) parliamentary sovereignty.[48] It devolved to the Assembly power over its own elections[49] and over how it wished to be called;[50] indeed, on 9 October 2019 the Assembly changed its name to Senedd Cymru/Welsh Parliament. The other major change was in the area of finance where the Act specifically removed the provision in section 12 of the 2014 Act for a referendum on the devolution of income tax powers.[51] We as a Government had always been lukewarm about this but the *quid pro quo* was greater borrowing powers. The UK Government was keen for us to take some responsibility over income tax (I suspect they were tired at attacks on their parsimony!) and so the power to vary income tax by up to 10p was devolved, but without power over the income tax bands themselves (unlike Scotland). This unlocked the ability to borrow up to £1 billion for capital projects, a significant change.[52]

7.3 The Future

The Welsh devolution journey has not yet reached its end. Jurisdiction remains a live issue and there are others, such as the devolution of the Crown Estate, a matter devolved in Scotland. Perhaps the most glaring difference between the devolved legislatures is in the field of justice and policing, neither of which is devolved in Wales. There is no doubt that the full devolution of justice would be a major change, given that the Welsh Government would have to build up civil service expertise in the area and issues such as the prison estate (Wales has neither a category A

[46] ibid, s 1.
[47] ibid, s 2.
[48] *R (on the application of Miller and another) v Secretary of State for Exiting the European Union* [2017] UKSC 5 [151].
[49] Government of Wales Act 2006, ss 5–8.
[50] ibid, s 16.
[51] ibid, s 17.
[52] ibid, s 18.

men's prison nor a women's prison) would need to be resolved. There is no reason in principle, however, that justice could not be devolved. The argument against it tends to focus on the view that has served Wales well (those of who saw multiple court closures in Wales over the last 20 years would take different view).

The argument against police devolution revolved around the inescapable fact that crime is international. Yet policing is devolved in Scotland and Northern Ireland. The key point is that there should be full co-operation between the different forces, which I witnessed during the NATO summit where police forces from around the UK came to Wales as part of the policing operation. There was no difficulty in organising that even though different governments were responsible for policing across the UK.

What was needed, then, was for more work to be done to look at the justice system in Wales and produce recommendations that would inform future political decisions. With that in mind I set up a Commission on Justice in Wales in December 2017. It was important that the review was headed by a credible figure and Lord Thomas of Cwmgiedd, the former Lord Chief Justice of England and Wales, agreed to lead it. In 2019 the Commission reported and recommended a number of changes in the justice system in Wales that could be implemented in criminal, civil, administrative and family justice as well as making suggestions to strengthen skills and knowledge in the legal sector in Wales.[53] Amongst those recommendations was that there should be 'legislative devolution of justice',[54] an innocuous-sounding phrase that actually recommended the devolution of justice. The Welsh Government embraced the recommendations while the UK Government rejected them, a situation that exists to the current day.

I have strayed beyond the strict boundaries of 2011–17 to give some context to the establishment and possible future direction of the Welsh devolution settlement. I entered an institution in 1999 which had secondary legislative powers in the same manner as a Secretary of State and with no revenue-raising powers whatsoever. I left an institution in 2021 which was a tax-varying, lawmaking Parliament. It was a long journey, and it has not yet reached its conclusion.

[53] www.gov.wales/sites/default/files/publications/2019-10/Justice%20Commission%20ENG%20DIGITAL_2.pdf.

[54] ibid, 469.

8

The Justice Committee in the 2019 Parliament: Bridging the Gap

JACK SIMSON CAIRD

8.1 Introduction

The Justice Committee is one of the House of Commons' departmental select committees, tasked with examining the expenditure, administration and policy of the Ministry of Justice.[1] This chapter outlines the role played by the Justice Committee in the extraordinary 2019 Parliament, which was defined by the turbulence caused by Brexit and the COVID-19 pandemic. Those events shaped the work of all departmental select committees. The departmental select committees share certain core features; for example, all have the same powers as defined by the standing orders. However, in practice, each committee is unique, and how it approaches its work is defined by a range of factors including the Chair and the membership, the particular policy areas that fall within its remit and the nature of the relationship with the department it scrutinises.

This chapter explores the constitutional significance of the Justice Committee's approach to its work in the 2019 Parliament. It begins by providing an overview of the membership of the Committee and its working methods, and then considers some of the most notable examples of the Committee's scrutiny work in the 2019 Parliament. The Justice Committee, this chapter argues, acted as an institutional link between the House of Commons and the legal system of England and Wales in the 2019 Parliament. The Committee's scrutiny work was underpinned by a commitment to both the rule of law and the separation of powers, which I argue is critical to bridging the gap between the legislature and the legal system. The Committee is an important constitutional actor within the House of Commons, acting as check on the Government's approach to justice policy and monitoring the operation of the justice system.

[1] Standing Order 152; it is also tasked with the expenditure and administration of the Attorney-General's Office.

8.2 The Composition of the Justice Committee in the 2019 Parliament

Once a general election is called and the House of Commons is dissolved, select committees cease to exist. After a general election, it can take some months for them to be established, their membership confirmed and for their scrutiny work to be up and running. The 2019 general election was held on 12 December 2019 and the House of Commons met for the first time on 17 December 2019. On 29 January 2020, Sir Bob Neill was re-elected as the Chair of the Justice Committee. The first formal meeting of the Committee after the December 2019 General Election took place on 3 March 2020, by which point COVID-19 cases were being reported across the UK. Including the chair, there were six Conservative Members of Parliament (MPs) on the Committee: Rob Butler, James Daly, Sarah Dines, John Howell and Dr Kieran Mullan. Of these, only one (excluding the Chair), John Howell, had been an MP prior to the 2019 election. There were four Labour members – Maria Eagle, Andy Slaughter, Marie Rimmer and Ellie Reeves – all of whom had been first elected prior to the 2019 general election. Kenny MacAskill from the Scottish National Party was the only member not from the Government nor the Official Opposition. The initial membership held two in-person meetings before moving online in April 2020.

The importance of the Chair to the operation of a parliamentary select committee is difficult to overstate.[2] The Chair plays a vital role in setting the agenda and approach of the committee to its work. Sir Bob Neill first became the Chair at the start of the 2015 Parliament, after four rounds of voting by the House of Commons on 17 June 2015. Neill succeeded Sir Alan Beith, who was the inaugural chair of the Justice Committee in 2007 after it was first established following the creation of the Ministry of Justice. Neill was first elected in June 2006 after more than two decades of practice at the criminal bar. Neill served as the planning minister between 2010 and 2012. Prior to becoming Chair of the Committee, Neill twice served as a member of the Committee, in 2007–10 and 2012–13. At the start of the 2019 Parliament, Neill was one of the most prominent lawyer parliamentarians in the House of Commons. He described himself as a 'lawyer first and a politician second'.[3] His criminal bar background meant he had a strong interest in all matters criminal justice, including prisons and probation, but he was also well connected across the legal professions. In January 2024, Neill was made an honorary Kings Counsel for 'his leadership of the Justice Select Committee, including his contributions in upholding the rule of law and as an advocate for the judiciary and legal profession'.[4]

[2] See for example M Geddes, *Dramas at Westminster: Select Committees and the Quest for Accountability*, (Manchester University Press, 2019).

[3] C Baksi, 'Legal Hackette Lunches with Bob Neill' (Legal Hackette, 16 November 2016), https://legalhackette.com/2016/11/16/legal-hackette-lunches-with-bob-neill.

[4] Ministry of Justice, New King's Counsel and Honorary King's Counsel welcomed by Lord Chancellor, 19 January 2024.

Of the 11 Members at the start of the 2019 Parliament, six were lawyers. While it is unsurprising that lawyers would put themselves forward to being members of the Justice Committee, it is undoubtedly a strength that a significant proportion of members have relevant professional experience. That said, it is worth stressing that non-lawyer members also bring to the Committee relevant experience from across the justice system; for example, Rob Butler was a former magistrate and member of the Sentencing Council. Over the course of the 2019 Parliament, the membership of the Committee changed significantly. The three changes of prime minister and the consequent changes to ministerial roles and parliamentary private secretaries had a knock-on effect on membership of select committees, though it should also be stressed that there were frequent changes of membership across all parties during the Parliament. Only the Chair and Kieran Mullan remained members of the Committee for the entire Parliament. The quorum for select committees is three members, and despite these frequent changes of membership, the Committee was always able to meet every week while the House was sitting, right up until the end of the Parliament.

The Committee is supported by a small secretariat, which includes clerks, specialists and operations staff. I joined the Office of Speaker's Counsel in May 2020, and I work as part of a team of lawyers that provides legal advice to select committees. The Justice Committee's work is commonly a mixture of policy and law, meaning that lawyers supporting the Committee work closely with clerks and committee specialists to provide research support for members.

8.3 The Committee's Powers and Working Methods

House of Commons select committees have wide discretion in both the methods used and subjects chosen in their scrutiny work. The standing orders set out the Committees' main powers to 'send for persons, papers and records', to publish evidence and to produce reports. In practice, these powers are used by select committees to conduct inquiries.[5] The standing orders do not set out any rules for how inquiries should be conducted, but the general approach is to launch an inquiry with a call for written evidence and a set of terms of reference, then to publish that evidence and to hold oral evidence sessions (including normally one with a Government minister) and, finally, produce a report which, by convention, the Government should produce a reply to within two months of publication. The basic components of an inquiry can be used in a myriad of different ways and combinations depending on the subject matter and the time available. The Justice Committee would normally have at least two inquiries ongoing at any one time, with one on prisons or probation and another with a more legal focus. One of the distinguishing features of the Justice Committee's approach to its work in the 2019

[5] House of Commons, Standing Orders, Public Business 2024 (HC 829) 152.

Parliament was that a significant proportion of its work was not done through inquiries. The Committee used one-off evidence sessions, typically with high-profile witnesses, and often followed up with letters to government ministers, as one of its main tools to undertake scrutiny. This account of the Committee's work in the 2019 is divided into three parts: non-inquiry work; inquiries; and working with the judiciary.

8.4 Non-Inquiry Work

One of the Justice Committee main tools to undertake scrutiny was one-off evidence sessions, often with high-profile witnesses and followed up with letters to government ministers. In the 2019 Parliament, the Committee held annual evidence sessions with the Lord and Lady Chief Justice and the Director of Public Prosecutions, each of which normally preceded an evidence session with the Lord Chancellor. Taken together, these sessions served a vital accountability function, enabling the Committee to hold the Government to account for the issues raised by the head of the judiciary and the Crown Prosecution Service (CPS).

Departmental select committees are tasked with examining their departments' 'associated public bodies' by the standing orders. In practice, each committee takes a different approach to scrutinising the public bodies within their remit. In 2024, the Institute for Government published a study showing the variation in approaches taken by committees to scrutinising the regulators within their remit.[6] Their analysis of 2019–24 showed that the Justice Committee had regularly held evidence sessions with the public bodies responsible for regulating and overseeing the justice system, in particular, the criminal justice inspectorates, who can provide crucial evidence of what is happening in prisons, probation and the CPS. In 2023, the Committee decided to hold a series of one-off evidence sessions with the main legal professional bodies and their regulators, following several high-profile disputes between them. The Committee then followed up on these sessions with a letter from the Chair to the Lord Chancellor, setting out a number of recommendations.[7] One of these was that the Government agree to add the Chair of the Legal Services Board (which oversees the work of all regulators of the legal professions in England and Wales) to the list of bodies subject to a pre-appointment hearing. In October 2024, the then Minister for Courts and Legal Services wrote to the Chair of the Justice Committee to say that the Government agreed with the previous Committee's recommendation.[8] Pre-appointment hearings can serve to create a connection between the relevant organisation and a committee,

[6] M Gill, M Bishop and C Parris, 'Parliament and regulators' (Institute for Government, April 2024), www.instituteforgovernment.org.uk/sites/default/files/2024-04/parliament-and-regulators.pdf.

[7] Letter from the Chair of the Justice Committee to the Lord Chancellor, 22 March 2024.

[8] In October 2024, the then Minister for Courts and Legal Services wrote to the Chair of the Justice Committee to say that the Government agreed with the previous Committee's recommendation: Letter from Heidi Alexander to the Chair of the Justice Committee, 29 October 2024.

which can provide a basis for the committee to undertake scrutiny of the relevant organisations' work.

The Committee also used one-off evidence sessions to scrutinise legislation. One of the most significant examples was the session on the Post Office (Horizon System) Offences Bill on 16 April 2024. The Bill was constitutionally unprecedented in that it provided for Parliament to quash convictions of subpostmasters and subpostmistresses after they were prosecuted by the Post Office during the period affected by the Horizon scandal. Following a public outcry generated in large part by the ITV drama on the subject, the Government fast-tracked the legislation through Parliament. As a bill of constitutional significance, its committee stage was held on the floor of the House, meaning that there was no public bill committee to gather evidence. The Committee's evidence enabled the gathering of evidence from legal experts on complex and constitutional significant provisions in the Bill. Following the session the Chair wrote to the Secretary of State for Business and Trade to outline the Committee's concerns with the constitutional and legal effect of the Bill and with the way the Government was justifying the measures.[9] The letter was then 'tagged' on the order paper for the Committee stage of the Bill on the floor of the House and was referred to a number of times during the debate on 29 April 2024.[10] While the Government did not make any concessions based on the points raised by the Committee, the Committee's scrutiny did require the Government to provide more detailed justifications for the constitutionally unprecedented measures in the Bill.

8.5 The Committee's Inquiries

The Committee has complete discretion in deciding on the subject of its inquiries. In the 2019 Parliament, the Committee's inquiries covered a mixture of broad topics that captured a core area of the Ministry of Justice's responsibility (for example, legal aid), as well as more narrowly focused topics such as whiplash reform. It is not possible to summarise all the Committee's inquiries here; instead, I highlight a range of inquiries that capture different aspects of the Committee's approach to scrutiny.

The Committee's inquiry on private prosecutions, launched in June 2020, was prompted by concerns raised by Helen Pitcher, the then Chair of the Criminal Cases Review Commission (CCRC), in a letter which suggested the Committee conduct an inquiry into prosecutions which are brought and investigated by the same organisation.[11] Her letter explained that the CCRC's review of convictions based on the Post Office's Horizon prosecutions had given rise to concerns over the

[9] Letter from Sir Robert Neill KC (Hon) MP, Chair of the Justice Select Committee to the Rt Hon Kemi Badenoch MP, Secretary of State for Business and Trade, dated 25 April 2024 relating to the Post Office (Horizon System) Offences Bill, 24 April 2024.

[10] *Hansard* HC Deb Vol 749, col 83 (29 April 2024).

[11] Letter from Helen Pitcher, Chairman, Criminal Cases Review Commission on Post Office private prosecutions, 24 June 2020.

lack of safeguards in place. The Committee's inquiry focused on the effectiveness of existing safeguards in place to ensure that private prosecutions are conducted fairly and in accordance with the relevant legal standards, and took evidence from a range of witnesses including the Association of Private Prosecutors. The Committee's report put forward several specific technical recommendations for how the legal framework should be strengthened, which were based on the expert evidence submitted to the inquiry.[12]

The Government's response accepted the majority of the Committee's proposals.[13] For example, the Government committed to creating a central register of private prosecutions so that it is possible to monitor which organisations are bringing cases before the courts.[14] One of the main recommendations – which the Government did not initially accept – that all defendants subject to a private prosecution be informed of their right to ask the CPS to review the prosecution, was taken forward and was ultimately implemented through statutory instrument in July 2022.[15] After the Court of Appeal's judgment in *Hamilton & Others v Post Office Ltd*, the Government referred to the Committee's report on a number of occasions and committed to taking forward the recommendations that remained to be implemented.[16] In 2025, the Government announced a consultation on the regulation of private prosecutions, and asked for views on the Committee's main recommendations on inspections and transparency.[17]

In 2021, the Committee launched a broadly framed thematic inquiry on open justice to consider how digital technology had affected the way that the courts are reported on. The Committee's report was positively received by the Government.[18] For example, the Committee recommended that HM Courts and Tribunals Service (HMCTS) produce 'a citizens' charter that outlines the public's rights to access information on the courts'.[19] In response, the Government committed to produce such a Charter and in February 2024 HMCTS issued a guide for members of public wishing to attend a court or tribunal.[20] In May 2023 the Government also decided to launch a consultation titled 'Open justice, the way forward', which sought to build on the Committee's report.[21]

[12] Justice Committee, Private prosecutions: safeguards (HC 497, 2 October 2020).

[13] Justice Committee, Private prosecutions: safeguards: Government Response to the Committee's Ninth Report (HC 1238, 4 March 2021).

[14] ibid, para 5.

[15] The Criminal Procedure (Amendment No 2) Rules 2022 (SI 2022/815).

[16] *Hamilton & Others v Post Office Ltd* [2021] EWCA Crim 577; see for example Kevin Hollinrake, then the Parliamentary Under-Secretary of State for Business and Trade, *Hansard* HC Deb Vol 743, col 90 (9 January 2024).

[17] Ministry of Justice, Oversight and regulation of private prosecutors in the criminal justice system consultation, 6 March 2025.

[18] Justice Committee, Open justice: court reporting in the digital age: Government Response to the Committee's Fifth Report of Session 2022–23 (HC 1040, 16 January 2023).

[19] Justice Committee, Open justice: court reporting in the digital age (HC 339, 1 November 2022) para 40.

[20] HMCTS, 'How you can attend or access courts or tribunal' (29 May 2024).

[21] Ministry of Justice, Open Justice: the way forward (11 May 2023).

Arguably the Committee's most influential work of the 2019 Parliament was the inquiry on Imprisonment for Public Protection (IPP) sentences. IPP sentences were introduced by the Criminal Justice Act 2003 and later abolished in 2012. However, many of those sentenced while the IPP sentence was available have never been released. When the Committee reported in September 2022, there were 2,926 IPP prisoners in England and Wales.[22] The call for evidence received more written evidence than any other inquiry by the Committee in the Parliament.[23] This was in part because the Committee received hundreds of handwritten submissions from IPP prisoners by post. The Committee's report had as its primary recommendation that the Government bring forward legislation to enable all IPP prisoners to be resentenced.[24] The Committee's report, and in particular the Committee's principal recommendation, was widely reported in the media and welcomed by organisations working in the criminal justice sector.

The Government's response to the report, published alongside a letter from the then Lord Chancellor Dominic Raab in February 2023, rejected the report's principal recommendation on resentencing.[25] That response also rejected the Committee's recommendation that the qualifying licence period for IPP prisoners be reduced from 10 years to five years.[26] In April 2023, Alex Chalk, a former member of the Justice Committee, replaced Dominic Raab as Lord Chancellor. On 27 April 2023, the Chair of the Committee led a Westminster Hall debate on the Committee's report where he decried the 'complete inadequacy' of the Government's response.[27] During the debate, Damian Hinds, the minister, reiterated the Government's position set out in the response.[28] Concluding the debate, the Chair of the Committee said that he planned to put down an amendment to the Victims and Prisoners Bill to give effect to the Committee's recommendation on resentencing.[29]

At that time, the Victim and Prisoners Bill was going through the House of Commons and awaiting its second reading. The Committee had an interest in the Bill, as it had conducted pre-legislative scrutiny of the draft Victims Bill.[30] As introduced to the House, the Victims and Prisoners Bill had a significantly broader scope than the draft bill, with Part 2 concerning the establishment of an independent public advocate and Part 3 containing reforms to the Parole Board. The Committee decided to follow up on its pre-legislative work by holding evidence sessions on the elements of the Bill that it had not previously scrutinised. House

[22] Ministry of Justice and HMPPS, Offender Management Statistics Quarterly: January to March 2022, Table 1.9a (Prison Population: 30 June 2022), 28 July 2022.

[23] Justice Committee, IPP sentences (HC 266, 28 September 2022) para 6.

[24] ibid, para 152.

[25] Justice Committee, IPP sentences: Government and Parole Board Responses to the Committee's Third Report (HC 933, 9 February 2023) 13.

[26] ibid, 8

[27] *Hansard* HC Deb Vol 731, col 444WH (27 April 2023).

[28] ibid.

[29] ibid.

[30] Justice Committee, Pre-legislative scrutiny of the draft Victims Bill (HC 304, 30 September 2022).

of Commons select committees do not routinely hold evidence sessions on bills once they have been introduced to Parliament, in part because of likely duplication of the work of the relevant public bill committee. However, scrutiny of bills is a core task of select committees, as defined by the Liaison Committee in 2012.[31] The Committee's evidence sessions on the Bill, held in May 2023, led to a letter to the Lord Chancellor, dated 7 June 2023, recommending significant changes to Parts 2 and 3 of the Bill.[32] On 12 July 2023, the Chair of the Committee's amendment to give effect to the Committee's recommendation on the resentencing of IPP prisoners was published ahead of the report stage in the Commons.

When the Victims and Prisoners Bill returned to the Commons for its report stage debate on 4 December 2023, the Government's position on number of key elements of the Bill had changed significantly. In relation to Parts 2 and 3 of the Bill, relating to the establishment of an independent public advocate and reform of the Parole Board, the Government had accepted many of the points made in the Justice Committee's letter of 7 June. The Government also announced that it was introducing amendments to reduce the licence period for IPP prisoners from 10 years to three years.[33] The Government's proposal therefore went further than the five years the Committee had originally recommended. The Government also indicated that it would not accept the amendment proposed by the Chair of the Committee on resentencing.[34] It can be difficult to establish causation when examining scrutiny and its effect on government bills, but in this case it would appear that the Justice Committee's work played a significant role in shaping the Victims and Prisoners Bill.

Not all of the Committee's inquiries led to changes in Government policy. In March 2021, the Committee launched an inquiry into how the Government has used the criminal law to respond to the COVID-19 pandemic. The Committee's inquiry examined the way lockdowns were enforced and prosecuted, and in particular the use of fines and the Single Justice Procedure to prosecute offences. The Committee's report was published in September 2021.[35] By convention, the Government is expected to provide its official response to a select committee report within two months of publication. In this case, the Government provided its response 10 months later in July 2022, and it was published in September 2022.[36] The Government told the Committee that the reason it was delayed was that it required the coordination of multiple departments.[37] In December

[31] Liaison Committee, Select committee effectiveness, resources and powers (HC 697, 25 October 2012) 11.

[32] Letter to Rt Hon Alex Chalk KC MP, Lord Chancellor and Secretary of State for Justice, dated 7 June 2023, on the Victims and Prisoners Bill.

[33] Edward Argar, the Minister of State, Ministry of Justice, *Hansard* HC Deb Vol 742, col 99 (4 December 2023).

[34] ibid.

[35] Justice Committee, Covid-19 and the criminal law (HC 71, 24 September 2021).

[36] Justice Committee, Covid-19 and the criminal law: Government Response to the Committee's Fourth Report of Session 2021–22 (HC 644, 8 September 2022).

[37] Letter from Dominic Raab MP, Lord Chancellor and Secretary of State for Justice, dated 9 June 2022, on Covid-19 and the Criminal Law Report response.

2021, the then Prime Minister announced an investigation into the allegations that parties in Downing Street had broken lockdown rules. The Sue Gray report was published in May 2022.[38] This example serves to illustrate that the political context of an inquiry plays a significant role in determining how, and when, the Government responds.

8.6 Working with the Judiciary

In the 2019 Parliament, the Justice Committee held 13 evidence sessions with judicial office holders. This does not include fee-paid judges, for example recorders and deputy district judges who appeared before the Committee.[39] While it has been increasingly common for judges to give evidence to parliamentary committees, the 2012 guidance from the Judicial Executive Board says that judicial appearances before select committees should be regarded as 'exceptional' and notes that 'until the last quarter of the twentieth century there were virtually no appearances by judges before parliamentary committees'.[40] As Hazell and O'Brien note in their 2016 study of judicial engagement with Westminster, it is far from normal practice in the common law world for judges to appear before select committees of the legislature. In some jurisdictions, for example Ireland and Australia, judicial evidence is either unheard of or very rare.[41] In this section, I assess each of the appearances of the senior judiciary before the Justice Committee in the 2019 Parliament. Looking at the 2019 Parliament as a whole, judicial appearances before the Justice Committee were not exceptional. On the contrary: they were a routine part of the Committee's work.

Lord Burnett of Maldon, then Lord Chief Justice, made his first appearance before the Committee in the 2019 Parliament on 22 May 2020 as part of the Committee's inquiry on the impact of COVID-19 on the courts.[42] Lord Burnett then appeared on three further occasions, each as part of the regular annual session following the publication of the Lord Chief Justice's annual report to

[38] Cabinet Office, Findings of Second Permanent Secretary's Investigation into Alleged Gatherings on Government Premises during Covid Restrictions, 25 May 2022.

[39] Kirsty Brimelow KC, who was appointed as Deputy High Court judge in 2021 and as Recorder in 2022, gave evidence on two occasions: on 8 February 2022 to discuss the Government's proposed human rights reform; and as Chair of the Criminal Bar Association on 6 September 2022 to discuss criminal barristers' strike action. Elizabeth Gallagher, a barrister and deputy district judge, participated in an evidence session on the Work of the County Court on 7 May 2024. Both appeared in their capacity as lawyers with expertise in the relevant area, rather than as judges.

[40] The Judicial Executive Board, Guidance to Judges on Appearances before Select Committees (2012) para 10.

[41] R Hazell and P O'Brien, 'Meaningful dialogue: judicial engagement with Parliamentary committees at Westminster' [2016] *Public Law* 54, 54

[42] Justice Committee, Oral evidence: Coronavirus (COVID-19): The impact on prison, probation and court systems, HC 299, 22 May 2020, The Rt Hon Lord Burnett of Maldon, Lord Chief Justice of England and Wales.

Parliament.[43] The effect of the pandemic and the growing backlog in the courts was a major theme in each of Lord Burnett's evidence sessions. Lord Burnett criticised successive governments for failing to fund the courts sufficiently.[44] He also used the sessions to outline the judiciary's position on the concordat process led by the Lord Chancellor to decide on the number of judicial sitting days to be funded in the upcoming financial year.[45] Across these sessions, Lord Burnett would provide an update on the situation in each of the jurisdictions and some commentary on what the Government and HMCTS were doing to resolve the problems facing the courts. The growing concerns of the increasing delays and lack of resources in the courts, in particular problems with the court estate and the limited judicial capacity, were a major area of interest of the Committee during the Parliament. Lord Burnett's oral evidence served to provide vital information and analysis to inform the Committee's work in scrutinising the Government's approach to court capacity. The Lord Chief Justice and the Committee had a shared interest in placing political pressure on the Government to do more to improve the resourcing of the courts. Lord Burnett's evidence formed a key part of the Committee's analysis and recommendations in its report on court capacity published in April 2022.[46]

Arguably the most high-profile judicial evidence session in the Parliament was Baroness Carr of Walton-on-the-Hill's first appearance as Lady Chief Justice on 16 January 2024. Dame Sue Carr was appointed as the first Lady Chief Justice on 15 June 2023, and took up the role on 1 October 2023. Baroness Carr's appearance on 16 January was not only her first appearance in Parliament as head of the judiciary, but it was also her first opportunity to speak publicly on the issues facing the justice system in England and Wales. The session began with the Chair restating the Committee's commitment to respecting the relevant constitutional principles: 'The Committee are very alert to the constitutional conventions that we do not ask the judiciary to come into the realms of politics or ask questions or comment upon any matters of potential political controversy or emerging Government policy.'[47] Baroness Carr's evidence session began with topical questions on the Government's legislation to quash the convictions resulting from the Post Office Horizon scandal and the deployment of judges to fast-track migrant appeals. On the Government's proposed legislation to quash convictions of subpostmasters and mistresses, Baroness Carr refuted the notion circulating in the press that the judiciary had approved the Government's approach: 'I am very grateful for the opportunity to make it absolutely clear that any suggestion the judiciary has given the proposed legislation the green light is simply not true.'[48] In relation to the deployment of

[43] Constitutional Reform Act 2005, s 5(1).

[44] Justice Committee Oral evidence: The work of the Lord Chief Justice, HC 868 (16 November 2021) Q41.

[45] Justice Committee Oral evidence: The work of the Lord Chief Justice, HC 226 (10 November 2020) Q144 .

[46] Justice Committee, Court Capacity (HC 69, 27 April 2022).

[47] Justice Committee Oral evidence: Work of the Lady Chief Justice, HC 466 (16 January 2024) Q4.

[48] ibid, Q5.

judges, Baroness Carr emphasised that it is the judiciary which decides how judges are to be deployed, rather than the Government: 'To be absolutely clear, matters of deployment of judges, the allocation of work for judges, and the use of courtrooms, are exclusively matters for the judiciary, and, more specifically, matters for myself and the Senior President of Tribunals.'[49] In these responses, the Lady Chief Justice showed that she was willing to use the evidence session as an opportunity to set out the judiciary's position on matters of live political debate where the judiciary had been implicated.

Other senior judges in leadership positions gave evidence to the Committee. On 17 November 2020, Mark Lucraft, the Chief Coroner between 2016 and 2021, gave evidence to the Committee alongside Derek Winter DL, Deputy Chief Coroner for England and Wales, and Alexia Durran, Deputy Chief Coroner for England and Wales as part of its inquiry into the Coroner Service. The Chief Coroner also provided written evidence to the inquiry. For this type of inquiry, where the Committee is seeking to undergo a detailed investigation into a less-well-understood part of the justice system, the cooperation and participation of the senior judiciary is vital. Unlike other expert witnesses, the judiciary will not always be able to put forward suggested recommendations for the Committee to adopt. However, the senior judiciary is able to offer criticism of how things operate. Mark Lucraft's successor as Chief Coroner, Thomas Teague KC, gave evidence to the Committee as part of its follow-up inquiry on 30 January 2024 and described the tripartite governance structure in the majority of coroner areas (between the coroner, the local authority and the local policing body) as 'archaic'.[50] This sort of observation from a senior judicial office holder is invaluable to the Committee's ability to build strong conclusions and recommendations on the operation of specific areas of the justice system.

On 25 April 2023, Sir Keith Lindblom, the Senior President of the Tribunals, gave evidence to the Justice Committee for a one-off session on the work of the immigration and asylum tribunals alongside Justice Ian Dove, Chamber President of the Upper Tribunal, Immigration and Asylum Chamber and Judge Melanie Plimmer, Chamber President of the First-tier Tribunal, Immigration and Asylum Chamber.[51] Sir Keith Lindblom answered questions on the current pressures facing the immigration and asylum tribunals. He also relied on the exception to the convention that judges do not comment on the merits of government bills set out that in official guidance unless 'the Bill or policy directly affects the operation of the courts or aspects of the administration of justice within the judge's particular area of judicial responsibility or expertise'.[52] Sir Keith Lindblom described the

[49] ibid, Q6.

[50] Justice Committee Oral evidence: The Coroner Service: follow-up, HC 490 (30 January 2024): His Honour Judge Thomas Teague KC, Q4.

[51] Justice Select Committee Oral evidence: Work of the immigration and asylum tribunals, HC 1152 (25 April 2023).

[52] The Judicial Executive Board (n 40) para 13.

Nationality and Borders Act and the Illegal Migration Bill as 'additional pressures'.[53] By contrast, the Senior President refused to be drawn as to whether any specific legislation was causing the judiciary problems in determining asylum and immigration cases.[54] As the guide to judges appearing before committees makes clear, the risk is that a comment on the substance of a specific provision could lead to a 'judge's impartiality from being called into question in the event of subsequently being asked to apply or interpret those provisions in a case in court'.[55]

The Master of the Rolls, Sir Geoffrey Vos, gave evidence to the Committee for the first time on 6 June 2023.[56] The session was used as an opportunity to discuss the current state of civil justice in England and Wales. The Committee's questioning focused on the County Court, and the evidence presented by Sir Geoffrey Vos helped to frame the Committee's inquiry on the work of the County Court, which was launched in October 2023.

Sir Andrew McFarlane, the President of the Family Division, gave evidence to the Committee on two occasions in the 2019 Parliament. On 11 January 2022, Sir Andrew McFarlane gave evidence to the Committee as part of its inquiry into open justice. The session provided an opportunity for the Committee to explore the proposal for reform set out in his report, 'Confidence and Confidentiality: Transparency in the Family Courts', published in October 2021.[57] The report proposed a pilot allowing reporting of certain cases in the Family Court, which represented a major change in operation of family justice in England and Wales. His second appearance, on 23 April 2024, was a one-off evidence session to explore the current issues in the Family Court. Despite the measures to improve transparency, there is still limited media reporting of family court cases, which means that Sir Andrew McFarlane's evidence on the operation of the Family Court to the Committee is particularly important for public understanding of the justice system.

The Justice Committee has a special relationship with the Sentencing Council for England and Wales. When the Sentencing Council was established by Parliament, it was decided that there should be some parliamentary oversight of the production of sentencing guidelines, which courts would be bound to follow. As a result, the Justice Committee is named as a mandatory consultee for all guideline changes produced by the Council, alongside the Lord Chancellor, in section 120 of the Coroners and Justice Act 2009. The 2009 Act requires that the Chair of the Council is a judicial member of the Council. Since it was established, the Chair of the Council has always been a Court of Appeal judge with a background in the criminal law. Lord Justice Holroyde, who was chair from 2018 to 2022, gave evidence on 2 February 2021. Lord Justice William Davis, Chair from 2022, gave

[53] Justice Select Committee (n 51) Q45.
[54] ibid, Q54–55.
[55] The Judicial Executive Board (n 40) para 10.
[56] Justice Committee Oral evidence: Work of the Master of the Rolls, HC 1387 (6 June 2023).
[57] President of the Family Division, Confidence and Confidentiality: Transparency in the Family Courts, 28 October 2021

evidence on 13 December 2022 as part of the Committee's inquiry into public opinion and understanding of sentencing. A key theme across both sessions was the need to promote awareness in Parliament and the wider public of how sentencing operates. Sentencing is a subject which often provokes fierce political debate; however, in both sessions the Chair of the Council used the opportunity to set out the institutional roles and boundaries that regulate how sentencing functions in England and Wales. Given the sensitivity of the subject matter, having the unique perspective of a serving senior judge answering questions on sentencing is a sign of the strength of the relationship between the Committee and the Council.

8.7 Conclusion

The Justice Committee's approach to its work in the 2019 Parliament was underpinned by a commitment to the rule of law and judicial independence. A good example of this was the Committee's decision, in September 2023, to pause its inquiry into the whiplash reform and the Official Injury Claim Service because of the pending appeal before the Supreme Court in case on the meaning of the whiplash reform legislation.[58] The *sub judice* rule, which is set out in a resolution of the House of Commons, prevents cases currently before the courts being discussed in parliamentary proceedings, including through the work of select committees.[59] The principle of comity, which underpins the *sub judice* rule, requires the House of Commons to respect the court's constitutional role and to avoid giving rise to any potential interference with the court's ability to decide cases. In this situation, the Committee wanted to avoid the perception that it was providing an alternative forum for the consideration of legal questions that were to be decided by the Supreme Court.[60] To be trusted by the senior judiciary as a forum to provide evidence, it is vital that the Committee is seen to uphold the constitutional norms that underpin the operation of the separation of powers.

In a parliamentary system, where the government of the day holds considerable power to set the agenda in the House of Commons, cross-party select committees represent a vital check on executive power. The remit of the Justice Committee to scrutinise the work of the Ministry of Justice enables it to make a contribution to the rule of law by identifying problems within the justice system and holding the Government to account for their approach to the administration of justice. Over the course of the 2019 Parliament, the Justice Committee's scrutiny work showed a focus on the operation of the justice system and a commitment to upholding the rule of law. The rule of law relies on the positive commitment of constitutional actors within the political system. Parliament, and the House of Commons in

[58] Justice Committee, Whiplash reform and the Official Injury Claim Service (HC 1140, 20 September 2023) para 7.

[59] House of Commons Standing Orders (Public Business), Appendix.

[60] Justice Committee (n 58) para 6.

particular as the democratically elected chamber, has a vital role to play in ensuring that the principles which underpin the rule of law are upheld. For example, the Lord Chancellor's statutory responsibilities, to uphold judicial independence and to ensure an effective and efficient system to support the courts, rely upon the scrutiny of parliamentarians to determine whether those duties are being fulfilled. The Justice Committee's scrutiny of the operation of the legal system, and its examination of the Government's policy-making on justice, is a core part of the political supervision that the rule of law depends upon.

PART III

The Executive

9

The Role of the Law Officers

ROSS CRANSTON

9.1 Introduction

The law officers are a critical part of the UK's constitutional arrangements. As the government's senior legal advisers in relation to policy, proposed legislation, and decision-making, they have a key role in maintaining the rule of law by ensuring that their colleagues, those in public service, and the institutions of the state comply with domestic and international law. The Attorney-General is the senior of the law officers, the Solicitor-General the junior. Following the Law Officers Act 1997, the Solicitor-General may lawfully exercise any function of the Attorney-General.[1] Prior to that Act the Solicitor-General's ability to act as the Attorney-General's deputy was limited, since most of the latter's functions are conferred personally, although from 1944 legislation allowed the Attorney-General to authorise the Solicitor-General to act in particular cases.[2] As the senior law officer, the Attorney-General decides how the work should be divided between the two.

A great deal has been written about the role of the law officers. One aspect has been the tension in England and Wales between the political and legal dimensions of the role and its implications, since both the Attorney-General and Solicitor-General are politicians. Both have typically been MP-politicians, but since 1997 a number have been members of the House of Lords; indeed, two were made peers so that they could assume the role (Lord Falconer KC as Solicitor-General in 1997 and Lord Hermer KC as Attorney-General in 2024). That contrasts with the position in places like Australia where Solicitors-General (but not Attorneys-General) are neutral, public office holders, albeit that they need to navigate political shoals.[3] In the last 20 years in England and Wales the debate has been whether the law officers should similarly be independent office holders. At one point a House of Commons select committee recommended that the law officers' legal functions

[1] s 1.
[2] Law Officers Act 1944, s 1(1)(c).
[3] See G Appleby, *The Role of the Solicitor-General. Negotiating Law, Politics and the Public Interest* (Hart Publishing, 2018).

concerning advice and prosecutions be carried out by an official who was outside party political life.[4] For good reasons the idea came to nothing.[5]

This account adopts a fairly conventional, functional approach to the law officers' role in the UK constitution, examining in turn ministerial, advisory, parliamentary, court-related, and public interest functions.[6] The focus is on England and Wales, although there is now a variety of law officers in the UK, each with their own idiosyncrasies.[7] What follows draws in part on my three years occupying the position of Solicitor-General between 1998 and 2001. Much has moved on since then – symbolised by the rather incongruous acquisition by the law officers in 2020 of special advisers (spads) – but the fundamentals remain.

9.2 Ministerial Role

The law officers in England and Wales are ministers in the Government but, as we will see, have (or at least should have) a degree of detachment from politics when performing the role.[8] They have a relatively small number of lawyers and staff in the Attorney-General's Office (previously, and more accurately in my view, called the Legal Secretariat to the Law Officers). In my time there were around a dozen or so lawyers in the Legal Secretariat, with about the same number of support staff, making a total of under 30.[9] Traditionally, the law officers have not been members of the Cabinet, but would attend when their advice was required or when matters within their responsibility were being considered. They would leave with the next item of business. That was the approach maintained by my first Attorney-General, John Morris KC, MP (later Lord Morris of Aberavon).

Although not formally a member of Cabinet, the Attorney-General now regularly attends its meetings. Arguments favouring this arrangement include that an Attorney-General's advice will be better because of their greater knowledge of its political context, and that members of the Cabinet are more likely to heed that advice because they are all colleagues in Cabinet. By contrast, it might be thought that the independence of the Attorney-General's advice – or at least the

[4] House of Commons, Constitutional Affairs Committee, *Constitutional Role of the Attorney General*, Fifth Report of the Session 2006–07, HC 306, 19 July 2007.

[5] eg, House of Lords, *Select Committee on the Constitution, The roles of the Lord Chancellor and law officers*, 2022–23 Session, HL 118, 18 January 2023, para 232. In 2007 I chaired a committee of the Bar Council which, by majority, rejected the idea of a non-political Attorney-General: *The Governance of Britain. The Role of the Attorney General*, Report of a Working Group of the Bar to the Chairman, Geoffrey Vos QC, November 2007 (unpublished). See also C Casey, *Between Law and Politics. The Future of the Law Officers in England & Wales* (Policy Exchange, 2023).

[6] Conor McCormick adds to this a more sophisticated framework of independence, accountability, and trust: *The Constitutional Legitimacy of Law Officers in the United Kingdom* (Hart Publishing, 2022).

[7] C McCormick and G Cowie, *Law Officers: A Constitutional and Functional Overview* (House of Commons Library, 14 February 2025).

[8] Ministerial and other Salaries Act 1975, Sch 1; House of Commons Disqualification Act 1975, s 2(1) and Sch 2.

[9] The Law Officers' Departments. Departmental Report, Cm 5108, 2001, 3.

appearance of independence – is adversely affected by what is their greater political involvement through their regular attendance at Cabinet. The arguments are finely balanced. The House of Lords Select Committee on the Constitution was neutral on the matter, but rightly observed that what was important was that the office holder prioritised adherence to the rule of law over governmental priorities and was willing and able to operate independently of government when required.[10]

As well as the Cabinet itself, those obligations apply to the law officers' membership of Cabinet committees. Of particular importance is the Parliamentary Business and Legislation (PBL) Committee. One of its functions is to consider the final (or near-final) draft of bills. If satisfied that a bill is ready and that other legal and procedural issues have been resolved, the committee will approve the Bill's introduction subject to any necessary minor and drafting changes.[11] Initially the legal issues which I as a law officer would need to consider for the committee was whether a bill conferred too wide a discretion on ministers, contained a power by secondary legislation to amend or repeal other Acts (a Henry VIII clause), or was retrospective or reversed the onus of proof. Parliamentary Counsel was conscious of these issues so that rarely, if ever, was it necessary to raise them as concerns for the committee. Once the Human Rights Act 1998 was in force the task became more demanding since it was necessary to opine on the accuracy of a minister's statement in relation to a bill, required by section 19(1)(a) of that Act, that the Bill was compatible with the rights conferred under the European Convention on Human Rights (ECHR). As well as the cabinet committees of which they are members, the law officers may be invited to attend others. During the Kosovo War that meant that John Morris and I attended the committees associated with the conflict, with an eye on the international and humanitarian law aspects.[12]

The administrative responsibilities of the law officers are various. There are four government departments for which the law officers are accountable to Parliament – the Government Legal Department (GLD), the Crown Prosecution Service (CPS), the Serious Fraud Office (SFO), and HM Crown Prosecution Service Inspectorate. The head of the GLD is the Treasury Solicitor, the most senior legal official in the UK Government, with the status of a permanent head.[13] GLD's function is to provide legal advice to most government departments, including instructing Parliamentary Counsel on primary legislation, drafting secondary legislation, and conducting most government litigation. As with the guidance on legal risk, discussed later, the law officers may give indications to the GLD about giving legal advice, as well as on other matters such as important litigation.

The terminology that the law officers 'superintend' the CPS and SFO underlines that they are not involved in the decisions taken in individual cases, except

[10] HL Select Committee on the Constitution, 2022–2023 Session, *The Roles of the Lord Chancellor and Law Officers*, HL 118, 18 January 2023, para 257.

[11] Cabinet Office, Legislative Process: Taking a Bill through Parliament, Guidance, 2013 (2023 version).

[12] Lord Morris of Aberavon, *Fifty Years of Politics and Law* (University of Wales Press, 2011) 198.

[13] J Jones, 'The Role of the Treasury Solicitor' (2024) 29 *Judicial Review* 75.

where statute expressly provides that their permission is a pre-condition to a prosecution. A protocol between the Attorney-General and the Director of Public Prosecutions (DPP) and SFO, introduced in 2009, was replaced in 2019 by Framework Agreements between the Attorney-General and each of them. Under the agreement with the DPP, for example, the Attorney-General appoints the DPP, supports and holds the DPP to account for the running of their organisation and the discharge of its functions, is consulted on changes to the Code for Crown Prosecutors, and answers Parliamentary Questions, questions from Select Committees, and correspondence from MPs about the CPS. The agreement states explicitly that the DPP exercises independence in individual casework decisions, and that the law officers are responsible for safeguarding the independence of CPS in its prosecution function and in taking individual prosecution decisions in accordance with the agreement.[14]

There are policy aspects to the law officers' ministerial functions. One aspect is ensuring the implementation of government policy. For example, I visited the 42 CPS areas in the different geographical parts of England and Wales to meet CPS staff, the police, and court staff, to encourage, first, the speeding up of the time from arrest to sentence for youth offenders (one of the five pledges given when the Government was elected in 1997), and secondly, the delivery of a joined-up criminal justice system at the local level through local inter-agency partnerships and closer co-operation between the CPS, the police, and the courts in matters like file preparation, case management, witness warning, and witness care (following the Government's adoption of the Glidewell Report).[15]

A second aspect is policy development, which had added force after my time in office. For example, Lord Goldsmith launched a major review of fraud, which recommended a national fraud strategy, a National Fraud Strategic Authority, the better reporting of fraud, a lead police force to tackle fraud on a national scale, and plea bargaining.[16] Important aspects of the report were adopted. The law officers do not currently have overall responsibility for policy areas, but play a role in ensuring the implementation of government priorities to halve violence against women and girls, tackle economic crime, drive up performance across the criminal justice system, improve support for victims of crime, and promote the rule of law nationally and internationally.[17] Too great an involvement in policy matters risks undermining the political detachment which the law officers need to perform their constitutional role as guardians of the rule of law.

[14] *Framework agreement between the Law Officers and the Director of Public Prosecutions* (Attorney General's Office & CPS, 13 March 2019), paras 13, 20.

[15] *The Review of the Crown Prosecution Service*, chr: Sir Iain Glidewell, Cm 3960, 1998. See also *Crown Prosecution Service, Annual Report for the period April 1998 - March 1999* (Stationery Office, 1999). I was also the 'Green minister' for the Law Departments, seeking to integrate sustainable development into their work: see *Crown Prosecution Service. Annual Report for the period April 1999 - March 2000* (Stationery Office, 2000).

[16] *Fraud Review. Final Report* (The Attorney General's Office, 2006).

[17] *Report and Business Plan 2024 - 2026* (Attorney General's Office, 2025) 11.

9.3 Legal Advisor to Government

Law authorises but also channels the actions of government. As its principal legal advisers the law officers advise in relation to both aspects as government goes about making law (through preparing bills for Parliament and secondary legislation) and implementing government policy. Legislation must be consistent with legal obligations such as those contained in the ECHR and in implementing policy government must act within the law's bounds. As a practical matter the huge expanse of government activity means that the law officers can only advise on a limited range of matters. Most legal advice in government is given by lawyers in the different government departments who, apart from those in the Foreign, Commonwealth and Development Office and HM Revenue and Customs, are all members of the GLD. It is only the most important, complex, or sensitive issues which are referred to the law officers, or those where there is no consensus as to the correct approach between departments.

At one time the law officers gave advice on a wide range of matters by way of formal opinions, as do barristers, often drawing on their own knowledge or research by themselves or their juniors. These days law officer advice is sought relatively informally by a government department. A draft of the advice itself is prepared, in the main by the members of the GLD in the law officers' department, based on what the ministries seeking advice have provided by way of background. In some cases the assistance of outside, specialist counsel may be sought in the preparation of the advice. The advice will be approved by a law officer and then given to the department. Advice by the law officers is regarded as the last word within government until there is later law officer advice or a judicial decision to the contrary. Since most advice will not be tested in court, the advice can determine the government's actions.

In giving advice, an obvious truism is that the law officers should ensure that the Government acts within the law. There are various aspects to this. As ministers in the Government the law officers will seek to facilitate its policies. A range of legal possibilities may be explored to achieve this. If there are legal obstacles to a particular path, a law officer will, like any good lawyer, seek to find another path or suggest a modification so that the Government can comply with the law. If it is likely that the policy will be challenged in court, the advice may canvass contingency arrangements should the outcome be unfavourable.[18]

In giving advice, however, there must be limits to what the law officers should do, limits which are more restrictive than those which apply in private lawyering. The template was set by the long-standing Shawcross principle, associated with the law officers' role in criminal prosecutions, that they must take into account matters of public interest, and must not be swayed (even less pressured) by ministerial colleagues. Their role is not to secure a conviction at all costs but to act

[18] D Seymour, 'Whitehall, Transparency, and the Law' in D Feldman (ed), *Law in Politics, Politics in Law* (Hart Publishing, 2013) 107.

independently and to contribute to the fairness of the criminal justice system.[19] With criminal proceedings the law officers act in a quasi-judicial capacity, but the standards applicable in that context have resonance in the context of giving advice.

In other words, in giving legal advice a law officer should not be acting with excessive zeal in their client's interests. They are not acting on behalf of a private client whose aim is to maximise their personal, financial, or corporate interests by taking advantage of the inconsistencies, ambiguities, and gaps in the law.[20] Rather, their client is the Government, which is entrusted to act in the public interest. One public interest is to enable people to enjoy the rights and freedoms accorded to them by law. Another public interest is to maximise fundamental values such as the rule of law. A third public interest is maintaining high standards of government behaviour. In the case of ministers those standards of behaviour are most clearly imposed by the Ministerial Code – to maintain high standards of personal behaviour, to embody the principles of public service, and to set a positive example of governing in the national interest.[21]. These public interests should mould how the law officers perform their task of advising government. They do not have the same force when the private lawyer advises a client. Ultimately, of course, it is up to ministers whether to accept and act in line with law officers' advice.

Like private lawyers, those in government have to be concerned with legal risk. The client may be seeking to push the boundaries of the law in pursuit of a particular goal. Risk about outcome may be heightened because the goal enters new legal territory, the law is in a state of flux, a statutory provision is ambiguous or open-textured, or the area of law is complex. In such cases the lawyer may advise an alternative path, if there is one. The first edition of the well-known booklet, *The Judge over your Shoulder*, was published by the Treasury Solicitor in 1987 to give guidance to civil servants about the principles of judicial review, which the courts had been extending in previous years. In particular, the guidance said, it was designed 'to highlight the danger areas where you are particularly at risk of laying your minister open to a challenge in the courts'.[22] In other words, like the private lawyer, the government lawyer needs to make a professional assessment about what a court might do if the advice, or at least a course of action based on the advice, is challenged in court. Is it likely to survive challenge, are the chances even, or will it likely fail?

In 2015 the GLD developed formal guidance on risk to ensure greater consistency and clarity in giving advice about risk. That included the use of colour coding, standard language (low, medium-low, medium-high, and high risk) and percentage ranges in assessing the risk of a challenge, its success, and its impact.

[19] Sir Hartley Shawcross, *Hansard*, HC Vol 483, col 681 (29 January 1951).

[20] Of course, private lawyers are not unconstrained: see R Cranston, 'Legal Ethics and Professional Responsibility' in R Cranston (ed), *Legal Ethics and Professional Responsibility* (Clarendon Press, 1995) 20–23.

[21] *Ministerial Code*, 2024 edn, paras 1.1–1.3. That includes upholding the Nolan Principles of public life: selflessness, integrity, objectivity, accountability, openness, honesty, and leadership: ibid, para 1.4.

[22] D Oliver, 'The Judge over your Shoulder' (1989) 42 *Parliamentary Affairs* 302, 304.

The guidance provided that 'If there is no respectable legal argument that we could put to the Court, then you will need to advise that the proposed action is unlawful.'[23] One reason for the need for the guidance was that government lawyers were now much more likely to enter the policy-making process at an earlier stage than in the past. Another was the nature of the advice given, less a formal quasi-'judgment' on an issue, increasingly a calculation of the chances of a policy meeting legal requirements.[24]

Risk is a necessary but difficult concept in giving legal advice. It is never entirely certain what arguments will stand up in court if a matter gets that far. However, in 2022 the Attorney-General, Suella Braverman KC MP, superseded the GLD guidance with the Attorney-General's Guidance on legal risk with the intention of moving to a private sector approach to risk. By contrast with the 2015 guidance, a proposal was only to be described as unlawful if there was no respectable legal argument capable of being put before a court, and the guidance advised that this would be rare.[25] In 2024 the new Attorney-General, Lord Hermer, took the view that the advice on risk needed to reflect the centrality of law and the importance of the rule of law to what government does, and that the Braverman approach might lead to a dilution of standards.[26] His revised guidance states that government lawyers must advise that a proposed course of action is unlawful if no tenable legal argument can be advanced – described as the position where no argument could be advanced consistently with a lawyer's professional obligations. However, the guidance adds, proceeding with a merely tenable argument should be a last resort.[27] In the guidance great importance is attached to the UK's commitment to its international, as well as its domestic law obligations.[28]

Confidentiality in law officer advice has raised its head at times of political crisis. The so-called law officers' convention is that neither the content of law officers' advice nor the fact that advice has (or has not been) given may be disclosed.[29] The justification is so that it ensures that full and frank legal advice can be given. Also persuasive is that, as with any client, law officer advice is protected by legal professional privilege.[30] The convention was much agitated at the time of the Iraq War where there was parliamentary and public pressure for the publication of the Attorney-General's advice about the lawfulness of the UK's participation.[31] As a backbencher during that period I defended the convention on the standard public

[23] Government Legal Department, Guidance Note on Legal Risk, revised July 2015. See Jones (n 13).

[24] B Yong, *Risk Management Government Lawyers and the Provision of Legal Advice within Whitehall* (Constitution Society & UCL Constitution Unit, 2013) 48, 52.

[25] Attorney General's Guidance on Legal Risk, 2022, paras 2 and 13,16. For controversy surrounding the guidance see McCormick and Cowie (n 7) 82–83.

[26] Justice Committee, Oral evidence: Work of the Law Officers, HC 577, 15 January 2025, Q16–17.

[27] Attorney General's Guidance on Legal Risk, 6 November 2024, paras 8 and 21.

[28] ibid, paras 9 and 13.

[29] Now in the Ministerial Code, para 5.14.

[30] See D Kenealy and S MacLennan, 'Legal Professional Privilege of Advice of the Attorney General' (2019) 24 *Coventry Law Journal* 81.

[31] See KA Kyriakides, 'The Advisory Functions of the Attorney-General' (2003) 1 *Hertforshire Law Journal* 73.

interest ground that if the advice were to be published it would leave governments in difficulty in obtaining full and frank legal advice on major matters of public and international law. I also argued that the disclosure was unnecessary in that case since the Government's legal position had already been published by the Foreign Affairs Select Committee of the House of Commons.[32]

Subsequently, however, I was persuaded by Lord Bingham's view that in a matter so important as war, the law officers' advice as to its lawfulness (or otherwise) should be made public.[33] In fact for some time the convention has recognised that disclosure may take place where ministers identify that there are overwhelmingly strong public interest considerations in favour of this course and they obtain law officers' consent.[34] Sir Geoffrey Cox's advice on the legality of proroguing Parliament during the Brexit negotiations is an example.[35] To my mind the convention would be undermined if a law officer needed to disclose that, because of a conflict of interest arising from their representing certain interests prior to appointment, they were disqualified from advising on a matter.[36]

9.4 Duties to Parliament

In 1946 Prime Minister Attlee issued a directive that the law officers should give priority to their parliamentary duties.[37] In subsequent years the law officers advised Parliament, when requested, as to the implications of particular legislative provisions, in particular those where the UK's international legal obligations were in play. In the late 1970s and early 1980s there was still much ink spilt on how extensive were the duties of the law officers to Parliament. Should they be in attendance at public bill (previously known as standing) committees and select committees when the relevant minister thought that this might be of assistance? Should they be ready at any time to give non-partisan advice to the whole House? For obvious reasons there was a consensus among law officers in successive Labour and Conservative governments that there were practical boundaries to their duties and these did not oblige law officers to advise beyond the constitution of, and conduct of proceedings in the House of Commons, the conduct and discipline of members, and the meaning and effect of proposed legislation.[38]

[32] eg, *Hansard* HC Deb Vol 418, cols 1429–32 (9 March 2004).

[33] Lord Bingham, 'The Rule of Law', Sixth Sir David Williams Lecture Centre for Public Law, 16 November 2006, 32–33. In fact, the Iraq advice was published on 28 April 2005 on the Prime Minister's Office website.

[34] R Mitchell and M Stockdale, 'A Privileged and Conventional Relationship: Legal Professional Privilege and the Law Officers' Convention' (2023) 87 *Modern Law Review* 111.

[35] J Hand, 'The Attorney-General, Politics and Logistics – A Fork in the Road?' (2022) 42 *Legal Studies* 425, 432.

[36] cf C Casey, *Conflicts of Interest and the Law Officers' Convention* (Policy Exchange, 2025).

[37] J Edwards, *The Law Officers of the Crown* (Sweet & Maxwell, 1964) 51.

[38] J Edwards, *The Attorney General, Politics and the Public Interest* (Sweet & Maxwell, 1984) 219–24.

By the time I occupied the position of Solicitor-General there was no suggestion that the law officers should attend public bill or select committees to give advice. The one occasion when over three years I acted on behalf of the House of Commons was to appear with the Treasury 'devil', Philip (now Lord) Sales as an intervener on behalf of the Speaker and the authorities of the House in a defamation action by a former MP, who wished to use a report by the Parliamentary Commissioner for Standards which was protected by Parliamentary privilege.[39] Otherwise my duties were to appear on a regular basis to answer oral questions by MPs (and to ensure answers were given to parliamentary written questions). The major focus of questions concerned the law officers' activities as government ministers and the activities of those for whom we had responsibility, notably the CPS.

During two of those three years I answered oral questions myself, since the Attorney-General, Lord Williams of Mostyn QC, was in the House of Lords – the fate, as well, of the current Solicitor-General, Ellie Reeves KC MP, since her Attorney-General, Lord Hermer KC, is in the House of Lords. As well, I took the Crown Prosecution Service Inspectorate Bill through the House of Commons, an easy task since it was a short and uncontroversial bill, and I also assisted Foreign Office ministers with a walk-on part during the passage of the International Criminal Court Bill.[40]

9.5 Relationship with the Courts

The role of the King's Attorneys from the thirteenth century was to conduct cases in court on behalf of the Crown. From the King's Attorney came the Attorney-General, and by the early sixteenth century a Solicitor-General was appointed to assist the Attorney-General. Given the history of these two offices and their occupants coming from the practicing bar, it was natural that along with giving advice in non-contentious matters they should conceive as their primary function appearing for the Government in court. That did not preclude appearing for other clients. It was only at the very end of the nineteenth century that the law officers were no longer permitted to conduct private litigation, and only in the mid-twentieth century that the method of remunerating them was by way of an all-inclusive salary, as with other ministers, instead of a salary plus the fees for litigious work normally payable to a barrister.[41] In the mid-twentieth century it was said that the Attorney-General or Solicitor-General should lead in cases of particular importance, ones which involved constitutional matters or legal questions of special difficulty, or prosecutions involving serious constitutional or public order issues, treason and perhaps murder by poisoning.[42]

[39] *Hamilton v Al Fayed* [2001] 1 AC 395.

[40] eg, *Hansard* HC Deb Vol 350, col 880 (23 May 2000); HC, Standing Comm D, International Criminal Court Bill (Lords) (3 May 2001) respectively.

[41] Edwards (n 37) 118.

[42] H Shawcross, 'The Office of the Attorney-General' (1953) 7 *Parliamentary Affairs* 380, 383–84; J Edwards (n 37) 306–08.

From early times it was clearly impossible for the law officers to appear in all the litigation in the name of the Crown. Prosecutions were undertaken by private counsel briefed in each case. By the second part of the nineteenth century the position at the Central Criminal Court (the Old Bailey) was formalised and Senior Treasury Counsel – now Treasury Counsel (Crime) – were appointed full time to conduct prosecutions there. With civil matters, the law officers from the mid-eighteenth century had a First Treasury Counsel (the Treasury 'devil') to assist with litigation and advisory work. The position became full time. During my time as a law officer there was a First Treasury Counsel (common law) and a First Treasury Counsel (Chancery), the positions occupied respectively by two outstanding lawyers, Philip Sales KC (now Lord Sales) and Jonathan Crow KC. From November 2025 the First Treasury Counsel, Sir James Eadie KC, is supported by six specialist counsel appointed to the Attorney-General's Senior Treasury Counsel (Civil) Group.

With the growth of government departments, the law officers were also involved with the standing counsel appointed to advise on the lawfulness of their department's activities and to conduct litigation on their behalf. Additional counsel could be briefed in the ordinary way. To avoid cronyism in the appointment of counsel for advisory and litigation work, from 1999 those wanting to undertake government work apply to become members of the A, B, or C panels, the panels ranked according to the experience of the applicants but reflecting as well the complexity of the work to be undertaken.[43] The upshot is that appointment from the position of Senior Treasury Counsel through to the most junior member of the C panel is now on the basis of open competition.

The law officers' function of appearing in court in serious cases for the Government and in the public interest has been in significant decline for some time. Factors include the pressure of other business, the experience of the law officers, and their own inclination.[44] During my time as Solicitor-General, my first Attorney-General, John Morris, appeared to briefly open the Government's case in the leading constitutional and human rights case, *R v DPP Ex p Kebeline*,[45] but left Lord Pannick KC to undertake the burden of the Government's submissions. John Morris also appeared in the International Court of Justice and the European Court of Human Rights.[46] The appearances of my next Attorney-General, Lord Williams KC, who was a leader of the bar, were also slight, including a case in the Committee of Privileges about the rights of hereditary peers, and one before the European Court of Human Rights about improperly obtained evidence.[47] By contrast Lord Goldsmith KC, Attorney-General between 2001 and 2007, undertook a heavy burden of important litigation in the House of Lords and elsewhere, unmatched

[43] R Cranston, 'The Attorney-General's Panels: The New Regime' (1999) 4 *Judicial Review* 272.

[44] The issue is covered in detail in Hand (n 35) 437–40.

[45] [2000] 2 AC 326, 358.

[46] *Yugoslavia v United Kingdom, Order, Provisional Measures* [1999] ICJ Rep 826, 832; *Hashman and Harrup v United Kingdom* (2000) 30 EHRR 241; *Re Lord Mayhew of Twysden's Motion* [2002] 1 AC 109 respectively.

[47] *Khan v United Kingdom* (2001) 31 EHRR 45.

by his successors, whose appearances have been mainly concerned with relatively short applications before the Court of Appeal, Criminal Division, that particular sentences imposed by judges are unduly lenient and should be varied.[48]

Appearances by Solicitors-General before the court have also been in sharp decline, with some not undertaking any court work. As Solicitor-General I appeared in the domestic courts on 11 occasions, twice in the European Court of Justice[49] and once in the European Court of Human Rights.[50] Five of the domestic cases were in the House of Lords;[51] five in the Court of Appeal, Civil Division.[52] Without the excellent support of Treasury Counsel, standing counsel, other counsel on the Attorney-General's panels, and the government lawyers involved, this would have been impossible. My motives were mixed. In my view it was important that the Government should retain the trust of the courts, which was bolstered by appearing before them, and that the law officers should also appear to underline the importance of particular cases. At a personal level, as well, I found the work to be a challenge and one of the most intellectually stimulating aspects of being an MP and member of the Government.

9.6 Public Interest Duties

Law officers have a number of public interest duties which are independent of government, such that the doctrine of collective ministerial responsibility does not apply. On the criminal law side these duties fall into various categories.[53] As mentioned earlier, statute requires that the law officers must give their consent if certain prosecutions are to be undertaken. National security and terrorism offences offer examples.[54] A second example is that the law officers may apply

[48] But Dominic Grieve KC as Attorney-General 2010–14 also appeared in the Supreme Court on at least two occasions: (*R (Chester) v Secretary of State for Justice* [2013] UKSC 63, [2014] AC 271; and *Attorney General for England and Wales v Counsel General for Wales* [2014] UKSC 43, [2014] 1 WLR 2622) and before the Lord Chief Justice in several contempt applications.

[49] Case 273/97 *Sirdar v Secretary of State for Defence* EU:C:1999:523, [1999] ECR I-7403 (women in armed forces); Case C-376/98 *Federal Republic of Germany v European Parliament and Council of the European Union* ECLI:EU:C:2000:544, [2000] ECR I-08419 (tobacco advertising).

[50] *Rowe v United Kingdom* (2000) 30 EHRR 1. *cf Hansard* HC Deb Vol 376, col 990W (13 December 2001), which is inaccurate. See also *Hansard* HL Deb Vol 609, col 162W (17 February 2000).

[51] *R v Secretary of State for Transport Ex p Factortame Ltd* (No 5) [2000] 1 AC 524 (EU law); *Hamilton v Al-Fayed (No 1)* [2001] 1 AC 395 (Parliamentary privilege); *Steed v Secretary of State for the Home Department* [2000] 1 WLR 1169 (ban on handguns); *R v Governor of Brockhill Prison Ex p Evans (No 2)* [2001] 2 AC 19 (damages if judge-made law changes); *Attorney General v Blake* [2001] 1 AC 268 (restitution of profits made by spy's memoirs).

[52] *R v Customs and Excise Commissioners Ex p Shepherd Neame* Ltd [1999] 1 CMLR 1274 (EU law and excise duty); *Hamilton v Al-Fayed (No 1)* [1999] 1 WLR 1569 (Parliamentary privilege); *Director General of Fair Trading v First National Bank Plc* [2000] QB 672 (unfair terms); *Trustees of BT Pension Schemes v Clark (HM Inspector of Taxes)* [2000] STC 222 (taxation); *Southwood v Attorney General* (2000) Times, 18 July (charities law).

[53] See McCormick and Cowie (n 7) 24–25.

[54] eg, Anti-Terrorism, Crime and Security Act 2001, ss 47, 50, 79, 80 and 113; Official Secrets Act 1911; Official Secrets Act 1920; Official Secrets Act 1989. There is a partial list at www.cps.gov.uk/

for leave to appeal against what they regard as an unduly lenient sentence and refer points of law to the Court of Appeal where a person tried on indictment has been acquitted in respect of the whole or part of it.[55] Unduly lenient sentences are now an important aspect of the law officers' work and, as indicated earlier, provide an occasion for them to make relatively short appearances in court in an area which may have political advantage. Thirdly, the law officers may institute proceedings where there are certain types of interference with the administration of justice.[56]

As regards the civil law, these public law duties are in some respects less important than in the past, with an expanding common law and enlarged regulatory regimes. For example, the law officers can give their approval (fiat) to legal action when a person is aggrieved about a matter of public interest but could not otherwise bring an action themselves. The leading case is *Gouriet v Union of Post Office Workers*,[57] where the House of Lords held that a law officer's decision whether to consent to a relator action was not subject to supervision by the courts. The relator action is less important than previously given the expanded ambit of standing which the courts now accord to complainants. However, the principle in *Gouriet*, that there are a category of law officers' functions immune from judicial review, justified by their unique constitutional position, has been applied when a claimant sought review of the Solicitor-General's refusal to quash a coroner's finding at an inquest and order a fresh investigation.[58] As with giving their approval to act in the *Gouriet* sense, the law officers' role in acting on behalf of the Crown to represent the interests of charities is less important now that the regulatory role of the Charity Commission has expanded.[59]

Under statute the law officers may refer devolution matters to the UK Supreme Court, and may intervene in court cases when devolution issues arise in the course of litigation. Thus they may refer a devolved bill to that court before it is presented for Royal Assent to determine whether its provisions are within the competence of a devolved legislature or would engage a protected subject matter.[60] Other aspects of the law officers' role to act in the public interest include the powers to protect against vexatious litigants.[61] The courts can also request the law officers to appoint special advocates (for example, in cases where parties and their lawyers cannot see material for national security reasons) and *amicus curiae* (in cases where a difficult point of law arises and there is no party able to argue it). In one case I had to advise the Crown on a peerage claim after considering the evidence and submissions of the parties.

prosecution-guidance/consents-prosecute#_cons7.

[55] Criminal Justice Act 1988, s 35 and Criminal Justice Act 1972, s 36(1) respectively.

[56] eg, Contempt of Court Act 1981, s 7.

[57] [1978] AC 435.

[58] *R (on the application of Campbell) v Attorney General* [2025] EWHC 1653 (Admin).

[59] See *Southwood v Attorney General* (n 52).

[60] McCormick and Cowie (n 7) 84–85.

[61] Senior Courts Act 1981, s 42(1).

9.7 Conclusion

The constitutional role of the law officers is widely acknowledged.[62] Among the politicians it is they who are at the forefront of ensuring adherence to the rule of law. As ministers in the Government they are expected to facilitate its policies and priorities. Like any good lawyer, therefore, they will seek to further their client's goals by suggesting alternative paths or mitigations if the obvious path risks being regarded by a court as unlawful. Unlike private lawyers, their client is the Government, which is entrusted to act in the public interest. That means enabling people to enjoy the rights and freedoms accorded to them by law, maintaining high standards of government behaviour, and maximising fundamental values such as the rule of law. All of this may act as a brake on government action. Moreover, the law officers also have responsibilities where they must act in a quasi-judicial capacity (for example, in approving prosecutions) or in the public interest (for example, in referring arguably unduly lenient sentences to the Court of Appeal or devolution issues to the Supreme Court).[63] The tensions may be managed in different ways at different times, although I have indicated where, having been a law officer, I think the lines should be drawn.

[62] T Daintith and A Page, *Executive Self-Government and the Constitution* (Oxford University Press, 2005) 256–74.

[63] eg, Appleby (n 3); PSC Lewis and L Mulcahy, 'Government lawyers: Technicians, Policy Shapers and Organisational Brakes' (2021) 28 *International Journal of the Legal Profession* 23; M Groves, 'The Changing Role of the Attorney-General' (2024) *Federal Law Review* 131.

10

Future Challenges for the Monarchy

ROBERT HAZELL

10.1 Introduction

The death of Queen Elizabeth II in 2022 led to an outpouring of tributes to her lifelong service, her powerful sense of public duty, and the exemplary way in which she performed her role. This was reflected in the tributes of British politicians, and the messages which poured in from leading statesmen from around the world.

Alongside these tributes, there was also an upsurge of questions about the monarchy's future. Journalists repeatedly asked whether the succession should skip to Prince William; whether the monarchy should be slimmed down; whether Charles had to be Supreme Governor of the Church of England; and whether he might prove to be a meddlesome monarch. They also asked how he would respond to the threatened disintegration of the Union, from Scottish independence or Irish reunification; and to the possibility of some of the 14 realms (the other countries around the world where the British monarch is also head of state) becoming republics during his reign.

Underlying these questions is the implicit assumption that the new monarch has some agency, that these are issues where he can influence the outcome. But the UK is a constitutional monarchy in which the King has relatively little autonomy. Critics who blame the monarchy for its cost, its pomp and pageantry, or its ties to the Anglican church, should first blame the Government and Parliament for setting the legal and financial framework within which the monarchy operates. The monarch as head of state appears on paper to be a powerful figure, summoning and dissolving Parliament, giving royal assent to laws, appointing the Prime Minister and all the other ministers; but everything the monarch does as a constitutional actor is tightly circumscribed by law and by convention. Section 10.2 of this chapter explains how tightly regulated the monarchy is, through laws passed by Parliament over the last 350 years; section 10.3 then explores how much autonomy is left to the individual monarch; the third part considers future challenges.

10.2 The Monarchy is Tightly Regulated by Law

Ever since the civil war in the seventeenth century and the glorious revolution at its end, which led the throne to be offered to William and Mary, the monarchy has been subject to regulation by Parliament. Parliament has changed the rules of succession four times; it has set and subsequently amended the religious tests required of a new monarch; it has revised and updated the Regency Acts; it has changed the funding basis for the monarchy, in 2011; it has abolished the prerogative power of dissolution in 2011, and restored it in 2022.

10.2.1 The Rules of Succession

When William and Mary were invited to assume the throne, they did so subject to the Declaration of Right, which subsequently became the Bill of Rights 1689. This barred Roman Catholics from the throne, as 'it hath been found by experience that it is inconsistent with the safety and welfare of this Protestant kingdom to be governed by a papist prince'. William and Mary had no children; when none of Queen Anne's children survived, Parliament passed a new law to bypass the more distant Catholic heirs to ensure the Protestant succession.

The Act of Settlement 1701 provided instead that the Crown would go to Princess Sophia, Electress of Hanover (granddaughter of King James I), and her descendants. In changing the line of succession Parliament thus ushered in the Hanoverian dynasty, who still reign over us. The next occasion that Parliament changed the line of succession was in 1936, in His Majesty's Declaration of Abdication Act 1936, to ratify the abdication of Edward VIII, and pass the succession to his brother George VI.

The fourth and most recent change happened in the Succession to the Crown Act 2013. This replaced the rule of male primogeniture with succession by the eldest child, whether male or female. It also ended disqualification of those who had married a Roman Catholic; but the ban on Catholics becoming monarch remained, as did the requirement for the monarch to be in communion with the Church of England.

10.2.2 The Accession and Coronation Oaths

On the accession of a new monarch, there are three religious oaths which must be taken, requiring the monarch to swear to be a true and faithful Protestant, and to uphold the Church of England, and in Scotland the Presbyterian Church of Scotland.[1] These oaths all go back to the time of William and Mary, when conti-

[1] R Hazell and R Morris, 'Swearing in the new King: The Accession Declaration and Coronation Oaths' (The Constitution Unit, UCL, May 2018).

nental Europe was largely Catholic and seen as an existential threat. They are statutory oaths required by the Coronation Oath Act 1689, Acts of Union 1707, and Accession Declaration Act 1910: any change to the oaths would require amending legislation.

By tradition the first oath sworn by a new monarch is the Scottish oath, taken by King Charles at his Accession Council on 10 September 2022 to preserve the Church of Scotland. The second is the Accession Declaration Oath, required by the Bill of Rights 1689 to be taken at a new monarch's first state opening of Parliament or at their coronation, whichever occurs first. The original oath was a lengthy denunciation of the Church of Rome, amended at George V's insistence by the Accession Declaration Act 1910 to read as follows:

> I do solemnly and sincerely in the presence of God profess, testify and declare that I am a faithful protestant, and that I will [uphold and maintain] the enactments which secure the protestant succession ...[2]

The third oath is one taken at the coronation, which also dates back to the time of William and Mary and the Coronation Oath Act 1689. It is a three-part oath, of which the third part requires the monarch to maintain the settlement of the Church of England, its doctrine, and all its rights and privileges.

10.2.3 The Regency Acts

The Regency Acts provide for a substitute monarch, a regent, in the event of the reigning monarch being incapacitated or underage.[3] The Regency Act 1937 introduced for the first time a general provision that the regent should be the person next in line of succession who was of age. The Act also established the office of Counsellor of State, a number of whom could deputise when the monarch was absent from the realm or experiencing a temporary illness. When Charles became King, the potential Counsellors of State became Queen Camilla, and the next four adults in line of succession: Prince William, Prince Harry, Prince Andrew and Princess Beatrice. Because of difficulties with the last three, Parliament swiftly added Prince Edward and Princess Anne to the list, in the Counsellors of State Act 2022.

10.2.4 Funding the Monarchy

In 2012 the arrangements for funding the monarchy were fundamentally changed, by the Sovereign Grant Act 2011. The new system is designed to be a more permanent arrangement than the old Civil List, which was reign-specific. Funding for the Sovereign Grant comes from a percentage of the profits of the Crown Estate,

[2] Accession Declaration Act 1910, Sch.

[3] A new Regent has also to swear an oath on taking office, in the Schedule to the Regency Act 1937. It commits the Regent to the same political and religious obligations as a sovereign.

initially set at 15 per cent. In 2017–18 the percentage was increased to 25 per cent, to pay for the 10-year refurbishment of Buckingham Palace, costing £370 million. The grant is reviewed every five years by the Royal Trustees (the Prime Minister, Chancellor of the Exchequer and Keeper of the Privy Purse): the next review will be in 2027.

The Sovereign Grant for 2024–25 is £86.3 million, but thanks to buoyant revenues from the Crown Estate, it will increase to £132 million in 2025–26. This led to critical comment in *The Guardian*, but officials said the extra money would be funnelled into the 10-year refurbishment of Buckingham Palace.[4] It meets the central staff costs and running expenses of the royal household. It also covers maintenance of the royal palaces in England and the cost of travel to carry out royal engagements.

Separately, the King benefits from the profits – currently £28 million a year – from the Duchy of Lancaster fed into the Privy Purse for the support of monarchy. At accession, King Charles lost the equivalent income from the Duchy of Cornwall, which has transferred to Prince William. The Duchy generates an annual income of £24 million.[5]

The Sovereign is not legally liable to pay income tax, capital gains tax or inheritance tax. Since 1993, however, the monarch has paid income and capital gains tax, on a voluntary basis. The Prince of Wales also pays tax voluntarily on his income from the Duchy of Cornwall to the extent that it is not used to meet official expenditure. Under a 2023 memorandum of understanding with the Treasury no inheritance tax is payable on assets held by the King as Sovereign. The official residences, the Royal Archives, the Royal Collection of paintings and similar assets fall into this category. The Treasury memorandum of understanding also provides that inheritance tax will not be paid on gifts or bequests from one sovereign to the next. The reasons given are that:

> Private assets such as Sandringham and Balmoral have official as well as private use, and the Monarchy as an institution needs sufficient private resources to enable it to continue to perform its traditional role in national life, and to have a degree of financial independence from the Government of the day.[6]

10.2.5 The Dissolution of Parliament

The law on dissolving Parliament has changed twice in the last 10 years. Under the Fixed-term Parliaments Act 2011 (FTPA 2011) the monarch's prerogative power of dissolution was abolished, and control over dissolution passed to Parliament.

[4] D Lavelle, 'Cost of taxpayer-funded grant for UK monarchy to rise by £45m' *The Guardian* (23 September 2024), www.theguardian.com/uk-news/2024/sep/23/cost-of-grant-that-funds-uk-monarchy-to-rise-by-more-than-53.

[5] Duchy of Cornwall, Annual Report 2024.

[6] Memorandum of Understanding on Royal Taxation, July 2023, para 1.11, www.gov.uk/government/publications/memorandum-of-understanding-on-royal-taxation-2023.

The FTPA 2011 allowed for early dissolution in only two circumstances: if two thirds of all MPs voted for an early general election; or if the House passed a formal no confidence motion, and no alternative government could be formed within 14 days. Theresa May easily obtained a two-thirds vote (by 522 votes to 13) for an early dissolution in April 2017; but her successor Boris Johnson failed on three occasions in 2019 to obtain the necessary two-thirds majority, and eventually side stepped the FTPA 2011 in the Early Parliamentary General Election Act passed in October 2019.

These difficulties brought the FTPA 2011 into disrepute, leading both Labour and the Conservatives to commit to its repeal in the December 2019 election. The Johnson Government published a draft FTPA (Repeal) Bill intended to revert to the previous system. As the Government's foreword explained:

> The Bill makes express provision to revive the prerogative power to dissolve Parliament. This means once more Parliament will be dissolved by the Sovereign, on the advice of the Prime Minister. This will enable Governments, within the life of a Parliament, to call a general election at the time of their choosing.

The Government's suggestion that dissolution would be on the advice of the Prime Minister was heavily criticised by a joint committee of both Houses, which reminded the Government that dissolution was a discretionary power, exercisable in accordance with the Lascelles principles.[7] These had been published in a letter to *The Times* in 1950 from the King's private secretary, Sir Alan Lascelles, writing under the pseudonym Senex. The letter explained that 'a wise Sovereign' might justifiably refuse dissolution in three circumstances:

> (1) the existing Parliament was still vital, viable, and capable of doing its job; (2) a General Election would be detrimental to the national economy; (3) he could rely on finding another Prime Minister who could carry on his Government, for a reasonable period, with a working majority in the House of Commons.[8]

The FTPA (Repeal) Bill was subsequently passed as the Dissolution and Calling of Parliament Act 2022. How much discretion the monarch might have to refuse a dissolution is discussed in the next section.

10.3 How Much Discretion or Autonomy does the Monarch Have?

This section considers how much autonomy the monarchy still enjoys, despite the tight legal framework described above. It begins with the new King's constitutional role, as head of state, before considering how much latitude the monarch enjoys in his wider ceremonial role, as head of the nation.

[7] Joint Committee on Fixed-term Parliaments Act, Report, HC 1046, HL 253, paras 124–35.
[8] A Lascelles, 'Dissolution of Parliament: Factors in Crown's Choice' *The Times* (2 May 1950).

10.3.1 The Monarch's Prerogative Powers

The most important constitutional powers of the monarch are: to appoint and dismiss ministers, in particular the Prime Minister; to summon, prorogue and dissolve Parliament; and to give royal assent to bills passed by Parliament. The first and third can be swiftly dealt with, because the monarch no longer has any discretion. The last time the monarch exercised any personal choice in the appointment of the Prime Minister was when King George V pressured Ramsay MacDonald to remain in office in 1931. As for royal assent, it is granted automatically once a bill has passed through all its stages in both Houses.

Prorogation and dissolution are different. It is true that Queen Elizabeth acceded to the Johnson Government's request to prorogue Parliament in August 2019; but the Supreme Court subsequently ruled that the prorogation was unlawful.[9] If in future a Prime Minister has the temerity to take a chance, the court laid down clear guidelines by which to judge any questionable request:

> [T]he relevant limit on the power to prorogue is this: that a decision to prorogue (or advise the monarch to prorogue) will be unlawful if the prorogation has the effect of frustrating or preventing, without reasonable justification, the ability of Parliament to carry out its constitutional functions as a legislature and as the body responsible for the supervision of the executive.[10]

Those guidelines will apply as much to the monarch considering any future request for prorogation, as to a Prime Minister asking for it: no monarch will want their order of prorogation to be declared unlawful.

Dissolution is also a discretionary power, with the Lascelles principles suggesting the circumstances in which it might properly be refused. So far as we know, dissolution has never been refused in the UK; but it has been in other Westminster countries, and indeed it was precedents from Canada and South Africa which informed the principles announced by Sir Alan Lascelles in *The Times*.[11]

10.3.2 The Accession and Coronation Oaths

The three religious oaths taken by a new monarch on accession and coronation were described above. They are statutory oaths, and only the Government and Parliament can amend them. But the oath-taker is not without agency, as King George V demonstrated in 1910. When he objected to taking the original oath required under the Bill of Rights and Act of Settlement with its fierce denunciation

[9] *R (on the application of Miller) v The Prime Minister; Cherry v Advocate General* [2019] UKSC 41.
[10] ibid [50].
[11] The precedents were Sir Patrick Duncan's refusal of a dissolution to General Hertzog in South Africa in 1939, and Lord Byng's refusal to Mackenzie King in Canada in 1926; both referred to in Sir Alan Lascelles' letter.

of the Church of Rome, the Asquith Government toned down the oath in the Accession Declaration Act 1910. If in time Prince William has reservations about the oaths, he could ask the Government to change them, as George V did in 1910. Because the oaths are taken soon after accession, the change would need to be made in the current reign, or very swiftly in the new reign: the law was changed for George V within three months of his accession.

10.3.3 Abdication

In his address to the nation, King Charles appeared to rule out any question of abdication when he said:

> As the Queen herself did with such unswerving devotion, I too now solemnly pledge myself, throughout the remaining time God grants me, to uphold the constitutional principles at the heart of our nation.[12]

He repeated the commitment to lifelong service at his inaugural meeting of the Privy Council. But the public take a different view: one in three think that at some point he should retire and hand over to Prince William.[13] If at any time Charles decided that he had done his duty, and wished to pass on the baton, it is inconceivable that the Government would stand in his way. No monarch can be forced to reign against his will, as Japan reluctantly acknowledged in allowing Emperor Akihito to abdicate in 2019. In acceding to his wishes, the Government would have to pass amending legislation (as in 1936) to recognise the abdication and proclaim William as the new monarch.

10.3.4 Size of the Royal Family

Charles was reported as wanting to slim down the royal family long before he became King.[14] There could be two reasons for this: a smaller royal family reduces the reputational risk to the monarchy when individuals like Prince Andrew get into trouble; and it could help to reduce costs. But a smaller royal team will mean that we see less of the royal family, when demand for royal visits already exceeds supply; and any savings will be very small, when set against the total costs of the monarchy.

It is for the monarch to decide who are the working members of the royal family, as Prince Harry and Meghan found when the Queen ruled that they could

[12] HM The King's Address to the Nation and Commonwealth, 9 September 2022, www.royal.uk/news-and-activity/2022-09-09/the-kings-address-to-the-nation-and-the-commonwealth.

[13] M Smith, 'Britons' first impressions of King Charles III' YouGov (13 September 2022).

[14] L Keay, 'Prince Charles plans to strip back the royals to just William, Harry and their wives and children when he becomes King' *Mail Online* (1 December 2019).

not be half in and half out.[15] Before their departure in 2020, and Prince Andrew's stepping aside in 2019, there were 15 working royals. There are now 10 recorded in the Court Circular as carrying out royal duties. Seven are full time working royals: Charles (aged 76) and Camilla (78); William (43) and Catherine (43); Edward Earl of Wessex (61) and his wife Sophie (60); and Princess Anne (75). And there are three older royals who contribute part time: the Duke of Kent (90); and the Duke (77) and Duchess (79) of Gloucester.

The reason for recording their ages is to note how elderly they are: one is 90, five are in their 70s, with only two under the age of 60. So Charles's wish for a slimmed-down royal family is going to happen naturally: when the Duke of Kent and Duke and Duchess of Gloucester retire, there will be only seven working royals. In 2019–20 the royal family carried out some 3,200 official engagements.[16] That number was down to 2,170 in 2024, partly because of cancer afflicting the King and the Princess of Wales; but it will be hard to reach the previous level with a smaller team. This matters because there is strong demand for royal visits throughout the UK, as any Lord Lieutenant will testify. Countries like Norway (population 5 million) and Denmark (6 million) can manage with a small royal family because they have much smaller populations to serve; the UK, with a population of 67 million, is over 10 times the size – and in addition there are the realms. So, mindful of Queen Elizabeth's maxim that 'to be seen is to be believed', there will need to be careful management of expectations if a smaller royal family means that we see less of them.

10.3.5 State Visits

In March 2022 Prince William and Princess Catherine went on a controversial tour to three of the realms: Belize, Jamaica and the Bahamas. It attracted a lot of criticism, in the host countries and back in the UK, with local protests and calls for slavery reparations, and it was depicted as a colonial hangover, strengthening Jamaica's wish to become a republic.[17]

It seems likely that the tour was proposed by the Palace, as part of the Queen's Platinum Jubilee celebrations, which also included a visit in April by Prince Edward and Sophie to the other realms in the Caribbean, where they also met with a hostile reception.[18] But most state visits are planned not by the Palace but by the Foreign Office:

> The programme of overseas visits (other than Realm visits) which is funded by the Sovereign Grant is determined by the Foreign, Commonwealth and Development

[15] R Hazell and R Morris, 'Prince Harry and Meghan Markle: Why half in, half out just isn't an option for royals' Constitution Unit Blog (13 January 2020).

[16] D Clark, 'Number of official engagements of British royal family' Statista (8 September 2022).

[17] R Hall and A Gentleman, 'Perfect storm: royals misjudged Caribbean tour, say critics' *The Guardian* (25 March 2022).

[18] E Burack, 'The Backlash to Prince Edward and Sophie's Royal Caribbean Tour Grows' *Town and Country* (26 April 2022).

> Office (FCDO) and undertaken on behalf of Government, and is approved by the Royal Visits Committee according to agreed priorities.[19]

During Queen Elizabeth's long reign she went on official visits to over 100 countries, and received more than 100 visits from incoming heads of state. The monarch has no choice in which heads of state are invited. Guests hosted by the Queen included President Putin (twice), President Muzorewa from Zimbabwe, Nicolae Ceausescu from Romania, President Xi Jinping of China, and her last state visitor in 2019 was President Donald Trump.

We know from Liz Truss's decision that King Charles should not attend COP27 how much control the Government has over state visits.[20] The royals may be able to express reservations, but ultimately they must act on advice and go where they are sent. Prince Andrew in his 10 years as trade envoy was sent on trade missions to many countries with doubtful human rights records. Trade missions are a danger zone, which have also landed other royal families in trouble, in Sweden and in Spain.[21]

10.3.6 Ceremonial Role as Head of the Nation

By contrast, in his ceremonial role as head of the nation, King Charles has a lot more latitude to develop his own style and determine his own programme. This was particularly in evidence during the first week of his reign, when he embarked on his whistlestop tour of the nations, visiting Scotland, Wales and Northern Ireland within days of accession.

Charles's tour of the nations was part of a wider plan to make the new King as visible and accessible as possible, and a huge contrast to the Queen's accession in 1952. On the day after the Queen died, he gave a televised address to the nation; the Queen's first broadcast in 1952 was her Christmas message, 10 months after accession.[22] The next day, at the Accession Council in St James's Palace which proclaimed Charles King, the proceedings were televised; in 1952 it had met behind closed doors. Two days later, the new King visited Westminster Hall to receive messages of condolence from both Houses; in 1952, those messages were delivered to the Palace, rather than the Palace coming to Parliament. And repeatedly, in London, Edinburgh, Cardiff and Belfast, Charles got out of his car to greet the crowds, to the evident dismay of his protection officers.

[19] Royal Household, The Sovereign Grant and Sovereign Grant Reserve, Annual Report and Accounts 2021–22, HC 429 (June 2022) 17.

[20] C Wheeler and R Nikkah, 'Liz Truss advised King Charles to stay away from COP27 climate summit' *Sunday Times* (2 October 2022).

[21] S Jones, 'Former Spanish king faces questions over €6.7bn Saudi rail deal' *The Guardian* (8 June 2020); Agence France Presse, 'Spain's Felipe Meets Saudi King Salman as Warship Sale Mooted' (16 January 2017); and 'King of Sweden stresses statements in Brunei misinterpreted' Kuwait News Agency (10 February 2004).

[22] D Torrance, 'A Tale of Two Accessions 1952 and 2022' UK Constitutional Law Blog (28 September 2022).

10.3.7 Royal Patronage and Causes

One further respect in which the King can develop his own style is in the causes he chooses to support. As Prince of Wales he was famous for his interest in a wide range of causes: the environment, farming, architecture, homeopathy, and more. In his first address to the nation he recognised that 'It will no longer be possible for me to give so much of my time and energies to the charities and issues for which I care so deeply';[23] but he need not abandon them altogether. Without being outspoken, he can continue to be patron of charities and causes close to his heart; he can include them in his programme of royal visits; he can invite them to receptions at Buckingham Palace.

10.4 Future Challenges for the Monarchy – and for the Government

10.4.1 Maintaining Popular Support

This final section records some of the main challenges facing the monarchy during Charles's reign. The first and most obvious challenge is to maintain popular support. Modern monarchy no longer depends on divine grace, but the consent of the people. During Queen Elizabeth's reign the monarchy consistently obtained support ratings of 60–80 per cent, declining slightly in her last decade. Sixty-four per cent still support continuation of the monarchy.[24] More worrying is the lower levels of support amongst the young, with 43 per cent of 18–24 year olds favouring a republic compared with 35 per cent for the monarchy; but John Curtice suggests this age gap has been there for at least 30 years, with support for the monarchy growing as people get older.[25]

10.4.2 Threats to the Union: Scottish Independence or Irish Reunification

The next big challenge is the threat of an increasingly disunited Kingdom. Charles's tour of the nations was seen by some as a bid to save the Union. If the Scottish Government succeed in its wish to hold a second independence referendum, can the monarchy remain neutral? The first referendum was famously an occasion

[23] HM The King's Address to the Nation and the Commonwealth (9 September 2022).

[24] YouGov, 'Do you think Britain should continue to have a monarchy in the future, or should it be replaced with an elected head of state?' (January 2026).

[25] J Curtice, 'King Charles inherits crown with support for monarchy at record low; but future not set in stone' UK in a Changing Europe (20 September 2022) Fig 2.

when Queen Elizabeth's impeccable neutrality seemed to slip for a moment. As someone who has been proclaimed King of the United Kingdom of Great Britain and Northern Ireland, can Charles pretend to be unconcerned if he becomes King of a Lesser Britain? The standing of the monarchy will inevitably be damaged, even if responsibility for the break-up lies with the politicians and not the monarch. So it will be hard to stand idly by; but a greater risk to the monarchy would be to allow itself to be coopted by unionist politicians, as Liz Truss attempted to do when she sought to join Charles's inaugural tour of the nations.[26]

It will be small consolation that the Scottish National Party wishes to retain the monarchy, so that an independent Scotland would become one of the realms, with Charles as its head of state.[27] That would be a hard role to fulfil if the break-up leads to a difficult divorce, as with Brexit, with Charles trying to remain above the divisions of his fractious kingdoms. It would be less of a blow if Northern Ireland votes for reunification with the south, since the monarchy has looser ties than with Scotland, whatever the unionist community might like to think.

10.4.3 Realms becoming Republics

It may be a different story with the other realms, the 14 countries around the world where Charles is now head of state. Here too it may be seen as a blow to the monarchy's prestige if some of the realms choose to reject Charles as King; but talk of the realms rushing to become republics is overblown, and for the monarchy their departure may even come as a relief.

Barbados became a republic in November 2021, and Charles attended the celebrations to wish them well. The next countries seen as likely to become republics are Australia, Antigua and Jamaica, but none is moving fast. In July 2024 the Australian Prime Minister, Anthony Albanese, abolished the post of assistant minister for the republic, which he had created, in tacit acknowledgement that a referendum on the issue was not going to be held following the defeat of the referendum on the Voice (for aboriginal communities) in October 2023.[28] In Antigua and Barbuda the Prime Minister Gaston Browne said in 2022 that he would call for a referendum in the next three years, but this has not happened.[29] Jamaica has gone furthest, charting the way in the May 2024 report of its constitutional reform committee, followed by a government bill in December of that year. But it will require support from the opposition to be carried, because the process of

[26] J Elgot, 'Liz Truss not accompanying King Charles on UK tour' *The Guardian* (11 September 2022).

[27] Scottish Government, 'Creating a modern constitution for an independent Scotland' (19 June 2023).

[28] K Middleton, 'Albanese's new lineup signposts Labor's areas of greatest weakness and effectively concedes he made mistakes' *The Guardian* (28 July 2024).

[29] Press Association, 'Antigua and Barbuda to hold republic referendum within three years' *The Guardian* (11 September 2022).

constitutional amendment requires a two-thirds vote in both houses of Parliament, followed by a referendum.[30]

The main reason why the monarchy might privately be relieved if the realms become republics is the reduction in workload. It is a lot of additional work being head of state of 14 other countries, and keeping up to speed with their politics and their societies. And it is an additional burden making regular visits. Queen Elizabeth made 22 official visits to Canada, 16 to Australia, 10 to New Zealand, six to Jamaica. Each visit will have involved long absences, and required careful preparation and briefing.

A secondary reason for relief is shedding the reputational risk involved with some of the more unstable realms. Take just two examples, Fiji and Grenada. Fiji has seen four *coups d'etat* in the last 40 years; it must have been a relief to the monarchy when the second coup in 1987 resulted in removing the Queen as head of state. Grenada was subject to a military coup in 1979, followed by invasion by the US in 1983; more recently, the royal tour of Grenada by the Wessexes had to be cancelled at the last moment in April 2022.

10.4.4 The Religious Oaths

The final items are challenges for the Government as much as for the monarchy, but are not currently on the Government's agenda. There was no adverse comment when Charles on accession took the oath to uphold the Presbyterian church in Scotland. It similarly passed without remark when he took an oath before Parliament to be a true and faithful Protestant, and when he swore at his coronation to uphold the rights and privileges of the Church of England. But these oaths are hangovers from a bygone age, when Catholicism was seen as an existential threat to the security of the state. The UK faces many serious threats in the modern age, but Catholicism is not one of them. In our more secular and pluralist society, the oaths need to be revised and updated; or dropped altogether.

Because the oaths are statutory, this is primarily a matter for Government and Parliament; but the next monarch as oath-taker could prod them into action. In 2017–18 the Constitution Unit undertook an 18-month study, consulting all interested parties, to see how the oaths might be revised and updated, if they are not repealed altogether. We suggested that new legislation could adapt each oath to its context.[31] The Scottish oath, taken before the inaugural Privy Council, could become a wider oath about the Union. The Accession Declaration, traditionally taken before Parliament, could become an oath to uphold the constitution and our laws. And the coronation oath, in a ceremony watched by millions, could become an oath to the people.

[30] 'Republicanism in Jamaica' Wikipedia, https://en.wikipedia.org/wiki/Republicanism_in_Jamaica.

[31] R Hazell and R Morris, 'Swearing in the new King: the Accession Declaration and Coronation Oaths', 2nd edn (The Constitution Unit, October 2022).

10.4.5 Dissolution and Prorogation

This last item will not be on the agenda of the Government, after passage of the Dissolution and Calling of Parliament Act 2022. The monarchy might be expected to welcome restoration of the prerogative power of dissolution, but experience elsewhere (such as the King-Byng affair in Canada) shows the risks involved. What follows is a truncated discussion; for detailed analysis see the chapter on dissolution and prorogation in our book on the prerogative.[32]

The risks to the monarchy were emphasised by expert witnesses to the Joint Committee on the Fixed-term Parliaments Act.[33] The central issue before the committee was whether dissolution should be decided by the Executive or by Parliament. As the committee acknowledged, 'Retaining a role for the House of Commons commanded a great deal of support in evidence to this Committee as well as PACAC and the Constitution Committee'.[34] It would shield the monarch from controversy; and ensure that the decision to dissolve was non-justiciable (as a proceeding in Parliament protected by Article 9 of the Bill of Rights). But the Johnson Government stuck to its policy of excluding the courts through an ouster clause, leaving the monarch as the only check on a doubtful request for dissolution.

The courts remain a check on prorogation, but the same central issue arises: whether the Executive should have the power to control the sittings of Parliament. The UK is almost alone among European parliamentary democracies in allowing the Executive to suspend Parliament through prorogation.[35] If in future a government is minded to reform prorogation, Parliament itself could be given power to decide when it was suspended. Or if the power remains with the Executive, Parliament could have power to veto prorogation or to un-prorogue itself.[36] As with dissolution, giving Parliament control over prorogation would remove the risk of the monarch being drawn into political controversy, avoiding a repeat of what happened in 2019.

[32] R Hazell and T Foot, *Executive Power: The Prerogative, Past, Present and Future* (Hart, 2022).

[33] See the written evidence of Andrew Blick, Robert Hazell, Thomas Fleming and Petra Schleiter; and oral evidence of Robert Hazell and Peter Hennessy, Philippe Lagassé and Anne Twomey, and Gavin Phillipson, Joint Committee on Fixed-Term Parliaments Act, Report (March 2021) 112–33.

[34] ibid, 84.

[35] T Fleming and P Schleiter, 'Prorogation: Comparative Context and Reform' (2021) 74 *Parliamentary Affairs* 964.

[36] R Hazell and M Russell, Written evidence to the Joint Committee on the Fixed-Term Parliaments Act, HC 1046 HL 253, FTP0003 (December 2020) paras 31–32.

PART IV

Judges, Law Reformers and Lawyers

11

The Effect of Pre-Hearing Publicity on Criminal Trials

SIR JOHN SAUNDERS

The right to trial by jury is one of our most treasured rights. It may be that financial constraints will limit the range of offences for which it is available but, for the most serious offences, it is likely to remain. Trial by jury will only remain a treasured right if we make sure that it is fair and achieves the correct result according to the evidence.

I have been concerned for some time about an increase in pre-trial publicity in high-profile prosecutions because of the effect it may have on the fairness of the trial. Finding an answer to the potential effects of pre-trial publicity on the outcome of trials is something that the criminal justice system has struggled with for some time and is still struggling with. Does pre-trial publicity affect the outcome of criminal trials? The problem is that no one knows the answer for sure.

This is not an academic treatise. That is much better done by academics who look at problems in a great deal more depth than most practicing lawyers. These are the concerned views of a former barrister and judge who has been involved in a number of high-profile trials where the problems of pre-trial publicity have been very evident. I shall start with an analysis of the case law to show how our courts have responded to pre-trial publicity and how they are now responding.

11.1 What Does the Case Law Tell Us?

There have been a number of cases where judges have had to deal with the possible effect of pre-trial publicity on the fairness of a trial. In *R v Kray*[1] an application was made to Lawton J, the trial judge, by the defence to challenge jurors for cause in a second trial for murder. Ronald Kray, a notorious criminal, had previously been convicted of murder in a heavily reported, sensational trial. The reporting of that trial after conviction not only included a report of what had been given in evidence in the trial and the verdict, but also included other matters which were described in the judgment of Lawton J dealing with pre-trial publicity as being

[1] (1969) 53 Cr App R 412.

'discreditable' to the defendant and not being in evidence in the trial. Unusually, the judge gave leave to the defence to question prospective jurors on the re-trial to establish whether there were grounds for a challenge for cause because a prospective juror was not impartial. Memorably in his judgment Lawton J, later to be a very influential Lord Justice of Appeal, said:

> It is, however, a matter of human experience, and certainly a matter of the experience of those who practice in the criminal courts, first, that the public's recollection is short, and, secondly, that the drama, if I may use that term, of a trial almost always has the effect of excluding from recollection that which went before. A person summoned for this case would not, in my judgment, disqualify himself merely because he had read any of the newspapers containing allegations of the kind I have referred to; but the position would be different if, as a result of reading what he had, his mind had become so clogged with prejudice that he was unable to try the case impartially.[2]

While later judgments have built on this by referring to a 'fade' factor which becomes more important the longer after prejudicial publicity the trial takes place, I think that few would now claim that the drama of the trial would itself exclude recollection of prejudicial material. One thing that does recur in judgments relating to the fairness of trials is that judges rely on their own beliefs as to the effect of prejudicial material on the minds of jurors. A good example of this is to be found in the next case that I consider.

After he was promoted to the Court of Appeal, Lawton LJ presided over the appeal in the case of *Coughlan and Young*.[3] The appeal was in part over the decision of the trial judge not to grant a stay because of prejudicial publicity following an unsuccessful plea of *autrefois convict*. The Court of Appeal upheld the decision of the judge and, in the judgment of the court, Lawton LJ again took a robust view, saying

> We do not rest our decision on this point solely on whether the exercise of the judge's discretion has been shown to have been wrong. We would have thought it right to take the appropriate action if we had been satisfied that this untoward piece of reporting had resulted in a miscarriage of justice. It is our experience that juries in general understand the responsibility which rests upon them. They know that they have to be sure of guilt on the evidence before returning a verdict of guilty. The fault with juries nowadays lies not in convicting when they should acquit but in acquitting when they should convict. Juries are capable of disregarding that which is not properly before them. They are expected to disregard what one accused says about another in his absence. If they can do that, which is far from easy, they can disregard what has been said in a newspaper.[4]

I doubt whether any Court of Appeal today, whatever their private views, would accuse juries publicly of acquitting when they should convict. As has been accepted in later cases, deciding whether to order a stay because of the effect of prejudicial

[2] ibid, 415.
[3] (1976) 63 Cr App R 33.
[4] ibid, 37.

publicity is not an exercise of a discretion but a judgment, and it is for the Court of Appeal to make a judgment as to whether it would have reached the same conclusion as the trial judge on the material it sees.

I do not intend to conduct an exhaustive review of the cases, but instead concentrate on those cases which seem to me to be the most important and highlight any possible weaknesses in the decisions.

There have been a few cases where a judge has ordered that a case should not proceed because of prejudicial material in the media. These are a small minority and may be thought to be extreme examples on their facts. In *McCann (John Paul)*[5] convictions were quashed because of remarks made by Lord Denning and the Secretary of State for Northern Ireland, reported in the media, in which they equated the exercise of the right of silence with guilt. These remarks were made during the trial of the appellants who had exercised their right to silence. There could have been no doubt of the possible effect on the fairness of the trial because of the timing of the remarks. In *Michelle and Lisa Taylor*[6] the Court of Appeal quashed a conviction on the basis of fresh evidence which was not contested by the Crown, but refused to allow a re-trial on the basis of the sensational and inaccurate press reporting during the trial.

Taylor was described as a decision on its own facts by the Court of Appeal in *R v Stone*,[7] another very high-profile case in which a conviction was quashed but a re-trial was ordered despite a great deal of publicity after the first trial, some of which was sensational and inaccurate. Describing an appeal as decided on its own facts is shorthand for saying it should not be used as a precedent in subsequent cases.

In the majority of cases trials or re-trials have proceeded despite high levels of prejudicial publicity.

I will now turn to what I consider to be the two most important authorities.

The Privy Council considered prejudicial publicity in the case of *Montgomery v HM Advocate and another*.[8] The background was unusual. In 1998 an Asian man suffered fatal injuries following an attack. Although three men were investigated only one was charged. After a trial the one who had been charged was convicted of assault but acquitted of murder. At the conclusion of the trial the trial judge criticised the Crown for not indicting the other two men, one of whom was Montgomery. The Lord Advocate publicly responded to the judge's criticism and there was then a great deal of publicity about the case and the part played by the other two in the killing. The case was compared in the media to the Stephen Lawrence killing and protest groups were set up. In July 1999 Montgomery and the other man were charged with murder. The two men brought an action against the Lord Advocate claiming that they could not get a fair trial because of all

[5] (1991) 92 Cr App R 239.
[6] Known as *R v Taylor* (1994) 98 Cr App R 361.
[7] [2001] EWCA Crim 297.
[8] [2003] 1 AC 641.

the publicity which had been generated about the case. Montgomery lost in the Scottish Court of Appeal and appealed to the Privy Council.

The Privy Council upheld the decision of the Court of Appeal and dismissed the appeal, but it is an important decision, and the reasoning has influenced cases not only in Scotland but also in England and Wales. It is important because it was decided by reference to Article 6 of the European Convention on Human Rights (ECHR) which establishes the right to a fair trial by an independent and impartial tribunal. That is an unqualified right, and the Court found that that right cannot be balanced against the importance of trying serious cases in order to detect and suppress crime. When applying a common law test courts have tended to carry out just that sort of balancing act. Courts rightly regard it as important in the public interest that cases, particularly high-profile ones, are heard and decided. That should no longer be a consideration in deciding on a stay, but it will be interesting to see whether it is still a factor even if not expressly acknowledged in any ruling. The decision in *Montgomery*, which has been followed by the Court of Appeal, Criminal Division in England and Wales makes clear that the public interest in deciding serious criminal cases should play no part in the decision whether to stay a case because of the effect of prejudicial publicity. The sole issue is whether the defendant can have a fair trial by an independent and impartial jury.

Despite the widespread publicity in Montgomery's case the Privy Council still decided that the test for an independent and impartial tribunal was met. Lord Hope, who gave the leading judgment, said that judges were entitled to assume that juries will faithfully follow directions given by the judge. He said 'the entire system is based on the assumption that the jury will follow the instructions which they receive from the trial judge and that they will return a true verdict in accordance with the evidence'.[9] In reaching its decision the Privy Council relied on some research commissioned by the New Zealand Law Commission as to the way that juries reach their decisions. The difficulty in relying on research about juries is that it is very difficult to find reliable research in this area because of restrictions on interviewing jurors. There is other research which reaches different conclusions to the New Zealand research.

The same view as to the beliefs and behaviours of jurors was expressed in the Court of Appeal for England and Wales in the case of *In the matter of B*.[10] Lord Judge, while he was President of the Queen's Bench Division, said:

> There is a feature of our trial system which is sometimes overlooked or taken for granted. The collective experience of this constitution as well as the previous constitution of the court, both when we were in practice at the Bar and judicially, has demonstrated to us time and time again, that juries up and down the country have a passionate and profound belief in, and a commitment to, the right of a defendant to be given a fair trial. They know that it is integral to their responsibility. It is, when all is said and done, their birthright; it is shared by each one of them with the defendant. They guard it faithfully.

[9] ibid, at 674.
[10] [2006] EWCA Crim 2692.

> The integrity of the jury is an essential feature of our trial process. Juries follow the directions which the judge will give them to focus exclusively on the evidence and to ignore anything they may have heard or read out of court.[11]

With great respect for the views of Lord Hope and Lord Judge, two of our greatest judges, they cannot know with any degree of certainty the way in which juries approach reaching their verdicts and particularly whether they always follow the directions of the judge. They will almost certainly never have served on a jury, and jurors are not permitted to reveal details of their discussions in the jury room.

Another case decided in 2006 by the House of Lords threw doubt over the assumption made by the judges in those two cases that juries faithfully follow directions given to them by judges in reaching their decisions. In *R v Coutts*[12] the House of Lords quashed a conviction for murder because the judge had failed to leave the jury an alternative of manslaughter in circumstances when the House of Lords decided the judge should have done. The judge had given what were accepted to be entirely accurate directions on what the jury had to be sure of before they could convict of murder. They convicted, and if it was correct that they had followed the directions faithfully, they would not have convicted of manslaughter and the conviction for murder could not have been unsafe. The House nevertheless found that the verdict was unsafe. A consequence of this decision was that the courts needed to look again at their confident and oft-repeated assertions that juries follow directions given by the judge. Combined with that decision of the House of Lords were the increased number of cases when jurors were found to have looked up things to do with the case on the internet before the case was over. Jurors are given clear directions by the judge not to carry out such searches, so the inevitable conclusion has to be that not all jurors follow the directions of the judge all of the time.

In the case of *Abu Hamza*[13] the Court of Appeal tried to reconcile what it accepted to be a tension between the decisions in the cases of *Coutts* and *Montgomery*.

Abu Hamza had been convicted in February 2006 after a trial presided over by Hughes J. The trial took place before the decision in *Coutts* had been given and promulgated. The adverse pre-trial publicity in Abu Hamza's case was extensive. The trial judge did not stay the proceedings saying, inter alia, that his experience of juries was that 'almost universally, they approach their task and their oath with conspicuous fairness'.[14] The Court of Appeal found that the judge was entitled to be satisfied that with proper direction a jury would be able to bring impartial judgment to the case and decide whether, despite being labelled by some as a public enemy, the defendant really did commit the offences with which he was charged. Of course, the trial judge had not considered the judgment in *Coutts* as it had not been delivered, and it was left to the Court of Appeal to take account of it in reaching its decision.

[11] ibid [31].
[12] [2006] UKHL 39.
[13] [2006] EWCA Crim 2918.
[14] Reproduced in the Court of Appeal's decision at [98].

The Court of Appeal set out how *Coutts* should be factored into decisions on prejudice. At [93] it said:

> It seems to us that there is a degree of tension between the approach of the House of Lords in Coutts and Lord Hope's observations in respect of the trust that can properly be placed on the jury's ability to perform their duty to reach a decision in accordance with the evidence and the directions of the judge. We suggest that the answer to this tension is as follows. The risk that members of a jury may be affected by prejudice is one that cannot wholly be eliminated. Any member may bring personal prejudices to the jury room and equally there will be a risk that a jury may disregard the directions of the judge when they consider that they are contrary to what justice requires. Our legal principles are designed to reduce such risks to the minimum, but they cannot obviate them altogether if those reasonably suspected of criminal conduct are to be brought to trial. The requirement that a viable alternative verdict be left to the jury is beneficial in reducing the risk that the jury may not decide the case in accordance with the directions of the judge. Prejudicial publicity renders more difficult the task of the court, that is of the judge and jury together, in trying the case fairly. Our laws of contempt of court are designed to prevent the media from interfering with the due process of justice by making it more difficult to conduct a fair trial. The fact, however, that adverse publicity may have risked prejudicing a fair trial is no reason for not proceeding with the trial if the judge concludes that, with his assistance, it will be possible to have a fair trial. In considering this question it is right for the judge to have regard to his own experience and that of his fellow judges as to the manner in which juries normally perform their duties.

The Court of Appeal concluded that a fair trial was possible, saying:

> The judge was correct to conclude that the adverse media publicity attendant upon the events that had occurred between 2000 and the bringing of charges against the appellant in October 2004 had put at risk the fairness of his trial. The challenge posed to the judge of taking appropriate steps to neutralise the effect of these matters by appropriate directions and guidance in the course of his summing up was considerable. The task was an exacting one. The judge was confident that he would be able to discharge it. We have concluded that his assessment of the position was correct. The circumstances did not require the judge to stay the prosecution on the ground that there could not be a fair trial.[15]

So what effect, if any, will the decision in *Coutts* and the misuse of the internet by juries have on applications to stay a case on the basis of adverse prejudicial material? It may be that the answer is very little. That was certainly the case in the application for leave to appeal by Lucy Letby against her conviction on a re-trial for attempted murder.

In August 2023 Lucy Letby was convicted of seven counts of murder and seven counts of attempted murder. The convictions were greeted with a torrent of publicity not simply restricted to the convictions but to descriptions of her which were likely to be highly prejudicial to her on any re-trial. In September 2023 the Crown Prosecution Service announced that it would seek a re-trial on a count of attempted murder on which the jury had failed to reach agreement. The re-trial

[15] ibid [104].

started on 10 June 2024 and the defence applied for a stay on the basis, in part, that it was impossible for her to have a fair trial because of the prejudicial publicity following her convictions.

The judge refused the stay. The trial judge, giving his reasons, said:

> I am satisfied that any prejudice to the defendant from the publicity in the media is not such as to preclude the defendant from having a fair trial. The evidence of her convictions will be in evidence before the jury. It will be subject to the necessary directions to the jury as to the use to which they may and may not put this evidence; they will also receive a direction as to the importance of reaching their verdict on, and only on the evidence placed before them and nothing else. Experience has shown that juries can be relied upon faithfully to follow such directions. The media coverage will, in any event, have been diluted by the 'fade factor' since the verdicts in the original trial were reported.[16]

The application for leave to appeal on the basis that a fair trial was not possible because of the prejudicial publicity received short shrift.[17] The fact that the convictions would be in evidence in the re-trial was a significant factor in the decision but, more controversially, the Court of Appeal said that 'In relation to the more emotive language used, the fade factor would be significant', and said later in its judgment:

> We take into account the fact that almost all of the material of which complaint now is made emerged in the week immediately following conviction. The prosecution relied on what they termed 'the fade factor'. We consider that they were right to do so.[18]

At paragraph 26 of its judgment the Court of Appeal said:

> The judge identified that to stay a criminal trial because it would offend the integrity of the justice system always will be the remedy of last resort. It is an exceptional step to take. It was not justified by the circumstances in this case.[19]

The fade factor relies on the belief that memories of newspaper headlines are brief. (Today's news is tomorrow's chip paper.) How far this is justified in a high-profile case like the Letby case perhaps needs independent verification from research, but some of the headlines at the end of Lucy Letby's trial went far beyond the facts of her convictions and, if remembered, would certainly be capable of prejudicing a jury. Is it sufficient simply for a judge and the Court of Appeal to say that the details will quickly fade from a jury's memory?

The Court of Appeal did not mention Article 6 ECHR and the absolute right to an independent and impartial tribunal in their judgment, and it is not easy to see how paragraph [26] of the judgment (see above) fits in with that absolute right. The remark gives the impression that both the trial judge and the Court of Appeal were carrying out a balancing act between the need to have a trial and the right to an independent and impartial tribunal. The decision in the case of *Abu Hamza* was

[16] Reproduced in the Court of Appeal's decision in *R v Letby* [2024] EWCA Crim 1278 [10].
[17] *R v Letby* [2024] EWCA Crim 1278.
[18] ibid [26].
[19] ibid [13].

not mentioned and the problems which have become evident following *Coutts* in being satisfied that jurors will follow directions of judges. It seems as if, in this case, the Court of Appeal may have gone back to ignoring the problems identified in *Montgomery* and *Abu Hamza*. It is right to say that this was an application for leave to appeal and therefore it is not usual for the Court to go into as much detail as the Court of Appeal, Criminal Division would in giving judgment in a full appeal, but in a case of this importance it might have been thought that the principles could have been identified by reference to the most significant authorities.

Are we doing enough to ensure that juries are not prejudiced by publicity prior to the trial? In my view we are not.

As indicated above, in *Montgomery* the Privy Council relied on research carried out in New Zealand to suggest that juries are less influenced by prejudicial publicity than some people might think. The difficulty with most research into this subject is that it has to be done with mock juries as genuine juries cannot be questioned about what went on in the jury room.

There is however now some research available with actual juries, such as Professor Cheryl Thomas's 2010 report, 'Are juries fair?', commissioned by the Ministry of Justice and published as part of the Ministry of Justice research series.[20] Professor Thomas looked at a number of different questions, but I will set out her key findings on the areas covered herein.

Media Reporting of Jury Trials and Juror Use of the Internet

The study was conducted in three different locations (Nottingham, Winchester and London), and included 62 cases and 668 jurors. The sample included both long, high-profile cases and standard cases lasting less than two weeks with little media coverage.

- Jurors serving on high-profile cases were almost seven times more likely to recall media coverage (70 per cent) than jurors serving on standard cases (11 per cent).
- Most jurors who recalled media reports of their case saw or heard reports only during the time their trial was taking place. This provides the first empirical evidence in this country of the 'fade factor' in jury trials (the further away media reports are from a trial the more likely they are to fade from jurors' memories).
- In contrast, a third of jurors (35 per cent) on high-profile cases remembered pre-trial coverage.
- In high-profile cases, jurors recalled media reports of their cases from a range of media outlets, with television (66 per cent) and national newspapers (53 per cent) the two main sources. This contrasts with jurors' recall of media reports in standard cases, where local newspapers accounted for almost all (77 per cent) coverage recalled.

[20] Cheryl Thomas, 'Are Juries Fair?' Ministry of Justice Research Series 1/10 (February 2010).

- Most jurors (66 per cent) in high-profile cases who recalled media coverage either did not or could not remember it having any particular slant. Where jurors did recall any emphasis, almost all recalled it suggesting the defendant was guilty.
- In high-profile cases, 20 per cent of jurors who recalled media reports of their case said they found it difficult to put these reports out of their mind while serving as a juror.[21]

The findings show that in high-profile cases over two-thirds of jurors will be aware of media coverage of their case. It would be helpful to know how these jurors perceive this media coverage, what particular type of pre-trial coverage jurors' recall and what type of coverage some jurors find difficult to put out of their minds. While no doubt most jurors would say that the publicity they read would have made no difference to their decision, the reliability of such statements may be doubtful.

While most contemporaneous reports of cases may be reasonably accurate and therefore unlikely to affect any verdict, other older material may well remain on the internet as will comments by celebrities, politicians and others whose views are often followed by more people than read newspapers. The courts cannot ignore the effect of the internet and judges do their best to persuade jurors against internet searches by giving them very strict directions. Again, Professor Thomas has carried out invaluable research into the use of the internet.

The Internet

All jurors who looked for information about their case during the trial looked on the internet.

- More jurors said they saw information on the internet than admitted looking for it on the internet. In high-profile cases 26 per cent said they saw information on the internet compared to 12 per cent who said they looked. In standard cases 13 per cent said they saw information compared to five per cent who said they looked.
- In the study jurors were admitting to doing something they should have been told by the judge not to do. This may explain why more jurors said they saw reports on the internet than said they looked on the internet.
- Among all jurors who said they looked for information on the internet, most (68 per cent) were over 30 years old. Among jurors on high-profile cases, an even higher percentage (81 per cent) of those who looked for information on the internet were over 30.[22]

These findings suggest that in 2010 more than a minimal number of jurors did not follow directions given to them by the judge, and shows that it is a matter for concern. Since 2010 Professor Thomas has worked closely with the senior judiciary

[21] ibid, vii.
[22] ibid, viii.

to try and ensure that juries understand the directions of the judge on what they can and cannot do. The results of those efforts are reported by Professor Thomas in an article in the *Criminal Law Review*.[23] Her conclusions from her research are that there is now an appreciably better understanding by jurors of their responsibilities and their understanding of what they can and cannot do. What is missing, however – and it is impossible to determine – is a proper understanding of what percentage of jurors look up matters relating to the case on the internet despite those warnings, or what influence prejudicial material has on the verdicts of jurors.

It is insufficient, I suggest, to try to deal with these issues by bland assertions that jurors do what judges say, and if judges tell them to ignore prejudicial material and decide the case on the evidence juries will be able to achieve this. In many of the cases I have included, judges have included remarks about how juries concentrate on the issues and do not allow extraneous material to interfere with their decision. How do judges know what juries take into account? My experience is that some jurors look really engaged, others look bored, and some have even been known to go to sleep, but there is no way of deciding by looking at them how conscientious they are. The judges who say that juries are very conscientious no doubt believe it, but that belief cannot be objectively verified. That is why having high-class research with genuine jurors may provide some degree of reassurance. Our system of justice depends on jurors carrying out the directions of judges and the fact that the House of Lords in *Coutts* cast doubt on that is worrying for the future of criminal trials.

While, as was said in *Abu Hamza*, it will never be possible to ensure that no jury is influenced in the decisions they make as a result of prejudicial material, we should do everything we can to prevent that happening. That requires two things. First, much more policing of the press to ensure that they abide by the strict liability rule under the Contempt of Court Act 1981. This Act provides that strict liability for contempt applies to a publication which creates a substantial risk that the course of justice in the proceedings in question will be seriously impeded or prejudiced when proceedings are active. Proceedings are active after a person has been arrested.

Who polices this? It is the Attorney-General's office who brings contempt proceedings where there is a breach, but it does not have the resources to track prejudicial material. The police are not going to do it. Currently, the only person who might do it is a defendant, but he/she must be rich. In the phone hacking trial where the defence had a very large team working constantly on the case including monitoring press reports and social media, they were constantly bringing to my attention as the trial judge reporting in papers and on social media which was said to be inaccurate. If it was inaccurate then it would be taken down immediately, reducing the risk of the jury seeing it and being affected by it. Rebekah Brooks made an application to stay the proceedings on the basis of a large amount of

[23] C Thomas, 'The 21st century jury: contempt, bias and the impact of jury service' (2020) 11 *Criminal Law Review* 987.

pre-trial media publicity which was adverse to her and the *News of the World*. I allowed the trial to continue and that was clearly the right decision as she was acquitted, but the jury was told a number of times how important it was to ignore pre-trial publicity. Further, the trial was very long and detailed, which I think makes it less likely that a jury would remain affected by pre-trial publicity.

In high-profile cases somebody needs to be looking at reporting in the media after an arrest to see whether the strict liability rule which is relied on in the authorities as providing protection is actually being complied with.

If there has been a breach, there needs to be proper enforcement. At present, proceedings for contempt can only be brought by the Attorney-General. The Law Commission is presently considering possible legislative change in relation to contempt of court.[24] One of the changes it is proposing is to remove the Attorney-General's role as the person who can instigate contempt proceedings. The role of a politician always has the potential for conflict, particularly where it may be his/her colleagues in government who may be in contempt. Before the trials arising out of the parliamentary expenses scandal, a number of senior politicians, including senior ministers, saw fit to comment disapprovingly on the fact that most of the defendants were claiming parliamentary privilege. Those comments were unfair and capable of affecting the fairness of the trial. As the trial judge I had to warn the politicians to stop. It should not have been my job: the Attorney-General should have intervened to ensure that the stream of comments did not occur. The Attorney-General is clearly compromised in those circumstances, as he may be in taking action against influential newspapers.

In the phone hacking case after the conviction of Andy Coulson on one count, but while the jury was still considering another count, David Cameron, who was then Prime Minister, made a public statement that he had been deceived by Andy Coulson. This statement was capable of affecting the fairness of the continuing trial, but it might be unrealistic to expect the Attorney-General to take action against his Prime Minister. He would certainly be compromised. Taking the responsibility away from the Attorney-General seems to me to be the correct course. After David Cameron's unwise intervention, a powerful application to discharge the jury without deciding the further charge on the basis of prejudice was made.

Further in an appropriate high-profile case where the amount of prejudicial information in the media clearly risks creating a bias in the jury, a judge needs to be brave enough to stay the trial. That is a very difficult step for any judge to take but he/she can no longer, I suggest, blandly rely on the view that juries ignore prejudicial press comment and follow judicial directions. To stay a case is not a last resort. If there cannot be a fair trial by an independent and impartial tribunal, and that means an unbiased tribunal, then the trial has to be stayed. Realistically there will always be pressure on the trial judge to let a high-profile case continue. There would be considerable public concern if a judge were to stay the proceedings.

[24] 'Cameron apologises over Andy Coulson appointment' BBC News (24 June 2014), www.bbc.co.uk/news/uk-politics-27998411.

The alternative is to accept the inevitable and live with it. There will always be prejudicial publicity in high-profile cases, not just in mainstream media but also on the internet. People now use the internet to look things up to such an extent that it may be that we have to accept that it is impossible to stop them doing it. Will that lead to a reduction in the fairness of the gold standard of jury trials? Only time will tell. If we just accept the inevitable and live with it, this may be used as a lever to further restrict the right to trial by jury which many people would find unacceptable.

12

The Constitutional Role of the Law Commission

ALISON L YOUNG*

12.1 Introduction

As independent bodies with advisory roles, it may seem odd to regard the Law Commission of England and Wales (LCE&W), the Scottish Law Commission (SLC) and the Northern Ireland Law Commission as playing a role in the UK constitution. Although they play an important role in law reform, they cannot initiate either primary or secondary legislation. Nor can the law commissions implement their reforms in other ways, for example by changing the common law.

Nevertheless, I will argue that the law commissions play an important constitutional role, being uniquely placed to reform the law. I will draw predominantly on the work of the LCE&W, with reference to the SLC, as the Northern Ireland Law Commission is currently non-operational. When carrying out their law reform role, the law commissions shore up the rule of law, helping to ensure that law is accessible, clear, certain and modern. Furthermore, the process through which the law commissions conduct their work facilitates democratic decision-making, particularly through enhancing deliberative and participatory democracy.

However, to succeed in these roles requires the law commissions to be both independent from, whilst also maintaining good relations with, the various governments of the UK. This delicate balance can only be maintained where there is an understanding of the relative constitutional roles of the law commissions, governments and legislatures, combined with effective transparency and oversight.

12.2 The Role of the Law Commissions

The LCE&W and SLC were established by the Law Commissions Act 1965, for the purpose of 'promoting the reform of the law'.[1] The Law Commissions are given an ambitious task: 'to take and keep under review all the law' in their respective

* I would like to thank Ethan George and Georgina Withers-Boalch for their outstanding legal research on this project, and Sir Peter Fraser and Matthew Jolley for their comments on an earlier draft.

jurisdictions.[2] In particular, they are required to consider the 'systematic development and reform' of the law, including 'codification', the 'elimination of anomalies', the 'repeal of obsolete and unnecessary enactments' the 'reduction of the number of separate enactments', and, more generally, the 'simplification and modernisation of the law'.[3] The Law Commission of Northern Ireland was established in 2007, with the same role.[4] However, it has not been operational since April 2015.

Law reform projects can be initiated in two ways. First, the law commissioners develop programmes of law reform.[5] Second, they can receive references from government departments.[6] Programmes of law reform are developed after a public consultation exercise. This would appear to provide the law commissions with *carte blanche* to develop programmes of law reform. However, programmes of law reform have to be agreed by either the Lord Chancellor, or the Scottish Ministers, and laid before either Parliament or the Scottish Parliament respectively.[7] This provides a veto power of the relevant government over these law reform projects. References from government ministers may be initiated by government, but the law commissioners enjoy a discretion as to whether to accept these references.[8] The origin of a project also has funding implications for the LCE&W. Governmental referrals are normally funded by the government department making the referral.[9] There is a greater ability for programme projects to be funded by the core funding granted to the LCE&W from the Ministry of Justice, although best endeavours should also be used to secure funding from the relevant government department, meaning that there may be little difference in practice.[10]

The LCE&W exercises its discretion according to the criteria set out in the Protocol agreed between the LCE&W and the UK Government in 2010.[11] When considering projects for inclusion in a programme, the LCE&W notifies the minister with policy responsibility for that area of the law. Before approving the project, the minister will need to agree to provide departmental support throughout the project. This is in the form of regular meetings, providing information as to the Government's policy. Departments also provide an undertaking that 'there is serious intention to take forward law reform in this area'.[12]

[1] Law Commissions Act 1965 (LCA 1965), s 1.
[2] ibid, s 3.
[3] ibid.
[4] Justice (Northern Ireland) Act 2002 (JNIA 2002), ss 50–52.
[5] LCA 1965, s 3(1)(b) and JNIA 2002, s 51(2)(b).
[6] LCA 1965, s 3(1)(c) and JNIA 2002, s 51(2)(c).
[7] LCA 1965, ss 3(2) and 3A.
[8] See S Wilson Stark, *The Work of British Law Commissions. Law Reform…Now?* (Hart Publishing, 2017) 54–61.
[9] Unless these are projects for the Ministry of Justice which provides core funding to the LCE&W.
[10] Ministry of Justice, 'Framework Document. Ministry of Justice and the Law Commission for England and Wales' (July 2015), paras 4.4–4.6.
[11] Protocol between the Lord Chancellor (on behalf of the Government) and the Law Commission (Law Com No 321)(Protocol), https://lawcom.gov.uk/corporate-document/protocol-between-the-lord-chancellor-on-behalf-of-the-government-and-the-law-commission.
[12] ibid, para 6.

The LCE&W initially selects from this range of possible projects, according to the following criteria:

- the extent to which the law is unsatisfactory;
- the potential benefits that will flow from law reform;
- the suitability of the project for the law commission;
- the expertise of the law commission to take on a project in this area;
- whether project funding is available;
- the degree of departmental support;
- relative priority of each project;
- whether there is a Scottish or Northern Irish dimension and, if so, whether there is a need to work with the Scottish or Northern Irish Law Commission; and
- whether there is a Welsh dimension that would need the involvement of the Welsh ministers.[13]

The same criteria are used by the LCE&W when determining whether to accept a referral from a government department.[14] There is no equivalent protocol for the SLC. In its recent eleventh programme, the SLC stated that it selected projects for law reform according to their relative importance, suitability and resources.[15]

Law reform projects normally follow three stages. First, in the pre-consultation stage, lawyers, legal assistants and research assistants (referred to as 'legal assistants' in the SLC) working for the law commission carry out detailed legal research in the area, including comparative research, determining the relevant legal issues and questions. At this stage, there are meetings with key stakeholders and relevant government departments. There may also be a call for evidence. This stage culminates in the production of a consultation paper, referred to as a discussion paper by the SLC. This contains provisional proposals of law reform, as well as asking broader questions regarding potential legal reforms. Second is the consultation stage, which normally takes three months. The aim is to consult as widely as possible, encouraging responses from the wider public in addition to stakeholders, legal and academic experts and relevant social and public interest groups. Third, is the analysis of consultation responses, where provisional proposals are modified in the light of consultation. This stage leads to the production of a report, making recommendations as to future law reform. Some reports may also include draft legislation designed to implement these law reforms.

The law commissions are advisory bodies.[16] Matthew Dyson describes them as possessing five unique elements: independence; expertise; collective responsibility;

[13] ibid, para 5.

[14] ibid, para 9.

[15] Scottish Law Commission, 'Eleventh Programme of Law Reform' (Scot Law Com 264), May 2023 (SLC 11th Programme).

[16] S Cretney, 'The Politics of Law Reform – a View from the Inside' (1985) 48 *Modern Law Review* 493.

consultation mechanisms; and a wide scope.[17] The above discussion demonstrates the wide scope of their roles and the use of consultation. The independence and expertise of the law commissions stems from their composition. Law commissioners for the LCE&W and SLC are appointed from those holding judicial office, or having relevant experience as a solicitor, barrister, or teacher of law in a University.[18] There are four commissioners and one chair of the LCE&W and no more than four commissioners and a chair of the SLC.[19] The Law Commission in Northern Ireland requires the Commission to consist of one solicitor, one barrister, one teacher of law in a University and one further individual who does not hold these qualifications.[20]

Appointments are made on merit, following an open application process, by the Lord Chancellor for the LCE&W, and the Scottish Ministers for the SLC.[21] Commissioners are appointed for a term of five years which may be renewed for a further period of up to five years. The chair of the LCE&W is a judge of the Court of Appeal or the High Court, by convention elevated to the Court of Appeal on appointment.[22] There is no statutory requirement for the chair of the SLC to be a member of the Scottish judiciary. However, the chair is normally a Senator of the College of Justice in Scotland.

The collective responsibility of the law commissions derives from the process of law reform. Each publication of the law commission is scrutinised and agreed by all the commissioners. Publications go through a rigorous process of peer review, where commissioners debate and agree provisional proposals and recommendations.

Baron Etherington referred to the establishment of the law commissions as a 'fundamental change in constitutional arrangements'.[23] Lord Scarman, the first chair of the LCE&W, regarded the law commissions as playing an important constitutional role by moving law reform from a piecemeal and ad hoc process to a coherent and consistent programme of law reform. Law reform would no longer solely be initiated by the government of the day, facilitating a better means of reforming, codifying and consolidating the law.[24] Lord Scarman also foresaw a further possible constitutional change – the move from a legal system primarily dependent on the common law to one which relied more on statutes and statutory interpretation.[25]

[17] M Dyson, 'The Future is a Foreign Country, They Do Things Differently There' in M Dyson, J Lee and S Wilson Stark (eds), *Fifty Years of the Law Commissions. The Dynamics of Law Reform* (Hart Publishing, 2016) 494.

[18] LCA 1965, ss 1(2) and 2(2).

[19] ibid, ss 1(1) and 2(1).

[20] JNIA 2002, s 50(4).

[21] LCA 1965, ss 1(2) and 2(1)–(2).

[22] ibid, s 1(1A).

[23] T Etherington, 'Law Reform in England and Wales: a Shattered Dream or a Triumph of Political Vision' (2008) 73 *Amicus Curiae* 3, 3.

[24] L Scarman, 'The Law Commission' (1972) 1 *Anglo-American Law Review* 31, and 'The Law Commission: its aims and achievements' (1974) *City of London Law Review* 7.

[25] ibid, and L Scarman, 'Law Reform by Legislative Techniques' (1967) 32 *Saskatchewan Law Review* 217.

The first of these roles is clearly taking place. The LCE&W has, to date, produced 257 law reform reports. Of those, 63 per cent have been implemented in whole or in part, and eight per cent have been accepted and are awaiting implementation. Only 12 per cent of these reports have been rejected, and three per cent have been accepted in whole or in part but will not be implemented, with four per cent having been superseded by other developments.[26] The SLC has produced 195 reports, of which 82 per cent were implemented in whole or in part, five per cent were superseded and 15 per cent were unimplemented.[27]

The second potential constitutional change predicted by Lord Scarman is less marked and harder to demonstrate. As discussed below, there has been a change in direction of the work of the law commissions away from consolidation and codification towards simplification and modernisation of the law. This includes work on potential regulatory frameworks for new emerging technologies. Whilst there has been a growth in legislation, it is difficult to see this as stemming solely from the work of the law commissions. This is understandable. The work of the law commissions, whilst important, represents only a small proportion of legislation made by the UK's four parliaments/legislative assemblies.

Lord Scarman also recognised two further constitutional roles for the law commission which I wish to explore in more detail: the facilitation of the rule of law; and of democracy.

12.3 The Law Commissions and the Rule of Law

When presenting the Law Commission Bill to the House of Commons for its second reading, Sir Eric Fletcher recognised the importance that laws 'should not only be just, but should be up to date, accessible and intelligible'.[28] For Fletcher, the ideal was to ensure that 'the law on any subject can be found in a single Statute'.[29] Lord Gardiner, the then Lord Chancellor, focused on a similar role for the law commissions when presenting the Bill for second reading in the House of Lords.[30] Baron Etherington referred to a constitutional right of citizens to have law that is accessible, intelligible and in accordance with modern needs.[31] The need to ensure law is accessible, modern and intelligible has consistently been of importance to the law commissions, as noted by the current chair of the Law Commission of England and Wales, Sir Peter Fraser, in his lecture marking the sixtieth anniversary of the law commissions, which also set out how the work of the law commissions furthers the rule of law.[32]

[26] Annual Report of the Law Commission, 2024–25.
[27] Scottish Law Commission, Annual Report 2024, 10.
[28] *Hansard* HC Deb Vol 706, col 47 (8 February 1965).
[29] ibid, col 54.
[30] *Hansard* HL Deb Vol 264, col 1140 (1 April 1965).
[31] Etherington (n 23) 8.
[32] P Fraser, 'The Future of Law Reform' SLS Hale Lecture 2025.

In his account of the rule of law, Lord Bingham referred to the need for law to be accessible, intelligible, clear, and predictable.[33] The connection between legal certainty, clarity and predictability is found in other accounts of the rule of law, including those which recognise their importance for personal autonomy.[34] If the law is unclear and uncertain, individuals may not be aware of when they are breaking the law. This is even more problematic given that ignorance of criminal law is not a valid defence. Law is used to regulate relations between individuals, and between individuals and the Government. If the law is clear and certain, individuals can plan their lives. Business relations are forged where there are clear and predictable rules, providing confidence and security, thereby facilitating economic growth.

Law reform clearly reinforces the rule of law through making the law clearer and more accessible. As Parliament makes more laws, greater fragmentation arises. Even with the creation of an online source of primary and secondary legislation, it can be difficult to access the law on any particular topic, this being found across a range of primary and secondary legislation.[35] The work of the law commissions facilitates the accessibility of the law. The first report of the LCE&W, for example, proposed the abolition of certain ancient criminal offences, implemented in the Criminal Law Act 1967. Its first programme focused on the consolidation and codification of the law of contract, the law of landlord and tenant and family law.[36] The consolidation of legislation is facilitated through special parliamentary procedures in Westminster, the Scottish Parliament, and the Senedd Cymru.[37]

There are now fewer projects that focus purely on consolidation or codification, although the current law reform programme of the SLC includes a project on the consolidation of nature conservation legislation.[38] The LCE&W also recently produced a report on modernising wills, which consolidates the law relating to wills and includes a draft bill.[39]

A clear example of where consolidation and codification is playing an important role is the work of the LCE&W in relation to Wales.[40] The Form and Accessibility of the Law in Wales report recommended that the Welsh Government pursue a policy

[33] T Bingham, *The Rule of Law* (Penguin, 2011) ch 3.

[34] J Raz, 'The Rule of Law and its Virtue' in J Raz, *The Authority of Law: Essays in Law and Morality* (Oxford University Press, 1979) ch 11 and L Fuller, *The Morality of Law* (Yale University Press, 1977).

[35] Lord Toulson, 'Democracy, Law Reform and the Rule of Law' in M Dyson, J Lee and S Wilson Stark (eds), *Fifty Years of the Law Commissions. The Dynamics of Law Reform* (Hart Publishing, 2016) 176.

[36] First Programme of the Law Commission (LC no 1).

[37] Standing Order Nos 58 and 140 (Westminster Parliament), Rule 9.17A (Scottish Parliament), SO26C (Senedd Cymru).

[38] SLC 11th Programme (n 5).

[39] Law Commission of England and Wales, 'Modernising Wills Law', Law Com No 409, HC 861 (2025).

[40] Lord Lloyd-Jones, 'Codification of Welsh Law', https://supremecourt.uk/uploads/speech_180308_5c867a3261.pdf.

of codification.[41] The LCE&W has worked on the codification of planning law in Wales,[42] and recently completed a project on the codification of Agricultural Law in Wales.[43] It has also worked on tribunals in Wales, facilitating access to justice.

More recently, both law commissions have undertaken work which aims to pave the way for new technologies, providing legal certainty to facilitate innovation and the use of modern technologies in business and trade. The LCE&W and SLC worked together on projects relating to automated vehicles, leading to the Automated Vehicles Act 2024. The LCE&W has also worked on digital assets, electronic trade documents, aviation autonomy and new funerary methods.

The constitutional and institutional features of the law commissions demonstrate how they are better placed than other institutions of the constitution to carry out law reform that can enhance the rule of law through helping to make the law more accessible, clear, certain and modern. Law commissions were specifically devised to perform this role, composed of legal experts, including legislative drafters from the Office of Parliamentary Counsel, producing reports and draft bills. They advise governments and ultimately legislatures on law reform projects. They are institutionally suited to this role through their composition and manner of working.

Legislatures mostly enact Government bills. Governments are focused on politics, initiating legislation that has political salience or fits with policy proposals set out in manifestos. They are less likely to initiate bills which mainly aim to reform the law. Governments are also split into departments focusing on specific policy areas. They do not have the same ability to examine the law holistically, potentially failing to realise when law reform is needed.[44] It is unlikely that consolidation and codification will be proposed by ministers wishing to change the law to fulfil policy objectives. It is also unlikely that such bills will be able to compete with other more politically salient bills for parliamentary time or drafting resources. Parliamentary legislation is also forward-looking. It may also be based on compromise and last-minute drafting, which may detract from rather than promote clarity and legal certainty, regardless of the outstanding expertise of the Office of Parliamentary Counsel.[45]

The judiciary may also be able to play a role in making the law. This may provide a quicker means of law reform than waiting for Parliament.[46] However, law reform

[41] The Law Commission, 'The Form and Accessibility of the Law in Wales', 'Ffurf a Hygyrchedd y Gfraith s'yn Gymys yng Nghymru', Law Com No 366, HC 469 (2016), Rec 1.

[42] The Law Commission, 'Planning Law in Wales/Cyfraith Cynllunio yng Nghymru Adroddiad Terfynol' HC 1788, Law Com No 383 (November 2018) and the Planning (Wales) Act 2026.

[43] The Law Commission, 'Agricultural Law in Wales: Scoping Report', 'Adroddiad Cwmpasu Cyfraith Amaethyddol yng Nghymru' Law Com no 424 (February 2026).

[44] See the statements of Sir Eric Fletcher, *Hansard* HC Deb Vol 706, cols 50–53 (8 February 1965). See also, Lady Hale, 'Fifty Years of the Law Commissions: The Dynamics of Law Reform Now, Then and Next' in M Dyson, J Lee and S Wilson Stark (eds), *Fifty Years of the Law Commissions. The Dynamics of Law Reform* (Hart Publishing, 2016) 39, and P Orterton, *A Lament for the Law Commission* (Countrywide Press, 1987).

[45] See P North, 'Is law reform too important to be left to lawyers?' (1985) 5 *Legal Studies* 119.

[46] ibid.

by the judiciary is ad hoc and haphazard, relying on a litigant to raise the issue before the courts, as well as having the time and the money to argue cases up to the Supreme Court. Settlement of disputes between litigants, which is encouraged, is also an impediment to final decisions on appeal. Judicial law reform is also incremental and not suited for reaching consensus across a wide range of views, focusing instead on an evaluation of competing legal arguments from the parties before the court.[47]

Law commissions, like the judiciary, are independent and in a good position to analyse laws which need clarity and certainty, but which would otherwise find it difficult to make it onto the legislative agenda. Law commissions have the legal expertise and time to carry out research in areas that cut across different governmental departments. They also refer to work carried out by law commissions in other nations, alongside extensive comparative law research evaluating solutions to similar legal problems in other jurisdictions. Their expertise, coupled with consultation, enables the law commissions to provide clear solutions to complex legal problems. Unlike the judiciary, they can hear from the wider public.

Law commission reports are still dependent on governments and legislatures for implementation into statutes. However, the use of special procedures, the use of draft bills accompanying reports, and the expert quality of the work of the law commissions can help ensure law reform is placed on the governmental and legislative agenda. The reliance on governments and legislatures to implement reports also acts as a safeguard to ensure law commissions act within their sphere of expertise and legitimacy.

12.4 The Law Commissions and Democracy

The consultation process used by the law commissions provides a means of enhancing democratic law-making. Consultation provides factual evidence that can help to ensure that law reform recommendations are more likely to reach the right outcomes. This is furthered through the process of constructive criticism from consultees, analysed by legal experts at the law commissions and further scrutinised through the process of peer review of the commissioners. It provides authority to law commission reports, alongside strong arguments in favour of their recommendations, aiding their acceptance by governments and legislatures.

In addition, as Lord Scarman argued, consultation can facilitate democracy in four ways.[48] First, it enables the voice of everyone to be heard, including those who are not experts in a particular area of the law. Second, it provides a means for stakeholders and those most affected by a particular law to criticise both the

[47] A Burrows, 'Post-legislative Scrutiny, Legislative Drafting and the "Elusive Boundary"' in M Dyson, J Lee and S Wilson Stark (eds), *Fifty Years of the Law Commissions. The Dynamics of Law Reform* (Hart Publishing, 2016) 252.

[48] Scarman (1972) (n 24).

current law and possible law reforms. In Scarman's words, proposals are 'subject to the criticism of those who know where the shoe pinches'.[49] Third, it can help to dispose of misconceptions of law commissions' proposals, helping to make proposed law reforms more politically acceptable. Fourth, it helps to stimulate interest in law reform.[50]

As North and Palmer recognise, this adds democratic legitimacy to the work of the law commissions. First, the wide consultation process aids participatory democracy. Law commissions use traditional and social media and online consultation forms to encourage participation as widely as possible. This encourages citizens to participate in the democratic process, having an ability to express their view as to why specific laws may not be working effectively and how they can be changed to better achieve their policy objective. This can include consultation with marginalised groups who may find it harder to have their voice heard in the ordinary lawmaking process. The public may also suggest possible law reform projects, helping to place issues that concern them onto the law reform and potentially future policy agendas.[51]

Consultation exercises also facilitate deliberative democracy. Consultation encourages deliberation and debate. Smaller groups of consultees enable open discussion and an exchange of ideas informed by experts and stakeholders. These help to reach an informed consensus through discussions in consultations and analysis of consultation responses by the law commissions before the publication of reports. This process is further refined through the peer review process within the law commissions.

Consultation exercises carried out by law commissions may be better able to facilitate deliberative democracy than the ordinary legislative procedure. There is no legal duty upon lawmakers to consult before making either primary or secondary legislation.[52] Nor are courts required to consult before making judgments. Whilst there is no legal duty on the law commissions either, this practice is deeply embedded in the work of the law commissions and is a key means of ensuring its reports are persuasive. It provides a means through which the law commissions can demonstrate their legitimacy, alongside their independence and expertise. This may be furthered in Northern Ireland through the presence of a lay member of the commission. Consultation is therefore more likely to take place. The law commissions' consultation process is also transparent, with the publication of consultation responses alongside consultation analysis and reports. Law commission reports also demonstrate how consultation responses can lead to changes to

[49] ibid, 36.

[50] ibid. See also, P Mitchell, 'Strategies of the Early Law Commissions' in M Dyson, J Lee and S Wilson Stark (eds), *Fifty Years of the Law Commissions. The Dynamics of Law Reform* (Hart Publishing, 2016) 55; Burrows (n 47); G Palmer, 'The Law Reform Enterprise: evaluating the past and charting the future' (2015) 131 *Law Quarterly Review* 402; and North (n 45).

[51] North (n 45) and Palmer (n 50).

[52] *Bates v Lord Hailsham* [1972] 1 WLR 1373; *R (National Council for Civil Liberties) v Secretary of State for the Home Department* [2025] EWCA Civ 571.

provisional proposals. For example, in the LCE&W's report on the Arbitration Bill, a provisional proposal to prohibit terms in an arbitration agreement that required a discriminatory appointment was not followed up as a recommendation in the final report. This was in response to consultation which indicated the rarity of these clauses, as well as arguments from stakeholders that such a change may not make sufficient difference to the diversity of arbitral appointments and may be unmanageable.[53]

Deliberative democracy requires an environment in which participants can contribute their own perspective and reflect on the views of others.[54] The larger the group participating, the harder it can be to find the time to ensure all views are heard. It also requires reflection on the views which emerge from deliberative processes, including a willingness to change policy directions in the light of deliberations and to seek consensus.[55] For deliberation to succeed in helping to form better solutions, it needs to take place in a forum where there is mutual respect, no imbalance of power and no recourse to power other than the persuasive force of an argument to ensure its acceptance.[56]

The consultation process carried out by the law commission is better able to meet these conditions than the judiciary or the legislature. The judiciary is best placed to balance the arguments of two parties concerning the interpretation or implementation of the law. It provides a neutral format in which these views are evaluated according to their rationality and persuasive force, but it is not as well equipped to take account of a wide range of views. Whilst legislatures can take account of a wider range of views, these are indirectly as opposed to directly represented. The Westminster legislature, in particular, is best understood as adversarial, scrutinising viewpoints rather than aiming to find consensus. Although bills may go through a pre-legislative process where there is wider direct participation, these consultation exercises may not have the same transparency as those carried out by the law commissions which normally publish responses to consultation exercises.[57] Government consultation exercises also tend to focus on testing established policy views and government responses to consultation exercises are more likely to rely on governmental policies and political allegiances than those of the law commissions.

[53] Law Commission, 'Review of the Arbitration Act 1996: Final Report and Bill' Law Com No 413, HC 1787 (2023) paras 4.55–4.66.

[54] JS Dryzek, 'Introduction' in A Bächtiger, JS Dryzek, J Mansbridge and ME Warren (eds), *The Oxford Handbook of Deliberative Democracy* (Oxford University Press, 2018); J Dryzak, *Discursive Democracy* (Cambridge University Press, 1990); R Forst, 'The Rule of Reasons. Three Models of Deliberative Democracy' (2001) 14 *Ratio Juris* 345,;and J Habermas 'Three Normative Models of Democracy' (1994) 1 *Constellations* 1.

[55] RE Goodin, *Reflective Democracy* (OUP 2003), R Goodin and J Dryzak, *Innovating Democracy: Democratic Theory and Practice after the Deliberative Turn* (Oxford University Press, 2008) ch 2.

[56] Goodin and Dryzak (n 55) ch 4; and J Habermas, *The Theory of Communicative Action* (Beacon Press, 1984).

[57] Where consultation responses are not published, this is normally due to the need to redact these responses in order to protect the rights of stakeholders.

This is not to argue that the law commissions carry out perfect consultation exercises that provide an ideal of deliberative democracy. Some topics of law reform are more likely to give rise to deliberation and discussion by the general public than others. It may also be challenging for the law commissions to reach all stakeholders. There is also a limited timeframe for broad public consultation which may hinder the ability the ability of the law commissions to cover all viewpoints.

12.5 Challenges

If the law commissions are to continue to fulfil their constitutional role, they need to balance the competing pressure of maintaining their necessary independence, whilst being able to effectively work with governments and legislatures to ensure their proposals are implemented. As Mumby notes, the law commissions stand at the interface of law and politics.[58] If this balance is not maintained, the law commissions risk becoming politicised or being subject to regulatory capture. Both may undermine their constitutional role.[59]

Legislation provides the law commissions with a very broad remit, which could include law reform of highly controversial areas of the law. Interpreted too broadly, law commissions may stray into law reform issues best left to democratically elected bodies.[60] Debates at the second reading of the 1965 Act in both the House of Commons and the House of Lords recognised this potential problem. These debates proposed that the ambit of the law commissions was 'lawyers' law' – making the law accessible, consolidation, modernising terminology and making technical changes. Issues such as correcting social injustice, or making pure policy choices, were not best suited to law commissions but to governments and legislatures.[61]

This is an understandable division. Law commissioners are not elected and are not democratically accountable, making law commissions unsuited to determining political policies or making purely moral choices.[62] This gives rise to the further risk of the law commissions becoming politicised, or being perceived as just another arm of government.[63] Governments may be less willing to approve and implement law reform projects, even those that fall firmly within the scope of 'lawyers' law', if it is perceived that the law commissions are no longer independent

[58] J Munby, 'Introduction' in M Dyson, J Lee and S Wilson Stark (eds), *Fifty Years of the Law Commissions. The Dynamics of Law Reform* (Hart Publishing, 2016) 288.

[59] J Lee, '"Not Time to Make a Change?" Reviewing the Rhetoric of Law Reform' (2023) 76 *Current Legal Problems* 129.

[60] D Lloyd Jones, 'Looking to the Future' in M Dyson, J Lee and S Wilson Stark (eds), *Fifty Years of the Law Commissions. The Dynamics of Law Reform* (Hart Publishing, 2016) 464.

[61] *Hansard* HC Deb Vol 706 cols 47–158 (8 February 1965) and HL Deb Vol 264 cols 1140–223 (1 April 1965).

[62] Lloyd Jones (n 60).

[63] E Clive, 'Law Reform and Social Policy' in M Dyson, J Lee and S Wilson Stark (eds), *Fifty Years of the Law Commissions. The Dynamics of Law Reform* (Hart Publishing, 2016) 98.

and are not basing their conclusions on expertise and evidence. There is even a possible danger of calls to disband the law commissions if they are perceived to be merely replicating the work of government departments.[64]

However, a focus on 'lawyers' law' prioritises the constitutional role of the law commissions of enhancing the rule of law over that of facilitating deliberative and participatory democracy. It also limits the ability of the law commissions to achieve social policy law reform. The law commissions have successfully worked in these areas – for example, through their work on the Children Act 1989, as well as extensive work in family law ranging from divorce to surrogacy. There are also ways through which law commissions can achieve law reform in these areas without the risk of politicisation, particularly through their use of consultation, their focus on the evaluation of evidence, and indications of where legal reform requires governmental intervention to determine purely political or moral issues.[65]

This balance is left to the self-restraint of the commissions, combined with governmental vetoes over programmes of law reform, the ability to limit the scope of law reform projects referred from government departments, the need for governmental funding, and for the law commissions to work with governments to ensure the implementation of law reform recommendations. Discussion of terms of reference can also be used to provide a policy steer from departments.[66] This enables the law commissions to propose law reform projects in controversial areas without taking pure policy decisions.[67] There is also further general oversight of the work of the law commissions through the transparency of their work. Consultation responses can be published, and reports provide a clear account and evaluation of possible areas of controversy, using evidence to weigh up competing views to reach conclusions, including explaining when no clear conclusion can be reached. Annual reports laid before the Westminster Parliament, the Scottish Parliament and the Senedd Cymru provide a further means of political oversight.[68]

However, the complex relationships between the law commissions and governments may give rise to concerns as to regulatory capture.[69] This risk can be

[64] In his Denning lecture of 2011, 'Shaping the Law – the Law Commission at the Crossroads', Lord Justice Munby noted the then recent review of arm's length bodies which had potentially threatened the existence of the Law Commission. In 2025, a further review of arm's length bodies was announced (see Cabinet Office and The Rt Hon Pat McFadden MP, 'Hundreds of quangos to be examined for potential closure as Government takes back control' Press release (7 April 2025), www.gov.uk/government/news/hundreds-of-quangos-to-be-examined-for-potential-closure-as-government-takes-back-control), although this is not specifically directed at disbanding the law commissions.

[65] See, for example, Law Commission, 'Disabled Children's Social Care', Law Com no 422, HC 1287 (September 2025), https://lawcom.gov.uk/publication/disabled-childrens-social-care-final-report.

[66] Lloyd Jones (n 60).

[67] See, for example, the Terms of Reference relating to the report, 'Celebrating Marriage: a New Weddings Law', para 1.4, https://webarchive.nationalarchives.gov.uk/ukgwa/20250109114306mp_/https:/cloud-platform-e218f50a4812967ba1215eaecede923f.s3.amazonaws.com/uploads/sites/30/2019/07/Terms-of-reference-for-the-Law-Commission-review-of-weddings-FINAL.pdf.

[68] LCA 1965, s 3(3).

[69] J Beatson, 'Challenges for Independent Law Reformers from Changing External Priorities and Shorter Timescales' in M Dyson, J Lee and S Wilson Stark (eds), *Fifty Years of the Law Commissions. The Dynamics of Law Reform* (Hart Publishing, 2016) 324.

illustrated by the evolution of the work of the LCE&W. Originally, the LCE&W worked predominantly on projects from its programmes of law reform. These programmes were produced on a frequent basis, supplemented by less frequent references from government departments. However, more recently, the LCE&W has produced programmes on a less frequent basis.[70] There is also a higher percentage of projects originating from departmental references.[71] The funding model of the LCE&W also illustrates the risks of potential regulatory capture. The current model was agreed in 2020, following concerns raised by the 2019 independent review of a 'perception that the current funding model is incentivising the Law Commission away from pursuing those projects of most importance and towards those which are the most able to pay', with both stakeholders and the LCE&W suggesting that the LCE&W's then funding arrangements had a negative impact on its independence.[72] The new funding model aimed to remedy this perception, by moving to a situation where funding is provided from the Ministry of Justice. However, the Ministry of Justice seeks to recharge other government departments to recover marginal costs of the work of the LCE&W.[73] The LCE&W should also endeavour to recover 20–33 per cent of its overall costs from costs paid by other government departments. Political and budgetary pressures may also influence departments to seek shorter timetables. They might also foster the perception that the LCE&W provides a service for government departments rather than seeking to pursue law reform where it is most needed, irrespective of which department is responsible for the relevant policy area and whether funding is available from that governmental department.[74]

The growing number of departmental references, alongside the need for departmental protocol support, budgetary commitments and a serious intention to bring forward law reform might help facilitate implementation of law commissions' reports. Without implementation, the law commissions will not achieve their constitutional purpose of law reform, undermining their ability to facilitate the rule of law and democracy. However, these may also influence the scope of projects that the law commissions can undertake.[75] This potentially undermines independence, which may have the contradictory outcome of undermining the persuasive force of law commissions' reports. Moreover, it would risk damaging the ability of the law commissions to facilitate participatory and deliberative democracy.

[70] The 12th programme was published in 2014, the 13th in 2017 and the 14th in 2025.

[71] 'Memorandum of Understanding between the Law Commission and Lord Chancellor (on behalf of Government): Law Commission funding model' para 14, https://cloud-platform-e218f50a4812967ba1215eaecede923f.s3.amazonaws.com/uploads/sites/54/2025/03/MoU-between-the-LC-and-Commission-final-version.pdf.

[72] Ministry of Justice, 'Tailored Review of the Law Commission of England and Wales' , para 7.5, https://assets.publishing.service.gov.uk/media/5c5c1cc040f0b676bfcd3caf/tailored-review-of-the-law-commission-of-england-and-wales.pdf.

[73] 'Memorandum of Understanding' (n 71) para 8.

[74] ibid, para 22.

[75] See S Wilson, 'Reforming the Law (Commission): A Crisis of Identity' [2013] i 20.

12.6 Conclusion

This chapter has illustrated both how the law commissions' constitutional role contributes to the maintenance of the rule of law and facilitates participatory and deliberative democracy. It has also noted the potential dangers of politicisation and regulatory capture, both of which may undermine their constitutional role. If the law commissions are to flourish, they need proactively to explain the benefits that legal experts can bring to law reform. This includes the benefits of structured, reasoned analysis of controversial issues, supplemented by transparent governmental policy steers where needed and the broad use of consultation. They also need to protect their independence, not only when exercising their discretion as to the law reform projects they undertake, but also in terms of their funding, particularly when faced with budgetary cuts and other constraints.

When reflecting on his role as chair of the Australian Law Reform Commission, Palmer argued that politicians and ministers, civil servants and lawyers spoke different languages.[76] Politicians communicate in terms of political persuasion and compromise. Civil servants communicate in terms of policy decisions, weighing up the costs and benefits of different policies and seeking consensus. Lawyers raised in a common law system are taught analytical common law reasoning, structuring questions into specific legal doctrines and outcomes. The work of the law commissions flourishes when there is an understanding of and effective communication between, the law commissions, ministers, politicians and civil servants. This enables each to perform their important distinct constitutional roles.

[76] Palmer (n 50).

13

Reimagining the Rule of Law: Substantive Equality, Feminism and Critical Race Theory

KARON MONAGHAN KC

13.1 Introduction

There is academic literature and judicial *dicta* on which some commentators rely in arguing that there exists a freestanding, substantive and justiciable principle of equality at common law. That principle is said, variously, to derive from democratic values,[1] a thicker conception of the rule of law,[2] and from fundamental rights said to be immanent in 'a new British constitution'.[3] However, as I explore below, if any common law principle of equality exists at all, case law suggests that it is, at most, procedural in content and instrumental in function. In the main, substantive equality is treated by the courts as a normative principle, not a justiciable right. Whether that position is consonant with contemporary iterations of the rule of law is doubtful. A more muscular conception of the rule of law – one in which fundamental rights are understood to inhere – would be more likely to foster the development of a constitutional, freestanding and substantive principle of equality. Such a principle would meet in part the criticisms advanced by some feminist and critical race theorists that the orthodox, Diceyan, conception of the rule of law entrenches disadvantage and reinforces existing power relations.

[1] J Jowell, 'Is Equality a Constitutional Principle?' (1994) 47 *Current Legal Problems* 1.

[2] TRS Allan, 'Questions of Legality and Legitimacy: Form and Substance in British Constitutionalism' (2011) 9 *International Journal of Constitutional Law* 155.

[3] V Bogdanor, *The New British Constitution* (Hart Publishing, 2009) xi, 270, providing an account of what Bogdanor argues is a 'New Constitution'.

13.2 Fundamental Rights and a Principle of Equality

There are a number of rights and principles that the common law regards as fundamental and, in that sense, constitutional.[4] Those recognised by the courts as constitutional include the rights of unimpeded access to a court,[5] liberty,[6] freedom of speech[7], assembly and association (usually said to be linked to the right to individual liberty and free speech[8]), privacy[9] and the right to vote (albeit, surprisingly, not including 'a right of universal and equal suffrage').[10] Further, unsurprisingly, the common law treats as fundamental the principle that by 'the exercise of state power the life or health of a person should not be taken away, impaired or endangered, except under clear authority of the law'.[11] While the content of some of these rights is contested, and none are absolute, the fact of their existence is generally not; nor is it controversial that each has the quality of a substantive right.[12] Some, at least, of these rights and freedoms indisputably inhere in the rule of law; access to a court being an obvious example.[13]

The elevated status accorded constitutional rights and principles at common law means that the principle of legality is engaged where legislation, on an ordinary construction, would interfere with them. Parliament is presumed not to intend to interfere with fundamental rights, and legislation will be interpreted in that light. While Parliament can, in principle, legislate as it chooses, including in a way that would abrogate fundamental rights, where it does so it must do so in express and unambiguous terms. Fundamental rights cannot be overridden by general words:

[4] See, for example, of the right to access a court; 'it is a principle of our law that every citizen has a right of unimpeded access to a court… Even in our unwritten constitution it must rank as a constitutional right' (*R v Secretary of State for the Home Department, ex parte Leech* [1994] QB 198, 210A–210D).

[5] *R (UNISON) v Lord Chancellor (Equality and Human Rights Commission and another intervening) (Nos 1 and 2)* [2020] AC 869 ('*UNISON*') [66]–[85].

[6] Magna Carta (1215), cls 39 and 40, cited in D Feldman, D Bailey and L Norbury, *Bennion, Bailey & Norbury on Statutory Interpretation*, 8th edn (LexisNexis, 2020) 892. AV Dicey, *Introduction to the Study of the Law of the Constitution*, 8th edn (MacMillan, 1915) (reprint by Liberty Fund, Inc to which edition the page references herein refer) 124. Such a right has been explicitly stated to be an aspect of the rule of law; *R v Secretary of State for the Home Department ex parte Muboyayi* [1992] QB 244, 254E–254G; *Bank Mellat v Her Majesty's Treasury (No 2)* [2014] AC 700, 773, [26].

[7] *R v Secretary of State for the Home Department, ex parte Simms* [2000] 2 AC 115 ('*Simms*') 126E–126G.

[8] Dicey (n 6) 170; *Re F (a minor) (publication of information of information)* [1976] 3 WLR 813, 834C–834D.

[9] See discussion in Feldman, Bailey and Norbury (n 6) 902–04.

[10] *Moohan v Lord Advocate (Advocate General for Scotland intervening)* [2015] AC 901, 924 [34], [35].

[11] Feldman, Bailey and Norbury (n 6) 894. It is doubtful that the two-child benefit cap would be thought to fall under this rubric though it impoverishes children. See, *R (SC) v Secretary of State for Work and Pensions* [2022] AC 223; Child Poverty Action Group, 'State of the Nations: Lessons in Tackling Child Poverty from Across the Four Nations' (October 2024), https://cpag.org.uk/sites/default/files/2024-10/State_of_the_nations.pdf ('The two-child limit is the main driver of rising child poverty. The rise in child poverty from 3.6 million in 2010/11 to 4.5 million in 2023/24 was almost exclusively concentrated in families with more than two children.').

[12] PG Polyviou, *The Equal Protection of Laws* (Duckworth, 1980) 3.

[13] *UNISON* (n 5).

'This is because there is too great a risk that the full implications of their unqualified meaning may have passed unnoticed in the democratic process.'[14] Instead, 'Parliament must squarely confront what it is doing and accept the political cost.'[15]

The Supreme Court has gone so far as to say that statutory powers interfering with fundamental rights should be read as 'subject to implied limitations, adopting an approach amounting in substance to a requirement of proportionality'.[16] This means that, at least in the case of some constitutional rights, the courts 'may interpret … legislation as requiring that any such interference should be no greater than is objectively established to be necessary to achieve the legitimate aim of the interference: in substance, a requirement of proportionality'[17] or, put another way, 'interpreted as authorising only such a degree of intrusion as is reasonably necessary to fulfil the objective of the provision in question'.[18]

Further, on a public law rationality challenge, a court is likely to subject any act done by a public authority that interferes with a fundamental right to 'heightened scrutiny',[19] with the range of rational decisions narrower than might ordinarily be the case.[20]

Fundamental rights therefore enjoy enhanced protection at common law.

Most strikingly, as Lord Woolf observed, 'if Parliament did the unthinkable', 'the courts would also be required to act in a manner which would be without precedent'.[21] The Supreme Court has acknowledged out loud that it might be compelled to intervene to prevent the abrogation of the most fundamental of rights even in the face of unequivocal primary legislation.[22] Although difficult to imagine in the foreseeable future (through an optimistic lens), and heretical as it may seem,[23] its very contemplation reflects the special status constitutional rights enjoy at common law.

The quest for a substantive and justiciable principle of equality at common law, then, is an important one. This is not to overlook Article 14 of Convention for the Protection of Human Rights and Fundamental Freedoms (1950) ('the Convention'),[24] but the common law carries particular weight within a common

[14] *Simms* (n 7) 131D–131G.
[15] ibid, 131E–131F.
[16] *Pham v Secretary of State for the Home Department* [2015] 1 WLR 1591 ('*Pham*') [118]. See too, *Simms* (n 7) 131D–131G.
[17] ibid [119].
[18] *UNISON* (n 5) [80].
[19] *R (Spitalfields Historic Building Trust) v Tower Hamlets London Borough Council and A'or* [2025] PTSR 700, 716 [54].
[20] *Pham* (n 16) [107]. See too, *Kennedy v Information Comr (Secretary of State for Justice intervening)* [2014] 2 WLR 808.
[21] H Woolf, 'Droit Public – English Style' [1995] *Public Law* 57, 68.
[22] *Moohan v Lord Advocate (Advocate General for Scotland intervening)* [2015] AC 901, 925 [35] (prisoner voting rights). See too, *R (Jackson) v Attorney General* [2006] 1 AC 262 [102], per Lord Steyn and [104]–[107], per Lord Hope.
[23] Parliamentary sovereignty being a key pillar of the constitution, as is uncontroversial; Dicey (n 6) 107.
[24] 'The enjoyment of the rights and freedoms set forth in this Convention shall be secured without discrimination on any ground such as sex, race, colour, language, religion, political or other opinion,

law system because of the breadth and depth of its legal reach, and its normative force. Presently, however, there is no compelling argument that the law recognises any such principle. There are cases where the senior courts have emphasised the importance of equality to democracy. Since democracy is fundamental to the UK's constitutional order, and occupies a central place in Dicey's conception of the rule of law, one might expect the common law to recognise a substantive and justiciable principle of equality. But it does not.

If one looks hard enough, it is possible to find cases from the early part of the twentieth century holding that the common law prohibits race discrimination in the granting of access to certain places of public resort.[25] But though referred to in later literature,[26] these cases go nowhere near establishing that a fundamental principle of equality exists, less so a principle of substantive equality. A number of cases decided at the end of the last century and the beginning of this century are regularly adverted to by those arguing that such a principle exists, at least in nascent form. The Privy Council case of *Matadeen v Pointu and O'rs*,[27] is generally regarded as the first of these because of the oft-cited passage in Lord Hoffmann's speech in which he emphasised the importance of the principle of equality before the law as follows:

> 'Equality before the law requires that persons should be uniformly treated, unless there is some valid reason to treat them differently.' Their Lordships do not doubt that such a principle is one of the building blocks of democracy and necessarily permeates any democratic constitution. Indeed, their Lordships would go further and say that treating like cases alike and unlike cases differently is a general axiom of rational behaviour. It is, for example, frequently invoked by the courts in proceedings for judicial review as a ground for holding some administrative act to have been irrational.[28]

The emphasis here is on the relationship between a principle of equal treatment, democratic values, and rationality as a ground of review. Lord Hoffmann does not declare or recognise equality as a freestanding justiciable principle at common law. Indeed, as Lord Hoffmann went on: 'The fact that equality of treatment is a general principle of rational behaviour does not entail that it should necessarily be a justiciable principle.'[29] It would be an exercise in futility to suggest that much can be gleaned from *Matadeen* save that Lord Hoffmann considered that formal equality in treatment might be a necessary criterion for rationality in a particular case.

national or social origin, association with a national minority, property, birth or other status' (Human Rights Act 1998 (HRA 1998), Sch 1).

[25] A Lester and G Bindman, *Race and Law* (Penguin Books, 1972) 63. See, S Atrey, 'A Common Law Principle of Racial Equality?' [2025] *Public Law* 215, noting that these cases were not decided on the basis of any common law principle of racial equality.

[26] Jowell (n 1).

[27] [1999] 1 AC 98 (Privy Council) ('*Matadeen*'). The case concerned provisions of the Constitution of Mauritius but the observations here seem to be of general applicability.

[28] ibid, 109C–109D.

[29] ibid, 109F.

Ghaidan v Godin – Mendoza[30] is also routinely cited in judicial and academic discourse on the question whether there exists a constitutional principle of equality. However, again, though an expression of the importance of equality as a democratic value, it does not provide comfort for those looking for a constitutional principle of equality. In *Ghaidan*, the House of Lords held that provisions of the Rent Act 1977 treating same-sex partners of deceased protected tenants less favourably than 'surviving spouses', a term defined to include those living with a protected tenant of a property 'as his or her wife or husband', violated the Convention rights under Articles 8 and 14[31] of same-sex partners. In the course of her speech, Baroness Hale, echoing the words of Lord Hoffmann in significant part, stated that,

> [A] guarantee of equal treatment is … essential to democracy. Democracy is founded on the principle that each individual has equal value. Treating some as automatically having less value than others not only causes pain and distress to that person but also violates his or her dignity as a human being. … Second, such treatment is damaging to society as a whole. Wrongly to assume that some people have talent and others do not is a huge waste of human resources. It also damages social cohesion, creating not only an under-class, but an under-class with a rational grievance. Third, it is the reverse of the rational behaviour we now expect of government and the state. Power must not be exercised arbitrarily. If distinctions are to be drawn, particularly upon a group basis, it is an important discipline to look for a rational basis for those distinctions. Finally, it is a purpose of all human rights instruments to secure the protection of the essential rights of members of minority groups, even when they are unpopular with the majority. Democracy values everyone equally even if the majority does not.[32]

There is no doubt that this is an important passage, particularly on the role of dignity and the significance of democratic values in the construction of fundamental rights. For present purposes, however, it is important to observe that this part of Baroness Hale's speech formed no part of the *ratio*, and its discernible relevance to the common law is, as with *Matadeen*, the relationship between equality and rationality as a ground of review.

For some, more promising was the case of *A v Secretary of State for the Home Department*.[33] At issue in *A* was the lawfulness of an order made by the Government derogating from Article 5(1) of the Convention and thereby permitting the indefinite detention of non-national terrorist suspects who could not be deported because of fears for their safety or other practical considerations.[34] The House of

[30] [2004] 2 AC 557 ('*Ghaidan*').

[31] Art 8: '(1) Everyone has the right to respect for his private and family life, his home and his correspondence. (2) There shall be no interference by a public authority with the exercise of this right except such as is in accordance with the law and is necessary in a democratic society in the interests of national security, public safety or the economic well-being of the country, for the prevention of disorder or crime, for the protection of health or morals, or for the protection of the rights and freedoms of others.'

[32] *Ghaidan* [132].

[33] [2005] 2 AC 68 ('*A*').

[34] Human Rights Act 1998 (Designated Derogation) Order 2001, SI 2001/3644, designating the UK's proposed derogation, under Art 15, from the right to personal liberty guaranteed by Art 5(1) of the

Lords concluded that while there were proper grounds for the derogation order, the statutory measures authorising indefinite detention were discriminatory, since they allowed for the indefinite detention of non-nationals but not UK nationals posing the same threat. For that reason, the House of Lords held that the measures did not rationally address the threat to security and were disproportionate. Since there had been no derogation from Article 14, the order was quashed and the statutory measures declared incompatible with Articles 14 read with Article 5. Lord Bingham recited, seemingly approvingly,[35] part of the passage in the speech of Lord Hoffmann in *Matadeen*, set out above, 'with reference to the principle of equality'[36] and also to Professor Hersch Lauterpacht's 'An International Bill of the Rights of Man',[37] in which Lauterpacht wrote that 'the claim to equality before the law is in a substantial sense the most fundamental of the rights of man'.[38] There was nothing else in the judgment from which the existence of any common law principle of equality could realistically be inferred.

By itself, then, *A* does not meaningfully advance the development of any substantive common law principle of equality. Perhaps because *A* has been relied upon by advocates and scholars so frequently, it has come to be viewed as evidencing a shift; that is, it has been afforded the status of important through the mere fact of its repetition.

Whether there is any residual common law principle of equality is in any event now doubtful in light of two recent decisions of the Supreme Court.

In *R (Gallaher Group Ltd and others) v Competition and Markets Authority*,[39] the claimants entered into early resolution agreements (ERAs) with the Competition and Markets Authority admitting liability and cooperating with the Office of Fair Trading (OFT) in return for substantial reductions in the financial penalties to which they would otherwise be subject. They were not given any assurance that if they did not appeal they would be given the benefit of any successful appeal by any of the other parties to the OFT's decision on breaches that led to the admissions being made. This was in contrast to the treatment afforded a third-party retailer which had entered into an ERA with the OFT to whom such an assurance had been given. When a number of parties did appeal and those appeals were allowed by the Competition Appeal Tribunal, the OFT settled with the third-party retailer reimbursing the sum which it had paid by way of penalty with interest and costs. The claimants asked the OFT to withdraw the decisions against them and refund the penalties paid since they ought to be treated in the same way as the third-party retailer, otherwise there would be inequality in treatment. The OFT refused. The question arose whether any inequality in treatment was substantively unfair and/or justiciable in public law proceedings as a free-standing ground. The Court of

Convention. See too, the Anti-terrorism, Crime and Security Act 2001, s 23.

[35] *A* (n 33) 113A–133B.

[36] ibid, 113D–133E.

[37] (1945) 115.

[38] *A* (n 33) [46].

[39] [2019] AC 96 ('*Gallaher*').

Appeal held that the principle of equal treatment applied, that there was no principled basis for limiting the requirements of fairness and equality to matters of process and methodology, and that the inequality in treatment was not objectively justified. The Supreme Court allowed the OFT's appeal, holding that:

> Whatever the position in European law or under other constitutions or jurisdictions, the domestic law of this country does not recognise equal treatment as a distinct principle of administrative law. Consistency … is a 'generally desirable' objective, but not an absolute rule.[40]

Where issues of consistency might arise at common law, they were to be treated as factors that might be relevant to rationality only.[41] Further, any principle of fairness was limited to the procedural so that whether as a matter of fact there had been unfairness was 'not a distinct legal criterion'.[42]

Even if a minimal common law principle of equal treatment were to have survived *Gallaher*, it could only have been as an aspect of rationality and, as is clear from the judgments overall, procedural.[43] Lord Sumption, in a concurring judgment, stated that the 'common law principle of equality is usually no more than a particular application of the ordinary requirement of rationality imposed on public authorities'.[44] As Elliott has commented, the implication now is that courts will 'confront issues of equality/consistency through the prism of rationality whereas legitimate expectation [an issue in *Gallaher*] amounts to a doctrine or lens in its own right'.[45] Elliott asks, and answers, the question whether it really matters whether consistent /equal treatment is regarded as an administrative law principle in its own right in the sense of being a separate ground of review:

> For three reasons, it does matter. First, recognising consistent/equal treatment as a free-standing principle would be fitting recognition of its normative importance. Secondly, it would facilitate the development of a suitable doctrinal superstructure, as occurred with legitimate expectation. This would enable courts to approach in a more systematic and predictable manner such issues as the circumstances in which a policy or practice should be regarded as sufficiently clear and settled as to render deviations from it prima facie 'inconsistent'. Thirdly, carving out a principle of consistent/equal treatment from the generality of rationality review would place less weight on the latter and, as a result, would aid legal transparency. It is now more than 30 years since Jowell and Lester [1987] P.L. 368, 372, highlighted the dangers of allowing the normative reasons for judicial intervention to remain obscured within the folds of the ***Wednesbury*** doctrine's 'ample cloak'. It is high time that the principle of consistency stopped lurking therein.[46]

[40] ibid [24], per Lord Carnwath JSC with whom the other Justices agreed.

[41] ibid [26], citing Lord Hoffmann in *Matadeen*, and [29].

[42] ibid [41], citing Lord Dyson MR below ([2016] Bus LR 1200 [53]).

[43] Lord Carnwath, who gave the leading judgment, did appear to elide objective justification (which would impose a proportionality assessment) and rationality when considering any difference in treatment (adopting the approach of Lord Dyson MR below), but did so fairly peremptorily ([43]).

[44] *Gallaher* (n 39) [50].

[45] M Elliott, 'A "Principle" of Consistency? The Doctrinal Configuration of the Law of Judicial Review' (2018) 77 *Cambridge Law Journal* 444, 447.

[46] ibid.

Gallaher can be criticised for the reasons given by Elliott. Although Elliott's focus is on formal equality in treatment, his concern about the absence of equality as a distinct ground of review would apply with equal force to any substantive principle of equality.

On one view, given the criticisms made by feminist and critical race theorists discussed below, *Gallaher* might be lauded as demonstrating a move away from a rule of formal equality in treatment through consistency. But that would be too simplistic an analysis. *Gallaher* did not discard formal equality in favour of a principle of substantive equality; rather, it foreclosed any immediate prospect of a freestanding justiciable principle of equality, even in its most minimal form.

In *Pathan v Secretary of State for the Home Department*[47] the Supreme Court was concerned with the substance of the principle of fairness and concluded that it imposed a duty of procedural fairness only; it did not impose a 'positive duty' or confer any 'substantive benefit'.[48] Lord Briggs referred in his judgment to a 'supposed principle of equal treatment' (although not relied upon in *Pathan*, so obiter) doubting 'whether, as a separate principle, it survives the detailed analysis of it in the *Gallagher* case'.[49] Even if any such principle could be rescued, it can be inferred from the Court's approach to fairness that its content would be formal and not substantive.

So far as case law is concerned, then, there is no sign of even the barest principle of equality. The merits of a principle of equal treatment are considered below, but for now it is sufficient to note that any hope that it could be used as a building block in the development of a common law principle of substantive equality is presently futile.

While there is some academic literature suggesting that there might exist a substantive and justiciable constitutional principle of equality, it is relatively sparse.

The best-known academic contribution is Jeffrey Jowell's article published in 1994: 'Is Equality a Constitutional Principle?'.[50] Jowell acknowledges the importance of formal equality to the rule of law, but argues nonetheless that 'is too thin a concept to deal with substantive inequality'.[51] I come back to the width of the rule of law later in this chapter. Jowell's conception of the principle of equality,

> is directed not only to the way the law is applied but also to the content of the laws themselves. It forbids not only the unequal application of equal laws, but also forbids unequal laws. Just like free speech, it is a principle that derives from democracy itself. Basic to democracy is the requirement that every citizen has an equal vote, and therefore an equal opportunity to influence the composition of the government. The notion of

[47] [2020] 1 WLR 4505 ('*Pathan*').
[48] ibid [108] and [140]–[141].
[49] ibid [168].
[50] Jowell (n 1).
[51] ibid, 6.

> equal worth is thus a fundamental precept of our constitution. It gains its ultimate justification from a notion of the way individuals should be treated in a democracy. It is constitutive of democracy.[52]

Jowell finds this conception of equality in directly effective provisions of the Treaty of Rome 1957 and measures enacted thereunder, in the Convention, and in common law duties imposed on inn-keepers and common carriers to receive and lodge all travellers and to accept passengers for carriage.[53] To those were added a smattering of public law cases 'invoking substantive inequality…struck down under the ground of judicial review known as "unreasonableness"'.[54] So far, so orthodox. But Jowell goes on to state that 'the application of a principle of equality'[55] lay behind them and that frequently 'substantive equality was the standard by which administrative decisions have been tested'.[56] The difficulty with Jowell's analysis is that the leap to substantive equality from rationality is not clearly explained.

There is, then, very little in the case law or scholarly commentary that points to the existence of equality as a fundamental right with the elevated status of those fundamental rights referred to above. As I discuss later in this chapter, the rule of law is potentially capacious enough to make room for such a principle, but this would require its reimagining.

13.3 The Rule of Law and Feminist and Critical Race Theories

As conceived of by Dicey, a principle of equal treatment is an essential component of the rule of law and that in turn is a 'guiding principle' which 'pervade[s] the modern constitution of England'.[57] Dicey's principle of equal treatment is 'the principle that all men are in England subject to the law of the land'.[58] This means 'the equal subjection of all classes to the ordinary law of the land administered by the ordinary law courts',[59] 'whatever be his rank'.[60]

Dicey's principle of 'legal equality'[61] seems intuitively unobjectionable. However, as feminist and critical race theorists have pointed out, in conceiving of legal equality in that way, Dicey presumes a 'society without *any* previous history

[52] ibid, 7, internal footnote removed.
[53] ibid, 9. See too, Lester and Bindman (n 25) 63.
[54] ibid, 10.
[55] ibid, 12.
[56] ibid, 13.
[57] Dicey (n 6) xxv.
[58] ibid, 115.
[59] ibid, 120.
[60] ibid, 115.
[61] ibid, 114.

of injustice'.[62] Instead, in Dicey's rule of law, that is simply 'assume[d] away'.[63] This sleight of hand is exposed well enough by what Conaghan describes as 'One of the enduring puzzles of feminist historical enquiry', namely,

> how the inequality of the sexes appeared to co-exist quite comfortably with the principle of equality before the law. By what "patriarchal trick" was it possible to deny women the full bundle of rights and duties associated with legal personhood while simultaneously extolling the virtues of legal equality?[64]

Dicey himself stated in his introduction to *The Law of the Constitution* of the demand for women's suffrage:

> It treats as insignificant for most purposes that difference of sex which, after all, disguised the matter as you will, is one of the most fundamental and far reaching differences which can distinguish one body of human beings from another.
>
> …
>
> The real strength (and it is great) of the whole conservative argument against the demand of votes for women lies in the fact that this line of reasoning, on the face thereof, conforms to the nature of things.[65]

The patriarchal trick is exemplified by the regulation of women's lives at common law. Paradigm examples include the rule that a wife was deemed to have consented irrevocably to sexual intercourse with her husband and that therefore a husband could not be convicted of the rape of his wife, even where as a matter of fact she had not consented; a rule in place until 1992.[66] Others included the common law doctrine of 'coverture', under which 'marriage constituted of a legal obliteration of women's identity',[67] so that 'The very being or legal existence of the wife is suspended during the marriage or at least incorporated and consolidated into that of the husband under whose wing, protection and cover she performs everything.'[68] The common law:

[62] CW Mills, *Black Rights/White Wrongs, The Critique of Racial Liberalism* (Oxford University Press, 2017) 140 (emphasis in the original), in critiquing Rawls' Theory of Justice and, in particular, his construct of the 'veil of ignorance' (J Rawls, *A Theory of Justice* (Harvard University Press, 1999) 118). See too, S Okin, *Justice, Gender, and the Family* (Basic Books, 1989). It was not until later that Rawls acknowledged the significance of race and sex, though contending that this was not 'as such a fault' (J Rawls, *Justice as Fairness: A restatement* (ed E Kelley) (Harvard University Press, 2011), cited in Mills (ibid) 146–47).

[63] KA Appiah, *As If, Idealisation and Ideas* (Harvard University Press, 2017) 114, when critiquing Rawls' Theory of Justice (n 62) but applying equally to Dicey's rule of law.

[64] J Conaghan, *Law and Gender* (Oxford University Press, 2013) 132–33. Internal citation, SA Gavigan, 'Petit Treason in the Eighteenth Century England: Women's Inequality before the law' (1989) 3 *Canadian Journal of Women and the Law* 335, 339.

[65] Dicey (n 6) lxxxiii.

[66] *R v R* [1992] 1 AC 599. The starkness of the issue was apparent from the point of law on which leave to appeal was granted: 'Is a husband criminally liable for raping his wife' (Conaghan (n 64) 59).

[67] S Fredman, *Discrimination Law* (Oxford University Press, 2002) 27.

[68] W Blackstone, *Commentaries on the Law of England*, 15th edn (T Cadell and W Davies, 1809), Bk 1, ch XV, 430, cited in Fredman (n 67) 27.

> [R]egarded husband and wife as one person, and that person was the husband. He acquired ownership or control over all his wife's property and income, along with liability for her pre-marriage debts. She had no contractual capacity of her own and so of course they could not make contracts with one another.[69]

While gradually dismantled from the late nineteenth century onwards, vestiges of the principle of coverture remained in place until the second half of the twentieth century.[70]

To patriarchy can be added racial inequality. Slavery had been abolished little more than 50 years before Dicey published the first edition of *Introduction to the Law of the Constitution*.[71] As Sharma says, 'Nowhere were the limits of the rule of law clearer than when the concept met the everyday racial inequalities that sustained the empire.'[72] This inequality included 'everyday forms of racial violence'.[73] Kolsky argues that:

> The notion of a rule of law as a system of principles designed to govern and protect equal subjects – a notion introduced to India by Britons themselves – was blatantly contradicted by the institutionalisation of racial distinctions in the statutory law and the overt partiality of white police, judges and juries.[74]

As Raz put it:

> [T]he rule of law is just one of the virtues which a legal system may possess and by which it is to be judged. It is not to be confused with democracy, justice, equality (before the law or otherwise), human rights of any kind or respect for persons or for the dignity of man. A non-democratic legal system, based on the denial of human rights, on extensive poverty, on racial segregation, sexual inequalities, and religious persecution may, in principle, conform to the requirements of the rule of law better than any of the legal systems of the more enlightened Western democracies. This does not mean that it will be better than those Western democracies. It will be an immeasurably worse legal system, but it will excel in one respect: in its conformity to the rule of law.[75]

The principle of equal treatment, then, as articulated by Dicey, Raz and others, is unconcerned with the content of legal rules; it is not concerned with the substance or distributive consequences of legal rules, and leaves untouched inequalities under the law.

[69] *Granatino v Radmacher (formerly Granatino)* [2010] UKSC 42 [139], per Baroness Hale.

[70] The Married Women's Property Act 1870 allowed married women to keep earnings and some property in their own right. The Married Women's Property Act 1882 allowed women to own, buy, sell and sue in their own name, and to be treated as separate legal persons. Vestiges of the principle remained thereafter so it was only in 1962 that spouses were able to sue each other for wrongful acts (Law Reform (Husband and Wife) Act 1962).

[71] (1885). The Slavery Abolition Act 1833 came into force on 1 August 1834. The apprenticeship system (compulsory labour) was not abolished until 1838 (Slavery Abolition Act 1838).

[72] K Sharma, 'The Rule of Law and Racial Difference in the British Empire' in S Wheatle and E O'Loughlin (eds), *Diverse Voices in Public Law* (Bristol University Press, 2023) 15–34, 27.

[73] ibid.

[74] E Kolsky, *Colonial Justice in British India: White Violence and the Rule of Law* (Cambridge University Press, 2010) 12, cited in Sharma (n 72) 27.

[75] J Raz, *The Authority of Law* (Oxford University Press, 1979) 211.

The façade of neutrality upon which the principle of equality before the law rests makes it indifferent to the societal disadvantages experienced by women and people of colour. As MacKinnon says, that 'Neutrality, including judicial decision making that is dispassionate, impersonal, disinterested, and precedential, is considered desirable and descriptive. Courts, forums without predisposition among parties and with no interest of their own, reflect society back to itself resolved.'[76] Not only does that neutrality in the institutions of justice sustain inequalities, but it also produces them. As Conaghan puts it:

> Law does not merely *reflect* the social (understood widely to include political, economic, cultural, and so on) but helps to construct it. Law is no shy imitator of some 'external reality'; as an authoritative form of knowledge which presents itself as scientific and objective, law directly influences how we see and make sense of the world. ... [L]aw is no mere reflection of the sex/gender order but actively involved in its construction and maintenance. Moreover, law does not simply mirror gendered norms and assumptions but may be their primary source and legitimation.[77]

The principle of equality before the law does the job of legitimatising law, whether its contents are just or not, all the while ignoring race and sex and societal disadvantage:

> Through the tion of the maxim of equality before the law, sex /gender is effectively removed from legal theoretical consideration while adherence to a gender - neutral account of law emerges as a virtue by conforming to the rule of law ideal.[78]

The authority law commands is maintained in part through a belief in the general population 'in the essential integrity and impartiality of law'.[79] For Farley, 'subjugated people conjure up "the idea of the rule of law"[80] – understood as "equality of right and due process" – as the means by which they will be released from their subordinate status'.[81] However, 'Farley … believes that hope in the rule of law functions to quiet the revolutionary demands of those who are dispossessed; … that it counsels them to delay the "General Strike" that will bring about their true liberation'[82] when 'There is no rule of law save as the disguise for the rule of one group over another'.[83] In this way, the principle of equality before the law produces, sustains and legitimises inequality.

[76] CA MacKinnon, *Toward a Feminist Theory of the State* (Harvard University Press, 1989) 162 (internal footnote removed).
[77] Conaghan (n 64) 195–96, emphasis in the original.
[78] ibid, 78.
[79] ibid, 134, citing D Hay, 'Proper Authority and Criminal Law' in D Hay et al (eds), *Albion's Fatal Tree: Crime and Society in Eighteenth Century England* (Random House, 1975) 17.
[80] AP Farley, 'Accumulation' (2005) 11 *Michigan Journal of Race and Law* 51, 54.
[81] Farley (ibid) cited in Bridges (n 82) 367.
[82] KM Bridges, 'Critical Race Theory and the Rule of Law' in J Meierhenrich and M Loughlan (eds), *The Cambridge Companion to the Rule of Law* (Cambridge University Press, 2021) 357–74, 367–68 (fn 29), discussing Farley (n 80) 54, 67.
[83] Farley (n 80) cited in Bridges (n 82) 367.

Further, the 'deference to formal equality' inherent in Dicey's principle introduces a comparative logic: those who are similarly situated must be treated similarly, and those who are materially different, differently; 'gender neutrality for sex, colorblindness for race'.[84] Women must be compared with men, and Black people with white people, applying to sex and race 'the broader legal norm of neutrality'.[85] Where they are differently situated, differential outcomes are tolerated. As MacKinnon observes:

> Missing in how Aristotle's theory has developed under law over time is an account of the original distribution of goods according to particular traits, a theory of the social creation of difference, a critical awareness of the way attribution of difference can support systematically worse treatment, an understanding of the standard against which anything else is deemed different, hence less, as being a strategy for social dominance, a grasp of the resulting system as reproducing social superiority and inferiority, and any conception of the fact that those who set the dominant standard presumptively get first-class treatment without having to be the same as anyone. Principle, in this approach, has been defined as ignoring whether a given group begins or ends better or worse off, termed 'neutrality'. Crucially as applied to sex, the worst inequalities of women as a group, such as lack of equal pay for sex-segregated work of comparable value and the failure of equal protection of the law for crimes of gendered violence, become unrecognizable as sex inequalities because they are merged with the sex difference. Treating such situations less well becomes treating unalikes unalike, hence equal ...
>
> Historically, this approach has rationalised segregation in the United States on the view that Black people are 'different' from white people, claiming equal but separate is equal ... This is an approach that seeks to have law mirror life: likes in life treated as likes in law, unlikes in life treated as unlikes in law. But what if social life is unequal? Legal equality then becomes a formula for reinforcing, magnifying, and rigidifying the social inequalities it purports to be equalizing and might have rectified.[86]

Munro makes the same point:

> The rule of law seeks to treat citizens equally irrespective of status, power or resource. In a world in which access to such things is unevenly distributed, the transactional rationality of the many may support preserving this operational principle, albeit that its realisation to date has been somewhat lacking (including in particular in respect of gender equality). Framing each individual as an abstract rights- bearer with an entitlement to receive equal respect and protection in exchange for reciprocal duties and responsibilities can facilitate this.[87]

For feminist and critical race theorists then, in conforming to Dicey's principle of equality, the law produces, sanctions and legitimises gender and racial injustice,

[84] CA MacKinnon, *Are Women Human?* (Harvard University Press, 2007) 105–07 (internal footnotes removed).
[85] MacKinnon (n 76) 217 (internal footnotes removed).
[86] MacKinnon (n 84) 106–07 (internal footnotes removed).
[87] VE Munro, 'Feminist Critiques of the Rule of Law' in J Meierhenrich and M Loughlan (eds.), *The Cambridge Companion to the Rule of Law* (Cambridge University Press, 2021) 340--356, 350.

and it does not step into the ring when the content of law is unjust. Further, adding insult to injury, it requires of those seeking a remedy for racial or gender discrimination that they prove that they are comparatively disadvantaged; that is, that they are in materially the same position as those already privileged over them. This creates an insurmountable barrier for many disadvantaged by history and circumstances who seek gender and racial justice.

13.4 Envisaging a New Rule of Law

As the above discussion shows, the concept of equality as envisaged in Dicey's account of the rule of law is positively unhelpful as a basis for challenging racial and gender injustice.

Modern case law eschews the idea of a discrete and justiciable substantive principle of equality at common law, and shoehorns any formal distinctions in treatment into rationality. There is now, apparently, no remnant of a principle of equality lurking somewhere waiting to be discovered.

However, the rule of law is uncontroversially a feature of our constitution[88] and it does not take much imagination to suppose that a principle of substantive equality might be fostered within it. While as Waldron says, the rule of law is an 'essentially contestable concept',[89] it is that contestation that opens a space for the development of a modern and more muscular principle of equality.

It is common to speak of a 'thin' or 'thick' definition of the rule of law.[90] The former being formal and instrumental, and the latter incorporating substantive commitments. Dicey's rule of law is paradigmatically thin,[91] and Lord Bingham's influential exposition thick.[92]

Lord Bingham defines the rule of law as 'all persons and authorities within the state, whether public or private, should be bound by and entitled to the benefit of

[88] Section 1, Constitutional Reform Act 2005.

[89] J Waldron, 'Is the rule of law an essentially contested concept (in Florida)? (2002) 21 *Law and Philosophy* 137.

[90] House of Lords Select Committee on the Constitution 13th Report of Session 2024–2026, *The Rule of Law: Holding the Line Against Tyranny and Anarchy* (2025) HL Paper 2011, paras 20 et seq.

[91] ibid, para 15; J Sumption, *The Challenges of Democracy and the Rule of Law* (Profile Books, 2025) 99–100. For Lord Sumption the 'real question is what rights are truly fundamental to the subsistence of civil society so that they should not depend on political choice. It does not matter what label we give them' (101). They do not include 'race relations' (105). Lord Sumption devoted a whole book to the subject of equality with his co-author, the right-wing Conservative politician who held ministerial office under the premiership of Margaret Thatcher (K Joseph and J Sumption, *Equality* (John Murray, 1979). However, it is of little help on this subject, regrettably. One academic reviewer described the book's arguments, aptly, as 'like pub conversations, disjointed and overflowing with bad humour ... There may be a semblance of prejudiced coherence for a paragraph or two, but then the short-term memory circuits fail and the authors seemed to lose interest in what they have just said, and they reshuffle the pack, or simply contradict themselves' (G Pearson, 'Reviews: Equality. Keith Joseph and Jonathan Sumption. London: John Murray, 1979, pp. 130, £4.95.' (1981) 1 *Critical Social Policy* 118, 118). But this was over 45 years ago.

[92] T Bingham, *The Rule of Law* (Penguin Books, 2011).

laws publicly made, taking effect (generally) in the future and publicly administered in the courts'.[93] For Lord Bingham, the ingredients of the rule of law include a principle of equality before the law, reflecting in essence Dicey's principle of equal treatment, as well as, more controversially, the adequate protection of human rights, drawing in this context on the Convention, including Article 14.

Bogdanor adopts a somewhat different position, but the substantive conclusion is the same.[94] Bogdanor argues that 'the era of constitutional reform[s] [since 1997[95]], together with Britain's entry in 1973 into the European Communities[96] has had the effect of replacing one constitution, a constitution whose origins lie far in the past, with a new constitution'.[97] For Bogdanor, 'Dicey's analysis, which perhaps offered a reasonably accurate account of Britain's constitutional arrangements in the past, has been made irrelevant'[98] by those changes.[99] Bogdanor's assessment is that we are 'now in transition from a system based on parliamentary sovereignty to one based on the sovereignty of a constitution, albeit a constitution that is inchoate, indistinct and still in large part uncodified'.[100] This means that 'the term "rule of law" [now] has a broader interpretation than that given to it by Dicey. It implies recognition of those basic human rights which ought to be acknowledged in any liberal society'.[101] It could barely be denied that equality is one of those.

There is also a growing international acceptance that the rule of law, referred to in numerous international and regional instruments,[102] is linked to both democracy and human rights.[103] According to the Venice Commission, 'The rule of law would be an "an empty shell" without permitting access to human rights.'[104] The Venice Commission's rule of law 'checklist'[105] includes, among other entitlements, equality before the law and non-discrimination.[106] Its equality and non-discrimination standard requires that states' constitutions enshrine the principle of equal treatment, including both a commitment to promote equality and a right to be free from discrimination,[107] as well as a guarantee of equality before the law.[108]

[93] ibid, 8.
[94] Bogdanor (n 3).
[95] The reforms to which Bogdanor refers included the enactment of the HRA 1998.
[96] The book was written before Brexit. On this point, his argument is reminiscent of Jowell (n 1).
[97] Bogdanor (n 3) xi.
[98] ibid, xiii.
[99] ibid.
[100] ibid.
[101] ibid, 63.
[102] European Commission for Democracy Through Law (Venice Commission), The Rule of Law Checklist (2016) ('Venice Commission Checklist') paras 9–32.
[103] ibid, para 33.
[104] ibid, para 31.
[105] The Checklist apparently includes the requirement for a written constitution, ibid, 17–18. It is not clear how the UK fits into this model.
[106] Venice Commission Checklist (n 101) 30–32.
[107] ibid, 30–31.
[108] ibid, 32.

Conceiving of the rule of law at common law as embracing a principle of equality would mean that such a principle does not depend upon Parliamentary approval, unlike the Human Rights Act 1998 and the Equality Act 2010.[109] The rule of law is preciously guarded by the courts and is not so vulnerable.[110] Further, treating a substantive principle of equality as an ingredient of the rule of law would mean that equality occupies a domain increasingly associated with fundamental rights, namely the common law. Recent judicial *dicta* places emphasis on the common law as the starting point in the search for fundamental rights.[111] As Lord Briggs, speaking extrajudicially,[112] has said, it would be wrong to suggest that the 'normative reach of the common law is more modest than that of the Convention'.[113] Indeed, it may extend further, 'particularly in "horizontal" scenarios where private individuals seek to assert their human rights against one another'.[114]

Further, the common law evolves over time[115] and so may itself be described as a 'living instrument', a description usually reserved for human rights instruments.[116] This leaves room for the progressive development of a principle of equality. While equality is shunted into rationality, the scope for its development as a substantive principle at common law is more limited.

This still leaves unresolved the vexed question of the shape and content of any substantive principle of equality. This too has been the subject of much debate.[117] Drawing on regional and international instruments, and the contributions of feminist and critical race scholars, any substantive principle of equality should aim to include a guarantee of *equality before and under the law (forbidding unequal laws)*; equal treatment; equal opportunity; (equal) dignity;[118] equal *recognition*;[119]

[109] Further, the Equality Act 2010 (EqA 2010) and the HRA 1998 have their own limitations. The possibilities for challenging governmental acts are closely circumscribed under EqA 2010, Sch 22, para 1, Sch 23, para 1 and Sch 3, Pt 1. Article 14 will only apply where the act complained of falls within the ambit of another protected right.

[110] See, for example *UNISON* (n 5) [66]–[68].

[111] *R (Daly) v Secretary of State for the Home Department* [2001] 2 AC 532 [30].

[112] Lord Briggs of Westbourne JSC, 'Justice Annual Conference – 25 years of the Human Rights Act. Protecting Human Rights: The Common Law As the Starting Point' (10 November 2025).

[113] ibid, 1

[114] ibid.

[115] *UNISON* (n 5) [61]–[63].

[116] See, for example, of the Convention: *In re McCaughey and another (Northern Ireland Human Rights Commission and others intervening)* [2012] 1 AC 725 [2] and [136] ('the Convention is a living instrument').

[117] See, for a discussion, K Monaghan, *Monaghan on Equality Law*, 2nd edn (Oxford University Press, 2013) paras 1.27–1.52 and 6.08–6.22.

[118] Fredman (n 67) 17; MP Foran, *Equality Before the Law: Equal Dignity, Wrongful Discrimination, and the Rule of Law* (Hart Publishing, 2023) 90.

[119] See, discussion in N Fraser and A Honneth, *Redistribution or Recognition? A Political-Philosophical Exchange* (Verso, 2003).

democratic participation;[120] redistribution and social justice;[121] and *equal respect for human entitlements (including life, health, emotion, thought, among others)*.[122]

13.5 Conclusion

Even some of the most sceptical feminist and critical race theorists see some 'emancipatory potential'[123] in a more just conception of the rule of law.[124] A rule of law with a substantive principle of equality as one of its ingredients would go some way towards realising that potential. MacKinnon, one of the most sceptical, remarks that 'while legal change may not always make social change, sometimes it helps and law *un*changed can make social change impossible'.[125]

It would be naive to think that a substantive principle of equality at common law would introduce radical change any time soon. The response of the senior courts to claims under Article 14 has become increasingly conservative, particularly in welfare benefits cases,[126] and there is little reason to believe that this position will fundamentally change, at least in the short term. But leaving the law unchanged may very well make social change impossible.

[120] See, 'the most celebrated footnote in constitutional law' (L Powell, '*Carolene Products* Revisited' (1982) 82 *Columbia Law Review* 1087, 1087): 'Prejudice against discrete and insular minorities may be a special condition, which tends seriously to curtail the operation of those political processes ordinarily to be relied upon to protect minorities, and which may call for a correspondingly more searching judicial inquiry' (*United States v Carolene Products Co* [1938] 304 US 144).

[121] See discussion in Fraser and Honneth (n 118).

[122] M Nussbaum, *Frontiers of Justice, Disability, Nationality and Species Membership* (Belknap, 2006) 70, 75–77.

[123] Bridges (n 82) 374.

[124] ibid.

[125] Munro (n 87) 355.

[126] *RR v Secretary of State for Work and Pensions* [2019] UKSC 52; *R (SC) v Secretary of State for Work and Pensions* [2022] AC 223; and *A v United Kingdom* (App nos 32949/17 and 34614/17).

14

Trust in the UK Supreme Court after Brexit

In memoriam Conor Gearty: 4 November 1957 to 11 September 2025

AIDAN O'NEILL KC*

14.1 Introduction

The late Professor Conor Gearty KC – a great Irish jurist whom I counted as a friend and colleague – wrote two articles for the *London Review of Books* on the post-Brexit UK Supreme Court (UKSC): respectively, 'In the Shallow End: on the UK Supreme Court' which was published in January 2022;[1] and 'Unwelcome Remnant: on the threat to the Human Rights Act', which came out (tragically, posthumously) in October 2025.[2]

In these two pieces, Conor highlighted what he identified as the determining influence of Robert Reed (Baron Reed of Allermuir) – President of the UKSC for the seven years between January 2020 and January 2027 – in rolling back much of that Court's (and that of its predecessor, the Appellate Committee of the House of Lords) pre-Brexit and post-Human Rights Act constitutional case law. As Conor put it in his 2022 article:

> Johnson's Brexit administration is in many ways an exercise in nostalgia, a search for a lost England, and the Supreme Court under Reed is similarly backward-looking. It has

* Aidan O'Neill KC (Scotland), KC (England and Wales), Barrister-at-law (Ireland) appeared as senior counsel in the following cases mentioned in this chapter: *Shindler v Chancellor of the Duchy of Lancaster* [2016] EWHC 957 (Admin), [2016] EWCA Civ 469, UKSC 2016/0105 PTA; *R (Miller) v Secretary of State for Exiting the European Union* [2017] UKSC 5; *Wightman v Secretary of State for Exiting the European Union* [2018] CSIH 62, Case C-621/18 EU:C:2018:999; *Cherry v Advocate General for Scotland* [2019] CSOH 20, [2019] CSIH 49, [2019] UKSC 41; *Dale Vince v Advocate General for Scotland* [2019] CSOH 77, [2019] CSIH 51; and *For Women Scotland v Scottish Ministers (No. 2)* [2022] CSOH 90, [2023] CSIH 37, [2025] UKSC 16.

[1] C Gearty, 'In the shallow end: on the UK Supreme Court' (2022) 44 *London Review of Books* (27 January 2022), www.lrb.co.uk/the-paper/v44/n02/conor-gearty/in-the-shallow-end.

[2] C Gearty, 'Unwelcome Remnant: on the threat to the Human Rights Act' (2025) 47 *London Review of Books* (9 October 2025), www.lrb.co.uk/the-paper/v47/n18/conor-gearty/unwelcome-remnant.

> reverted to an approach rooted in legal formalism, an extremely narrow reading of the rule of law, while displaying an old-school lack of interest in the lived experiences of those whose plights have brought them to the judges' attention.

And in his October 2025 piece Conor again referenced 'the court's powerful president, Lord Reed' who, 'remains by far the most important influence' over a 'Supreme Court [which] is quietly editing the Human Rights Act out of existence. In cases where human rights cannot be ignored entirely … new modes of reasoning are being used to ensure that the law under scrutiny cannot be found in breach of human rights.'

Lord Reed has himself stated – as Conor highlighted – that judges 'have to accept that responsible criticism of judicial decisions is an aspect of judicial accountability', albeit that Lord Reed also said this:

> Whether it is directed from the left or the right, the criticism rarely attempts to engage with the court's reasoning, but focuses instead on the outcome of court cases, and praises or blames the judges according to whether the outcome is politically welcome or unwelcome.[3]

Conor's work undoubtedly engaged with, and tested, the reasoning presented by the UKSC by way of justification for its conclusions in a run of cases decided since the UK ceased to be a Member State of the EU. In so doing Conor performed one of the primary responsibilities of legal scholars of our constitution, which is to maintain the fundamental democratic principle of judicial accountability even (especially?) of courts of final instance.

In this chapter I do not seek to call into question Conor's general thesis. His critique has been backed by other academics' detailed scholarly analysis of the UKSC's post-Brexit case law.[4] Indeed, it has received confirmation from a (former) horse's mouth. In a letter from the now retired (if not retiring) UKSC Justice Jonathan Sumption to the *London Review of Books*[5] (responding critically – and

[3] Lord Reed of Allermuir, 'Trust in the courts in an age of populism' The Peter Taylor Memorial Address 2025 (Delivered at Inner Temple on 12 June 2025), https://supremecourt.uk/uploads/speech_lord_reed_13062025_88f834d8f5.pdf.

[4] See for example L Graham, 'Has the UK Supreme Court Become More Restrained in Public Law Cases?' (2024) 87 *Modern Law Review* 1073 and the papers cited there at pages 1073–74. After an exhaustive survey of the Court's output from January 2020 to a cut-off point of January 2023, Graham's paper concludes as follows (at 1109–10): 'There is little evidence that the Court is advocating for judicial restraint across the board, or a wholesale reduction of its powers or jurisdiction (there is little evidence, for example, of a general deference towards lower courts or a tightening of the Court's inherent jurisdiction); equally, it is not always conservative when it comes to developing law, exercising discretion or departing from precedent *generally* – it is only really reluctant to do this when the outcome would intrude upon political issues upon which the executive has competence, or the sovereignty of the legislature, or the dualist nature of the constitution. The Court *has* become more restrained, but only in certain respects. The Court is not a political court; it is a *political constitutionalist* Court. As indicated at the outset, this gives rise to huge questions: is this acceptable? What is the cause of this? And what, if anything, *could*, or *should*, be done about it? I hope not to disappoint the reader too much by leaving these enormous issues unanswered for others to determine.'

[5] J Sumption, 'On the court' (2022) 44 *London Review of Books* (10 February 2022), www.lrb.co.uk/the-paper/v44/n03/letters.

in defence of the court – to Conor's article) Sumption admits that there have been radical shifts in position taken by the post-Brexit UKSC from the approach taken by the top courts in earlier years. Sumption notes:

> In the last few years there has been an almost complete turnover in the personnel of the UK Supreme Court at every level. In the three decades which began in about 1985, the appellate courts were dominated by a highly interventionist generation of judges. The generation that has succeeded them is well placed to look back on the achievements of their predecessors, and to review them in the light of experience. This is a perfectly normal process of life of any deliberative institution.
>
> The essential feature of the UK Supreme Court's recent decision on public law has been a renewed emphasis on the centrality of Parliament in our constitution, not just as the supreme legislative organ of the State but as the ultimate source of the political legitimacy of governments. Some of the more aggressive judicial interventions of the past have had the effect of appropriating to the courts the right to decide where the public interest lies. …
>
> What the UK Supreme Court has done is to require judges to have more regard than hitherto to the proper distribution of constitutional responsibilities in the State. Responsibilities which are conferred by law on ministers politically answerable to Parliament should not be shifted to judges politically answerable to no-one. The function of the courts is <u>not</u> to review the social or economic merits of government policy.

In this chapter I want to look more generally at the issue of *trust* in the UKSC after Brexit. In particular, I want to see if Conor's focus on the person of the court's first post-Brexit President (as being, in Conor's view, the prime and decisive mover behind the UKSC's changed overall constitutional vision and approach since Brexit) can be substantiated, and so justified. In this way, I hope this piece can be seen as building on Conor's work.

14.2 Can we Properly Talk of a *Reed* Supreme Court?

In September 1998 Robert Reed, at the age of 42, was appointed a Senator of the College of Justice (as judges of the Court of Session are formally known). In February 2012, aged just 55, he took up appointment as a Justice of the UKSC, becoming its Deputy President in May 2018. On 13 January 2020, the new Baron Reed of Allermuir, now 63 years old, succeeded Baroness Hale as President of the UKSC. Two weeks later, on 27 January 2020 – in a triumph for the discreet charm of the *Edimbourgeoisie* – his fellow Scots lawyer on the UKSC since October 2013, Patrick Hodge (the Right Honourable Lord Hodge) was appointed Deputy President of the Court. And on 31 January 2020, at 11pm, the UK left the EU.

In US Constitutional scholarship it is standard to survey trends in the case law of the US Supreme Court by reference to its Chief Justice: whether 'the Roberts court', referencing the current Chief Justice John Roberts, or the 'Rehnquist Court' for his immediate predecessor as Chief Justice, William Rehnquist. Not so in the

UK, however. Here it appears to be considered rather 'bad form' to assess (still less critique) court judgments by direct reference to the individuals making up the bench which produced them.[6] This may simply be an application of the 'sausage principle' that 'laws, like sausages, cease to inspire respect in proportion as we know they are made': *das Wurst-Prinzip* (as Bismark did *not* call it).[7] Or, as Conor put it – to continue the culinary metaphors – 'Judges, whether serving or retired, tend not to speak out. Barristers know on which side their bread is buttered.'

But, if anything, there may be *more* reason within UK constitutional scholarship – compared to US constitutional scholarship – to refer to our respective Supreme Courts under reference to the name of their presiding judge. This is because in the US context the serving Chief Justice has *no* role to play in the selection of those who will serve alongside him/her on the SCOTUS bench. Instead, Justices of the US Supreme Court are nominated by the serving US President and – after confirmation hearings before the Judiciary Committee of the US Senate, and if and only if their nomination passes the confirmation vote in the Judiciary Committee – the full Senate debates and votes on whether POTUS's nominated candidate should be appointed to the Court. In the past 40 or so years Presidential nominations to the SCOTUS bench have been made on an openly partisan basis (is this proposed Justice perceived to be "Republican" or "Democrat" in their sympathies ?). And, since the Senate 1987 rejection of the nomination of Robert Bork, Senate confirmation votes for such nominees have largely split on those same ideological/party political lines.

By contrast, in the UK the Supreme Court (Judicial Appointments) Regulations 2013 (SI 2013/2193) ('the 2013 Regulations') give the President of the UKSC the key role in the appointment of other members of the court (including appointment to the position of Deputy President).[8] The President of the Supreme Court

[6] Though see more recently L Graham, *Judicial Individuality on the UK Supreme Court* (Hart Publishing, 2025). See too A Paterson, 'Creating a group oriented Supreme Court – Lord Neuberger's legacy' (2021) 28 *International Journal of the Legal Profession* 107, 108, https://doi.org/10.1080/09695958.2021.1877716 referencing, among other works; Arvind and Stirton, *Lawyers and the Legal Model: Judicial Ideology, Judicial Professionalism and Institutional Strategy Among the Law Lords*, 14 May 2012 https://extranet.sioe.org/uploads/isnie2012/arvind_stirton.pdf; C Hanretty, 'The decisions and ideal points of British Law Lords' (2013) 43 *British Journal of Political Science* 703; C Hanretty, *A Court of Specialists: Judicial Behaviour on the UK Supreme Court* (Oxford University Press, 2020); R Cahill O'Callaghan, 'The influence of personal values on legal judgments' (2013) 40 *Journal of Law and Society* 596; and R Cahill O'Callaghan, *Values in the Supreme Court: Decisions, Divisions and Diversity* (Hart Publishing, 2020).

[7] A remark by the mid-19th-century American poet John Godfrey Saxe, subsequently (and wrongly) attributed to Count Otto von Bismarck in the form: 'Laws are like sausages: it is best not to know how they are made.'

[8] For the background to these provisions see P O'Brien, 'Changes to judicial appointments in the Crime and Courts Act 2013' [2014]Unite *Public Law* 179 who notes, at 188: '*Supreme Court* Under the old system *the President and Deputy President* were obliged to sit on all ad hoc Supreme Court appointments commission ('SCACs') including those to select their own successors, together with a member each from the Judicial Appointments Commission for England and Wales, the Scottish Judicial Appointment Board and Northern Ireland Judicial Appointments Commission. This requirement was widely regarded as inappropriate and, as President of the Court, Lord Phillips argued for its removal in his evidence to the Lords Constitution Committee. The Committee itself noted that it is 'contrary to well-recognised principles of appointments for an individual to select his or her successor': Committee

ex officio chairs the required five-person Selection Commission. The President is the *only* member of the UKSC involved in the appointment. And it is the President who – after due regard to the territorial composition of the selection commission – nominates to be the 'senior UK judge' to sit with the President on any particular Selection Commission one of: the Lord Chief Justice of England and Wales; the Master of the Rolls; the Lord President of the Court of Session; the Lord Chief Justice of Northern Ireland; the Lord Justice Clerk of the Court of Session; the President of the Queen's Bench Division; or the Chancellor of the High Court. The remaining three places on the Selection Commission are filled by: one member of the Judicial Appointments Commission for England and Wales; one member of the Judicial Appointments Board for Scotland; and one member of the Northern Ireland Judicial Appointments Commission. All of these Judicial Appointment Commissions members have to be nominated to sit on the Selection Commission for the UKSC by their respective bodies. At least two of these three nominees must be 'non-legally qualified' (which is to say that they have *never* practised or been employed as a lawyer, and have *never* held any relevant judicial office).[9]

Once the name of the sole individual chosen by the Selection Commission for appointment to the Court has been passed to the Lord Chancellor's office, in theory the Lord Chancellor has the power to reject its nomination, but only 'on the ground that, in the Lord Chancellor's opinion, the person selected is not suitable for the office concerned': 2013 Regulations, Regulation 21(1). Regulation 21(2) provides that the nomination may be referred back to the Selection Committee for it to 'reconsider' if in the Lord Chancellor's opinion—

Report 4.3. The Act responds to this by removing the obligation that the President *and Deputy President* sit on Supreme Court selection commissions, replacing it with a requirement only that *one judge of the court must sit* and explicitly prohibiting the President and Deputy President from sitting on commissions to select their successors. SCACs under the amended Constitutional Reform Act 2005 will closely resemble those under the old system apart from this. The regulations specify further that *the President is to chair all SCACs other than those to appoint a new President.* For the appointment of a new President the SCAC will be chaired by a lay member from the JAC, JAB or NIJAC and the Deputy President will sit. The regulations also provide that a senior UK judge will take up a second judicial place on a SCAC. This policy was announced in the MoJ's *Appointments and Diversity* paper: Appointments and Diversity 'A Judiciary for the 21st Century' response to consultation paper. A plan to have seven members on the SCAC to appoint the President has not been followed through in the regulations.'

[9] Whether as: Judge of the High Court of Justice or Court of Appeal; Judge of the Court of Session, or Temporary Judge in Scotland; Judge of the High Court of Justice or Court of Appeal in Northern Ireland; Judge of the Court Martial Appeal Court; Chairman of the Scottish Land Court; Circuit Judge; Sheriff principal, sheriff, summary sheriff, temporary sheriff principal, part-time sheriff or part-time summary sheriff in Scotland; County Court Judge or deputy County Court Judge in Northern Ireland; District Judge (magistrates' courts) (but not Deputy District Judge (magistrates' courts)); district judge (magistrates' courts), or deputy district judge (magistrates' courts), in Northern Ireland; Chief or other Child Support Commissioner for Northern Ireland or Deputy Child Support Commissioner for Northern Ireland; Chief or other Social Security Commissioner (not including a Deputy Commissioner); Chief or other Social Security Commissioner for Northern Ireland or Deputy Social Security Commissioner for Northern Ireland (excluding a person appointed in pursuance of the Social Security Act 1980, s 13(5)).

(a) there is not enough evidence that the person is suitable for the office concerned;
(b) there is evidence that the person is not the best candidate on merit; or
(c) there is not enough evidence that if the person were appointed the judges of the Supreme Court would between them have knowledge of, and experience of practice in, the law of each part of the United Kingdom.

As far as anyone not-in-the-know knows, neither of these 'bounce-back' powers of the Lord Chancellor has ever been used (presumably on the basis that it would again be thought to be 'bad form' for the Lord Chancellor to reveal, or express, any lack of confidence in the Selection Commission's wisdom and good judgement). So what happens, *in practice*, is that once the Selection Commission (chaired by President of the Court) has selected the individual who is to be appointed as a Justice to the Court the name is then passed by the Lord Chancellor to the Prime Minister who – per the Constitutional Reform Act 2005, section 26(3) – '(a) must recommend any person who has been selected as a result of the convening of a Selection Commission and (b) may *not* recommend any other person'. Formally, appointment as a Justice of the UKSC is then made by the King on this recommendation made by the Prime Minister.

In stark contrast to the situation which prevails on the other side of the Atlantic, the legislative and regulatory framework is designed to insulate the issue of the appointment of Justices of the UKSC from *political influence* (from the Government) or *prior open public scrutiny* (from Parliament). The mechanism which has been put in place is to have two senior judges (assisted by two or three non-lawyers from among the great and the good) privately deliberating and selecting who gets appointed to judicial office on the UK's apex court.

The non-public way in which UKSC Justices are selected for appointment may be an example of a precautionary application of the *Wurst-Prinzip*. It is also said to encourage otherwise shy and retiring – but still the best and brightest individuals among the serving judiciary – to put their hats in the ring to be UKSC Justices; knowing that few will *know* – and no one outside the process will *see* – how their candidacy fares; and confident that they will never be subjected to the degree of hostile scrutiny visited on, for example, Robert Bork, Clarence Thomas and Brett Kavanaugh in their respective confirmation hearings before the US Senate Judicial Committee.[10] But what all this 'don't ask, don't tell' 'under-the-radar process' means is that, *in practice*, the Selection Commission chaired (and, in part, selected) by the

[10] See Andrew Burrows (who was appointed direct from academic life to be a UKSC Justice in June 2020) in 'Numbers sitting in the Supreme Court' (2013) 129 *Law Quarterly Review* 305, 308: 'In contrast to the position with the politicised Supreme Court of the United States, it is very hard to predict – perhaps with some rare exceptions – how any particular Supreme Court judge would have decided a case in which he or she did not sit. As the political views of UK Supreme Court judges are, in general, unknown and are not relevant to their appointment – so that the judges do not split on political lines – it may be powerfully argued that there is simply no need to be concerned about the 'what might have been' argument.' On the contrary, see L Graham, 'Lessons from Lord Hope's Diaries: judicial ideology and panel selection', *UK Const L Blog* (18th June 2020) (available at https://ukconstitutionallaw.org/).

President of the Supreme Court, has a significant – indeed *determining* – influence on the ultimate decision as to who will (and who will *not*) become a Justice of the Supreme Court.[11] Yet the inherent problem with such a system, say its critics, is that it favours what might be described as 'judicial cloning'; that is to say, judges appointing as judges people who are just like them: the same old, same old, late-middle-aged, upper middle-class, privately educated, Oxbridge graduate, well-off, white men.

14.3 All Change in the Post-Brexit UK Supreme Court

The second point to note about the post-Brexit UKSC is there has been vast change, over a very short period, in the composition of the Supreme Court judicial bench since the UK left the EU.[12] The only judges who had served on it for more than a decade at the time of writing were its President Lord Reed and its Deputy President Lord Hodge. Lord Hodge retired after 12 years as a UKSC Justice on 31 December 2025. He was replaced as the Court's required second Scottish Justice by Lord Doherty who began sitting in January 2026. At the same time, Lord Sales succeeded Lord Hodge to become Deputy President of the court. There were eight vacancies for UKSC Justices filled on the court in the six years between the start of 2020 and the end of 2025. Further retirements have since been announced. Lord Richards, Lord Lloyd Jones and Lord Reed are all scheduled to leave the court by January 2027. What this will mean is that from January 2027 all but two (Lord Briggs and Lord Sales) of the full complement 12-strong UKSC bench will be post-Brexit appointees. Perhaps, more significantly yet (since Lord Briggs did not take part in the decision) Lord Sales will be the *only* judge who was part of the unanimous 11 judge UKSC decision in *Cherry v Advocate General for Scotland/R(Miller) v Prime Minister* which ruled that the pre-Brexit attempted prorogation of Parliament in 2019 under the Johnson premiership to be void and of no effect.[13] And this chronology also tells

[11] Lord Reed said this in his Evidence to the House of Lords Constitution Committee's Annual evidence session with the President and Deputy President of the Supreme Court on Wednesday 22 April 2026, available at https://committees.parliament.uk/event/27087/formal-meeting-oral-evidence-session/: 'This may sound immodest – I do not want it to – but I got a letter saying that I was regarded as the embodiment of judicial integrity ... I would be inclined to caution against opening up what might be a bit of a Pandora's box. The system that we have, I can tell you, is one envied by other judiciaries around the world. We are very unusual in having a process by an independent commission rather than political nomination.'

[12] As at 1 January 2026 the serving UKSC judges in order of seniority of (re)appointment were: Lord Reed (February 2012, retiring January 2027); Lord Lloyd-Jones (October 2017 to January 2022; August 2022, retiring January 2027); Lord Briggs (October 2017); Lord Sales (January 2019); Lord Hamblen (January 2020); Lord Leggatt (April 2020); Lord Burrows (June 2020) Lord Stephens (October 2020); Lady Rose (April 2021); Lord Richards (August 2022 to June 2026); Lady Simler (November 2023); and Lord Doherty (January 2026). Richard Snowden LJ, a corporate law specialist judge on the Court of Appeal of England and Wales, was appointed to fill Lord Richards' place on the UKSC with effect from July 2026.

[13] See BC Jones, 'Judicial review and embarrassment' [2022] *Public Law* 179, 187–88: 'A unanimous Supreme Court (11-0) [in *Cherry v Advocate General for Scotland/R (Miller) v Prime Minister* [2019] UKSC 41, [2020] AC 373] decided that the prorogation was unlawful and quashed the decision,

us that Lord Reed as President of the UKSC will *necessarily* have been *directly* involved as Chair of this UKSC Justices Selection Commission in the post-Brexit recommendations for appointments (or, in the case of Lord Lloyd-Jones, reappointment) of around three-quarters of the Justices who make up the full 12 judge complement of the UKSC from January 2027 on.

When giving evidence before House of Lords Constitution Committee in 2022 Lord Reed was asked whether, when considering candidates for appointment as Justices to the UKSC, he (and his colleagues from the Judicial Appointments Commissions) 'take into account whether their judicial history shows a tendency towards activism or a tendency towards restraint'. He said this:

> I would take that into account. For example, for the exercise this week, we asked them to give a presentation on judicial activism and its impact on the relationship between the courts, the Government and Parliament. We are expecting them not only to have talked the talk but to have walked the walk, if I can put it that way. Obviously, the judges – myself and the Master of the Rolls – are well aware of people's track record, and I certainly take that into account. … They do have to demonstrate—we specifically test them on this — a proper understanding of constitutional roles. If I am aware from somebody's record that they have been issuing judgments that demonstrate a lack of such an understanding, I would take that into account.[14]

In May 2024, Lord Reed told the House of Lords Constitution Committee:

> People have become aware of the work that the top court does, to an extent, when they were never aware of it previously. Some people have the impression that the court is activist and has taken on a new constitutional role. This is a consequence of the visibility of our work.
>
> Let us compare it with the Appellate Committee in the 1960s, when the principles of judicial review were revolutionised by the Appellate Committee under the chairmanship of Lord Reid of Drem, or in the early 2000s, when the leading cases on the effect of the Human Rights Act were decided. The senior Law Lord at the time was Lord Bingham but most of the leading cases were actually presided over by Lord Nicholls. Compared

thus recalling Parliament. Although the court dropped the "improper motive" ground and "clandestine manner" language used by the Inner House [in *Cherry v Advocate General for Scotland* [2019] CSIH 49, 2020 SC 37 per Lord President (Carloway) at [54]], its unanimity—despite deep divisions in the lower courts [*Cherry v Advocate General for Scotland* [2019] CSIH 49, 2020 SC 37 v *R (Miller) v Prime Minister* [2019] EWHC 2381 (QB)] — suggested that it was responding to a constitutional threat. One prominent commentator called the decision "damning", and the "strongest possible condemnation" of the government's decision to prorogue Parliament: *Meg Russell,* 'The Supreme Court ruling in *Cherry/Miller (No.2)*, and the power of parliament' *(Constitution Unit Blog, 27 September 2019)*. The Supreme Court ruling in *Cherry/Miller (No.2)*, and the power of parliament | The Constitution Unit Blog. The unanimous nature of the decision and the complete nullification of the prorogation – thus recalling Parliament – was a significant embarrassment to the Prime Minister, who was undoubtedly the episode's constitutional villain.'

[14] See Lord Reed's response to Question 12 in the Oral evidence to the House of Lords Constitution Committee's Annual evidence session with the President and Deputy President of the Supreme Court on Wednesday 6 April 2022: committees.parliament.uk/oralevidence/10084/pdf.

> with those judgments of the Appellate Committee, we have on the whole been rather a conservative court.[15]

And by June 2025 Lord Reed felt able to tell the House of Lords Constitution Committee this:

> On our Court, there have been changes in judicial personnel over the years. I do not think the prevailing view has changed very much, but there were judges on the Court in the past who took a more expansive view of the Court's constitutional function than is certainly the prevailing view at the moment.[16]

From Lord Reed's own account to the House of Lords Constitution Committee, then, we may take the following:

(1) In his period as President of the UKSC, there has been a clear shift in the Court's self-understanding and self-presentation, involving a conscious repudiation of its predecessors' previous, more expansive view of its constitutional function to result in what Lord Reed now describes as 'rather a conservative court'.

(2) One of the factors which Lord Reed identifies as behind this apparent sift to becoming 'rather a conservative court' is the increased visibility of the UKSC and the rise in public scrutiny and (social) media comment to which its work is now subjected. The paradox results that the growing institutional transparency of the court at work has, on Lord Reed's account, led to greater circumspection on the part of the Justices who work there. This may not be surprising given that the open justice principle has long been seen as one means of ensuring that the judges themselves do not abuse their judicial power;[17] for, as Jeremy Bentham put it, publicity 'keeps the judge himself, while trying, under trial'.[18]

(3) But Lord Reed also identifies as another of the factors leading to this shift in the prevailing view within the Court as to it proper constitutional function is the *changes* in judicial personnel making up the Court. Writing extra-judicially the then Lord Justice Buxton observed that it is 'not necessary to be

[15] See Lord Reed's response to Question 2 in the Oral evidence to the House of Lords Constitution Committee's Annual evidence session with the President and Deputy President of the Supreme Court on Wednesday 1 May 2024: committees.parliament.uk/oralevidence/14736/pdf.

[16] See Lord Reed's response to Question 7 in the Oral evidence to the House of Lords Constitution Committee's Annual evidence session with the President and Deputy President of the Supreme Court on Wednesday 4 June 2025: committees.parliament.uk/oralevidence/16152/pdf.

[17] In his judgment in *Scott v Scott* [1913] AC 417 Lord Shaw of Dunfermline relied on two statutes of the pre-Union independent Scottish Parliament – the Court of Session (Scotland) Act 1693 and Act Anent Advising Criminal Processes with Open Doors of 12 June 1693 – as the basis for asserting 'open justice' to be a general constitutional principle across the UK, and noted that these two Scottish statutes of 1693 – passed as part of Scotland's (Glorious) Revolutionary post 1688/89 settlement –were intended: 'to secure civil liberties *against judges* as well as against the Crown'.

[18] See J Bentham, *Works*, vol 4 (1843) 316 quoted in *L v L - re ancillary financial relief and anonymity* [2015] EWHC 2621 (Fam), [2016] 1 WLR 1259 by Mostyn J at [5].

a fully signed-up American Realist in order to think that in some cases the result may be affected by the identity of the judges who hear the appeal'.[19] And as we have seen, as the *ex officio* Chair of the Selection Commission for the appointment of UK Supreme Justices, Lord Reed has necessarily been directly involved in those personnel appointments.

(4) In particular, when chairing the Selection Commission for appointment as a Justice of the Supreme Court, Lord Reed (and the other member of the Commission) avowedly take into account whether candidates' 'judicial history shows a tendency towards activism or a tendency towards restraint' and they require candidates to 'demonstrate … a proper understanding of constitutional roles', a matter on which they are 'specifically tested' by Lord Reed and the non-legally qualified individuals who have been chosen to sit on any particular Selection Commission with him and the other judge chosen by him.[20]

This 'testing' by the *ad hoc* Selection Commissions (which are convened whenever there is a need to fill a vacancy on the UKSC bench) of any aspirant UKSC Justices to ensure that they 'talk the talk' and can demonstrate that have 'a proper understanding' of the constitutional role to be played by the UKSC; and secondly the associated examination by Lord Reed and his colleagues from time to time nominated to these ad hoc Selection Commissions, of all candidates' past record as lower court judges, with a view to checking on where or not the candidates have, in fact, 'walked the walk' and applied that 'proper understanding' in their previous judicial decisions, appear to be designed to ensure and enforce (at least during Robert Reed's tenure as President) a new attitude of *judicial quietism*.

This testing and checking means that *judicial quietism* will be expected to characterise not just the past judicial approach of the individuals who get through the selection process to appointment as a UKSC Justice, but will have like effect on all

[19] R Buxton, 'Sitting *en banc* in the new Supreme Court' (2009) 125 *Law Quarterly Review* 288, 288

[20] See Lord Reed's response to Question 4 in the Oral Evidence to the House of Lords Constitution Committee's Annual evidence session with the President and Deputy President of the Supreme Court on Wednesday 22 April 2026, available at https://committees.parliament.uk/event/27087/formal-meeting-oral-evidence-session/:

> 'It is a matter of great importance … that whoever is appointed should have a good understanding of constitutional relationships between the courts, Parliament and the Government. One consequence of that has been that, as part of the selection process, we ask the shortlisted candidates to give us a presentation and we have very often chosen one on that very topic. I can remember asking something along the lines of, "Do you think that the relationship between the courts and Parliament has been damaged by an overenthusiastic interpretation of the Human Rights Act?". If the candidate says, "No, there's no problem. We had a wonderful relationship with Parliament, and the Human Rights Act had no impact on that whatever", you wonder, "What planet has this person been on?".

Lord Waldegrave of North Hill: My final point is that somebody living on that planet is rather unlikely to get on to the Supreme Court.

Lord Reed of Allermuir: So long as I am chairing the selection commission, I would be looking for people with a better awareness of constitutional realities.'

lower courts containing individuals who might harbour the hope or ambition, one day, themselves to be appointed to the top court.[21]

Robert Reed announced in early 2026 that he would step down as Presidency of the UKSC in January 2027. Until then, he continues to have the power directly to test and check the records of lower court judges seeking promotion to the UKSC for their adherence and commitment to the new post-Brexit neo-Diceyan constitutional orthodoxy which the UKSC has crafted during the seven years of the Reed UKSC Presidency. And even after stepping down as UKSC President, Robert Reed may continue to exert an indirect influence, as he would remain eligible to be called back to sit *ad hoc* on the UKSC bench since he does not reach the mandatory judicial retirement age of 75 until September 2032.

14.4 The Turning of the Tide

It all seemed so different not so very long ago, when the prospect of the UK's exit from the EU provoked a slew of litigation before the courts raising fundamental constitutional issues.

Prior to the Brexit referendum, the courts in England and Wales were asked in *Shindler v Chancellor of the Duchy of Lancaster* to rule on the lawfulness (in terms of its compatibility with EU law) of Parliament excluding from the Brexit referendum franchise UK nationals who had lived outside the UK for more than 15 years where they had done so in exercise of their free movement rights to work elsewhere in the EU. The case got as far as the Court of Appeal,[22] but the UKSC – after a half-day oral permission hearing before five judges[23] – denied the claimants' permission to appeal to it.[24]

[21] See now L Graham, 'Human Rights challenges after *R (SC) v. Secretary of State for Work and Pensions* [2012] UKSC 26' (20260 *Public Law* 48–65 for an empirical analysis highlighting just such a shift in the decision of lower courts.

[22] *Shindler v Chancellor of the Duchy of Lancaster* [2016] EWCA Civ 469, [2017] QB 226.

[23] *Shindler v Chancellor of the Duchy of Lancaster* UKSC 2016/0105 PTA refused on 24 May 2016 by Lady Hale, Lord Mance, Lord Sumption, Lord Reed, Lord Hughes: Permission to Appeal (PTA) results – The Supreme Court. Giving the Court's decision, Lady Hale (then Deputy President of the Supreme Court) said: 'We should make it clear that the question is not whether this particular voting exclusion is justifiable as a proportionate means of achieving a legitimate aim. The question is instead, firstly, whether European Union law applies at all, as only if it does so is there any possibility of attacking an Act of Parliament; and secondly, if so, whether there is any interference with the right of free movement. Assuming for the sake of argument that European Union law does apply, we have decided that it is not arguable that there is an interference with right of free movement, for the reasons given by the Divisional Court ([2016] EWHC 957 (Admin), [2016] 3 CMLR 22) and the Court of Appeal ([2016] EWCA Civ 469, [2017] QB 226). We do have considerable sympathy for the situation in which the applicants find themselves and we understand that this is something which concerns them deeply. But we cannot discern a legal basis for challenging this statute. Accordingly, the application for Permission to appeal is refused.'

[24] H Green, 'Expatriates Lose Supreme Court Bid for Right to Vote in EU Referendum' The University of Aberdeen Blog (2 June 2016), www.abdn.ac.uk/law/blog/expatriates-lose-supreme-court-bid-for-right-to-vote-in-eu-referendum.

After the Brexit referendum result, in *Miller (No 1)* a three-judge Divisional Court in England and Wales,[25] and separately the Northern Ireland courts,[26] and then an 11-judge UKSC bench – were asked to determine the following matters: first, whether or not it was within the existing prerogative powers of the Crown (that it is to say, the inherent powers of the UK Government) to notify the EU of the UK's intention to withdraw from, and cease to be a Member State of, the EU, or whether specific primary legislation passed by the UK Parliament was required before such notification could be made; and secondly, whether the consent of the Northern Ireland Assembly and/or of the majority of people of Northern Ireland had to be obtained before any such notification could validly be given.[27]

Then, in *Wightman v Secretary of State for Exiting the European Union*, the UKSC refused to grant[28] the UK Government's application for permission to appeal to it[29] against the decision of the Inner House of the Court of Session[30] to refer to a full 27-judge bench of the Court of Justice of the European Union,[31] the question of whether or not, as a matter of EU law, once the UK had duly notified the Council of its intention to leave the EU under Article 50 of the Treaty on European Union (TEU), that notice of intention to leave could itself unilaterally be withdrawn by the UK, at least during the two-year notice period for withdrawal required under the Treaty.

In *Cherry v Advocate General for Scotland* and in *R (Miller) v Prime Minister* the Inner House of the Court of Session and a Divisional Court of High Court of England and Wales had, respectively and separately, to determine: first, whether the decision by the then UK Prime Minister, Boris Johnson, to advise the Queen to prorogue Parliament (in the weeks immediately before the date when the UK would automatically to cease to be an EU Member State as the extended Article 50 TEU notice period ran out) was a justiciable matter for the courts; and, if so, whether it was lawful. The Court of Session found the decision to be both justiciable and unlawful.[32] The Divisional Court of England and Wales held it to be

[25] *R (Miller) v Secretary of State for Exiting the European Union* [2016] EWHC 2768 (Admin), [2017] 1 All ER 158.

[26] *In re McCord's application for judicial review re Article 50 TEU notification* [2016] NIQB 85, [2017] 2 CMLR 7, a case then referred by the Northern Ireland Court of Appeal (NICA) to the UKSC.

[27] *R (Miller) v Secretary of State for Exiting the European Union* [2016] EWHC 2768 (Admin), [2017] UKSC 5, [2018] AC 61.

[28] 'Case Comment: Permission to appeal determination in the matter of Secretary of State for Exiting the European Union v Wightman and others' UKSC Blog (23 November 2018), https://ukscblog.com/case-comment-permission-to-appeal-determination-in-the-matter-of-secretary-of-state-for-exiting-the-european-union-v-wightman-and-others.

[29] 'Wightman and Others v Secretary of State for Exiting the European Union - application for permission to appeal to the Supreme Court', UK Government Policy Paper, 26 November 2018, www.gov.uk/government/publications/wightman-and-others-v-secretary-of-state-for-exiting-the-european-union-application-for-permission-to-appeal-to-the-supreme-court.

[30] *Wightman v Secretary of State for Exiting the European Union* [2018] CSIH 62, 2019 SC 111.

[31] Case C-621/18 *Wightman and others v Secretary of State for Exiting the European Union* EU:C:2018:999, [2019] QB 199.

[32] *Cherry v Advocate General for Scotland* [2019] CSIH 49, 2020 SC 37.

essentially a political decision, and questions of its lawfulness were not for the courts to consider or determine.[33] Another 11-judge bench of the UKSC heard appeals against each of these decisions together and unanimously upheld the Scottish Court's position.[34]

And in *Dale Vince v Advocate General for Scotland* the Court of Session was faced with the question as to whether or not the courts: had the power to ordain the Prime Minister to sign and send a letter to the President of the European Council as required by the European Union (Withdrawal) (No 2) Act 2019, section 1(4);[35] and/or interdict the Prime Minister from doing anything to frustrate or undermine the will of Parliament as expressed in that Act; and finally whether it should exercise any such powers, in all the circumstances then before it.[36]

This repeated bringing before the courts of issues of, at times, neuralgic political sensitivity undoubtedly raised the courts' profiles in public consciousness and afforded the judges involved in these cases an unprecedented new visibility as their proceedings and their decisions were subject to intense public debate.[37] The attention was not all welcome. The three judges forming the Division Court in *Miller (No 1)* – the Lord Chief Justice Lord Thomas of Cwmgiedd, the Master of the Rolls Sir Terence Etherton, and the then Lord Justice Sales – were each pictured in their judicial robes on the front page of the *Daily Mail* under the banner headline 'Enemies of the people'. But, as Lord Reed put it, 'sadly, there was not much government defence of the judges at that time' and 'at that time we were being accused by many politicians and journalists of overreach and of being politically motivated, following *Miller 2*. A briefing from 10 Downing Street suggested that the [UK Supreme] Court might be radically altered or even abolished.' [38]

Against that background it is perhaps unsurprising that – after all the sugar-high excitement brought on by Brexit-related constitutional litigation – the current UKSC might appear to have cultivated, or at least to seek to present, a corporate personality and constitutional vision which mirrors that of Lord Reed as

[33] *R (Miller) v Prime Minister* [2019] EWHC 2381 (QB), [2019] 4 All ER 299 [60].

[34] *Cherry v Advocate General/R(Miller) v Prime Minister* [2019] UKSC 41, 2020 SC (UKSC) 1, [2020] AC 373.

[35] European Union (Withdrawal) (No 2) Act 2019, s 1(4) relevantly provides as follows: 'The Prime Minister must seek to obtain from the European Council an extension of the period under Article 50(3) of the Treaty on European Union ending at 11.00pm on 31 October 2019 by sending to the President of the European Council a letter in the form set out in the Schedule to this Act requesting an extension of that period to 11.00pm on 31 January 2020 in order to debate and pass a Bill to implement the agreement between the United Kingdom and the European Union under Article 50(2) of the Treaty on European Union.'

[36] *Dale Vince v Advocate General for Scotland* [2019] CSIH 51, 2020 SC 90.

[37] See, for example, J Finnis, 'The unconstitutionality of the Supreme Court's prorogation judgment' (Policy Exchange, 2019), https://policyexchange.org.uk/wp-content/uploads/2019/10/The-unconstitutionality-of-the-Supreme-Courts-prorogation-judgment.pdf, and R Ekins and S Laws, 'The Supreme Court has done lasting damage to our constitution: no principle justifies last week's radical legal intervention in high politics' *Prospect* (4 October 2019), www.prospectmagazine.co.uk/politics/39298/the-supreme-court-has-done-lasting-damage-to-our-constitution.

[38] Lord Reed of Allermuir (n 3).

its President: to be unshowy, to be cautious and quietly conservative, keen to avoid any suggestion of radicalism, happy to avoid attention, trusted not to unsettle the status quo, content to be thought 'mostly harmless'. He says this:

> It is worrying that there should be distrust of the courts, and it underlines the need for the courts to do what they can to build greater trust. But we should not deceive ourselves into thinking that the reasons for the distrust have nothing to do with the courts. Cases in which, for example, judges have said that they might disapply an Act of Parliament which they regarded as contrary to the rule of law, or in which they have interpreted ouster clauses so narrowly as to render them ineffective, have left a legacy. The courts' approach in recent years has been more attentive to the separation of powers; but the more ambitious decisions and dicta of the past have not been forgotten.[39]

By whom are these decisions and dicta 'not forgotten'? By the court? By its critics? Or by both? And just what does this 'not forgetting' mean for future judicial action? These questions are all left there studiously unanswered. Lord Hodge said that that he and Lord Reed 'have sought to address this perception by the Executive and supporters of the Executive that somehow the court has become more activist'.[40] And Lord Reed appears to see his primary mission as the first post-Brexit President of the UKSC to persuade the UK Government and Westminster Parliamentarians that, their having 'taken back control' from the EU, there is now nothing to fear from the Court and that instead they can have 'confidence that we are a body that knows what the constitutional boundaries are and respects them in practice'[41] All this is said against a background that Lord Reed was named as the co-author (with Baroness Hale) of the unanimous decision of the 11 judge UKSC bench (which also included Lord Hodge) in the prorogation case *Cherry v Advocate General for Scotland /R (Miller) v Prime Minister*

It seems that this means that Whitehall (or perhaps just Downing Street) has to be reassured that the Court is now 'more executive minded than the executive'[42] such that ministerial decisions will be deferred to even in the face of evidence of their severe adverse impact on individual cases.[43]

[39] ibid.

[40] See Lord Hodge's response to Question 8 (n 13).

[41] See Lord Reed's response to Question 4 (n 13).

[42] See *Liversidge v Anderson* [1942] AC 206 per Lord Atkin (dissenting) at 244: 'I view with apprehension the attitude of judges who on a mere question of construction when face to face with claims involving the liberty of the subject show themselves more executive minded than the executive.'

[43] See for example the following cases. *R (O (A Child)) v Secretary of State for the Home Department* [2022] UKSC 3 where the court rejected a challenge to the lawfulness of a Home Office scheme of charging fees for citizenship applications at a level (£1,012 per child) which the court was constrained to accept was set at a wholly unaffordable level for many children and their families (thereby effectively preventing them from taking out British citizenship). *R (Begum) v SIAC* [2021] UKSC 7, [2021] AC 765 where the court overturned the Court of Appeal's order that Shamima Begum be given permission to re-enter the UK from Al-Hawi Internally Displaced Persons Camp in Syria in order to contest the decision to deprive her of British citizenship made by the then Home Secretary, Sajid Javid. *Shvidler v Secretary of State for Foreign, Commonwealth and Development Affairs* [2025] UKSC 30, [2025] 3 WLR 346 where the Court upheld the lawfulness of an assets freeze imposed on a UK citizen under the Russia (Sanctions) (EU Exit) Regulations 2019 notwithstanding (in the words of Lord Leggatt dissenting at

And that Westminster Parliamentarians receive assurances that no Westminster legislation will ever be subject to 'judicial condemnation if it fails to meet a legal standard embodying international obligations to which Parliament has not chosen to give domestic legal effect' so as not to 'impose pressure on Parliament to avoid the opprobrium which such a finding would entail'.[44]

And that both Whitehall and Westminster are to be given the comfort to know that that it is unconstitutional for lawyers to seek to rely on international law in the domestic forum as if it imposed obligations, when it only gives voice to aspirations.[45] Lord Reed explained the decision in *R (SC) v Work and Pensions Secretary*[46] (rejecting a challenge to the two-child benefit cap):

> In that case, where there was a conflict between an Act of Parliament dealing with social security and a UN convention [on the Rights of the Child] that Parliament had not implemented, it was pretty obvious which one trumped the other. We have made that clear now in a way that it was not previously clear. It had been rather muddied by some previous judgments in our court. That has been clarified, and lower courts now know where they are.[47]

14.5 Trusting Women

Yet surely if the UKSC is really to be *trusted* – not just by the UK Government and Westminster Parliamentarians, but in society at large – and for its own continued credibility and relevance, not least among women, and for justice to be *seen* to be done – the number of women Justices on this now highly visible and newly exposed UKSC has to reach, at least, parity with men.[48] For as a pre-Brexit UKSC recognised in *R (C) v Secretary of State for Work and Pensions*:

> 'We lead women's lives: we have no choice'. Thus has the Chief Justice of Canada, the Rt Hon Beverley McLachlin, summed up the basic truth that women and men do indeed lead different lives.
>
> How much of this is down to unquestionable biological differences, how much to social conditioning, and how much to other people's views of what it means to be a woman

[324]) 'the devastating effect on Mr Shvidler and his family of depriving him, indefinitely, of access to his own funds and other economic resources on a worldwide basis except to such minimal extent as the Government allows' such as to 'strike at the very heart of his right to live his own life as he chooses'.

[44] See *Re UNCRC (Incorporation) (Scotland) Bill* [2021] UKSC 42, [2021] 1 WLR 5106, 2022 SC (UKSC) 1 per Lord Reed at [52].

[45] *R (SC) v Work and Pensions Secretary* [2021] UKSC 26, [2022] AC 223 per Lord Reed at [91] *et passim*

[46] [2021] UKSC 26, [2022] 2 AC.

[47] See Lord Reed's response to Question 9 (n 13).

[48] See the former Deputy President of the UK Supreme Court, Lord Hope of Craighead's Question 11 to Lord Reid (n 13). Lord Hope had said: 'I will come on to diversity. At the moment, the court has only one lady sitting in the court, whereas some years ago there were three, so it looks as though you are moving backwards.'

> or a man, is all debatable and the accepted wisdom is perpetually changing. But what does not change is the importance, even the centrality, of gender in any individual's sense of self.
>
> Over the centuries many people, but particularly women, have bitterly resented and fought against the roles which society has assigned to their gender.
>
> Genuine equality between the sexes is still a work in progress.[49]

In 2001 when giving the annual Mario G Olmos Law and Cultural Diversity Lecture at UC-Berkeley, Sonia Sotomayor, now a Justice of the US Supreme Court, made the following observation:

> I would hope that a wise Latina woman – with the richness of *her* experiences – would, more often than not, reach a better conclusion than a white male who hasn't lived that life.

In 2003, the then Chief Justice of Canada, Beverley McLachlin, put matters this way:

> The … most important reason why I believe we need women on our Benches is because we need the perspectives that women can bring to judging.
>
> …
>
> [J]urists are human beings, and, as such, are informed and influenced by their backgrounds, communities, and experiences.
>
> For cultural, biological, social and historic reasons, women do have different experiences than men.[50]

The main problem with the current appointments system which gives the current President of the UKSC such power over who else gets to sit on the UKSC is that it doesn't appear to be great in tackling that issue of ensuring diversity, in particular, the proper number of women as Justices of the UKSC. And this is despite the fact that section 27(5A)(b) of the Constitutional Reform Act 2005 provides in effect that where two candidates to be a UKSC Justice are found to be 'of equal merit' it is open to the Selection Commission, if it wishes, to prefer one of them over the other 'for the purpose of increasing diversity within the group of persons who are the judges of the Court'.

For a period – while Lord Reed was *Deputy* President of the Supreme Court – three of the full complement of 12 Justices of the Supreme Court were women: Baroness Hale, Lady Arden, and Lady Black. Baroness Hale resigned in January

[49] *R(C) v Secretary of State for Work and Pensions* [2017] UKSC 72, [2017] PTSR 1476, Baroness Hale delivering judgment in that case on behalf of a unanimous court (Baroness Hale of Richmond PSC, Lord Kerr of Tonaghmore, Lord Wilson, Lord Carnwath, Lord Hughes JJSC) at [1].

[50] Rt Hon Beverley McLachlin PC, Chief Justice of Canada, in prepared remarks to the Association of Women Barristers in a seminar at the House of Commons in London on 2 July 2003, quoted in Baroness Hale, 'Law Maker or Law Reformer: What is a Law Lady for?' (2005) 40 *Irish Jurist* 1, 1.

2020, Lady Black resigned in January 2021, and Lady Arden resigned in January 2022. This meant that for almost two years under Robert Reed's Presidency – from January 2022 until November 2023 – there was only one women Justice, Lady Rose (who had been appointed in April 2021). The problem of the fact of under-representation of women in and before the UKSC was abundantly clear in the hearing before the UKSC in the appeal in *For Women Scotland v Scottish Ministers (No 2)*[51] where before a majority male bench (Lord Reed of Allermuir, Lord Hodge, Lord Lloyd-Jones, Lady Rose of Colmworth and Lady Simler) the Court was addressed, in the main, by male counsel (reader, *je m'accuse* – only the Scottish Ministers had women counsel speaking on their behalf) on the legal issue of just who is to be considered a 'woman' for the purposes of the Equality Act 2010.

Yet when asked by the House of Lords Constitution Committee to explain this under-representation of women as Justices of the UKSC, Lord Reed said there was a dearth of applications from suitably qualified women and stated that, for some otherwise eligible women, there was:

> [A] reluctance to do the kind of work that the Supreme Court does. It is a very intellectual place. It is also a place where you have to do everything but some things more than others. You particularly do commercial law and the sort of work I have been describing.
>
> We do hardly any family law, which is an area where women have historically specialised. We do not do very much medical negligence or the like, which is another area where women have tended to work. We do not have very much crime in the Supreme Court, although there is crime in the Privy Council; again, that is an area where you tend to find that women have experience. … Not everybody is keen to do even more work, perhaps especially women who are of a certain age and have family responsibilities and so on.[52]

Returning to this theme the following year, Lord Reed said this to the Committee:

> If you have devoted your life to family law, for example, and that is what you want to do and find fulfilling, the Supreme Court is not for you; because we have maybe one case a year to do with family law.[53]

Perhaps, in all of this, it is best to leave the last word to Lord Reed's immediate predecessor as President of the UKSC, Baroness Hale, who, prior to her appointment to the bench, had a long and distinguished career as an academic and law commissioner specialising in family law.[54] Speaking extra-judicially in 2005 (in a talk subsequently published – appropriately enough, in this commemoration of Conor Gearty's work – in the *Irish Jurist*) she said this: 'One man's common sense is another woman's hopeless idiocy.'[55]

[51] [2025] UKSC 16, [2025] ICR 899.
[52] See Lord Reed's response to Question 11 (n 13).
[53] See Lord Reed's response to Question 15 in the Oral evidence to the House of Lords Constitution Committee's Annual evidence session with the President and Deputy President of the Supreme Court on Tuesday 4 July 2023: committees.parliament.uk/oralevidence/13449/pdf.
[54] See Lady Hale's profile on the Supreme Court's website: https://supremecourt.uk/justices/lady-hale-of-richmond-dbe.
[55] Hale (n 47) 4.

PART V

Designing Constitutions

15

The Pitfalls of Constitution Writing

GISELA STUART AND MATTHEW LLOYD

15.1 Introduction

This chapter is not the work of constitutional lawyers or historians, but of Gisela Stuart, a politician with over 30 years' experience in British and European politics, and Matthew Lloyd, who is a political science academic at Queen Mary University of London with a background in political practice. In 2002, the Labour MP Gisela Stuart became a member of the Presidium of the European Convention on the Future of Europe, representing the UK and parliamentarians. In the summer of 2003, the Convention produced A draft Treaty establishing a Constitution for Europe. The document was signed in Rome in 2004, but ultimately failed to be ratified by Member States. Those who drafted the document were more concerned with institutional self-interest than democratic accountability. As Gisela Stuart reflected in her 2003 Fabian Pamphlet, 'The Making of Europe's Constitution': The constitutional writing process needed to be 'more in tune with the aspirations of Europe's peoples and less designed to meet the inclinations and ambitions of its bureaucrats and politicians'.[1] Much of the draft was later incorporated into the Lisbon Treaty of 2007, which entered into force in 2009, before the UK formally left the EU in 2020.

Some of the seeds for the EU referendum in 2016 and the UK's decision to leave were sown in that period. Supranational institutions provide protection for smaller countries, fix broken states or create enduring interdependencies. The UK had a constitutional settlement that had been incrementally developed and refined over centuries and was deeply rooted in our collective understanding. The UK did not feel the need to hand over power to fix a problem.

Westminster strengthened the political identity of Scotland by re-establishing a Scottish Parliament in Holyrood in 1999. In Wales, the National Assembly, established in 1998, became the Senedd (Welsh Parliament) in 2020. The Northern Ireland Assembly was created in 1998, after the Belfast Agreement. Apart from the short-lived English Votes for English Laws (EVEL) experiment, there were no provisions for a distinct voice for England. The public space for a call for an English Parliament has, in the past, been claimed by those to the right of mainstream British politics.

[1] G Stuart, 'The Making of Europe's Constitution' (Fabian Society, 1 December 2003), https://fabians.org.uk/publication/the-making-of-europes-constitution.

Failure to seek ratification from the people on changes to EU governance and a failure to provide a meaningful political voice for England in British politics provided the dual constitutional failure of Westminster that contributed to the charge that 'Brexit was made in England'.[2] Constitutional reform must be rooted in purpose, shaped by consensus and attentive to democratic norms. Reform should modernise, but not disrupt; and strengthen trust rather than deepen division. While the temptation to legislate for short-term political advantage is strong, successful reform resists that pull. The creation of the Supreme Court in 2009 showed how change can respect tradition while looking forward.[3] Yet other efforts, from the Fixed-term Parliaments Act 2011 to the Brexit referendum, reveal what happens when reforms are rushed, ill-framed or driven by party political considerations.

The UK constitution is not a single rulebook, but a compact between the governed and those who govern. Reform must be careful and enabling, grounded in judgement and humility. Technical changes are never just technical; they carry political meaning and consequence. Constitutional reform is never neutral. At its best, it is an art that deepens legitimacy. When in doubt, it should always err in favour of the people.

This chapter argues that constitutional reform is most likely to succeed when it emerges from the demands of the people rather than being imposed by political elites. Devolution settlements written from the top down, at the wrong time or for the wrong reasons are doomed to fail. In the UK, we have seen poorly timed reforms that lacked popular support and delivered unintended adverse consequences. Constitutional change must be rooted in context. A constitution reflects not just institutional design, but also the political culture, history, and constraints of the time. No model can be transplanted or applied in isolation from these wider forces. The final argument is one of patience. Uncodified systems, like the UK's, allow for adaptation over time. In constitutional politics, the art lies not in a single act, but in the slow embedding of consent.

15.1.1 The EU Constitution that Never Was

In the Laeken Declaration of 2001,[4] the EU committed itself to bringing its institutions closer to the people by being more transparent and efficient. The Convention on the Future of Europe,[5] led by the former French President Valery Giscard

[2] B Wellings, 'Brexit and English Identity' in P Diamond, P Nedergaard and B Rosamond (eds), *The Routledge Handbook of the Politics of Brexit* (Routledge, 2018), https://research.monash.edu/en/publications/brexit-and-english-identity.

[3] Constitutional Reform Act 2005.

[4] Office for Official Publications of the European Communities, 'Laeken Declaration on the Future of the European Union' (15 December 2001), www.cvce.eu/en/obj/laeken_declaration_on_the_future_of_the_european_union_15_december_2001-en-a76801d5-4bf0-4483-9000-e6df94b07a55.html.

[5] V Giscard d'Estaing, 'The Convention and the Future of Europe: Issues and Goals' (2003) 1 *International Journal of Constitutional Law* 346.

D'Estaing, brought together parliamentarians and government representatives from the existing Member States, as well as those who had applied to join, including Turkey.

Giscard d'Estaing early on identified three key elements necessary to create a successful and enduring constitutional settlement:

(1) The Union required its own resources. Rather than regular painful budget negotiations, there should be a stream of income that, as a matter of course, flows to the Union's institutions. Member States would have to cede budgetary control over a particular tax stream.
(2) The political leadership of the Union, the Commission, should have no more than 15 members. Existing arrangements provided for every Member State, however large or small, to nominate one Commissioner. Some countries would have to give up the permanent right to have a Commissioner.
(3) This would be the last time that any treaty changes would be subject to a ratification process in every single Member State. Future changes should be ratified by convening a 'People's Congress', where representatives from all parliaments and governments give legal effect to the changes. This would have removed the veto of national parliaments.

None of these key elements were contained in the Draft European Constitution.[6] Reflecting on what went wrong for the EU provides valuable pointers for any constitution drafter. Democratic institutions require a *demos*. And even if there is no distinct *demos* at the outset, there needs to be structures to develop one. Elections to the European Parliament have national political parties on the ballot paper. There are political groupings at EU level, but they are a means of caucusing, rather than voter representation. Ultimately, pan-European political parties are required, or at a minimum level, naming their preferred candidate as Commissioner should their party win a majority. None of this was attempted. Instead, the creation of a single currency was hoped to establish irrevocable interdependencies in order to build a common European identity.[7] The EU has struggled to achieve this so far. Indeed, the Euro Crisis[8] that began in 2009 created hostility as 'core' states such as Germany felt they were bailing out profligate 'peripheral' states such as Greece, whilst parts of Greek society blamed states such as Germany for the austerity measures imposed upon their country.[9] As a result, the EU has struggled to establish a sense of

[6] Treaty Establishing a Constitution for Europe, https://eur-lex.europa.eu/legal-content/EN/TXT/?uri=oj:JOC_2004_310_R_TOC.

[7] M Ovidiu Cercel, 'The Role of the Euro in Strengthening the European Identity' (2023) 17 *Europolity - Continuity and Change in European Governance* 5.

[8] CFI Team, 'European Sovereign Debt Crisis' (Corporate Finance Institute, no date), https://corporatefinanceinstitute.com/resources/fixed-income/european-sovereign-debt-crisis.

[9] J Coleman, 'Greek Debt Crisis Triggers Memories of World War Two' BBC News (9 July 2015), www.bbc.com/news/blogs-eu-33467931.

demos,[10] shared identity[11] and united pro-EU civic society[12] that stretches across Member States.

The Laeken Declaration of 2001, committing to greater democracy, transparency and efficiency, was not the result of popular demand. It reflected a deep concern about low voter turnout in elections to the European Parliament, as well as frustration over decision-making processes in the institutions of the EU. Qualified majority decision-making had to be increased, the use of the veto by Member States reduced to a minimum, and the organisation representing Member States required more strategic leadership. All of these things in themselves are institutionally important, but it can hardly be claimed that the President of the Council was created in response to popular demand. However, a valid case could be made for the Commission President to be elected by voters across the Union.

In the 2005 UK general election, all three main political parties promised in their manifestos a referendum on the Constitutional Treaty. Such a referendum would have offered the voters a clear choice - continue with the existing arrangements or give consent to the constitutional changes enshrined in the new treaty. All three political parties reneged on their promise.

15.1.2 The Key Arguments

Constitutional changes should benefit the 'people', rather than the institutions. They should not be imposed 'top down' and they rarely succeed if they are merely the response to a current crisis.

A nation's constitution can only be understood by looking at its evolution in a historic context. There is no perfect model, and alternative structures of governance or voting systems will be key considerations for constitutional changes. A state's history, geography, ideology, institutions, political context and statehood all contribute to a particular constitutional settlement. A variety of arrangements emerge from different states and at different times. There will always be political, economic and societal factors and constraints. Constitutions do not exist in a vacuum, and we can only appreciate the different political trade-offs and compromises in the context of the political art of the 'possible'.

Lastly, assessing success requires the passage of time. Constitutions and any changes should rarely be seen as a 'big bang' political task, but aim to enshrine enduring values which are adapted to the needs and circumstances of the moment. The UK's uncodified constitution is inherently more flexible and allows for a more pragmatic and incremental approach. It is possible to impose time limits –

[10] M Jolly, 'A Demos for the European Union?' (2005) 25 *Politics* 12.

[11] D Lichtenstein and C Eilders, 'Lost in Uncertainty: How the Euro Crisis Affected European Identity Constructions in National Media Discourses' (2019) 81 *International Communication Gazette* 602.

[12] J Fitzgibbon, 'Citizens against Europe? Civil Society and Eurosceptic Protest in Ireland, the United Kingdom and Denmark' (2013) 51 *Journal of Common Market Studies* 105.

so-called sunset clauses – or require regular review or renewal of specific constitutional provisions. In 2015, a Standing Order of the House of Commons introduced a process of reserving the right to vote on English legislation to English MPs. The Standing Order was removed by a decision of the House of Commons in 2021. EVEL[13] serves to illustrate the ability to trial a constitutional change and allows the elected politicians of the day to decide whether to continue, adapt or abandon a particular proposal. Success is not restricted to embedding a change; not proceeding is an equally valid outcome.

15.2 A Very British Constitution

The UK's uncodified constitution, its norms and conventions, reflect Britain's history and pragmatic approach to politics. This strategy has been referred to as Britain 'Muddling Through'.[14] In the absence of clear legal rules, it relies on a shared understanding of what constitutes good behaviour in public and political life, the 'good chaps'[15] theory of the UK Government. From Henry VIII to Oliver Cromwell, from the Glorious Revolution to the Supreme Court's ruling on the lawfulness of the Prorogation of Parliament in 2019,[16] the UK has a long and proud history of pragmatic adaptability. Bogdanor[17] describes how Britain's uncodified constitution relies on statutes, parliamentary conventions, common law and works of authority rather than a single written document, as is the case in most modern democracies, most prominently the USA. The UK is an island nation with clearly defined borders, has not experienced a major land invasion for 1,000 years, or the complete failure of the nation-state, and was thus able to establish a long tradition of democracy. History sets it apart from mainland Europe. The flexibility to gradually evolve in a contemporary setting is probably best illustrated by Westminster's changing relationship with the four nations.

15.2.1 The Quest for English Devolution

'Who speaks for England?' remains an unanswered question. The Scottish Parliament was re-established in 1999, the Welsh Assembly was created in 1998, and in 2020 became the Senedd Cymru (the Welsh Parliament), and the Northern

[13] R Kelly, 'English Votes for English Laws' (House of Commons Library, 2025), https://commonslibrary.parliament.uk/research-briefings/cbp-7339.

[14] D Weldon, *Two Hundred Years of Muddling Through: The Surprising Story of Britain's Economy from Boom to Bust and Back Again* (Abacus, 2022).

[15] A Blick and P Hennessy, 'Good Chaps No More? Safeguarding the Constitution in Stressful Times' (The Constitution Society, 2019), https://consoc.org.uk/publications/good-chaps-no-more-safeguarding-the-constitution-in-stressful-times-by-andrew-blick-and-peter-hennessy.

[16] *R (on the application of Miller) v The Prime Minister* [2019] UKSC 41.

[17] V Bogdanor, *The New British Constitution* (Hart Publishing, 2009).

Ireland Assembly was established in 1998. Wales, Scotland and Northern Ireland have political identities that have become established within mainstream British politics. A distinct English identity has long been viewed with suspicion, as something owned and shaped by right-wing nationalist groups. And yet, there is consistent support for an English Parliament. In 2007, 61 per cent of English voters believed that there should be an English Parliament.[18] In 2021, 62 per cent of those who identified as English supported the forming of an English Parliament.[19] Westminster legislates for the whole of the UK. Scottish, Welsh and Northern Irish MPs have a vote even if the legislation only applies to England. What has become known as The West Lothian Question can only be answered by either creating new institutions for England or by making changes at Westminster.

The Greater London devolution referendum in 1998 gave London as the capital city a directly elected mayor and an assembly. Similar proposals by the New Labour Government for English regional assemblies failed. The initial referendum in the North East was rejected by more than three quarters of the voters.[20] The 2010 Coalition Government agreement included the creation of directly elected Police and Crime Commissioners[21] and referendums for directly elected regional mayors.[22] For Police and Crime Commissioners, the turnout in elections was low with little apparent support from the public.[23] The Coalition introduced a regional mayor in areas such as Greater Manchester even after the idea was rejected in a referendum.[24] The changes to the institutional arrangements for England were patchy and piecemeal.

The Government of David Cameron approached The West Lothian Question by bringing about changes to parliamentary procedures. New Standing Orders in the House of Commons in 2015 were designed to ensure that legislation that affected only England, or England and Wales, was approved by a majority of MPs representing English constituencies. Administratively, EVEL could be made to work, but it created a de facto two-tier system of MPs in Parliament. The system did not command much support or respect, arguably hastening a potential break-up of the UK, and it came to an end in 2021 when the Standing Order was not renewed.[25]

[18] BBC, 'Newsnight Poll on the Union' Press release (16 January 2007), www.bbc.com/pressoffice/pressreleases/stories/2007/01_january/16/union.shtml.

[19] Nation Cymru, '"Labour Should Appeal to English Identifiers" as Poll Shows 62% Would Vote for English Parliament' (1 October 2021), https://nation.cymru/news/labour-should-appeal-to-english-identifiers-as-poll-shows-62-would-vote-for-english-parliament.

[20] BBC News, 'Why Did the North East Shun Regional Assembly?' (8 November 2004), http://news.bbc.co.uk/1/hi/talking_point/3984991.stm.

[21] UK Government, 'Police and Crime Commissioners', www.gov.uk/police-and-crime-commissioners.

[22] M Sandford, 'Directly-Elected Mayors' (House of Commons Library, 2025), https://commonslibrary.parliament.uk/research-briefings/sn05000.

[23] R Garside, 'The End of an Undemocratic Experiment?' (Centre for Crime and Justice Studies, 27 November 2013), www.crimeandjustice.org.uk/end-undemocratic-experiment.

[24] BBC News, 'George Osborne: Greater Manchester to Have Elected Mayor' (3 November 2014), www.bbc.com/news/uk-england-manchester-29876939.

[25] Kelly (n 13).

Under the 2010 Coalition Government, a number of regional mayors were foisted on English regions even when some of the cities within those regions, such as Manchester and Birmingham, had rejected the idea of directly elected mayors in local referendums.[26] This was a significant intervention by Westminster to enforce top-down devolution on the regions of England. However, some regional mayors such as Manchester's[27] 'King of the North',[28] Andy Burnham, do seem to have become more established and high profile[29] than other regional mayors.[30] During the COVID-19 pandemic lockdowns, these regional leaders and local authorities played a significant role in coordinating local response efforts.[31] Richards et al[32] highlights how the top-down approach of English devolution left regional mayors arguing against the Treasury during COVID-19. The authors concluded that further devolution to regional mayors is needed. Andy Burnham continues to use his voice during the COVID-19 public inquiry to criticise what he viewed as the 'London-centric' COVID-19 response.[33] This exposed some of the weaknesses in Westminster's top-down devolution policy for England.

At the time of writing, Starmer's Labour Government has brought forward its 2025 White Paper on English Devolution[34] that marks a significant change of approach to English devolution and would end the bespoke 'deal-by-deal'[35] mayoral devolution policy started under the 2010 Coalition Government. It would give greater powers to regional mayors in policy areas such as housing and development, health and wellbeing, public service reform, and skills and employment. A new system of integrated settlements would give mayoral combined authorities greater control over multi-year funding across key policy areas like transport,

[26] Lords Select Committee, 'House of Lords - The Union and Devolution - Select Committee on the Constitution' (House of Lords, 2016) HL Paper 149, https://publications.parliament.uk/pa/ld201516/ldselect/ldconst/149/14911.htm.

[27] A Paun et al, 'Mayor of Greater Manchester' (Institute for Government, 4 May 2024), www.instituteforgovernment.org.uk/explainer/mayor-greater-manchester.

[28] A Nurse, 'Andy Burnham's Standoff with London Was Always about More than Just Lockdown Money' (University of Liverpool, 23 October 2020), https://news.liverpool.ac.uk/2020/10/23/andy-burnhams-standoff-with-london-was-always-about-more-than-just-lockdown-money.

[29] IPSOS, 'Andy Burnham More Popular in Manchester than Sadiq Khan in London or Andy Street in West Midlands' (30 April 2024), www.ipsos.com/en-uk/andy-burnham-more-popular-in-manchester-than-sadiq-khan-in-london-or-andy-street-in-west-midlands.

[30] B Allen and S Routley, 'Regional Mayors' (Institute for Government, 4 September 2024), www.instituteforgovernment.org.uk/explainer/regional-mayors-devolution.

[31] R Machin, 'UK Local Government Experience of COVID-19 Lockdown: Local Responses to Global Challenges' (2023) 38 *Local Economy* 80.

[32] S Warner et al, 'English Devolution and the Covid-19 Pandemic: Governing Dilemmas in the Shadow of the Treasury' (2021) 92 *The Political Quarterly* 321.

[33] P Walker, 'UK Covid Response Was London-Centric, Andy Burnham Tells Inquiry' *The Guardian* (27 November 2023), www.theguardian.com/uk-news/2023/nov/27/uk-covid-response-was-london-centric-andy-burnham-tells-inquiry.

[34] UK Government, 'English Devolution and Community Empowerment Bill: Guidance' (10 July 2025), www.gov.uk/government/publications/english-devolution-and-community-empowerment-bill-guidance/english-devolution-and-community-empowerment-bill-guidance.

[35] M Sandford and N Dempsey, 'Metro-Mayors and Devolution Deals' (House of Commons Library, 2017), https://commonslibrary.parliament.uk/metro-mayors-and-devolution-deals.

skills and regeneration. Instead of bidding into fragmented pots, high-performing authorities receive a single settlement with outcomes-based accountability. This approach deepens local autonomy, but still retains the Treasury's ultimate oversight through performance frameworks and eligibility criteria.

The Government's radical plans to simplify England's tiers of local government[36] represents one of the biggest overhauls[37] in local government organisation in the post-war era. The White Paper encourages the creation of unitary councils that merge district and county functions with the aim of simplifying governance, reducing duplication and improving accountability. Iversen and Soskice argue that regional mayors can provide key spokespeople to lobby for the economic needs of their designated region and that can contribute to the generation of growth and prosperity.[38] Local leaders, opposition parties and the District Councils' Network (DCN)[39] have voiced concern at the Government's proposals, arguing there is no clear evidence that such reorganisations deliver better outcomes, and that they risk eroding local identity. The White Paper does give a coherent political structure to the patchwork of English devolution initiatives, but still falls short of providing a distinct 'voice for England' analogous to an English Parliament.

15.2.2 Reflections on the British Case

Constitutions are a living thing, and every generation of elected politicians embarks on bringing about some changes to our constitutional arrangements. As they embark on the task, they may want to reflect on the successes and failures of the recent past. Demands for change should come from the electorate and be for their benefit if they are to stand a chance of becoming embedded in domestic political structures. There was a clear demand for devolution to Scotland and Wales, and both the Scottish and Welsh Parliaments are now well established within the British political-economic structures. They are legitimate political bodies that represent the demos of their respective nations.[40] Finding a voice for England remains a

[36] A Paun et al, 'Nine Things We Learned from the English Devolution White Paper' (Institute for Government, 17 December 2024), www.instituteforgovernment.org.uk/comment/english-devolution-white-paper.

[37] J Newman, 'English Councils and Planning Set to Be Transformed under Ambitious Devolution Plan – an Expert Explains' (The Conversation, 17 December 2024), <http://theconversation.com/english-councils-and-planning-set-to-be-transformed-under-ambitious-devolution-plan-an-expert-explains-246163.

[38] T Iversen and D Soskice, Democracy and Prosperity: Reinventing Capitalism through a Turbulent Century (Princeton University Press 2019) <https://www.jstor.org/stable/j.ctv4g1r3n> accessed 31 July 2025.

[39] DNC, 'No Evidence Exists to Support Mega Councils, Government Admits' (District Councils' Network, 31 January 2025), www.districtcouncils.info/no-evidence-exists-to-support-mega-councils-government-admits.

[40] D Difford, 'Where Do Scotland and Wales Stand on Devolution?' (YouGov UK, 17 September 2024), https://yougov.co.uk/politics/articles/50542-where-do-scotland-and-wales-stand-on-devolution.

work in progress. The answer can be found in either more regional devolution or a radical move to a more federal structure for the UK.

After the 2014 Scottish Referendum, the Constitution Reform Group (CRG) – a group of politicians and constitutional, legal and public finance experts – produced a fully worked out bill called The Act of Union Bill.[41] One of the authors of this chapter, Gisela Stuart, was a member of the steering group. Rather than devolving powers from the centre, the four parts of the UK would agree on the powers they needed to serve their citizens best. It included options to replace the House of Lords with a National Parliament; to establish an English Parliament; and the creation of a UK Central Bank to replace the Bank of England. The proposals would be subject to a post-legislative referendum. After enactment, a majority of 65 per cent of total votes cast, and a majority of votes cast in England, in Scotland, in Wales and in Northern Ireland, would be required to bring the new arrangements into effect. The Act of Union Bill was introduced as a Private Member's Bill in October 2018, but never progressed beyond the First Reading.[42] Brexit and COVID-19 shifted political attention to other, more urgent matters. The moment for radical changes designed to keep the UK together had passed.

Enduring constitutions involve checks and balances, and can provide stability and resilience, but they cannot prevent power struggles when the country is divided.

The Fixed-term Parliaments Act 2011,[43] introduced as part of the Coalition Government, and promoted by the Liberal Democrats, removed the right of a prime minister to seek the dissolution of Parliament for pure political gain. In the short term, it was intended to hold the coalition together, as noted by the evidence gathered by the Public Administration and Constitutional Affairs Committee.[44] In the long term, it was expected to bring greater stability to the political system. It also constrained the options of prime ministers who had lost the confidence of the House, but did not have enough votes to reach the two-thirds majority needed to trigger a general election. Norton set out this concern in 2016.[45] In the latter half of 2019 Prime Minister Johnson attempted three times to trigger a general election[46] to break the parliamentary deadlock over the Brexit withdrawal agreement. Despite the Prime Minister calling for the end of his Government and for judgement to be handed to the electorate in an early general election, he could

[41] Constitution Reform Group and Lord Lisvane, Act of Union Bill 2018.

[42] C Coleman, 'Case for a Referendum on the Outcome of EU Withdrawal Negotiations' (House of Lords, 2025), https://lordslibrary.parliament.uk/research-briefings/lln-2018-0107.

[43] N Clegg et al, Fixed-term Parliaments Act 2011 [Bill 64-EN].

[44] Public Administration and Constitutional Affairs Committee, 'The Fixed-Term Parliaments Act 2011' (House of Commons, 2020), https://publications.parliament.uk/pa/cm5801/cmselect/cmpubadm/167/16702.htm.

[45] P Norton, 'The Fixed-term Parliaments Act and Votes of Confidence' (2016) 69 *Parliamentary Affairs* 3.

[46] R Mason, 'Boris Johnson Fails in Third Attempt to Call Early General Election' *The Guardian* (28 October 2019), www.theguardian.com/politics/2019/oct/28/boris-johnson-third-attempt-general-election-fails.

not command a two-thirds majority as opposition parties refused to support the motion. The Fixed-term Parliaments Act 2011 was repealed in March 2022.

15.3 Conclusions on Assessing Constitutions

There are clear lessons that can be drawn from the EU's attempt to establish a constitution and the UK's pragmatic approach to allow constitutional arrangements to evolve. Constitution writing is a strategic long game, and changes should not be used as a tactical response to short-term political challenges. It requires the passage of time before success or failure can be judged. Recent examples, which did not stand the test of time, included the Fixed-terms Parliaments Act 2011 and EVEL.

15.3.1 Lessons from History

Constitution writing is a long game, and any government attempting to enact constitutional change in order to solve short-term political challenges or attempting to remove uncertainty will likely result in failure. It takes time to assess whether constitutional change has been successful. Only over the long run can we judge if any unintended adverse consequences have emerged. We need to ask whether the new mechanism is working as intended. Can the constitution still be changed in an orderly way? Has the change been accepted by the *demos*? And has it lasted? Any deep-seated problems left unsolved in constitution writing can become institutionalised and generate political challenges for future governments. Schulchuck contends that the EU suffers from a 'democratic deficit' because the institutional structures of the organisation are undemocratic and that the foundations for democracy do not exist in the EU.[47] This challenge continued to create problems for the EU and contributed to Brexit as growing numbers of 'Constitutional Brexiteers' such as Gisela Stuart felt frustrated by this process.

The House of Lords Act 1999 removed the right of most, but not all, hereditary peers to sit and vote in the House of Lords. Phase one allowed 92 hereditary peers, on a temporary basis, to remain. After 2002, whenever a vacancy arose due to death or resignation, a by-election would take place. The electorate is mostly limited to hereditary peers, and candidates are drawn from a narrowly defined group. In 2003 Lord Grantchester was elected by three votes.[48] The general expectation was, even amongst those who brokered the compromise, that the system would not last

[47] T Shelchuk, 'The Problem of "Democratic Deficit" in the European Union' (2019) *Economics. Finances. Law* 11.

[48] UK Parliament, 'Results of Labour Hereditary Peers By-Election' Press release (27 March 2003), www.parliament.uk/mps-lords-and-offices/offices/lords/house-of-lords-external-communications/hoflpressnotice301003.

long. It was not until 2025 that the Labour Government introduced the House of Lords (Hereditary Peers) Bill.[49] The bill passed and the House of Lords (Hereditary Peers) Act 2026 finally removed the remaining connection between hereditary peerage and membership of the House of Lords. Constitutional changes take up time and space in a government's legislative programme, and as the benefits tend to take more than a single parliament to manifest themselves, it's not unusual for the reforming zeal to wane rapidly. Relying on a 'phase two' is a high-risk strategy.

15.3.2 Lessons from our American Cousins

The US Constitution has endured since it was ratified in 1788 and implemented in 1789. It is the oldest still-active written constitution in the world. It provided the legal and institutional framework to hold together 13 former colonies and turn them into a functioning post-colonial republic. That endurance, now over 230 years, shows how a foundational legal text can last when it is broad in scope and rooted in principle rather than overly detailed. The framers focused on structure, rights and the separation of powers. They left room for interpretation and evolution over time. The original document is just over 4,000 words long, yet it continues to provide the legal foundations for the most powerful country in the world. Its longevity lies partly in its ability to combine flexibility with stability and to support both national unity and the decentralised identity of its constituent states.

It has held together a large and diverse country across different geographies, economies and political traditions. It provided a framework for unity during the most extreme conflicts in US history, including the Civil War, the Civil Rights Movement and the Vietnam era. It has allowed liberal and conservative states, industrial and agricultural economies, and different racial and cultural communities to coexist within a single legal and political system. Through the balance of powers between Congress, the Executive and the judiciary, and through the federal structure that empowers state governments, it has supported political pluralism and compromise.[50] Despite serious crises and clear injustices, the institutions have adapted, survived and retained their legitimacy among most citizens.

The US Constitution is very difficult to amend. Since its ratification, only 27 amendments have passed. The most recent was in 1992. Critics argue that this rigidity has led to policy deadlock and legal obstacles, particularly around issues like gun control, voting rights and campaign finance.[51] Others, however, point to

[49] P McFadden, Baroness Smith of Basildon and Cabinet Office, House of Lords (Hereditary Peers) Bill - Parliamentary Bills - UK Parliament 2025 [Bill 295].

[50] J Toobin, 'Our Broken Constitution' *The New Yorker* (1 December 2013), www.newyorker.com/magazine/2013/12/09/our-broken-constitution.

[51] M Pengelly, 'Erwin Chemerinsky on the Need for a New US Constitution: "Our Democracy Is at Grave Risk"' *The Guardian* (1 September 2024), www.theguardian.com/books/article/2024/sep/01/erwin-chemerinsky-no-democracy-lasts-forever.

this difficulty as one of the reasons the Constitution has endured. The process of change is so demanding that no side of the political divide can easily dominate the other or rewrite the rules in their own interest. In this sense, the Constitution protects the long-term balance of power by forcing change to be cautious and deliberate.[52]

It remains to be seen how well the constitution and its institutions fare in the face of the challenges presented by President Donald Trump. His significant use of executive orders in his second term, without bringing about enduring legislative changes, combined with his reliance on unilateral actions, challenges the wisdom of a unitary Executive.[53] At the same time, his heavy use of executive orders creates the risk that a future president could undo Trump's policy legacy,[54] while constitutional institutions endure the immediate political turbulence, much as they did during his first term.[55] Whilst constitutional structures are important for enduring democracies, such as America, the political-economic context cannot be ignored. If critical actors in the Republican Party feel unable to repeat their role in defending democratic norms, as they did during Trump's first term, according to Levitsky and Ziblatt,[56] then these constitutional institutions face an even greater test of resilience in the second term.

15.3.3 Avoiding the Pitfalls of Constitution Writing

Opportunities to write a constitution for a new nation-state are rare. Invariably, it's a case of adapting an existing document, or set of constitutional arrangements, to meet a particular deep-rooted need or respond to significant changes in circumstances. Altering the constitution rarely provides a lasting solution to problems of a given moment. The promise of a referendum on the voting system and the passing of the Fixed-term Parliaments Act 2011, both springing from the coalition

[52] J Madison and A Hamilton, 'The Federalist No. 51', http://founders.archives.gov/documents/Hamilton/01-04-02-0199; J Madison and A Hamilton, 'The Federalist No. 62', https://founders.archives.gov/documents/Hamilton/01-04-02-0212; SM Griffin, 'Constituent Power and Constitutional Change in American Constitutionalism' in M Loughlin and N Walker (eds), *The Paradox of Constitutionalism: Constituent Power and Constitutional Form* (Oxford University Press, 2008), https://doi.org/10.1093/acprof:oso/9780199552207.003.0004; J Lepore, 'The United States' Unamendable Constitution' *The New Yorker* (26 October 2022), www.newyorker.com/culture/annals-of-inquiry/the-united-states-unamendable-constitution; R Albert, 'The World's Most Difficult Constitution to Amend?' (Social Science Research Network, 2022), https://papers.ssrn.com/abstract=4323143; R Albert, *Constitutional Amendments: Making, Breaking, and Changing Constitutions* (Oxford University Press, 2019).

[53] J Paschold and A Sparacino, 'The Pace of Trump's Executive Orders during His First 100 Days Is a Significant Departure from His Recent Predecessors' (London School of Economics, 13 May 2025), https://blogs.lse.ac.uk/usappblog/2025/05/13/the-pace-of-trumps-executive-orders-during-his-first-100-days-is-a-significant-departure-from-his-recent-predecessors.

[54] A Payne, 'Trump Is at the Peak of His Power—But It Won't Last' (City St George's University of London, 13 February 2025), www.citystgeorges.ac.uk/news-and-events/events/2024/october/panel-discussion-series-american-election-2024/trump-is-at-the-peak-of-his-powerbut-it-wont-last.

[55] S Levitsky and D Ziblatt, *How Democracies Die: What History Reveals about Our Future* (Penguin, 2019).

[56] ibid.

agreement in 2010,[57] are cases in point. Constitutional changes advocated or resisted for party political purposes carry particular risks. Individual voter registration was resisted by the Labour Party, preferring the traditional system of household registration. Individual voter registration was argued to disadvantage households where, for some members, English was not their first language. The Conservative Party is not in favour of reducing the voting age for general elections from 18 to 16 years, as there is a general assumption that the young are progressive and will favour centre-left parties.

There are times when making fundamental changes to the constitution are right and appropriate. Few would argue today against the move of the judicial functions of the House of Lords to the Supreme Court of the UK. By adapting to more contemporary practices, the institution retained its legitimacy. Other reforms of the House of Lords have been less successful. Effective constitutional changes require clarity of purpose and careful expert drafting. The Constitutional Reform and Governance Act 2010[58] introduced reforms, including putting the Civil Service Commission on a statutory basis. The legislation established clear boundaries whilst being enabling, something Gisela Stuart came to value greatly during her period as the First Civil Service Commissioner. In our representative parliamentary democracy, the parliament of the day has the right to decide, without binding their successors. Participatory democracy, in the form of a referendum, is an option and has been tried in various settings. The referendum on our continued membership of the EU, better known as 'the Brexit vote' in 2016, demonstrated the need for thoughtfully prepared options and a government willing and able to implement the outcome.

Constitutional reform is most likely to succeed when it is grounded in popular demand, rather than serving the interests of institutions or political elites. In the UK, attempts to impose top-down constitutional change have often backfired, leading to adverse unintended consequences. This chapter has argued that many reforms are pursued at the wrong moment or for short-term political reasons, rather than as part of a genuine process of national renewal. Understanding a constitution also means understanding its historical, cultural and political context. Each settlement reflects the constraints and trade-offs of its time. Reforms do not occur in a vacuum. Finally, the durability and legitimacy of constitutional change can only be judged over time. Change should not be viewed as a one-off event. Instead, it must be tested in practice, embedded in political life and accepted by citizens if it is to endure. A constitution reflects the balance of power between the people and those who govern. Constitution writing, like politics, is an art and not a science and if in doubt, it should always err in favour of the people!

A constitution is a nation's life story. And like life, to paraphrase Kierkegaard, it is not a problem to be solved; it can only be understood backwards and must be lived forwards.

[57] UK Government, 'The Coalition Documentation' (20 May 2010), www.gov.uk/government/publications/the-coalition-documentation.

[58] Jack Straw, Lord Bach and Ministry of Justice, Constitutional Reform and Governance Act 2010.

16

The Poison Pill in Commonwealth Caribbean Constitutions

RICHARD ALBERT

16.1 Introduction: British Entrenchment and Colonial Quasi-Independence

An extraordinary scene unfolds in *King Richard II*,[1] Shakespeare's dramatisation of the reign of Richard of Bordeaux, King of England from 1377 to 1399. In the play, the King makes a remarkable declaration. He renounces his throne and relinquishes all royal powers vested in him:

> I give this heavy weight from off my head,
> And this unwieldy sceptre from my hand,
> The pride of kingly sway from out my heart;
> With mine own tears I wash away my balm,
> With mine own hands I give away my crown.[2]

Rare is the monarch who voluntarily resigns his dominion over peoples and lands. This has proven true particularly for British sovereigns in relation to their colonial subjects. It took a bloody revolutionary war in the eighteenth century for the US to win independence from the empire of King George III. Two centuries later, as the new global model of lawful decolonial constitutionalism replaced revolutionary self-determination as the prevailing path toward decolonisation,[3] the UK continued to find great difficulty in fully ceding power to its former colonies – even as the UK agreed to colonial demands for constitutional independence.

When the UK and its colonies negotiated a peaceful path to independence, the new post-colonial constitutions commonly retained the British monarch as head of state, with day-to-day operations led by a local prime minister in the role of head of government. This arrangement is not unusual, nor unexpected, given that preserving a strong bond to the monarchy can bring the former colony stability, unity, and needed continuity on the heels of dramatic change to the status quo.[4]

[1] W Shakespeare, *King Richard II* (AW Verity ed, Cambridge University Press, 1899).
[2] ibid, IV.1.73.
[3] See R Albert, 'Decolonial Constitutionalism' (2025) 25 *Chicago Journal of International Law* 341, 345.
[4] See T Ginsburg et al, 'The Functions of Constitutional Monarchy: Why Kings and Queens Survive in a World of Republics' (2023) Northwestern Public Law Research Paper No 23–29, 18, 27, 36.

Like virtually every constitution enacted since 1789,[5] these post-colonial constitutions also codified a set of procedures for their own amendment. Yet there is something quite peculiar about the content and design of their amendment procedures: they contain a poison pill that makes it significantly more difficult ever to replace the British monarch with a locally chosen head of state.

In this chapter, I draw from my experience as a member of the 15-person Constitutional Reform Committee of Jamaica to illustrate the effects of the decolonial poison pill on the most recent effort to give the people of Jamaica a head of state of their own choosing instead of a foreign monarch.

16.2 The Design of Post-Colonial Commonwealth Caribbean Constitutions

A poison pill is a defensive tactic used by corporations to thwart a hostile takeover.[6] Innovated by Martin Lipton of the American corporate law firm Wachtell, Lipton, Rosen & Katz, a poison pill is a shareholder rights plan that makes it exceedingly costly and complex for a potential buyer to acquire a target company.[7] The poison pill is triggered when a potential buyer builds momentum toward seizing a majority of the target corporation stock. At that moment, existing shareholders are given special rights to protect their company.[8] These special rights, if exercised, increase the difficulty of completing the acquisition, and may ultimately discourage it. In the context of post-colonial constitutions, the poison pill is the higher degree of difficulty that applies to any effort to remove the British monarch as head of state, while most other constitutional reforms may be accomplished considerably more easily using one or more lower thresholds of approval.

16.2.1 An Escalating Structure of Constitutional Amendment Rules

Consider the Constitution of Canada, a former British colony whose post-colonial constitution retains the British monarch as head of state. The Constitution codifies an escalating structure of constitutional amendment difficulty consisting of five procedures of amendment, each one restricted in its application to specific parts or principles of the Constitution.[9] These five amendment procedures grow more onerous in the thresholds of legislative approval they require from provincial and

[5] See F Giovannoni, 'Amendment Rules in Constitutions' (2003) 115a *Public Choice* 37, 37.

[6] RS Ruback, 'An Overview of Takeover Defenses' in AJ Auerbach (ed), *Mergers and Acquisitions* (University of Chicago Press, 1987) 49, 58–60.

[7] See C de Kay Wilson, 'Marty Lipton's Poison Pill' (1984) 3 3 *International Financial Law Review* 10.

[8] See H Nixon and PC Shoback, 'The Reasonable Pill' (1989) 1 *DePaul Business Law Journal* 1, 1–5.

[9] Constitution Act 1982, ss 38–49 (Canada).

federal actors to enact a reform: from a simple provincial majority, to a simple parliamentary majority, to three configurations of federal-provincial majorities of increasing difficulty. This complex design makes the Canadian Constitution one of the world's most rigid.[10]

For instance, Parliament alone, by simple majority vote, may enact a constitutional reform to its own internal constitution,[11] for instance matters of legislative procedure and parliamentary privilege.[12] But matters deemed more important to the architecture of the Canadian Constitution are more strongly entrenched under higher thresholds of legislative approval. For example, in order to enact a reform to the more highly valued principle of proportional provincial representation in the House of Commons, the Constitution requires approval resolutions from both chambers of Parliament as well as approval resolutions from seven out of 10 provinces whose aggregate population amounts to at least half of the population of all provinces combined.[13]

Here is the poison pill in the Canadian Constitution: if Canadians one day wish to substitute the British monarch with a locally chosen head of state – and consequently to change the system of government from constitutional monarchy to parliamentary republic – constitutional actors will be legally required to do something unprecedented in the history of Canada: they will have to satisfy the most demanding of the five amendment procedures. This most onerous of all five amendment procedures requires the unanimous approval of Parliament in addition to approval resolutions from each of the 10 provincial assemblies.[14] Constitutional actors failed to complete the journey the only time they ventured into this gauntlet of pan-Canadian legislative coordination.[15]

16.2.2 The Prevalence of Poison Pills

Similar poison pills are codified in post-colonial Commonwealth Caribbean constitutions. There are currently eight Caribbean Commonwealth Realms for which King Charles III serves as head of state: Antigua and Barbuda; the

[10] See R Albert, 'The Difficulty of Constitutional Amendment in Canada' (2015) 53 *Alberta Law Review* 85.

[11] Constitution Act 1982, s 44.

[12] See I Greene, 'Constitutional Amendment in Canada and the United States' in SL Newman (ed), *Constitutional Politics in Canada and the United States* (State University of New York Press, 2004) 249, 251.

[13] Constitution Act 1982, s 42(1)(a).

[14] ibid, s 41(a). This procedure may have been informally amended to also require approval resolutions from the territories of Canada. See R Albert, 'The Theory and Doctrine of Unconstitutional Constitutional Amendment in Canada' (2016) 41 *Queen's Law Journal* 143, 202. It may have also been informally amended to require a national popular referendum. See R Albert, 'The Conventions of Constitutional Amendment in Canada' (2016) 53 *Osgoode Hall Law Journal* 399, 413–15.

[15] For an account of the dramatic failure of the Charlottetown Accord, see PH Russell, 'The End of Mega Constitutional Politics in Canada?' (1993) 26 *Political Science & Politics* 33. For an account of the larger history of constitutional reform failures in Canada, see PH Russell, *Constitutional Odyssey: Can Canadians Become a Sovereign People?*, 3rd edn (University of Toronto Press, 2004).

Bahamas; Belize; Grenada; Jamaica; Saint Kitts and Nevis; Saint Lucia; and Saint Vincent and the Grenadines. All eight countries have post-colonial independence constitutions that codify an escalating structure of constitutional amendment.[16] Each constitution codifies two or more amendment procedures, each one expressly designated for use in relation to specifically enumerated rules, principles, or parts of the constitution. What results from this escalating structure of constitutional amendment is a hierarchy of constitutional rigidity: some rules, principles, and parts of the constitution are more difficult to amend than others. Importantly, the choice of which amendment procedure applies to a particular rule, principle, or part of the constitution is not made at random. It is the product of careful aforethought and indeed negotiation by those around the constitution-making table at the enactment of the new constitution.

Table 16.1 illustrates the prevalence of this escalating design of constitutional amendment. Seven out of the eight Commonwealth realms codify a post-colonial constitutional poison pill that raises the difficulty of replacing the foreign King with a native president. The exception is the Constitution of Belize, enacted in 1981, which establishes three separate procedures of constitutional reform: two-thirds approval in the House of Representatives for any constitutional rule except a special category of rules that require either three-quarters approval in the House of Representatives or three-quarters approval in the House of Representatives plus simple majority approval in the Senate.[17] Should Belizeans wish to change their system of government from constitutional monarchy to parliamentary republic, the Constitution authorises them to make this transformative change using only the easiest procedure of constitutional reform requiring two-thirds approval in the House of Representatives. Yet is worth noting that both major political parties have committed to holding a voluntary referendum in addition to this parliamentary vote if ever the country undertakes the process replace the monarch with a locally chosen president.[18]

Seven Commonwealth realms therefore embed in their constitution a poison pill that makes it comparatively more legally onerous to transition from a constitutional monarchy to a republic than it is to enact constitutional reforms using the general default process for constitutional change. Table 16.2 shows just how comparatively more onerous it is to become a republic in these seven countries: all require the additional step of a popular referendum, and in some cases also a higher threshold of legislative approval in order to authorise the referendum at all. While none of the seven Commonwealth realms requires a

[16] See Constitution of Antigua and Barbuda (1981), s 47; Constitution of Belize (1981), s 69; Constitution of The Bahamas (1973), s 54; Constitution of Grenada (1973), s 39; Constitution of Jamaica (1962), s 49; Constitution of Saint Kitts and Nevis (1983), s 38; Constitution of Saint Lucia (1978), s 41; Constitution of Saint Vincent and the Grenadines (1979), s 38.

[17] Constitution of Belize (1981), s 69(3)–(4).

[18] See D Vernon, 'From a Queen to a King to What? Belize Stil Waiting in 2024' Belize Breaking News (22 April 2024).

Table 16.1 Do Caribbean Commonwealth realms require a special process to become a republic?

Commonwealth realm	**Does the Constitution require a special process to become a republic?**	**If yes, is this special process *less* or *more* legally onerous than the default process for constitutional reform?**
Antigua and Barbuda	Yes	More onerous
Bahamas	Yes	More onerous
Belize	No	—
Grenada	Yes	More onerous
Jamaica	Yes	More onerous
Saint Kitts and Nevis	Yes	More onerous
Saint Lucia	Yes	More onerous
Saint Vincent and the Grenadines	Yes	More onerous

Table 16.2 What does the Constitution require for a Caribbean Commonwealth to become a republic?

Country	**What is the default process to reform the Constitution?**	**What is the special process to become a republic?**
Antigua and Barbuda	2/3 vote of Parliament	+ Referendum with 2/3 approval
Bahamas	Majority vote of Parliament	3/4 vote of Parliament + Referendum with majority approval
Belize	2/3 vote of House of Representatives	None
Grenada	2/3 vote of Parliament	+ Referendum with 2/3 approval
Jamaica	Majority vote of Parliament	2/3 vote of Parliament + Referendum with majority approval
Saint Kitts and Nevis	2/3 vote of National Assembly	+ Referendum with 2/3 approval separately in islands of Saint Christopher and Nevis
Saint Lucia	2/3 vote of Parliament	3/4 vote of Parliament + Referendum with majority approval
Saint Vincent and the Grenadines	2/3 vote of all Representatives	+ Referendum with 2/3 popular approval

referendum as part of their default process for constitutional reform, all seven countries require a successful referendum in order to replace the monarch with a homegrown head of state. What is more, a majority of Commonwealth realms (four out of seven) sets a 2/3 supermajority threshold in order for the referendum to pass. Some of these Commonwealth realms moreover raise the legislative threshold to detach from the British monarchy. In The Bahamas, for instance, the default process for constitutional reform requires a simple majority vote of Parliament. Yet to become a republic, the poison pill requires a 3/4 supermajority vote of Parliament in addition to a simple majority popular vote in a referendum.

16.3 The Jamaican Independence Constitution of 1962

As displayed on Tables 16.1 and 16.2, Jamaica is one of the seven (out of eight) Caribbean Commonwealth realms whose post-colonial constitution contains a poison pill, making it markedly more complicated to complete the decolonial project by replacing King Charles III with a homegrown head of state. It was never going to be easy to change the constitutional status quo in Jamaica. It is a gargantuan task to mobilise constitutional actors behind any constitutional reform, let alone one that can be completed by design only with bipartisan legislative support in addition to a constitutional referendum in a country that has never held an amendment referendum.

16.3.1 The Order at Buckingham Palace

To this day, the Constitution of Jamaica is officially contained in a schedule appended to an imperial instrument issued as an Order in Council at Buckingham Palace.[19] Constitutional reform to create the Republic of Jamaica would patriate the Constitution and make it Jamaica's own, enacted by its people through its own institutions. The Constitution itself makes it hard to achieve this objective, by virtue of the rules of constitutional amendment enacted over six decades ago.

It is an understatement to describe as intricate the constitutional amendment rules codified in the 1962 Jamaican Constitution. These rules span over 1300 words distributed in more than 25 parts across nine sub-sections.[20] Together, they create a complex escalating structure of constitutional amendment featuring three distinguishable procedures of reform, each requiring a different configuration of legislative and popular majorities to reform to separate parts of the Constitution.

[19] The Jamaica (Constitution) Order in Council 1962, 1962 No 1550 (23 July 1962).
[20] Constitution of Jamaica (1962), s 49.

Some parts of the Constitution may be amended by an act of Parliament passed by simple majorities in both houses of the bicameral legislature.[21] For instance, a recent amendment with a simple majority in Parliament took a major step on the way to creating the Republic of Jamaica. The independence constitution of 1962 required that bills adopted by parliamentarians in Jamaica be enacted officially with a reference to the authority of the 'The Queen's Most Excellent Majesty'.[22] In 2024, parliamentarians amended the Constitution to replace any reference to 'The Queen's Most Excellent Majesty' in the declaration required for every bill enacted through the legislative process with a new reference either to 'the Parliament of Jamaica' or 'the Parliament and people of Jamaica' as the ultimate enacting authority.[23] This reform was appropriately hailed as a victory for the republican movement, as it tore down a pillar of the monarchy.[24] This package of amendments contained other reforms related to the words of enactment for bills passed under the law of the Constitution. All were formalised in an Act of Parliament approved by simple majorities votes in each house. This is the least onerous amendment procedure in the Constitution.

Other parts of the Constitution may be amended only by an Act of Parliament approved by a two-thirds supermajority in each house.[25] The Constitution specifies, for instance, that reforms to fundamental rights and freedoms are achievable only through this second procedure. The Constitution enumerates the dozens of sections and sub-sections entrenched under this amendment procedure of intermediate difficulty.[26] There are also specially designated waiting periods for amendment proposals enacted using this second of three procedures of constitutional reform.

16.3.2 The Amendment Labyrinth

The third and most difficult procedure of constitutional amendment must be used to amend those parts of the Constitution deemed most important. These rules accordingly enjoy the highest level of entrenchment against change.[27] They are protected by an amendment labyrinth that even the most determined constitutional actors in Jamaica have never been successfully traversed. Three factors make this procedure extraordinarily difficult: (1) temporal limitations; (2) bi-partisan supermajority requirements; and (3) popular approval. Each on its own is hard to

[21] ibid, s 49(4)(b).
[22] ibid, s 61.
[23] Constitution (Amendment of Section 61) Act 2024.
[24] See J Murphy, 'Senate Passes Bill for Constitutional Amendment to Formulate New Words of Enactment' (Jamaica Information Service, 20 July 2024); J Clark, 'Jamaica Moves Forward with Amendment to Constitution' *Caribbean National Weekly* (3 June 2024).
[25] Constitution of Jamaica, s 49(4)(a).
[26] ibid, s 49(2).
[27] ibid, s 49(3).

overcome but when combined into a package, as they are in Jamaica, they show why this third amendment procedure is a poison pill whose effect is to entrench the British monarch as head of state.

First, temporal limitations: an amendment bill to replace the foreign King with a locally chosen Jamaican president must be introduced in the House of Representatives, where the bill must sit for three months before debate can begin. Following this initial three-month waiting period, a further three months must elapse between the conclusion of parliamentary debate in the House and a final vote. If the vote is successful, only then may the bill be sent to the Senate for debate and ultimately a vote. These temporal limitations on the amendment process magnify the risk that the reform will be disrupted or derailed along the way.

Second, an amendment bill under this third procedure may be approved only with a two-thirds supermajority vote in the House of Representatives, and a special bi-partisan two-thirds supermajority vote in the Senate. Assembling such a high majority is challenging even in the best of times and circumstances. Yet the architectural design of the Senate makes it even more challenging to mobilise the support of two-thirds of that house. Jamaica's post-colonial constitution creates a Senate consisting of 21 members.[28] Two-thirds of the Senate, then, amounts to the approval of 14 members. Achieving this degree of support is unlikely when the Government and Opposition are divided on the amendment proposal. Of those 21 senators, 13 are chosen by the Government,[29] while the remaining eight are chosen by the Leader of the Opposition.[30] Securing the fourteenth vote will always be difficult, perhaps even improbable, when the Opposition opts to disagree with the Government on the proposed reform for reasons of principle or politics.

Third, no amendment proposed using this third procedure may be enacted without the approval of a majority of the people in a national referendum. Constitutional referendums are not easy to win. Amendment referendums fail 40 per cent of the time.[31] In Jamaica, the challenge posed by a referendum stems both from the unpredictability of its outcome when the Government and Opposition are divided on the question, and from the historical fact that no referendum has ever been held in the more than six decades since the country became independent. The year prior to independence in 1961, Jamaica held a referendum on whether to remain in the Federation of the West Indies – the people voted no.[32] But that was not a constitutional referendum nor was it held under the current Constitution of Jamaica. There are many unknowns in the holding of a constitutional referendum in Jamaica, and that will be a complicating factor if ever one is held. What is more,

[28] ibid, s 35(1).

[29] ibid, s 35(2).

[30] ibid, s 35(3).

[31] See Z Elkins and A Hudson, 'The Strange Case of the Package Deal: Amendments and Replacements in Constitutional Reform' in R Albert and R Stacey (eds), *The Limits and Legitimacy of Referendums* (Oxford University Press, 2022).

[32] See E Wallace, 'The West Indies Federation: Decline and Fall' (1962) 17 *International Journal* 269, 275.

the Constitution imposes a further temporal limitation on referendums under this third procedure of constitutional amendment: the referendum vote must be held no sooner than two months, and no later than six months, after its passage in both houses of Parliament.

This exceedingly difficult amendment procedure must be used to reform the nature of executive authority in Jamaica, specifically the vesting clause in the Constitution: 'The executive authority of Jamaica is vested in Her Majesty.'[33] Transforming the system of government from constitutional monarchy to parliamentary republic is therefore possible only through this onerous procedure. It applies also to reforming certain carefully enumerated parts of the Constitution, including the supremacy of the Constitution, the composition of the Parliament of Jamaica, the dissolution and extension of the life of Parliament, qualifications for membership in the Senate and the House of Representatives, and the constitutional amendment rules themselves, among other parts of the Constitution entrenched under this most rigid reform process.[34]

16.4 The Road to Republic, 2023–25

Every time Jamaica has sought to become a republic since the enactment of its independence constitution in 1962, the poison pill in its constitution has been a pivotal factor. Starting with reform efforts in the 1970s through the 1990s and most recently in the 2010s, the path to a republican form of government has been lined with significant barriers.[35] Still, the Government of Prime Minister Andrew Holness proclaimed its commitment to at last achieving successful reform when it created the new Ministry of Legal and Constitutional Affairs to lead the country to its long-awaited destination: replacing the foreign King with a local head of state.[36]

In March 2023, the Government of Jamaica announced a fresh effort at constitutional reform, to be guided by a Constitutional Reform Committee (CRC), to change the system of government from a constitutional monarchy into a parliamentary republic. At the press conference unveiling the members and mandate of the CRC, Prime Minister Holness emphasised the non-partisan objective of the reform process: 'This is not a partisan endeavor and I want to give the public the assurance that whatever we do, we will be acting in the best interests of the people of Jamaica.'[37] Consistent with the Prime Minister's pledge of non-partisanship, the

[33] ibid, s 68(1).
[34] ibid, s 49(3).
[35] See D O'Brien, 'Jamaica's Long and Winding Road to Becoming a Republic' ConstitutionNet (30 June 2022).
[36] A Smith, 'New Ministers and State Minister Sworn In' Jamaica Information Service (11 January 2022).
[37] C Patterson, 'PM Announces Members of Constitutional Reform Committee' Jamaica Information Service (23 March 2023).

CRC consists of 15 members spanning a broad range of interests and affiliations.[38] This latest reform effort is noteworthy for its innovation in constitutional design: a phased process of constitutional change.

16.4.1 A New Three-Phased Approach

Necessity, it is said, is the mother of invention. In much the same way, it was necessary for Jamaica to find a way somehow to overcome the poison pill in the Constitution, which makes it extremely difficult to replace the monarch with a local president as head of state. The solution was a Jamaican innovation in constitutional reform: a new phased approach to constitutional renewal. Recognising that the reforms associated with creating the Republic of Jamaica can be enacted only through the most onerous path of constitutional amendment, the Government chose prudently to divide the constitutional reform process into three phases.[39] In Phase One, all amendments requiring a referendum are grouped together into a single package for debate and ultimately a popular vote. In Phase Two, the focus turns to amendments that do not require a referendum to enact. Having completed the reforms in Phases One and Two, Phase Three entails a review of the entire legal landscape with a view to enacting a brand new Constitution for Jamaica.

This phased approach will help navigate the labyrinth of constitutional amendment. Insofar as the reforms needed to establish the Republic of Jamaica all require a referendum – patriating the Constitution, abolishing the constitutional monarchy, creating a new office of head of state – it was advisable to separate those reforms from others that require a different process of enactment. In addition, given that a majority of Jamaicans are fully behind the republican project, it was moreover advisable to seal those reforms from others for which there may not be similarly robust support at the initial stages of the process but for which a different tenor of discussion and debate would be needed to arrive at a consensus before proceeding with a plan for enactment. Moreover, this three-phased approach to constitutional reform has the advantage of clarity: the various steps on the long yet deliberate path to constitutional renewal are public, principled, and accessible.

The details of this three-phased approach are specified in the Terms of Reference issued by the Ministry of Legal & Constitutional Affairs concurrent with the launch

[38] The CRC includes Marlene Malahoo Forte, Chair of the CRC and Minister of Legal & Constitutional Affairs; Ambassador Rocky Meade, Co-Chair of the CRC; Derrick McKoy, Attorney-General; Senator Tom Tavares-Finson, President of the Senate and Commissioner of the Electoral Commission; Senator Ransford Braham, representing the Government; Senator Donna Scott-Mottley and Representative Anthony Hylton, both representing the Parliamentary Opposition; Nadeen Spence, representing Civil Society; David Henry and Elaine McCarthy, representing different faith-based communities; Sujae Boswell, as Youth Advisor; Laleta David Mattis of the National Reparations Committee; Hugh Small as a nominee of the Leader of the Parliamentary Opposition; Lloyd Barnett as the national constitutional law expert; and me as the international constitutional law expert.

[39] See Ministry of Legal & Constitutional Affairs, 'Terms of Reference for the Constitutional Reform Committee' (2023).

of the CRC. The Terms of Reference are short but specific, spanning eight single-spaced pages in total. The design and content of the Terms of Reference were the subject of long and thoughtful discussion at the initial meetings of the CRC. Each CRC member had the opportunity to review them separately, to comment on them in our group setting, to propose adjustments to them, and to persuade fellow members of the need to revise them in ways either large or small. By the time the CRC began its substantive deliberations on how to end Jamaica's status as a Commonwealth realm, the members of the CRC had arrived at unanimous agreement on the Terms of Reference.

Unanimity was a guiding principle for the work of the CRC, though not because the Government had required it. Rather, at the early meetings of the CRC, the members of the CRC agreed that our work would proceed only by consensus – that no decision would be made without the support of each member of the CRC, present and voting.[40] These auspicious beginnings to the work of the CRC – unanimous agreement on the Terms of Reference and a commitment to consensus – signalled that Jamaica might at last cross the finish line on the road to republic.

In Jamaica, as in the rest of the world, constitution-making is a political process, not a legal one. This became clear as the CRC initiated its work on Phase One. Within one month of the start of deliberations, all members had recorded their unanimous agreement on the fundamental issue at play in the constitutional reform process: to abolish the monarchical form of government and to create the Republic of Jamaica. CRC members from both the Government and the Opposition echoed similar points, both about their momentous agreement on a path forward and about their arrival at this agreement by consensus. An Opposition member of the CRC remarked with pride that 'it has been consensual. We have been able to make some decisions and the Opposition remains very much engaged and involved in this very important and historic process.'[41] But something happened soon thereafter to disrupt the momentum created by this landmark agreement.

16.4.2 Principle or Politics?

In a surprising move, the Leader of the Opposition announced that his party would no longer support replacing King Charles III with a locally chosen head of state unless Jamaica also withdrew concurrently from the Judicial Committee of the Privy Council and acceded to the appellate jurisdiction of the Caribbean Court of Justice: 'We in the PNP have no interest in moving to a republic while retaining the King's Privy Council in London as Jamaica's final court. That does not

[40] C Patterson, 'Constitutional Reform Decisions Based on Consensus – Malahoo Forte' Jamaica Information Service (17 April 2023).

[41] J Murphy, 'Up and Running—CRC Reaches Accord on Removing Monarchy; 15th Member Added' *Jamaica Gleaner* (15 April 2023).

make sense to any progressive person.'[42] He added that 'we the People's National Party will support both moving forward together. We have no interest in one without the other.'[43] This announcement caught observers by surprise, given that the Government and Opposition had earlier agreed on the Terms of Reference for the constitutional reform process – and the Terms of Reference purposely excluded from Phase One the matter of Jamaica's court of last resort, precisely because it is known by all to be a matter on which Jamaicans are divided. Phase One was intended to focus exclusively on those matters that may be reformed only by referendum, and for which popular and legislative approval is appropriately high. It was a deliberate choice to disentangle the matter of the final court from the abolition of the monarchy.

In response to the Leader of the Opposition's shocking revelation, the Chair of the CRC acknowledged, appropriately, that 'the issue of the final court of appeal is an important issue'.[44] The Chair added that CRC discussion and deliberation on the final court are 'set for phase two',[45] precisely to avoid derailing reforms like the creation of the Republic of Jamaica – a change that Jamaicans support by an overwhelming majority. The Chair wisely observed that 'constitutional reform work is complex, and it is lengthy. We can't do it all at once, and it makes sense to proceed on the matters on which we have consensus.'[46] A prominent member of the CRC – indeed, the leading authority on the Constitution of Jamaica – joined the Chair in advising that it is best to make progress on those important matters on which there is consensus, and to return at a later date to those matters requiring more discussion, debate, time to resolve. He illustrated the quandary with a vivid metaphor and concluded that it is best to proceed with abolishing the monarchy now:

> We have the King of England as our head of state. The second is that our Constitution is contained in a British instrument made in England. And the third is that our final court of appeal is the judicial committee of the Privy Council, which is a colonial institution. And my position is, although I support strongly the removal of these three vestiges of colonialism, I say that if I'm tied and I can release two of my limbs or three of my limbs, then the fact that the fourth is not also released doesn't convince me that I shouldn't get the ones that I can have released.[47]

The work of the CRC nonetheless continued apace with purpose, despite the tactics of the Opposition. Within roughly one year of the creation of the CRC, members had held 38 meetings, five public town halls, and over 80 stakeholder engagement

[42] 'PNP Will Not Support Removal of King Charles as Head of State Without Jamaica also Severing Ties from the Privy Council – Golding' *Jamaica Observer* (17 September 2023).

[43] ibid.

[44] 'Malahoo Forte Insists Privy Council Issue will be in Second Phase of Reform' *Jamaica Observer* (22 September 22, 2023)

[45] ibid.

[46] 'CCJ "Cass Cass": Ja's Political Chess Game Over Final Appellate Court' (Loop News, 30 October 2023).

[47] 'CRC Member Barnett Concerned PNP Stance Could Stall Constitutional Reform' (Radio Jamaica News, 19 September 2023).

sessions, alongside robust engagement with the people and the press on television, radio, in print, and online, including on social media through a dedicated website as well as platforms on Facebook, Instagram, X/Twitter, and WhatsApp.[48] These year-long discussions and deliberations culminated with the publication of a major CRC report setting out detailed recommendations on the path forward to Jamaicanising the constitution.[49] All recommendations were made by consensus, consistent with the initial commitment taken by all members of the CRC. Although there was unanimous support from the CRC for each of the recommendations, the Opposition Leader instructed Opposition members of the CRC not to sign the report; their names therefore appear on the report unaccompanied by their signatures.[50]

After the CRC submitted its report to the Cabinet and tabled it in Parliament, the Cabinet authorised the CRC to draft instructions for a parliamentary bill to enact the recommendations in the CRC report.[51] With the CRC report serving as guide, the CRC proceeded to prepare drafting instructions for the bill to transition Jamaica from a constitutional monarchy to a parliamentary republic.[52] Two bills were prepared: one to establish the Republic of Jamaica; and another that details the procedures for the country's first constitutional referendum to amend the Constitution.[53] The legislation was then tabled in the House of Representatives in order to formally begin the amendment process, which requires a three-month waiting period prior to parliamentary debate.[54] The significance of that moment cannot be overstated, as the Chair of the CRC recognised:

> The tabling of the Bill marks the greatest progress made, so far, in our effort to reform the Constitution of Jamaica to achieve the national goals of having a Jamaican as Head of State instead of the hereditary British Monarch and also having our supreme law taken out from under the cloak of the imperial Order in Council and placed in proper form.[55]

The reform bill is presently being reviewed by a Joint Select Committee of both houses of Parliament. The Opposition Leader and the Opposition members of the CRC have boycotted the Joint Select Committee, continuing to insist that the Opposition will not support the establishment of the Republic of Jamaica without concurrently withdrawing from the jurisdiction of the Judicial Committee of the

[48] *Report of the Constitutional Reform Committee on the Transition to the Republic of Jamaica and Other Matters* (May 2024).

[49] V McKenzie, 'Constitutional Reform Committee Recommendations Tabled in Parliament' *Our Today* (22 May 2024).

[50] 'Cabinet Reviewing Constitutional Reform Committee Report' (Loop News, 13 May 2024).

[51] J Murphy, 'Cabinet Approves Drafting Instructions for Transitional Bill' (Jamaica Information Service, 23 May 2024).

[52] 'CRC Preps Drafting Instructions for Bill to Make Jamaica a Republic' Loop News (14 June 2024).

[53] 'Two Draft Bills Submitted for Making Jamaica a Republic' *Our Today* (26 September 2024).

[54] L Linton, 'Legislation Facilitating Jamaica's Transition to a Republic Tabled in the Lower (Jamaica Information Service, 11 December 2024).

[55] ibid.

Privy Council.[56] The Government, for its part, continues correctly to point to the agreement codified in the Terms of Reference for the work of the CRC.

Faced with these disruptive dynamics, observers cannot help but wonder whether the position of the Opposition is driven by a political calculation to obstruct what is otherwise a clear path to creating the Republic of Jamaica – at a time when the country has come closer than ever before to achieving this longstanding goal. Or whether the Opposition is driven by the principle that constitutional decolonisation must be all-encompassing if it is to occur at all – that complete constitutional decolonisation must prevail over guaranteed incremental constitutional progress.

Observers of course have their own views on this question. Some believe the Opposition is impelled by pure politics, while others credit the Opposition for taking a principled stance. The matter cannot be resolved by politicians themselves, as the process remains for the moment stalled as a result of the Opposition's conditional support for abolishing the monarchy. Only the people can resolve this impasse with the direction they give their elected representatives for how to proceed. As it happens, the people will soon have the opportunity to decide between the Government and Opposition in the upcoming General Elections, to be held by the end of this year.

16.5 Conclusion – Unlocking Jamaica's Constitutional Handcuffs

The seven Caribbean Commonwealth Realms whose constitutions codify a special process to become a republic make that process considerably more difficult than the default process for constitutional reform. This escalating structure of constitutional amendment rules handcuffs the people to a foreign monarch who remains in the role of head of state absent constitutional heroics by an extraordinary mobilisation of legislative and popular actors. In Jamaica, replacing the foreign King with a homegrown president has proven just as difficult as intended. When Jamaica at last proclaims itself a republic – and that day will come, sooner or later – it will have been a remarkable feat of coordination, inspiration, and mobilisation of constitutional actors. No exercise of the power of decolonial constitutionalism can be more compelling than replacing the monarchy through a vote of the people in accordance with the onerous self-entrenching rules established by the monarchy itself with the aim of discouraging and frustrating the project of decolonisation.

[56] 'Opposition Members Boycott Meeting of Constitutional Reform Committee' Committee' (Loop News, 23 January 2025).

PART VI

Comparative Perspectives

17

Governance New Zealand Style

RT HON SIR GEOFFREY PALMER KC, KCMG, AC, PC*

17.1 Introduction

This chapter draws upon my experience of government and the law in New Zealand. As a professor of law, I taught constitutional law at Victoria University of Wellington and comparative constitutional law at the University of Iowa and the University of Virginia. When I returned from working for the Australian Government during the Whitlam administration I realised how different Australia's governance is from our own! In 1979, before becoming an MP, I published *Unbridled Power? An Interpretation of New Zealand's Constitution and Government.*[1] It complained among other things that New Zealand was the fastest lawmaker in the West. The problems outlined in that book still concern me after all these years. As an MP from 1979 until 1990, I learned first-hand how the New Zealand system worked. As Deputy Leader of the Opposition, I chaired the Labour Party's Policy Council and developed an open government policy, including a New Zealand Bill of Rights, enacted as the New Zealand Bill of Rights Act 1990. As Leader of the House, I was closely involved in the Government's legislative programme and was in charge of its progress.

As Minister of Justice and Attorney-General from 1984 until 1989, I learned how to put legislation together, including the Constitution Act 1986. During this time, we established the Law Commission. (As its president for five years much later, between 2005 and 2010, I again had close contact with legislation and its processes.) As Attorney-General, I was the titular head of the legal profession, and recommended lawyers for appointment to the judiciary. The Attorney-General is also a guardian of the rule of law: a matter of vital concern in any democracy. As Prime Minister and Minister for the Environment, I learned other things.

New Zealand is one of the world's oldest democracies and one of the most remote from the rest of the world. In 1893, it was the first country in the world to introduce universal adult suffrage. New Zealand consists of two main islands and many smaller ones in the South Pacific. It stretches a long way, approximately 1,600 kilometres from top to bottom. It has spectacular mountain scenery and seascapes.

* All references to legislation are to New Zealand instruments unless otherwise specified.

[1] Oxford University Press, 1979.

New Zealand is a country of 5.3 million people, and these days is highly diverse. It is an advanced Western country in which 17.8 per cent of the population now identify as Māori and 67.8 per cent as being European. Other major ethnic groups are Asians at 17.3 per cent and Pacific peoples at 8.9 per cent.[2]

Indeed, New Zealand is nation of immigrants, the first to arrive being Māori in 1200–1300 CE. They travelled in double-hulled canoes from Eastern Polynesia. British contact began with whalers and sealers and the settlement of Australia by the British. Te reo Māori, the Māori language, has been an official language of New Zealand since 1987.

17.2 New Zealand's Early Constitutional Context

New Zealand became a Crown Colony in 1841.[3] This was after the Colonial Office had negotiated the Treaty of Waitangi (te Tiriti o Waitangi) between Queen Victoria and Māori Chiefs. The purpose of the Treaty was to provide the British with the consent of Māori to allow British settlers to emigrate to New Zealand. As we shall see later, the Treaty remains a live political issue.

The New Zealand Constitution Act 1852 (UK) was enacted by the Imperial Parliament at Westminster, parts of which remained in force until 1986. The purpose was to provide for 'peace, order and good government'.[4] Unlike many British colonies, New Zealand enjoyed a quick march to self-government. The colonial Parliament first assembled in Auckland in 1853 which acted, at that point, as the capital city. It was moved to Wellington in 1865.

In 1857, Westminster agreed to responsible government for New Zealand. That meant that in general, only defence and foreign affairs remained beyond the competence of the New Zealand Parliament. Modern New Zealand still bears the imprint of England – its common law, its parliamentary institutions, and echoes of Westminster.

17.3 The Current Constitutional and Political Landscape

The New Zealand constitution is uncodified and relies heavily upon constitutional conventions for its practical operation, one characteristic it shares with the UK, although the political culture is quite different. New Zealand's small unicameral Parliament, usually confined to 120 members, with the Executive having 30 MPs at present, results in executive domination and diminished accountability. Despite these weaknesses, calls for a codified, written constitution have not been heeded.[5]

[2] Figures as at the 2023 New Zealand Census.

[3] AH McLintock, *Crown Colony Government in New Zealand* (Government Printer, 1958).

[4] Long title.

[5] G Palmer and A Butler, *A Constitution for Aotearoa New Zealand* (Victoria University Press, 2016); G Palmer and A Butler, *Towards Democratic Renewal: Ideas for Constitutional Change in New Zealand* (Victoria University Press, 2018).

New Zealand has a short, three-year electoral term. That often leads to short-term policy-making. And political parties exert strong control over their MPs. The strengths of the New Zealand system lie in its proportional representative electoral system, a free and open society with high levels of transparency, and low levels of corruption. The country has a credible rule of law with a strong, statutorily independent judiciary with security of tenure.

New Zealand has been something of a pioneer in some aspects of its rather egalitarian democracy, particularly in relation to electoral law. There is some relevant statute law but it impossible to understand New Zealand's governance without understanding its heavy reliance on constitutional conventions.

New Zealand has operated a mixed-member proportional (MMP) electoral system since 1996 based on a Royal Commission report that itself borrowed from the German electoral system. Such a system is unusual in Westminster-style countries. The present administration is a National Party-led majority coalition government between three political parties, comprising of National, ACT, and New Zealand First. The current distribution of seats is as follows:

- National: 49
- ACT: 11
- New Zealand First: 8
- Labour: 34
- Green: 15
- Māori: 6
- Total number of seats in the House of Representatives: 123 (due to an 'overhang').

The established pattern over the whole period of MMP has been that either National or Labour leads the Government but generally need confidence and supply agreements from one or more of the smaller parties represented in Parliament to achieve stability. The 2020 general election was the only one of the 10 MMP general elections in which a single party – Labour – secured a majority alone and could form a government. This was a rare result under MMP and one not likely to be easily achieved in the future. The COVID-19 pandemic was an influence on the 2020 election result.[6]

The unusual feature of the 2023 general election was that it produced a three-party coalition government with a majority in the House of Representatives. Up until this election, it had been thought the effect of MMP was to moderate the policies of the largest party in government by requiring support for confidence and supply, thus removing less widely supported policies of small parties from the Government's legislative agenda. But the Government elected in 2023 has a very

[6] G Palmer and G Palmer Steeds, *Democracy in Aotearoa New Zealand: A Survival Guide* (Te Herenga Waka University Press, 2022) 74.

different flavour about it.[7] This has been achieved by combining the policies of the three parties and requiring each of them to support the policies of the others. The coalition agreements that resulted were numerous and highly complex. The Coalition supports this programme with a disciplined majority in the House, with some of the most controversial policies coming from two small parties with small levels of electoral support. In some ways, this Government is more like a first-past-the-post government than an MMP government.

This chapter will now focus on a number of key aspects of New Zealand's governance:

- constitutional conventions and the Cabinet Manual;
- the Constitution Act 1986 and the monarchy;
- attempts at producing more checks and balances, including the New Zealand Bill of Rights Act 1990, and suggesting securing more MPs to increase the accountability of the Executive to the House; and
- the Treaty of Waitangi and its unsettled status.

17.4 Constitutional Conventions and the Cabinet Manual

The New Zealand *Cabinet Manual 2023* is regarded as something approaching holy writ as to how Cabinet government works in New Zealand. It is revised periodically and the present version was published in 2023.[8] It is used by ministers, staff in ministerial offices, MPs, and public servants as the first port of call when an issue arises. The New Zealand Cabinet Office is a well-oiled machine that keeps things ship-shape and advises on issues. The *Cabinet Manual*, in its Preface, states:

> The Cabinet Manual has been an authoritative guide to New Zealand's system of central government decision making since the publication of the first edition, then known as the Cabinet Office Manual, in 1979. This is the seventh edition of the Cabinet Manual. Successive governments have recognised the need for guidance to provide the basis on which they will conduct themselves while in office. The Cabinet Manual fulfils this need.

The *Cabinet Manual* goes to some pains to spell out several of the key conventions. It is not set in stone but is revised to reflect changes in political, administrative, and constitutional arrangements. The work done by convention in New Zealand is of basic importance. Cabinet government is a convention. There is no mention of Cabinet in any New Zealand statute. The same is true as to the role of the political party caucus – that strange Antipodean invention that Australia shares with New Zealand, where caucus members must agree to the introduction of government bills.

[7] G Palmer, 'The novel evolution of MMP under the Luxon government' [2024] *New Zealand Law Journal* 9.

[8] Cabinet Office, *Cabinet Manual* (2023), www.dpmc.govt.nz/sites/default/files/2023-06/cabinet-manual-2023-v2.pdf.

One cannot understand how the New Zealand Government works without understanding the conventions, yet they are not legally enforceable. They are norms that are usually followed. That the Monarch must act on the advice of His Majesty's responsible ministers is another critical convention, preserving the democratic character of the system. The caretaker convention is set out in the *Cabinet Manual*, as is the relationship of the Prime Minister to Cabinet. The conventions on ministerial responsibility, both collective and individual, are dealt with in the *Cabinet Manual*. But predicting what will happen on a particular set of facts can be hazardous. That has become more difficult since the introduction of the MMP electoral system in 1996 which has seen more political parties represented in the House.

The underlying principle of the *Cabinet Manual* is based on democracy. Crisply, that is expressed as:

- The King reigns …
- … but the government rules …
- … so long as it has the support of the House of Representatives.[9]

Each principle is supported by longer statements in the *Cabinet Manual* setting out what they entail from a practical point of view. The *Cabinet Manual* helpfully clarifies this rather untidy and uncertain mix of law and convention. Taking the above three principles and combining them with the six entrenched provisions of the Electoral Act 1993, we reach about as far as we can go with an uncodified constitution to producing a New Zealand constitutional *Grundnorm*. Those entrenched provisions protect essential democratic principles, including the three-year term of Parliament; the minimum voting age of 18 years; the division of the country into electoral districts; the required limits on statistical tolerance for electoral districts; the independent Representation Commission that ensures gerrymandering cannot occur by keeping MPs out of decision-making about electoral districts; and the method of voting, including the secret ballot.

A simple majority in Parliament is not sufficient to amend the six entrenched provisions in section 268. It requires either a 75 per cent majority in the House or a majority of the voters at a referendum. However, section 268 itself is not entrenched, meaning it could, in theory, be changed with a simple majority in the House. Despite that, entrenchment has always been followed since it was introduced in 1956.[10]

The literature on constitutional conventions is mainly British. The author has always thought that the British political scientist Geoffrey Marshall wrote the best book on conventions. It was he who characterised the convention on ministerial responsibility as 'like most British conventions, somewhat vague and slippery – resembling (to borrow a phrase) the procreation of eels'.[11]

[9] ibid, 3.

[10] See E McLay, *In Search of Consensus: New Zealand's Electoral Act 1956 and its Constitutional Legacy* (Victoria University Press, 2018).

[11] G Marshall, *Constitutional Conventions: The Rules and Forms of Political Accountability* (Clarendon Press, 1984) 54.

17.5 The Constitution Act 1986 and the Monarchy

New Zealand's unique set of constitutional arrangements allow for flexibility and are capable of quick adjustment. New Zealand lacks a codified superior law constitution as many countries have. In that respect it resembles the UK, which itself is an international outlier in that regard. The prime statute is the Constitution Act 1986. It is possible to discern the branches of government from that statute, but much of the detail is left to constitutional conventions which are sometimes vague and which can morph into something different over time.

The long title of the 1986 Act says:

> An Act to reform the constitutional law of New Zealand, to bring together into one enactment certain provisions of constitutional significance, and to provide that the New Zealand Constitution Act 1852 of the Parliament of the United Kingdom shall cease to have effect as part of the law of New Zealand.

The Act is divided into five parts:

- Part 1: The Sovereign
- Part 2: The Executive
- Part 3: The Legislature
- Part 4: The Judiciary
- Part 5: Miscellaneous provisions

The Act outlines the main structures of the institutions of the constitution but leaves much of the detail to be dealt with elsewhere by other means: by other statutes that could be regarded as having constitutional significance, by constitutional conventions, and by judicial decisions.

New Zealand has a tradition of following the rule of law with a high-quality judiciary rooted in English law, but with increasing New Zealand characteristics, particularly those known as tikanga Māori. New Zealand continues to lack the checks and balances that often characterise other constitutions. This feature increases the fragility of the rule of law, since the Executive easily dominates the small House of Representatives. Parliament can, and does in some instances, abuse its power. More MPs are necessary to redress the balance, but this is not popular with the general public.

Section 15 of the Constitution Act 1986 provides the 'Parliament of New Zealand continues to have full power to make laws'. And the New Zealand Bill of Rights Act in section 4 provides:

> No court shall, in relation to any enactment (whether passed or made before or after the commencement of this Bill of Rights),—

(a) hold any provision of the enactment to be impliedly repealed or revoked, or to be in any way invalid or ineffective; or
(b) decline to apply any provision of the enactment—

> by reason only that the provision is inconsistent with any provision of this Bill of Rights.

Charles III is King of New Zealand by New Zealand law as the constitutional monarch at the time of writing.

Section 2 of the Constitution Act 1986 lays down the modern essentials about the monarch:

> (1) The Sovereign in right of New Zealand is the head of State of New Zealand, and shall be known by the royal style and titles proclaimed from time to time.
> (2) The Governor-General appointed by the Sovereign is the Sovereign's representative in New Zealand.

The role involves a mixture of constitutional and ceremonial functions. There are some complications involved with the modern situation of the Crown and the monarchy. One is that the monarch does not live in New Zealand. The 'Crown' is a loose term and what it means depends upon the context in which the issue arises. The Office of Governor-General is constituted by the Letters Patent signed by the Queen of New Zealand in 1983 and countersigned by the then-Prime Minister.[12]

The Letters were also set up for the Realm of New Zealand which includes not only New Zealand but also the self-governing state of the Cook Islands; the self-governing state of Niue; Tokelau, technically a non-self-governing territory; and the Ross Dependency, which is in Antarctica.[13] The Royal Titles Act 1974 governs the title and style of the monarch in relation to New Zealand and recognises the monarch as the Head of the Commonwealth.

In summary, the Letters Patent as a part of the law of New Zealand constitute the office of the Governor-General and state, with the Governor-General as Commander-in-Chief of the Realm of New Zealand. They deal with the appointment and holding of the office, which is usually for a five-year period; and they set up the Executive Council, which is the institution that advises the Governor-General and the Sovereign. The advisers are the ministers of the Government in power.

The Letters Patent provide:[14]

[12] Letters Patent Constituting the Office of the Governor-General of New Zealand 1983 ('Letters Patent 1983'). Both the historical development of the Crown and the monarchy in New Zealand are dealt with in detail in a comprehensive work, with focus on the Letters Patent: A Quentin-Baxter and J McLean, *This Realm of New Zealand: The Sovereign, the Governor-General, the Crown* (Auckland University Press, 2017) 96–112. Other constitutional law texts that contain useful information and analysis include MSR Palmer and DR Knight, *The Constitution of New Zealand: A Contextual Analysis* (Cambridge University Press, 2022); and PA Joseph, *Joseph on Constitutional and Administrative Law*, 5th edn (Thomson Reuters, 2021).

[13] Letters Patent 1983, cl 19; Palmer and Knight (n 12) 37.

[14] Letters Patent 1983, cl 16.

> Our Ministers of the Crown in New Zealand shall keep Our Governor-General fully informed concerning the general conduct of the Government … and shall furnish Our Governor-General with such information as he may request with respect to any particular matter …

One mystery of the monarchy is the exercise of the royal prerogative.[15] The royal prerogative is subject to being defined, restricted, or amended by legislation passed by Parliament. Yet there remain important areas of public administration where the prerogative is used, particularly in relation to emergencies and some aspects of the public service.

The situation in relation to the role of Commander-in-Chief contains some ambiguities. The real power on defence lies with Cabinet and the Minister of Defence.[16] The monarch as a symbol of unity separate from the government of the day is of some importance.[17]

The Governor-General has important obligations to ensure the Crown is never without advisers. Scholars over the years have discussed the so-called reserve powers that may exist for independent action by the Governor-General contrary to or without ministerial advice.[18] Constitutional scholars have worried about the power of the Governor-General to make decisions in a situation of crisis or emergency that have great political consequences. One example of this is the case when Sir John Kerr, the Australian Governor-General dismissed Gough Whitlam, the Prime Minister of Australia, in 1975.[19] Widespread expressions of outrage occurred in many quarters and later led to Kerr resigning his office. A historian who had written a biography of Whitlam, after years of research in the Australian National Archives, brought a legal case to require the public release by the Archives of the correspondence between Kerr and the Palace concerning the dismissal.[20] Nothing like the Whitlam dismissal has ever occurred in New Zealand.

17.6 A Restricted Bill of Rights

The New Zealand Bill of Rights Act 1990 began life as a much more ambitious reform that had to be reduced due to political opposition. It was promoted in the White Paper as an entrenched Bill of Rights enforceable in the courts, and included the Treaty of Waitangi.[21] As enacted, the Bill of Rights is an ordinary

[15] See Palmer and Knight (n 12) 42–43.

[16] Defence Act 1990, Pt 1.

[17] Quentin-Baxter and McLean (n 12) 130–32, fn 1. See also T Arnold and G Palmer, *Report of the Government Inquiry into Operation Burnham* (2020).

[18] Quentin-Baxter and McLean (n 12) 170; Palmer and Knight (n 12) 43–44.

[19] C Madden, 'The dismissal: 45th anniversary' (*Flagpost: Parliament of Australia*, 11 November 2020), www.aph.gov.au/About_Parliament/Parliamentary_departments/Parliamentary_Library/Research/FlagPost/2020/November/The_dismissal.

[20] J Hocking, *The Palace Letters: The Queen, the governor-general, and the plot to dismiss Gough Whitlam* (Scribe Publications, 2020).

[21] G Palmer, 'A Bill of Rights for New Zealand: A White Paper' [1984–85] I AJHR A6.

statute, not entrenched, and can be altered by a simple majority of the House. The background will be canvassed and some brief account of its development since its enactment given below, but the jurisprudence as developed by the courts cannot be covered in detail here.[22] It is interesting that the New Zealand Bill of Rights Act made a significant contribution in the design of the UK legislation on the same topic.[23] Lord Lester of Herne Hill, the Liberal Democrat who promoted the British legislation, recognised his debt to the New Zealand Act.[24]

The purpose of promoting the Bill of Rights that was finally enacted in 1990 aimed to limit the powers of the Executive and Parliament and to ensure that human rights were given greater legal weight. The New Zealand constitution lacked checks and balances to a dangerous degree. The overweening power of the Executive caused the great Australian constitutional lawyer Professor Leslie Zines to label New Zealand an 'executive paradise'.[25]

New Zealand has a political constitution and any efforts to change it must result from political activity. With no written or codified constitution, New Zealand has few constitutional rules that cannot be altered easily. So the features of the constitution at any given time tend to reflect the outcome of political battles. The New Zealand constitution evolves and mutates remorselessly, like a living, breathing organism. The basic constitutional framework remains the same today as when the Bill of Rights Act was passed in 1990.[26]

A political market had been created for these changes by the high-handed and dubious constitutional behaviour of the 1975–84 Muldoon Government. The unconstitutional behaviour began early in the life of the Government, detailed in the classic decision of *Fitzgerald v Muldoon* in which the Prime Minister tried to stop the statutory superannuation scheme of the previous government by press statement, only to have the Chief Justice declare the action illegal because the Prime Minister was attempting to suspend the law by regal authority without the consent of Parliament and so breached the Bill of Rights 1689.[27]

After a prolonged period of parliamentary consideration and a process of extensive public submissions to a select committee that produced both an interim and final report, it was decided to water down the proposal to blunt the extensive criticisms that it received: namely, that it would make the law uncertain and

[22] For the case law, see A Butler and P Butler, *The New Zealand Bill of Rights Act*, 2nd edn (LexisNexis, 2014); and Joseph (n 12). The most useful guide to interpretation of the Bill of Rights Act can be found in the leading New Zealand Supreme Court case of *Hansen v R* [2007] NZSC 7, [2007] 3 *New Zealand Law Review* 1.

[23] KJ Keith, 'The New Zealand Bill of Rights Act 1990 – An Account of its Preparation' (2013) 11 *New Zealand Journal of Public and International Law* 1, 15 fn 70.

[24] A Lester, *Talking to Myself: A Life in Human Rights* (Biteback Publishing, 2022) ch 25; A Lester, 'The Magnetism of the Human Rights Act 1998' (2002) 33 *Victoria University of Wellington Law Review* 20.

[25] L Zines, *Constitutional Change in the Commonwealth* (Cambridge University Press, 1991) 47.

[26] See G Palmer, 'What the New Zealand Bill of Rights Aimed to Do, Why it did not Succeed and How it can be Repaired' (2016) 14 *New Zealand Journal of Public and International Law* 169, 171.

[27] *Fitzgerald v Muldoon* [1976] 2 *New Zealand Law Review* 615 (SC).

transfer power to the judges.[28] The proposal was vigorously opposed by the New Zealand Law Society.[29] So the restricted Bill of Rights was enacted in 1990 as an ordinary statute. It was not to be supreme law. Trimming the sails was politically necessary in order to pass the measure. It is noteworthy that the New Zealand Bill of Rights Act 1990 does not include property rights.

Despite its retention of parliamentary supremacy, the Bill of Rights has become an important ingredient of the constitutional architecture of New Zealand. It has changed the way in which the courts and Parliament deal with rights. As enacted, it had benign but limited effects upon the system of government. Departments were obliged to examine their legislative proposals to ensure they were rights-compliant. The judges breathed some life into the Bill of Rights, as it began to be relied upon by litigants in the courts. Broadly speaking, the Bill of Rights' accomplishments include:

- increased attention within government agencies to compliance with individual rights when designing legislative proposals;
- vetting of legislation by the Attorney-General to report on measures that do not comply, by the production of legal opinions tabled in the House drawing attention to breaches;
- an extensive body of case law spanning more than 30 years;[30]
- improved standards of rights-compliant policing by the New Zealand Police;
- consistency of secondary legislation with rights, otherwise it is ultra vires the empowering provision;
- a remedy of damages in some instances for breaches;[31]
- an influence in administrative law decisions of the courts;[32]
- the Act expressly binding the judiciary, influencing their statutory interpretation;[33] and
- a significant influence in court cases involving criminal procedure and punishments including search arrest and detention.

An increased voice for the Bill of Rights has been provided through the New Zealand Bill of Rights (Declarations of Inconsistency) Amendment Act 2022. Now

[28] ibid, 12.

[29] Justice and Law Reform Committee, 'Final Report of the Justice and Law Reform Select Committee on a White Paper on a Bill of Rights for New Zealand' [1988] I AJHR 8C. For an account as to how all this developed, see G Palmer, *New Zealand's Constitution in Crisis: Reforming our political system* (John McIndoe, 1992) 51–70. See also Justice and Law Reform Committee, 'Interim Report of the Justice and Law Reform Select Committee: Inquiry into the White Paper – A Bill of Rights for New Zealand' [1987] I AJHR 8A.

[30] Discussion of this case law can be found in G Palmer, *Reform: A Memoir* (Victoria University Press, 2013) 353–55. See also C Geiringer, 'On a Road to Nowhere: Implied Declarations of Inconsistency and the New Zealand Bill of Right Act' (2009) 40 *Victoria University of Wellington Law Review* 613.

[31] *Simpson v Attorney-General* [1994] 3 NZLR 667 (CA) (Baigent's case).

[32] Butler and Butler (n 22).

[33] New Zealand Bill of Rights Act 1990, ss 3(a) and 6.

there is a clear set of steps that must be gone through in the House, and which are reflected in the Standing Orders: where the Supreme Court makes a declaration of inconsistency, the Attorney-General presents the declaration to the House, a select committee considers it, and a government response is presented to the House.[34]

17.7 The 1840 Treaty of Waitangi and its Afterlife

Although the Treaty of Waitangi (te Tiriti o Waitangi) was negotiated in 1840 between the British Government and Māori, its position in the system of governance and law is not settled. This is a highly complex subject and the analysis here cannot be as full and complete as the subject matter demands.[35] The Treaty is a brief document containing a long preamble about the need for peace and good order between the settlers and Māori. There are three operative articles.

The English language translation of the first article says that the chiefs cede to Queen Victoria 'absolutely and without reservation all the rights and powers of sovereignty' they had. The second article, on the other hand, guaranteed to the Chiefs, families and individuals:

> [F]ull exclusive and undisturbed possession of their Lands and Estates Forests Fisheries and other properties which they may collectively or individually possess so long as it is their wish and desire to retain the same in their possession.

But if they wished to give them up, the Crown had the exclusive right of pre-emption. The third article extended to Māori the protection of the Crown and imparted to Māori 'all the Rights and Privileges of British subjects'.[36]

There exist serious inconsistencies between the English and Māori language versions of the Treaty. Māori did not understand they were being asked to cede sovereignty in the sense that the British understood that term. And the guarantees in the Māori version suggest Māori had greater rights than were contained in the English version. There is also a possible legal theory that the Treaty was a binding contract. The *contra proferentem* rule of interpretation should be applied, meaning that any ambiguity should be interpreted in the sense unfavourable to the party who drafted and put forward the document.

During the nineteenth century, the Treaty did not fare well in state practice, but in the latter half of the twentieth century it has been given greater weight and more legal recognition. Although the text of the Treaty appears in statute, the Treaty itself does not have the effect of statute law.

The Third Labour Government, elected with a clear mandate in 1972, had a policy to 'examine a practical means of legally acknowledging the principles set

[34] The measure was the result of the decision of the Supreme Court in *Attorney-General v Taylor* [2018] NZSC 104, [2019] 1 NZLR 213.

[35] MSR Palmer, *The Treaty of Waitangi in New Zealand's Law and Constitution* (Victoria University Press, 2008).

[36] The full text can be found in the Treaty of Waitangi Act 1975, Sch 1.

out in the Treaty of Waitangi'. The policy was worked through a caucus committee and a statute was passed, the Treaty of Waitangi Act 1975.

This created a commission of inquiry known as the Waitangi Tribunal to report on the role of the Treaty in particular contemporary situations. The Tribunal has done heavy work for many years and has both Māori and Pākehā members. In this way, the formal 'principles' of the Treaty entered the constitutional dialogue. The Treaty of Waitangi Act 1975 was a most significant step to reversing the trend that had dominated in previous years of trying to ignore the Treaty.

The preamble to the statute states the reasons for the approach. The brief three articles in the original Treaty were written in two languages and were not compatible with what was agreed. It was thought by taking the issues gradually and examining each issue individually and thoroughly before the Tribunal that it would be possible to make progress. And that proved to be correct.

The Tribunal initially, under the chairmanship of Sir Edward Durie, the Chief Māori Land Court Judge, made a number of important reports that produced recognition of the Treaty and convinced the Fourth Labour Government to extend the jurisdiction of the Tribunal back to 1840. This produced many claims for the palpable historic injustices that had been visited upon Māori. Large awards of money, land, and other assets were handed over in recompense.

Claims began to be negotiated directly between Māori and the Crown. This produced many settlements. The historic claims are now almost at an end and the Tribunal has produced many important reports on contemporary and historical issues. Contemporary breaches remain to be dealt with on a continuing basis as the law currently exists.

Some New Zealand statutes refer to the Treaty. For example, section 9 of the State-Owned Enterprises Act 1986 provided that 'Nothing in this Act shall permit the Crown to act in a manner that is inconsistent with the principles of the Treaty of Waitangi'. This provision led to a most significant legal decision in 1987, *New Zealand Māori Council v Attorney-General*, in which the Full Court of Appeal unanimously held that the Crown could not transfer assets to a state-owned enterprise without establishing a system to consider whether such a transfer would be inconsistent with the principles of the Treaty of Waitangi, and therefore unlawful.[37]

The result of this legal declaration was a negotiation with Māori followed by the passage of a statute that permitted transfers as long as titles to the lands and waters in question made it clear they were subject to Treaty claims. This meant the rights of claimants were expressly protected. There were other cases as well.

The Court determined that these principles include that the Treaty was a partnership between the Crown and Māori in which both must act reasonably, honourably, and in good faith. The parties owe each other a duty of good faith to ensure that. It includes active protection, as the Crown's right to govern involves a corresponding obligation to actively protect Māori interests. It includes redress, putting wrongs right. The Tribunal has identified other principles of reciprocity,

[37] *New Zealand Māori Council v Attorney-General* [1987] 1 NZLR 641 (CA).

mutual benefit, self-government, and the right of Māori communities to manage themselves and their territories and resources.

So, the present situation is that the Treaty and its principles are part of statute law for some purposes and not for others, and the applications of the Treaty may be inconsistent from one statute to the next. Furthermore, under some circumstances, the courts can consider the Treaty when interpreting other statutes, even when it is not specifically mentioned.

In recent decades, the Treaty has come to form a more important element of government decision-making. Decision-making processes set out in the *Cabinet Manual 2023* require attention to the consequences of decisions that affect Māori interests.

The Treaty has recently been the subject of intense political controversy that led to the largest protest march to the Parliament in the history of the country.[38] There were more than 40,000 people. The Principles of the Treaty of Waitangi Bill was roundly defeated in the House on 10 April 2025 by 112 votes to 11. Only one party in the Parliament voted for it: the ACT Party that introduced it. It had been the subject of agreed policy contained in the Coalition agreement, with the National Party agreeing only to support the Bill up to the second reading in the House.

The measure was condemned as racist, divisive, and a serious misrepresentation of the Treaty, which has now 185 years of history. One MP was ordered out of the House for calling the promoter of the Bill a 'liar' because of inaccuracies he had advanced about the Treaty in his Bill. The parliamentary debate was passionate, and in many respects hopeful for the future of the Treaty.[39]

More than 300,000 submissions were filed by members of the public with the Select Committee. They were overwhelmingly opposed to the measure. The enormous march on Parliament a few months earlier seems to have resulted in the Treaty being more widely supported than before.

Modern experts in international law are in broad agreement that the Treaty of Waitangi was a valid treaty under international law. The learned author Professor Ian Brownlie wrote:[40]

> There can be no doubt … that the Treaty of Waitangi presupposed the legal and political capacity of the chiefs of New Zealand to make an agreement which was valid on the international plane. As such, the Treaty created real rights and obligations at international law.

This means the rights and obligations the Crown took up in 1840 now belong to the Crown in right of New Zealand under international law: the Treaty is binding.[41] London cannot make decisions for New Zealand these days. New Zealand

[38] J MacManus, 'Was the hīkoi New Zealand's largest-ever protest?' The Spinoff (20 November 2024), https://thespinoff.co.nz/atea/20-11-2024/was-the-hikoi-new-zealands-largest-ever-protest.

[39] (10 April 2025) 783 NZPD (Principles of the Treaty of Waitangi Bill – Second Reading).

[40] I Brownlie, *Treaties and Indigenous Peoples: The Robb Lectures* (Clarendon Press, 1992).

[41] P McHugh, *The Māori Magna Carta: New Zealand Law and the Treaty of Waitangi* (Oxford University Press, 1991) 180.

is the successor to the obligations of the British Government which negotiated the Treaty. It is binding as a valid treaty at international law. And to cap it all off, the Treaty may be binding as a matter of contract law.[42]

The Crown has obligations to honour its guarantees of tino rangatiratanga (self-determination) and equal rights under New Zealand's existing constitutional arrangements.[43] These obligations cannot be easily dismissed. Rights and obligations arising from treaties cannot specifically be invoked and enforced in the domestic courts unless they have been incorporated in domestic law by Acts of Parliament. Many domestic laws do refer to the Treaty as matters now stand, although efforts are being made by the current Government to repeal some of them. The courts have often used the Treaty as both a source of principle and as an aid to interpretation of both statute and common law.[44]

The Treaty has been described by Lord Cooke, the distinguished New Zealand jurist, as 'simply the most important document in New Zealand's history' because it provided legitimacy for the British coming to settle in New Zealand in the first place.[45] Recent experience tells New Zealanders they cannot safely ignore its own history by trying to wipe it out, as the Treaty Principles Bill would have done.

[42] R Boast, *Buying the Land, Selling the Land: Governments and Māori Land in the North Island 1865–1921* (Victoria University Press, 2008) 448–50.

[43] The relationship between the Crown, sovereignty, and Māori monarchy is well discussed: B Patterson, RS Hill and K Patterson (eds), *After the Treaty: The settler state, race relations & the exercise of power in colonial New Zealand* (Steele Roberts, 2016), in particular Carwyn Jones at 132 and Vincent O'Malley at 205. See also M Stanton Turei, NR Wheen and J Hayward (eds), *Te Tiriti o Waitangi Relationships: People, Politics and Law* (Bridget Williams Books, 2024).

[44] Such as in *Huakina Development Trust v Waikato Valley Authority* [1987] 2 NZLR 188 (HC); *Fitzgerald v R* [2021] NZSC 131, [2021] 1 NZLR 551; *Ellis v R* [2022] NZSC 114, [2022] 1 NZLR 239.

[45] R Cooke, 'Introduction' (1990) 14 *New Zealand Universities Law Review* 1, 1.

18

Civil Servants as Actors in a Danish Constitutional Context

HENRIK SKOVGAARD-PETERSEN*

18.1 Introduction

In recent years, there has been a lively debate in many democracies about the 'deep state' undermining the will of the people and their elected representatives. A related discourse casts the civil service, in pejorative terms, as the 'blob', with connotations of civil servants as overly cautious, recalcitrant, dragging their heels while fretting about procedural minutiae, or even serving their own interests or agendas. However, this perspective overlooks the other side of the coin: that the civil service, along with other parts of 'the system' (such as judicial review and parliamentary and public scrutiny), plays an important role in guarding the constitution and upholding the rule of law.

From a Danish perspective – in particular if one zooms in on academic circles and traditional journalistic outlets – the debate centres on the balance which civil servants must strike between, on the one hand, serving their political masters and achieving workable results and, on the other hand, ensuring that the means employed are within the boundaries of legality. In other words, civil servants must navigate their duties as 'sherpas', who enable their political masters to develop and implement policies, and as 'shepherds' of the constitution who exercise a constraining function by identifying the outer limits of policy and legislation.

The aim of this chapter is to explain and illustrate how the Danish civil service – generally considered a well-functioning impartial civil service – grapples with some of these balancing exercises as actors in the constitutional landscape. The starting point of the chapter is a range of legal, empirical and academic sources, but it is also based on the author's own experience as a civil servant in different government departments. In particular, it draws on the author's experience as head of the Constitutional and Human Rights Law Division at the Danish Ministry of Justice

* The views expressed in this chapter are solely those of the author and do not represent the views of his employer.

(2019–23) which is responsible for advising on, inter alia, the constitutionality of legislative and other proposals.

The chapter will begin with a brief introduction to the relevant constitutional framework, in particular the role of the civil service in the Danish system of government. The fundamental obligations of civil servants are then introduced, followed by a brief summary of some recent studies and assessments of civil servants' observance of these duties. We then turn to two examples concerning legislative and executive functions, respectively.

This chapter refers to the Danish constitutional system. However, regardless of how our constitutional arrangements are shaped – and how we choose to reshape them in a world characterised by general upheaval and frequent challenges to the foundations of (western) liberal democracies – the question of constitutional stewardship remains.[1] Reflecting on how the civil service (and other actors) rise to this task is important for our understanding of the stabilising factors of the constitutional system and how to reconcile them with constant – and legitimate – ambitions for change and development.

18.2 The Constitutional Framework and the Danish Civil Service

The Danish Constitutional Act 1953 (CA 1953) contains only one express provision concerning the civil service: section 27 provides for certain employment protections for the very select group of civil servants formally appointed by the King.[2] However, important questions such as the role, competences and responsibilities of the civil service are not regulated by the CA 1953. The absence of such rules reflects the fact that the civil service is inextricably linked to the Government; indeed, the term 'government' is often applied in a broad sense to refer not only to ministers but also to the entire government apparatus, including ministers, ministries and civil servants.

Under Danish constitutional law ministers are individually responsible and accountable for the exercise of their constitutional powers (in Danish constitutional theory this is termed a ministerial system, which is contrasted with a system of cabinet government). Civil servants derive their competences from the minister whom they serve, and from a formal point of view each department (ministry) constitutes a hierarchical chain of delegation which in principle – depending on the matter at hand – extends from the minister at the

[1] The distinction between constitutional policy and constitutional stewardship is drawn from the House of Lords Select Committee on the Constitution, 'Executive oversight and responsibility for the UK constitution' (HL Paper 72, 28 January 2025).

[2] Except for permanent secretaries, civil servants in government departments are no longer appointed by the monarch, but subject to ordinary forms of employment. Denmark is a constitutional monarchy, and the involvement of the monarch in the exercise of constitutional powers is purely ceremonial (see especially CA 1953, ss 12–14).

top to junior civil servants at the bottom.[3] The fact that each ministry is considered a separate hierarchical legal entity also means that Danish civil servants do not form part of a single 'civil service' with an equivalent of the UK Cabinet Secretary at the helm.

The constitutional backdrop also explains the respective relationships of responsibility and accountability. Denmark has a parliamentary system of government which means that the Government as a whole (represented by the Prime Minister) and individual ministers can be subject to a vote of no confidence in Parliament (CA 1953, section 15). Parliament can also bring criminal proceedings before the Court of Impeachment against ministers for alleged breaches of legal duties incumbent on them.[4] These specific constitutional forms of responsibility apply only to ministers. Thus, it is a basic feature of Danish constitutional law that ministers are accountable to Parliament while civil servants are accountable to the minister whom they serve. One implication of this separation is that by convention civil servants do not give evidence before parliamentary committees on their own behalf, and when civil servants participate in committee meetings, they do so in their capacity as assistants to the minister who retains ministerial responsibility vis-a-vis Parliament.[5]

Finally, a few remarks on the functions and competences of the civil service. As noted above, the civil service essentially derives its competences from the government (individual ministers) and therefore assists ministers in exercising the powers vested in them. One important function which should be highlighted for the present purposes is the Government's role in the legislative process. Under CA 1953, section 3(1), legislative power is shared between the Government and Parliament. Although Danish governments typically do not command a majority in Parliament, the Government's formal and informal role in the legislative process is very prominent. In formal terms, ministers have the right to introduce bills before Parliament (CA 1953, section 21), and if a bill is passed, the Government decides whether it should receive Royal Assent (CA 1953, section 22). While the latter – in principle the power to veto a bill passed by Parliament – is de facto never applied, the former is of huge practical significance. Individual MPs are entitled to introduce bills (CA 1953, section 41(1)), yet the Government's important agenda-setting function is clearly borne out by the fact that 98–99 per cent of adopted bills are

[3] To a large extent this corresponds to the *Carltona* principle in the UK, according to which the civil service has no legal or constitutional personality separate from the Government or ministers (see *Carltona Ltd v Commissioners of Works* [1943] 2 All ER 560; D Torrance, 'The United Kingdom constitution – a mapping exercise' (House of Commons Library Briefing Paper No CBP 9384, 21 June 2025) 160, 181.

[4] See H Skovgaard-Petersen, 'Impeachment in Denmark: Law and Practice' in Ch Monaghan et al (eds), *Impeachment in a Global Context: Law, Politics and Comparative Practice* (Routledge, 2024).

[5] In some rare cases, civil servants participate without the presence of the minister in public hearings, etc organised by Parliament. Exceptions apply in particular to civil servants who enjoy an independent position, such as heads of independent (arm's-length) administrative agencies.

introduced by a minister.[6] As will be shown below, this means that the civil service plays a crucial role – and assumes great responsibility – in shaping bills and the legislative process.

18.3 The Fundamental Duties of Civil Servants

The legal framework governing the work of the civil service consists of a number of written and unwritten norms of administrative law and – depending on the subject matter in question – specific obligations laid down in primary or secondary legislation. The so-called Code VII, which can be considered the Danish equivalent of the UK Civil Service Code, summarises the fundamental obligations in the following seven key duties: legality, truthfulness, professionalism, development and cooperation, responsibility and management, openness about errors, and party-political neutrality.[7]

The duty of party-political neutrality merits particular attention here. Even though, as shown above, the civil service is derived from the Government, the Danish administrative model is that of an impartial civil service. The only exception is that each minister may employ between one and three[8] special advisers who are not subject to this duty, but may advise and assist ministers also with respect to party politics and the work of the minister's political party. They are employed only for as long as the minister in question remains in office, and employment terminates when a general election is called.

Given that there is only one or a few special advisers dedicated to assisting each minister in a political capacity, it is not hard to see why the ordinary – impartial – civil service cannot (and is not supposed to) shy away from offering what is typically called political and tactical advice, eg advice on how best to navigate political and parliamentary procedures to enact and implement policies.[9] There are clear benefits to this model, both from the point of view of individual civil servants and the system, given that the experience and knowledge accumulated by civil servants is retained when a new government takes over. However, it is not hard to see why it involves potential tensions as well as perceived tensions from the point of view of the public and other external observers. In order for the model to work, civil servants need to be individually and collectively resilient to any – actual

[6] Folketinget, 'Året, der gik, i Folketinget: Beretning om folketingsåret 2023–24' (Folketingets Administration, 2024) 34–36, www.ft.dk/-/media/sites/ft/pdf/publikationer/aarsberetning/aaret-der-gik-i-folketinget-2023_24.pdf.

[7] Medarbejder- og Kompetencestyrelsen, 'Code VII: Seven Key Duties' (Ministry of Finance, 2015). An official English translation is available at https://medst.dk/media/ut1ctzqn/kodex_vii_english_version.pdf. The Code is not legally binding, but in important respects it reflects underlying legal duties, breaches of which may result in disciplinary (or even criminal) sanctions. The Code is not an exhaustive reflection of all the norms and duties which apply to civil servants.

[8] Prime Minister's Office, 'Rammer for ansættelse af særlige rådgivere' (23 November 2023), https://medst.dk/media/eculw1zy/ansaettelse-af-saerlige-raadgivere_november-2023.pdf.

[9] Code VII (n 7) 10, 52.

or perceived – pressure from the incumbent minister and government to cross the boundaries set out in Code VII in the pursuit of their political agenda.

An important question, therefore, is to what extent the duties described in Code VII – and more generally the legal framework applicable to civil servants – are respected in practice. It is of course difficult to provide an answer with a great degree of certainty, and it would be far beyond the scope of this brief piece to delve into the vast literature on the subject.

In broader terms, based on the Worldwide Governance Indicators, Denmark is a very high scorer on the rule of law, regulatory quality and government effectiveness.[10] Furthermore, although there have been specific cases of maladministration etc also in recent years – some of which have been considered quite spectacular and controversial – the evidence does not point to a rise in the number of cases subject to commissions of inquiry or similar.[11] A number of studies in recent years have tried to provide an empirical picture of the extent to which the duties laid down in Code VII are upheld in practice. In an overview essay published as part of the so-called Democracy and Power Study[12] the authors provide an overview of a number of recent studies and surveys.[13] Unsurprisingly, it is hard to offer an unambiguous answer. According to a recent study commissioned by the union DJØF,[14] around 40 per cent of participants said that it was challenging (10 per cent) or somewhat challenging (31 per cent) to comply with the duties in Code VII at times when they had to provide assistance and advice to the minister under significant time pressure. The authors note that it is unclear how to interpret these numbers, but that they indicate that compliance with the norms can sometimes be under pressure. Moreover, they note that when the questions concerned specific duties, there seemed to be fewer problems. Furthermore, some studies suggest that civil servants, especially at the lower levels, sometimes find that their political neutrality is under pressure, and that the boundaries of the assistance provided are sometimes challenged. However, other studies suggest that higher-ranking civil servants who are in positions in which they need to be very aware of the risk of

[10] D Kaufmann and A Kraay, 'Worldwide Governance Indicators, 2023 Update' (2023), www.worldbank.org/en/publication/worldwide-governance-indicators, cited in J Grønnegård Christensen, *Embedsfolk* (Djøf Forlag, 2024) 193.

[11] JP Christensen, Ministre og Embedsmænd: Pligter og Ansvar (DJØF Forlag, 2022) 312. Grønnegård Christensen (n 10) 207 agrees that such spectacular cases do not reflect a serious and frequent problem in the day-to-day functioning of the administration.

[12] The study, the Danish title of which is Magtudredningen 2.0, is an update of a similar project conducted two decades earlier (Magtudredningen) which covers a broad range of issues. It is funded by the state budget, but the leader of the project has been appointed on recommendation by the Independent Research Fund Denmark.

[13] N Opstrup et al, 'Kodex VI: Et autoværn eller blot afstribning af kørebanen?' (2024) and the references cited therein, https://ps.au.dk/fileadmin/Statskundskab/Billeder/Forskning/Forskningsprojekter/Magtudredning/Essays/Tema3/Essay_af_Niels_Opstrup__Joergen_Groennega__rd_Christensen__Heidi_Houlberg_Salomonsen___Amalie_Trangbaek__1_.pdf. As part of the Democracy and Power Study, new studies concerning the interaction between the Government and civil servants will be published.

[14] DJØF literally translates to the Danish Association of Lawyers and Economists. It is the union which represents most of the civil servants with a union affiliation.

overstepping the boundaries of political neutrality have a highly developed sense of integrating legitimate political advice with professional advice.

The following two sections illustrate types of constitutional function exercised by civil servants in government departments and, in doing so, these sections aim to give an impression of the way in which the civil service performs its dual roles as 'sherpas' and 'shepherds' within the framework of their duties.

18.4 The Legislative Process: Constraining and Enabling

Under Danish constitutional law, all ordinary legislation must be in accordance with the CA 1953 and unwritten legal norms of a similar rank. From a constitutional point of view, these are the only formal – legal – limits to the powers of the Danish legislature.[15] All MPs must make a solemn declaration of loyalty to the CA 1953,[16] and ministers and civil servants are also under a legal duty to respect the constitution.

This is of course by no means a unique feature of the Danish constitutional system. From the perspective of this chapter, however, it is important to note that certain institutional and structural features mean that the civil service has an important role in this regard. First of all, there is no judicial or other authoritative mechanism for ex ante review of the constitutionality of bills introduced before Parliament.[17] Moreover, the CA 1953 is notoriously difficult to amend, particularly because of the requirement that a constitutional amendment must be approved in a referendum by a majority consisting of at least 40 per cent of the electorate.[18] Finally, ex post constitutional review of legislation, once enacted, may be performed by the ordinary courts, ultimately the Supreme Court. However, even if an applicant with standing brings a challenge to a legislative provision before the courts, Danish courts traditionally exercise judicial restraint vis-a-vis the choices made by Parliament owing to the latter's democratic mandate. Indeed, there is only one case in which Danish courts (the Supreme Court) have outright struck down a legislative provision as contrary to the CA 1953.[19]

[15] In practice, much of what is discussed in the following applies to Denmark's obligations under EU law and international law, in particular core conventions such as the European Convention on Human Rights. Indeed, it may be argued that the de facto limits imposed on the legislature by certain financial, technical or other constraints are equally important in practice. Be that as it may, the point is that constitutional limits merit a special status given their absolute legal nature.

[16] CA 1953, s 32(7).

[17] In practice, the process of ensuring that new policy proposals or initiatives comply with the CA 1953 is often carried out internally between government departments before the policy proposals are published or subject to political negotiations with the parties represented in Parliament. Constitutional advice may also be requested in connection with amendments proposed during the parliamentary process (often at the committee stage) or in a number of other situations, eg when responding to questions put by MPs to a minister.

[18] CA 1953, s 88.

[19] J Peter Christensen, '§ 3' in J Peter Christensen et al, *Grundloven med kommentarer*, 2nd edn (DJØF Forlag, 2025) 75.

Since the Government proposes virtually all bills which end up being passed by Parliament, the main responsibility for assessing the constitutionality of bills rests with civil servants. All government departments are responsible for constitutional questions within their respective remit, but for the purposes of consistency all government departments should consult a specialised division of the Ministry of Justice whenever a constitutional question arises.[20]

Civil servants have to navigate a number of challenges in performing this task. They must serve the minister and the Government, but given that Parliament does not perform its own constitutional review or assessment, civil servants have to be mindful of the fact that they are de facto advising both of the legislative institutions, ie Parliament as well as the Government. However, unlike Parliament, civil servants do not possess their own democratic mandate, nor do they have an indirect source of democratic legitimacy (as do ministers owing to the parliamentary system). Thus, civil servants are under an obligation to advise on the limits set by the constitution, such as civil liberties protected by the CA 1953, without showing undue deference to politicians, while remaining aware that an unnecessarily cautious approach to legal questions which give rise to doubts may place too many restrictions on the will of the majority. While this balancing act is inherent in processes of constitutional assessment or review, it would seem to be particularly acute when placed in the hands of civil servants. Although judges, too, lack a democratic mandate, their position is bolstered by the judiciary's constitutional independence and legitimacy; moreover, the advantage of court cases is that they are decided on the merits of the particular facts of the individual case.

How do civil servants discharge this responsibility in practice? There is not much systematic research into this question. One larger study was published in 2009,[21] and two former permanent secretaries at the Ministry of Justice have reflected on the Ministry's statements on questions of constitutional law in articles published in 1982 and 2007, respectively.[22] The following is largely based on this material and the author's own experience.

A main characteristic of the assessments of constitutional questions given by civil servants is that they are written and presented as advice rather than decisions or judgments, thus signalling that, ultimately, they defer to the legislature and the courts. Their proper role is to present the legal arguments and the most likely conclusion as regards the constitutionality of the bill.[23] The constitutional mandate

[20] This advisory role was established and formalised in 1960; N Madsen, 'Justitsministeriets udtalelser om grundlovsspørgsmål' in M Koktvedgaard (ed), *Festskrift til W.E. von Eyben* (Juristforbundets Forlag, 1982) 16. Even expert commissions commonly request from the Ministry of Justice a statement or memorandum on any constitutional issues considered in the commission's report. Unlike in the UK, there are no politically appointed law officers in the government or advising the Government.

[21] T Elbæk-Jørgensen, 'Rådgivningen af Folketinget om statsretlige spørgsmål – En undersøgelse af praksis 1998–2006' (October 2009), www.justitsministeriet.dk/sites/default/files/media/Arbejdsomraader/Forskning/Forskningspuljen/2011/2009/Statsretlig_raadgivning.pdf.

[22] Madsen (n 20) 13; M Lunn, 'Justitsministeriets rolle i lovgivningsprocessen' in E Werlauff and S Bønsing (eds), *Festskrift til Claus Haagen Jensen* (Jurist- og Økonomforbundets Forlag, 2007).

[23] Madsen (n 20) 21–22; Lunn (n 22) 318–19.

to legislate is vested in the Government and Parliament, and it is ultimately for these political institutions to decide whether to propose and pass a given bill, and, in turn, it is ultimately for the courts to give an authoritative ruling if a relevant and admissible case is brought.

These features shine through in the way in which the advice is presented. The relevant source material is described in detail, and the conclusions are set out in carefully crafted language. For instance, it will sometimes be concluded that a proposal would 'give rise to weighty/serious questions with respect to the CA',[24] which essentially reads as a strong recommendation (or warning) not to proceed. Previously, in difficult cases without an obvious answer supported by the relevant material, it would regularly be concluded that the civil service was 'more inclined'[25] to support one view rather than the other. In an effort to make the language more accessible to lawmakers, such expressions have gone out of fashion in recent years, but that does not detract from the fact that the civil service's assessments are presented as the view of the ministry, and there are often express qualifications or reservations, eg when there is a lack of authoritative judicial decisions or unambiguous legal source material.[26]

From the perspective of the civil service, an added benefit to this cautious approach is credibility. Credibility is crucial in order to command the respect of ministers and of all or most political parties in Parliament, and a cautious approach to constitutional interpretation also lowers the risk of the courts overturning the civil service's assessment. It is also very rare for the Ministry of Justice to have to change its view on the interpretation of the CA 1953. However, examples can be found, most recently in 2020 when the Ministry of Justice reconsidered its interpretation of CA 1953, section 70. The provision was previously found to contain a prohibition of discrimination on the grounds of ethnicity; however, after having revisited the relevant academic literature and the preparatory works, the ministry concluded that section 70 does not apply to differential treatment on the grounds of ethnicity.[27]

Based on the considerations above, it is not difficult to see why, despite the formalities, civil servants can be perceived as de facto gatekeepers constraining the legislature's freedom to enact legislation. Whatever the motivation – the convincing nature of the advice or the risk involved in going against the advice of civil servants concerning the constitutionality of a bill or an amendment – the

[24] The expression in Danish is 'rejser væsentlige spørgsmål i forhold til grundloven'. As is often the case, the linguistic nuances do not translate fully into another language.

[25] The expression in Danish is 'mest tilbøjelig til'.

[26] Moreover, when the Ministry of Justice advises on principles which are not strictly legal, civil servants take great pains to stress that these principles do not constitute legal limits in a strict sense; Madsen (n 20) 23; Lunn (n 22) 322. Such non-binding principles can to some extent be compared to constitutional conventions.

[27] Ministry of Justice, 'Notits om beslutningsforslag nr. B 32 om at afskære statsstøtte til visse friskoler, hvor over halvdelen af eleverne har udenlandsk baggrund' (16 June 2020). Given that the ECHR contains a prohibition of discrimination on the grounds of ethnicity, the practical implications of the revised interpretation are limited, and none of the relevant political initiatives have been implemented.

reality is that the legislature chooses to defer to the civil service's advice. Given that questions of constitutional law are not always clear-cut, this means that much depends on the choices made by the civil service in analysing and interpreting the legal source material, the margin chosen in the interpretation and the language in which the conclusions are presented.

However, it is for precisely the same reason that civil servants can also play an important enabling role. This is probably one of the most important developments throughout the years, as evidenced if one compares the previously mentioned articles written by two former permanent secretaries at the Ministry of Justice. Perhaps the most important difference between them is the emphasis placed in the most recent contribution (from 2007) on civil servants as creative and constructive actors; not merely as 'naysayers' poised to shoot down proposals. If civil servants find it questionable whether a proposal is in conformity with the CA 1953, they should engage actively in considering whether it can be reshaped in a legally acceptable manner.[28] Such adjustments typically happen as part of the internal government processes, but there are a number of publicly available examples of this sort of constructive and open advice. For instance, in 2023 the Ministry of Justice answered a question from Parliament regarding the constitutionality of a prohibition of Muslim headscarves in schools. While the Ministry concluded that such a prohibition would be incompatible with the CA 1953, it went on to state that it would be possible within the framework of the CA 1953 to consider a general prohibition of visible symbols of political, ideological or religious views.[29]

Some will undoubtedly argue that this enabling and constructive role illustrates the pertinence of the debate, previously alluded to, concerning the 'politicisation' of the civil service. Needless to say, civil servants are required to be acutely aware of their responsibility not to compromise with their integrity and professional legal approach when engaging in such constructive advice. However, there is nothing constitutionally improper about civil servants trying to serve their political masters with finding workable solutions to the problems which politicians wish to solve – provided, of course, that they scrutinise alternative proposals rigorously. In fact, it can be argued that the practice of searching for feasible and constitutional alternatives may reduce the pressure on civil servants when their task is not merely confined to a binary assessment of the constitutionality of one particular proposal.

The role of the Ministry of Justice in advising other government departments and Parliament on constitutional questions has evolved over the decades, and while there is no constitutional requirement that the Ministry of Justice possesses

[28] Lunn (n 22) 316–18.

[29] Ministry of Justice, 'Answer to question no 3 relating to proposal no B8' (13 April 2023), www.ft.dk/samling/20222/beslutningsforslag/b8/spm/3/svar/1947695/2689951/index.htm. A similar example is cited by M Hansen Jensen, '§ 70' in Christensen et al (n 19) 475, 485, concerning a proposal to criminalise the use of burqas in the public space (which, according to the Ministry of Justice in 2009, gave rise to 'serious doubts' as to the compatibility with CA 1953, s 70) as opposed to a general prohibition of full face-covering in the public space (which was introduced in 2018 after the Ministry of Justice had concluded that such a prohibition would not give rise to questions with respect to s 70).

this role, it has become firmly established. However, it has not been unchallenged. Since the early 1990s there have been several suggestions – typically by opposition MPs – that the de facto monopoly on constitutional advice should be broken, eg by establishing a constitutional council under the auspices of Parliament in order to provide external advice or second opinions with complete independence from the Government.[30] So far, the political appetite for such fundamental changes has not been sufficient. Whether it will remain so is probably to a large extent dependent on the ability of the civil servants at the Ministry of Justice to continue to navigate the many demands involved in providing high-quality and credible advice.

18.5 The Exercise of Executive Powers: Between Law and Political Intentions

The functions performed by civil servants with respect to the exercise of executive powers are often constitutional in a less direct sense than the situations described in the previous section. Thus, the relevant legal framework and limits are usually to be found in ordinary legislation rather than the CA 1953. However, in a more abstract sense, the responsibilities incumbent on the civil service with respect to executive actions are undoubtedly of constitutional significance. In particular, civil servants must ensure the legality of executive actions which, ultimately, underpins the rule of law and protects from abuse of powers.

Compared to the legislative context discussed above, there are differences with respect to the institutional backdrop, affecting the circumstances in which civil servants perform their duties. One important difference is the fact that the courts do not exercise the same kind of judicial restraint. Furthermore, the legislative process involves both the Government and Parliament whereas executive decision processes are typically internal to the ministry in question. As a result, civil servants who identify limitations to executive action may be perceived as more directly responsible for any obstacles identified to the preferred course of action. Finally, executive action is often of direct consequence to the rights of individuals; indeed, this has typically been the case in the administrative 'scandals' which have been under scrutiny in recent years, and in the two most recent impeachment cases (decided in 1995 and 2021, respectively).

It is important to stress that a huge number of executive decisions are taken in the day-to-day work of government departments, and rarely do they give rise to the kinds of dilemmas described below. Nevertheless, history shows that there is a small proportion of hard cases which typically involve, on the one hand, a minister's intention to introduce or change a certain policy by executive action,

[30] See eg the following proposals (none of which were adopted by the Danish Parliament): Proposal no B 49 (28 January 1992), proposal no B 7 (20 October 1992) and proposal no B 69 (10 January 2020). Moreover, the question was debated in the Danish Parliament in 2021; see interpellation no F 24 (26 November 2020, debated on 12 January 2021).

and, on the other hand, difficult legal questions concerning the boundaries set by legislation or international conventions.

Evidently, a civil servant faced with a request to take an illegal course of action must refuse to do so. However, in those very difficult cases where there is no clear-cut legal solution, and in which there is an absence of authoritative sources such as judgments, etc, there is a genuine dilemma between the duty to comply with the instructions of superiors and the duty to observe the principle of legality.[31] Code VII contains directions regarding the correct course of action in such situations. Under the duty of responsibility of management:

> Civil servants must draw the attention of their superiors to any doubt about the lawfulness of an action or to doubt about professional issues or compliance with the duty of truthfulness in order that the superior may decide on the matter. In case of disagreement, a civil servant must as a general rule comply with his/her superior's decision.

Essentially, this expresses the so-called duty to warn. The Code continues with a description of the so-called duty to refuse:

> Civil servants must refuse to comply provided it is clear that a manager issues directions to carry out unlawful actions or to violate the duty of truthfulness. If the manager insists that his/her directions be complied with, the civil servant must inform the manager's immediate superior of the matter and at the same time inform the manager of this.[32]

It is very difficult to examine empirically how often such hard cases arise and in what proportion of them civil servants do not succeed in ensuring that the executive action in question remains within the boundaries of the law. In the experience of the present author, in the normal and well-functioning relationship between civil servants and the minister, the advice of civil servants is accepted, including when the advice is not to proceed with a given course of action. In particular, the fact that civil servants normally endeavour to point to possible alternatives (as discussed in the previous section) probably contributes to a recognition that civil servants are not simply risk-averse actors resistant to change, but genuinely interested in working constructively with the political intentions of the minister within the limits of the law.

Nevertheless, a number of commissions of inquiry or other special forms of inquiries over the years have shed light on cases in which civil servants and/or ministers have not lived up to their responsibilities. Space does not permit a

[31] In the real world, the problem will rarely present itself quite so obviously. At least initially, the situation typically arises after the minister has stated their intended course of action with a view to receiving the advice of the civil service. If the (preliminary) legal advice suggests that there are legal obstacles or caveats, discussions will typically follow in order to reach a result which does not give rise to legal concerns.

[32] Code VII (n 7) 41. In addition, it is generally accepted that permanent secretaries who are confronted with a minister who does not heed a warning must inform the permanent secretary at the Prime Minister's Office.

discussion of all of them,[33] and for the present purposes it is sufficient to illustrate the interplay between civil servants and the minister by referring to the example of the case which resulted in the most recent Court of Impeachment judgment from December 2021.

In very brief terms, the facts are as follows: In early 2016, there were media reports that Danish asylum centres were housing married or unmarried couples, one of whom was a minor woman (girl) and the other a man above the age of majority. The then Minister of Immigration, who was the minister responsible for the asylum system, wanted the Danish Immigration Service (an agency subordinate to the Ministry of Immigration) to introduce more restrictive accommodation arrangements, preferably an absolute rule that such couples should not be allowed to cohabitate. The minister was advised by the civil service that an absolute rule requiring separation, regardless of the individual circumstances of each case, could not be introduced within the relevant legal framework. Nevertheless, in February 2016, on the minister's insistence, the Ministry of Immigration issued a press release stating that such an absolute rule would now apply. The Ministry informed the Immigration Service of the press release, thereby effectively issuing an instruction to implement the rule.

There are many aspects to the case,[34] but for the present purposes it serves to illustrate an important element of the interaction and dynamics between the minister and civil servants, ie the significance of the advice given by the civil service and the potential of such advice to constrain and enable the minister to make specific choices.

The Court of Impeachment,[35] by 25 votes to one, found that the Minister of Immigration at the time was guilty of a violation of the Ministerial Responsibility Act 1964.[36] The minister's responsibility related to the fact that the Immigration Service had initiated and maintained an administration of the accommodation arrangements in the asylum system which resulted in the separation of a number of married or cohabiting couples, one of whom was aged 15–17, in violation of the right to respect for family life enshrined in Article 8 of the European Convention on Human Rights (ECHR) and general rules of administrative law. The Court of Impeachment majority referred to the advice given by the civil service in several respects. In particular, when assessing the *mens rea* of the former minister, the majority emphasised that the minister had been warned on several occasions that the relevant legal framework would not allow for an absolute rule requiring the separation of couples without a concrete assessment of each individual case. The

[33] Christensen (n 11) provides a thorough discussion and analysis of many of the recent cases. In absolute numbers, Christensen notes that 12 judge-led inquiries (ie not including other types of inquiries) have been initiated between 1999 and December 2021. Since then, one further such inquiry has been set up.

[34] Christensen (n 11) provides a thorough discussion.

[35] Court of Impeachment judgment of 13 December 2021, https://rigsretten.dk/media/of4lp4dn/rigsrettens-dom-af-13-december-2021.pdf.

[36] Act no 117 of 15 April 1964, as amended by Act no 433 of 31 May 2000.

fact that the minister decided, nevertheless, in favour of such an unconditional scheme, resulted, in the words of the Court, in 'short-circuiting' the procedure required by the ECHR and Danish administrative law.

The advice given by civil servants was also emphasised at the sentencing stage by a majority of 15 judges who considered it to be an aggravating circumstance that the minister had acted against the advice. On the other hand, these judges also noted that the civil service had inaccurately given the minister the impression that it would only be disproportionate to separate the couples in very few cases. This would normally constitute a mitigating circumstance for the minister; however, the judges added that the advice should be seen in the light of the pressure which the minister put on the civil service, eg by communicating on social media that she would direct the Immigration Service to put an end to cohabitation between minor girls and adult spouses or partners in asylum centres. Thus, the judges took note of the minister's role in shaping the circumstances in which civil servants gave their advice.

The Court of Impeachment does not have jurisdiction to decide on the responsibility of civil servants; however, commissions of inquiry may assess whether there are grounds for bringing criminal or disciplinary proceedings against civil servants, provided that their terms of reference so provide. The commission of inquiry which had examined the affair prior to Parliament's decision to bring impeachment proceedings was charged with performing such assessments, and the advice offered by civil servants to the minister also formed an important basis of the commission's conclusions. The commission found that the advice given to the minister prior to the press release and the instruction to the Immigration Service had been inadequate, given that the advice had given the minister the impression that the couples could be separated to a wider extent than what was actually possible. However, the commission also found that the civil servants had clearly warned the minister that an absolute scheme would not be legal. In conclusion, the commission did not find a basis for any disciplinary action against civil servants advising the minister prior to the press release and instruction being issued.[37]

On the other hand, with respect to the initial period of time (just over a month) when the new accommodation arrangements were implemented, the commission found that there were sufficient grounds for disciplinary proceedings against one of the civil servants involved in offering the minister legal advice. The commission essentially found that the senior civil servant in question should have continued to press the point after the press release and instruction had been issued. This could have been done by stating that the civil servant in question would not participate in initiating the new accommodation administration, by securing (written) documentation for the advice given, by contacting the Immigration Services directly, by formally involving the Ministry of Justice or by contacting the Prime Minister's Office. Seeing as these avenues were open, but none of them taken, the commission

[37] Instrukskommissionen, Beretning (vol 6, 2021) 3497–98.

concluded that the senior civil servant in question could be subject to disciplinary proceedings.[38]

Each case is unique, but the events briefly summarised above are illustrative of the complexities sometimes involved in the interaction between ministers and civil servants. The responsibility for upholding legality is ultimately a joint endeavour which must be carried out in good faith. Civil servants must advise – and, if need be, warn against a given course of action – and a minister who chooses to disregard the advice assumes the risk of being found responsible. On the other hand, the minister will usually be 'off the hook' if the civil service has not advised against the relevant course of action.[39] However, the latter point comes with the important qualification that civil servants must not be put under undue pressure to provide advice pointing in a particular direction. The enabling effect of advice cannot be obtained by pressure. Yet the civil service is also under an obligation to stand firm against such attempts. Civil servants' duty to uphold legality does not end with advising the minister and leaving the decision on the minister's desk. Even after a decision is made, active steps must be taken to reverse the decision and avoid any illegal administration in practice. In those rare cases in which such conflicts arise, it is evident that there are difficult professional, human and psychological obstacles which contribute to the risk that the system fails.

Accordingly, it is appropriate to end this section by highlighting quite a remarkable passage in the commission of inquiry's report. The commission decided to comment expressly on a statement contained in the explanations offered by the parliamentary committee which, based on the commission's initial findings, had decided to bring the impeachment case mentioned above. The committee had stated that the decision to impeach the minister in this specific instance should not alter the fact that a minister should still be able to question the assessments of the civil service and ask the civil service to consider alternative policy solutions.[40] The commission commented that the factual circumstances as described by the commission indicated that the civil service – even when instructions are clearly in violation of fundamental legal principles – is reluctant to give a clear refusal and instead goes too far in accommodating the minister's decision. Moreover, the commission stressed that, while a minister should evidently have the right to 'challenge' the civil service, it is of equal importance to have a culture which respects the professional expertise of the civil service, and in which it is legitimate for the civil service to point to a legal limitation whenever necessary.[41]

[38] Instrukskommissionen (n 37) 3499–500. The complexity of the assessment is highlighted by the fact that the commission emphasised a number of mitigating factors.

[39] See the analysis by Christensen (n 11) 102–03, 110–16, 291–94, which is based on a large number of cases.

[40] Standing Orders Committee report of 27 January 2021, Folketingstidende 2020–21, tillæg A, B 134 som fremsat.

[41] Instrukskommissionen (n 37) 3494; Christensen (n 11) 294–95.

18.6 Concluding Remarks

The Danish civil service is almost completely absent from the written constitution. In formal terms, this reflects the view of civil servants as mere extensions of ministers. This perception does not do justice to the importance of the functions which civil servants exercise – and are expected to exercise – in a complex society where there are significant demands on the state to develop and execute a wide range of policies and initiatives. As illustrated above, the Danish civil service is vital to the ability of both the legislature and the Executive to respond to these demands.

The conclusion would hold true with respect to the civil service's expertise in a range of fields, but the focus on constitutional questions has thrown into sharp relief the duality of civil servants' role as both 'sherpas' and 'shepherds', and of the enabling and constraining potential of their advice. It follows naturally from this observation that the way in which civil servants perform their role and navigate the necessary balancing acts is a legitimate subject of academic and public debate and scrutiny. In our view – which seems to find support in a number of the sources cited – the general picture is that the civil service is an important source of stability and that civil servants manage to provide efficiency and delivery while respecting the duties of legality and impartiality. In the vast majority of instances, the roles of 'sherpa' and 'shepherd' are not opposed to each other, and when a potential conflict arises, a solution is found within the boundaries of the law. There are occasional examples of problematic cases or even administrative 'scandals', but they are dealt with efficiently and may also serve to discourage others from similar behaviour.

Nevertheless, it must also be acknowledged that there are critical voices calling for adjustments or reforms, typically with a view to bolstering the legal and other professional elements of civil servants' roles – strengthening the shepherd's crook while relieving some of the sherpa's load.[42] Whatever constitutional policymakers choose to make of such suggestions to reshape the role of the civil service, civil servants will remain indispensable actors on the constitutional stage.

[42] See eg the discussion in Grønnegård Christensen (n 10) who takes a nuanced approach.

BIBLIOGRAPHY

Albert, R, 'The Difficulty of Constitutional Amendment in Canada' (2015) 53 *Alberta Law Review* 85.

– 'The Conventions of Constitutional Amendment in Canada' (2016) 53 *Osgoode Hall Law Journal* 399.

– 'The Theory and Doctrine of Unconstitutional Constitutional Amendment in Canada' (2016) 41 *Queen's Law Journal* 143.

– *Constitutional Amendments: Making, Breaking, and Changing Constitutions* (Oxford University Press, 2019).

– 'The World's Most Difficult Constitution to Amend?' (Social Science Research Network, 2022), https://papers.ssrn.com/abstract=4323143.

– 'Decolonial Constitutionalism' (2025) 25 *Chicago Journal of International Law* 341.

Allan, TRS, 'Questions of Legality and Legitimacy: Form and Substance in British Constitutionalism' (2011) 9 *International Journal of Constitutional Law* 155.

Allen, B and Routley, S, 'Regional Mayors' (Institute for Government, 4 September 2024), www.instituteforgovernment.org.uk/explainer/regional-mayors-devolution.

Appiah, KA, *As If, Idealisation and Ideas* (Harvard University Press, 2017).

Appleby, G, *The Role of the Solicitor-General. Negotiating Law, Politics and the Public Interest* (Hart Publishing, 2018).

Atrey, S, 'A Common Law Principle of Racial Equality?' [2025] 2026 *Public Law* 215.

BBC, 'BBC - Press Office - Newsnight Poll on the Union', www.bbc.com/pressoffice/pressreleases/stories/2007/01_january/16/union.shtml.

BBC News, 'George Osborne: Greater Manchester to Have Elected Mayor' (3 November 2014), www.bbc.com/news/uk-england-manchester-29876939.

– 'Why Did the North East Shun Regional Assembly?' (8 November 2004), http://news.bbc.co.uk/1/hi/talking_point/3984991.stm.

Baksi, C, 'Legal Hackette Lunches with Bob Neill' (Legal Hackette, 16 November 2016), https://legalhackette.com/2016/11/16/legal-hackette-lunches-with-bob-neill.

Bagehot, W, *The English Constitution* (Chapman and Hall, 1867).

Barber, N, Hickman, T and King, J, 'Pulling the Article 50 "Trigger": Parliament's Indispensable Role' (UK Constitutional Law Association, 27 June 2016).

Barnett, A, 'Sleaze, scandal and the man in the white suit' *The Guardian* (16 May 2004).

Bingham (Lord Bingham of Cornhill), 'The Rule of Law', Sixth Sir David Williams Lecture Centre for Public Law (16 November 2006).

Bingham, T, *The Rule of Law* (Penguin Books, 2011).

Blackburn, R, 'Enacting a Written Constitution for the United Kingdom' (2015) 36 *Statute Law Reform* 1.

Blackstone, W, *Commentaries on the Law of England*, 15th edn (T Cadell and W Davies, 1809).

Blick, A, 'The constitutional consequences of Mr. Johnson' (The Constitution Society, 7 July 2022).

Blick, A and Hennessy, P, 'Brexit and the Melting of the British Constitution' (The Constitution Society (no date).

– 'Good Chaps No More? Safeguarding the Constitution in Stressful Times' (The Constitution Society, 18 November 2019).

Bogdanor, V, *The New British Constitution* (Hart Publishing, 2009).

Bowers, J, *Downward Spiral. Collapsing Public Standards and How to Restore Them* (Manchester University Press, 2024).

Bowman III, FO, 'Presidential Pardons and the Problem of Immunity' (2021) 23 *Legislation and Public Policy* 425.

Bridges, KM, 'Critical Race Theory and the Rule of Law' in J Meierhenrich and M Loughlan (eds), *The Cambridge Companion to the Rule of Law* (Cambridge University Press, 2021).

Briggs (Lord Briggs of Westbourne JSC), 'Justice Annual Conference - 25 years of the Human Rights Act. Protecting Human Rights: The Common Law As the Starting Point' (10 November 2025).

Bruno, F, The Salisbury-Addison Convention Paper Five (The Office of the Convenor of the Crossbench Peers, 2024).

Bryan, C, *Code of Conduct: Why We need to Fix Parliament and How to Do It* (Bloomsbury, 2023).

Buchan, B and Hill, L, *An Intellectual History of Political Corruption* (McMillan 2014)

'CCJ "Cass Cass": Ja's Political Chess Game Over Final Appellate Court' (Loop News, 30 October 2023).

CFI Team, 'European Sovereign Debt Crisis' (Corporate Finance Institute, no date), https://corporatefinanceinstitute.com/resources/fixed-income/european-sovereign-debt-crisis.

'CRC Member Barnett Concerned PNP Stance Could Stall Constitutional Reform' (Radio Jamaica News, 19 September 2023).

'CRC Preps Drafting Instructions for Bill to Make Jamaica a Republic' (Loop News, 14 June 2024).

'Cabinet Reviewing Constitutional Reform Committee Report' (Loop News, 13 May 2024).

Casey, C, *Between Law and Politics. The Future of the Law Officers in England & Wales* (Policy Exchange, 2023).

– *Conflicts of Interest and the Law Officers' Convention* (Policy Exchange, 2025).

Cercel, MO, 'The Role of the Euro in Strengthening the European Identity' (2023) 17 *Europolity - Continuity and Change in European Governance* 5.

Christensen, JG, *Embedsfolk* (Djøf Forlag, 2024).

Christensen, JP, *Ministre og Embedsmænd: Pligter og Ansvar* (DJØF Forlag, 2022).

Christensen, JP, Jensen, JA and Jensen, MH, *Grundloven med kommentarer*, 2nd edn (DJØF Forlag, 2025).

Clark, J, 'Jamaica Moves Forward with Amendment to Constitution' *Caribbean National Weekly* (3 June 2024).

Cochrane, L and Belam, M, 'Say it with a brooch: what message was Lady Hale's spider sending?' *The Guardian* (24 September 2019).

Coleman, C, 'Case for a Referendum on the Outcome of EU Withdrawal Negotiations' (House of Lords, 2025), https://lordslibrary.parliament.uk/research-briefings/lln-2018-0107.

Coleman, J, 'Greek Debt Crisis Triggers Memories of World War Two' (BBC News, 9 July 2015), www.bbc.com/news/blogs-eu-33467931.

Commission on Political Power, *Options Paper: The Creation of a Senate*, March 2023

– *Options Paper: Executive Reform*, September 2022

Conaghan, J, *Law and Gender* (Oxford University Press, 2013).

Cranston, R, 'Legal Ethics and Professional Responsibility' in R Cranston (ed), *Legal Ethics and Professional Responsibility* (Clarendon Press, 1995).

– 'The Attorney-General's Panels: The New Regime' (1999) 4 *Judicial Review* 272.

DNC, 'No Evidence Exists to Support Mega Councils, Government Admits | District Councils' Network' (31 January 2025), www.districtcouncils.info/no-evidence-exists-to-support-mega-councils-government-admits.

Darbyshire, P, *Sitting in Judgment: The Working Lives of Judges* (Hart Publishing, 2011).

Davies, C, 'King Charles's coronation invitation confirms use of title of "Queen Camilla"' *The Guardian* (4 April 2023).

Dicey, AV, *Introduction to the Study of the Law of the Constitution*, 8th edn (MacMillan, 1915).

Difford, D, 'Where Do Scotland and Wales Stand on Devolution?' (YouGov UK, 17 September 2024), https://yougov.co.uk/politics/articles/50542-where-do-scotland-and-wales-stand-on-devolution.

Dominiczak, P, Hope, C and McCann, K, 'Judges vs the people: Government ministers resigned to losing appeal against High Court ruling' *The Telegraph* (3 November 2016).

Dyson, M, Lee, J, and Wilson Stark, S (eds), *Fifty Years of the Law Commissions: The Dynamics of Law Reform* (Hart Publishing, 2016).

Edwards J, *The Law Officers of the Crown* (Sweet & Maxwell, 1964)
– *The Attorney General, Politics and the Public Interest* (Sweet & Maxwell, 1984).
Ekins, R and Laws, S, 'The Supreme Court has done lasting damage to our constitution: no principle justifies last week's radical legal intervention in high politics' *Prospect* (4 October 2019), www.prospectmagazine.co.uk/politics/39298/the-supreme-court-has-done-lasting-damage-to-our-constitution.
Elbæk-Jørgensen, T, 'Rådgivningen af Folketinget om statsretlige spørgsmål – En undersøgelse af praksis 1998-2006' (October 2009), www.justitsministeHriet.dk/sites/default/files/media/Arbejdsomraader/Forskning/Forskningspuljen/2011/2009/Statsretlig_raadgivning.pdf.
Elkins, Z and Hudson A, 'The Strange Case of the Package Deal: Amendments and Replacements in Constitutional Reform' in R Albert and R Stacey (eds), *The Limits and Legitimacy of Referendums* (Oxford University Press, 2022).
Elliott, M, 'A 'Principle' of Consistency? The Doctrinal Configuration of the Law of Judicial Review' (2018) 77 *Cambridge Law Journal* 444.
Erskine May, T, *A Treatise Upon the Law, Privileges, Proceedings and Usage of Parliament* (Charles Knight & Co, 1844).
Farley, AP, 'Accumulation' (2005) 11 *Michigan Journal of Race and Law* 51.
Feldman, D, Bailey, D and Norbury, L, *Bennion, Bailey & Norbury on Statutory Interpretation*, 8th edn (LexisNexis, 2020).
Finnis, J, 'The unconstitutionality of the Supreme Court's prorogation judgment' (Policy Exchange, 2019), https://policyexchange.org.uk/wp-content/uploads/2019/10/The-unconstitutionality-of-the-Supreme-Courts-prorogation-judgment.pdf.
Fitzgibbon, J, 'Citizens against Europe? Civil Society and Eurosceptic Protest in Ireland, the United Kingdom and Denmark' (2013) 51 *Journal of Common Market Studies* 105.
Folketinget, 'Året, der gik, i Folketinget: Beretning om folketingsåret 2023-24' (Folketingets Administration, 2024) 34–36, www.ft.dk/-/media/sites/ft/pdf/publikationer/aarsberetning/aaret-der-gik-i-folketinget-2023_24.pdf.
Foran, MP, *Equality Before the Law: Equal Dignity, Wrongful Discrimination, and the Rule of Law* (Hart Publishing, 2023).
Fowler (Lord), 'Report of the Speaker's Committee on the size of the House' *Hansard* Vol 785 (31 October 2017).
Fraser, N and Honneth, A, *Redistribution or Recognition? A Political-Philosophical Exchange* (Verso, 2003).
Fredman, S, *Discrimination Law* (Oxford University Press, 2002).
Gardiner, G and Martin, A (eds), *Law Reform now* (Gollancz, 1963).
Garside, R, 'The End of an Undemocratic Experiment?' (Centre for Crime and Justice Studies, 27 November 2013), www.crimeandjustice.org.uk/end-undemocratic-experiment.
Gavigan, SA, 'Petit Treason in the Eighteenth Century England: Women's Inequality before the law' (1989) 3 *Canadian Journal of Women and the Law* 335.
Gay, O and Leopold, P (eds)., *Conduct Unbecoming: The Regulation of Parliamentary Behaviour* (Politico's, 1994).
Gearty, C, 'In the shallow end: on the UK Supreme Court' (2022) 44 *London Review of Books* (27 January 2022), www.lrb.co.uk/the-paper/v44/n02/conor-gearty/in-the-shallow-end.
– 'Unwelcome Remnant: on the threat to the Human Rights Act' (2025) 47 *London Review of Books* (9 October 2025), www.lrb.co.uk/the-paper/v47/n18/conor-gearty/unwelcome-remnant.
Geddes, M, *Dramas at Westminster: Select Committees and the Quest for Accountability*, (Manchester University Press, 2019).
Gill, M, Bishop, M and Parris, C, 'Parliament and regulators' (Institute for Government, April 2024), www.instituteforgovernment.org.uk/sites/default/files/2024-04/parliament-and-regulators.pdf.
Ginsburg, T et al, 'The Functions of Constitutional Monarchy: Why Kings and Queens Survive in a World of Republics' (2023) Northwestern Public Law Research Paper No 23-29.
Giovannoni, F, 'Amendment Rules in Constitutions' (2003) 115a *Public Choice* 37.
Giscard d'Estaing, V, 'The Convention and the Future of Europe: Issues and Goals' (2003) 1 *International Journal of Constitutional Law* 346.

Gordon, R, *Repairing British Politics: A Blueprint for Constitutional Reform*, 2nd edn (Hart Publishing, 2025).
Gordon, R and Jack, M, *Parliamentary Privilege: Evolution or Codification?* (The Constitution Society, 2013).
Graham L, 'Has the UK Supreme Court Become More Restrained in Public Law Cases?' (2024) 87(5) *Modern Law Review* 1073–1110
Green H, 'Expatriates Lose Supreme Court Bid for Right to Vote in EU Referendum', The University of Aberdeen Blog, 2 June 2016, available at: https://www.abdn.ac.uk/law/blog/expatriates-lose-supreme-court-bid-for-right-to-vote-in-eu-referendum/.
Greene, I, 'Constitutional Amendment in Canada and the United States' in SL Newman (ed), *Constitutional Politics in Canada and the United States* (State University of New York Press, 2004).
Greenslade, R, 'How the press reacted to the article 50 verdict' *The Guardian* (24 January 2017).
Griffin SM, 'Constituent Power and Constitutional Change in American Constitutionalism' in Loughlin and N Walker (eds), *The Paradox of Constitutionalism: Constituent Power and Constitutional Form* (Oxford University Press, 2008), https://doi.org/10.1093/acprof:oso/9780199552207.003.0004.
Groves, M, 'The Changing Role of the Attorney-General' (2024) 52 *Federal Law Review* 131.
Haddon, C, 'The Brexit battle is fundamentally changing the constitution' (Institute for Government, 2 September 2019).
Hale (Baroness), 'Law Maker or Law Reformer: What is a Law Lady for?' (2005) 40 *Irish Jurist* 1.
Hale (Lady), 'The United Kingdom Constitution on the move', The Canadian Institute for Advanced Legal Studies' Cambridge Lecture 2017 (7 July 2017).
Hand, J, 'The Attorney-General, politics and logistics – a fork in the road?' (2022) 42 *Legal Studies* 425.
Hay, D, 'Proper Authority and Criminal Law' in D Hay et al (eds) *Albion's Fatal Tree: Crime and Society in Eighteenth Century England* (Random House, 1975).
Hazell, R and O'Brien, P, 'Meaningful dialogue: judicial engagement with Parliamentary committees at Westminster' [2016] *Public Law* 54.
Hazell, R and Sayers-Carter, C, *Reforming the Prerogative* (UCL, The Constitution Unit, 2022).
Hegel, GWF, *Outlines of The Philosophy of Right*, TM Knox, trans (Oxford University Press, 2008).
Heywood, J, 'Timeless values in an age of change' Civil Service Blog (24 May 2015).
Hine, D and Peele, G, *The Regulation of Standards in British Public Life - Doing the Right Thing?* (Manchester University Press, 2016).
Horder, J, *Misconduct in Public Office: Law and Politics* (Oxford University Press, 2018).
– 'Criminal Law at the Limit: Countering False Claims in Elections and Referendums' (2021) 84 Modern Law Review 429.
House of Lords Select Committee on the Constitution, 'Executive oversight and responsibility for the UK constitution' (HL Paper 72, 28 January 2025).
Institute for Government, 'Nine Things We Learned from the English Devolution White Paper' (17 December 2024), www.instituteforgovernment.org.uk/comment/english-devolution-white-paper.
Instrukskommissionen, *Beretning*, vol 6 (2021).
IPSOS, 'Andy Burnham More Popular in Manchester than Sadiq Khan in London or Andy Street in West Midlands' (30 April 2024), www.ipsos.com/en-uk/andy-burnham-more-popular-in-manchester-than-sadiq-khan-in-london-or-andy-street-in-west-midlands.
Iversen, T and Soskice, D, *Democracy and Prosperity: Reinventing Capitalism through a Turbulent Century* (Princeton University Press, 2019), www.jstor.org/stable/j.ctv4g1r3n.
James L, 'The Johnson legacy: the UK constitution' (UK in a Changing Europe, 1 September 2022).
Jolly, M, 'A Demos for the European Union?' (2005) 25 *Politics* 12.
Jones, BC, 'Our Forgotten Constitutional Guardians: Preserving Respect for the Law' (2021) 42 *Statute Law Review* 1.
– 'Judicial review and embarrassment' [2022] *Public Law* 179.
Jones, J, 'The Role of the Treasury Solicitor' (2024) 29 *Judicial Review* 75.
Jowell, J, 'Is Equality a Constitutional Principle?' (1994) 47 ***Current Legal Problems*** 1.

Kaufmann, D and Kraay, A, 'Worldwide Governance Indicators, 2023 Update' (2023), www.worldbank.org/en/publication/worldwide-governance-indicators.
Kavanagh, A, The Collaborative Constitution (Cambridge University Press, 2023).
de Kay Wilson, C, 'Marty Lipton's Poison Pill' (1984) 3 *International Financial Law Review* 10.
Kelly, R, 'English Votes for English Laws' (House of Commons Library, 2025), https://commonslibrary.parliament.uk/research-briefings/cbp-7339.
Kenealy, D and MacLennan, S, 'Legal Professional Privilege of Advice of the Attorney General' (2019) 24 *Coventry Law Journal* 81.
Khushal Murkens, JE, 'A written constitution: a case not made' (2021) 41 *Oxford Journal of Legal Studies* 965.
Kolskey, E, *Colonial Justice in British India: White Violence and the Rule of Law* (Cambridge University Press, 2010).
Kyriakides, KA, 'The Advisory Functions of the Attorney-General' (2003) 1 *Hertfordshire Law Journal* 73.
Labour, 'A New Britain: Renewing our Democracy and Rebuilding our Economy: Report of the Commission on the UK's Future' (5 December 2022).
Law Commission, 'Protocol Rhwng Gweinidogion Cymru a Comisiwn y Gfraith/Protocol between the Welsh Ministers and the Law Commission' (10 July 2015).
Lazarus, L, 'Constitutional Scholars as Constitutional Actors' (2020) 48 *Federal Law Review* 483.
Lee, J, '"Not Time to Make a Change?" Reviewing the Rhetoric of Law Reform' (2023) 76 *Current Legal Problems* 129.
Lepore, J, 'The United States' Unamendable Constitution' *The New Yorker* (26 October 2022), www.newyorker.com/culture/annals-of-inquiry/the-united-states-unamendable-constitution.
Lester, A and Bindman, G, *Race and Law* (Penguin Books, 1972).
Levitsky, S and Ziblatt, D, *How Democracies Die: What History Reveals about Our Future* (Penguin, 2019), www.penguin.co.uk/books/306746/how-democracies-die-by-ziblatt-steven-levitsky-and-daniel/9780241381359.
Lewis, PSC and Mulcahy, L, 'Government lawyers: Technicians, Policy Shapers and Organisational Brakes' (2021) 28 *International Journal of the Legal Profession* 23.
Lichtenstein, D and Eilders, C, 'Lost in Uncertainty: How the Euro Crisis Affected European Identity Constructions in National Media Discourses' (2019) 81 *International Communication Gazette* 602.
Linton, L, 'Legislation Facilitating Jamaica's Transition to a Republic Tabled in the Lower House' (Jamaica Information Service, 11 December 2024).
Lords Select Committee, 'House of Lords - The Union and Devolution - Select Committee on the Constitution' (House of Lords, 2016) HL Paper 149, https://publications.parliament.uk/pa/ld201516/ldselect/ldconst/149/14911.htm.
Lunn M, 'Justitsministeriets rolle i lovgivningsprocessen' in E Werlauff and S Bønsing (eds), *Festskrift til Claus Haagen Jensen* (Jurist- og Økonomforbundets Forlag, 2007).
MacKinnon, CA, *Toward a Feminist Theory of the State* (Harvard University Press, 1989).
– *Are Women Human?* (Harvard University Press, 2007).
McCormick, C, *The Constitutional Legitimacy of Law Officers in the United Kingdom* (Hart Publishing, 2022).
McCormick C, and Cowie, G, *Law Officers: A Constitutional and Functional Overview* (House of Commons Library, 14 February 2025).
McHarg, A, 'Reforming the United Kingdom constitution: Law, convention, soft law' (2008) 71 *Modern Law Review* 853.
McKenzie V, 'Constitutional Reform Committee Recommendations Tabled in Parliament' *Our Today* (22 May 2024).
Machin, R, 'UK Local Government Experience of COVID-19 Lockdown: Local Responses to Global Challenges' (2023) 38 *Local Economy* 80.
MacKinnon, C, *Women's Lives, Men's Laws* (The Belknap Press. 2007).
Madison, J and Hamilton, A, 'The Federalist No. 51', http://founders.archives.gov/documents/Hamilton/01-04-02-0199.

– 'The Federalist No. 62', https://founders.archives.gov/documents/Hamilton/01-04-02-0212.
Madsen, N, 'Justitsministeriets udtalelser om grundlovsspørgsmål' in M Koktvedgaard (ed), *Festskrift til W.E. von Eyben* (Juristforbundets Forlag, 1982).
'Malahoo Forte Insists Privy Council Issue will be in Second Phase of Reform' *Jamaica Observer* (22 September 2023).
Mason, R, 'Boris Johnson Fails in Third Attempt to Call Early General Election' *The Guardian* (28 October 2019), www.theguardian.com/politics/2019/oct/28/boris-johnson-third-attempt-general-election-fails.
Medarbejder- og Kompetencestyrelsen, 'Code VII: Seven Key Duties' (Ministry of Finance, 2015), https://medst.dk/media/ut1ctzqn/kodex_vii_english_version.pdf.
Ministry of Justice, 'Framework Document. Ministry of Justice and the Law Commission for England and Wales' (July 2015).
Mills, CW, *Black Rights/White Wrongs, The Critique of Racial Liberalism* (Oxford University Press, 2017).
Mitchell, R and Stockdale, M, 'A Privileged and Conventional Relationship: Legal Professional Privilege and the Law Officers' Convention' (2023) 87 *Modern Law Review* 111.
Monaghan, C, 'Muddling-Through Constitutionalism: The Importance of the Relationship Between the Monarch and the Prime Minister' in M De Visser et al (eds), *European Yearbook of Constitutional Law 2024: Varieties of Constitutionalism* (Springer, 2025).
Monaghan, K, *Monaghan on Equality Law*, 2nd edn (Oxford University Press, 2013).
Morris (Lord), *Fifty Years of Politics and Law* (University of Wales Press, 2011).
Munro, VE, 'Feminist Critiques of the Rule of Law' in J Meierhenrich and M Loughlan (eds), *The Cambridge Companion to the Rule of Law* (Cambridge University Press, 2021).
Murphy, J, 'Up and Running—CRC Reaches Accord on Removing Monarchy; 15th Member Added' *Jamaica Gleaner* (15 April 2023).
– 'Cabinet Approves Drafting Instructions for Transitional Bill' (Jamaica Information Service, (23 May 2024).
– 'Senate Passes Bill for Constitutional Amendment to Formulate New Words of Enactment' (Jamaica Information Service, 20 July 2024).
NationCymru, '"Labour Should Appeal to English Identifiers" as Poll Shows 62% Would Vote for English Parliament' (1 October 2021), https://nation.cymru/news/labour-should-appeal-to-english-identifiers-as-poll-shows-62-would-vote-for-english-parliament.
Neuberger (Lord), 'UK Supreme Court decisions on private and commercial law: The role of public policy and public interest', Centre for Commercial Law Studies Conference 2015 (4 December 2015).
Newman, J, 'English Councils and Planning Set to Be Transformed under Ambitious Devolution Plan – an Expert Explains' *The Conversation* (17 December 2024), http://theconversation.com/english-councils-and-planning-set-to-be-transformed-under-ambitious-devolution-plan-an-expert-explains-246163.
Nixon, H and Shoback, PC, 'The Reasonable Pill' (1989) 1 *DePaul Business Law Journal* 1.
Norton, P, 'The Fixed-term Parliaments Act and Votes of Confidence' (2016) 69 *Parliamentary Affairs* 3.
Nurse, A, 'Andy Burnham's Standoff with London Was Always about More than Just Lockdown Money - University of Liverpool News' (23 October 2020), news.liverpool.ac.uk/2020/10/23/andy-burnhams-standoff-with-london-was-always-about-more-than-just-lockdown-money.
Nussbaum, M, *Frontiers of Justice, Disability, Nationality and Species Membership* (Belknap, 2006).
O'Brien, D, 'Jamaica's Long and Winding Road to Becoming a Republic' ConstitutionNet (30 June 2022).
O'Brien, P, 'Changes to judicial appointments in the Crime and Courts Act 2013' [2014] *Public Law* 179.
Office for Official Publications of the European Communities, 'Laeken Declaration on the Future of the European Union' (15 December 2001), www.cvce.eu/en/obj/laeken_declaration_on_the_future_of_the_european_union_15_december_2001-en-a76801d5-4bf0-4483-9000-e6df94b07a55.html.
Okin, S, *Justice, Gender, and the Family* (Basic Books, 1989).

Oliver, D, 'The Judge over your Shoulder' (1989) 42 *Parliamentary Affairs* 302.
– 'Constitutional Guardians: The House of Lords' (The Constitution Society, 2015).
'Opposition Members Boycott Meeting of Constitutional Reform Committee' (Loop News, 23 January 2025).
Opstrup, N, Christensen, JG, Salomonsen, HH and Trangbæk, A, 'Kodex VI: Et autoværn eller blot afstribning af kørebanen?' (2024), https://ps.au.dk/fileadmin/Statskundskab/Billeder/Forskning/Forskningsprojekter/Magtudredning/Essays/Tema3/Essay_af_Niels_Opstrup__Joergen_Groennega__rd_Christensen__Heidi_Houlberg_Salomonsen___Amalie_Trangbaek__1_.pdf.
'PNP Will Not Support Removal of King Charles as Head of State Without Jamaica also Severing Ties from the Privy Council – Golding' *Jamaica Observer* (17 September 2023).
Paine, T, *The Rights of Man, The Writings of Thomas Paine*, Vol 2 (1779–92).
Paschold, J and Sparacino, A, 'The Pace of Trump's Executive Orders during His First 100 Days Is a Significant Departure from His Recent Predecessors' (London School of Economics, 13 May 2025), blogs.lse.ac.uk/usappblog/2025/05/13/the-pace-of-trumps-executive-orders-during-his-first-100-days-is-a-significant-departure-from-his-recent-predecessors.
Paterson, A, 'Creating a group oriented Supreme Court – Lord Neuberger's legacy' (2021) 28 *International Journal of the Legal Profession* 107.
Paun, A et al, 'Mayor of Greater Manchester' (Institute for Government, 4 May 2024), www.instituteforgovernment.org.uk/explainer/mayor-greater-manchester.
Payne, A, 'Trump Is at the Peak of His Power—But It Won't Last' (City St George's University of London, 13 February 2025), www.citystgeorges.ac.uk/news-and-events/events/2024/october/panel-discussion-series-american-election-2024/trump-is-at-the-peak-of-his-powerbut-it-wont-last.
Pearson, G, 'Reviews: Equality. Keith Joseph and Jonathan Sumption. London: John Murray, 1979, pp. 130, £4.95.' (1981) 1 *Critical Social Policy* 118.
Pells, R, 'Daily Mail's "Enemies of the People" front page receives more than 1,000 complaints to IPSO' *Independent* (10 November 2016).
Pengelly, M, 'Erwin Chemerinsky on the Need for a New US Constitution: "Our Democracy Is at Grave Risk"' *The Guardian* (1 September 2024), www.theguardian.com/books/article/2024/sep/01/erwin-chemerinsky-no-democracy-lasts-forever.
Perry, A and Tucker, A, 'Top-Down Constitutional Conventions' (2018) 81 *Modern Law Review* 765.
Polyviou, PG, *The Equal Protection of Laws* (Duckworth, 1980).
Powell, L, '*Carolene Products* Revisited' (1982) 82(6) *Columbia Law Review* 1087.
Prime Minister's Office, 'Rammer for ansættelse af særlige rådgivere' (23 November 2023), https://medst.dk/media/eculw1zy/ansaettelse-af-saerlige-raadgivere_november-2023.pdf.
Public Administration and Constitutional Affairs Committee, 'The Fixed-Term Parliaments Act 2011 (House of Commons, 2020), https://publications.parliament.uk/pa/cm5801/cmselect/cmpubadm/167/16702.htm.
Rawls, J, *A Theory of Justice* (Harvard University Press, 1999).
– *Justice as Fairness: A restatement* (ed E Kelley) (Harvard University Press, 2011).
Raz, J, *The Authority of Law* (Oxford University Press, 1979).
Reed (Lord), 'Trust in the courts in an age of populism' The Peter Taylor Memorial Address 2025 (delivered at Inner Temple on 12 June 2025), https://supremecourt.uk/uploads/speech_lord_reed_13062025_88f834d8f5.pdf.
Report of the Constitutional Reform Committee on the Transition to the Republic of Jamaica and Other Matters (May 2024).
Reynolds, S, 'The high-profile private individual as constitutional actor' (2025) 36 *King's Law Journal* 104.
Ridley, FF, 'There is no British Constitution: A Dangerous Case of the Emperor's Clothes' (1988) 41 *Parliamentary Affairs* 340
Rozenberg, J, 'Judges need help to counter the dark arts' *The Law Society Gazette* (9 September 2025).
Ruback, RS, 'An Overview of Takeover Defenses' in AJ Auerbach (ed), *Mergers and Acquisitions* (University of Chicago Press, 1987).

Russell, PH, 'The End of Mega Constitutional Politics in Canada?' (1993) 26 *Political Science & Politics* 33.
– *Constitutional Odyssey: Can Canadians Become a Sovereign People?*, 3rd edn (University of Toronto Press, 2004).
Russell, M, 'A Stronger Second Chamber; Assessing the Impact of House of Lords Reform in 1999 and the Lessons for Bicameralism' (2010) 58 *Political Studies* 866.
– *The Contemporary House of Lords* (Oxford University Press, 2013).
– 'House of Lords reform: navigating the obstacles' (Institute for Government, 2023).
Sampson, A, 'Why everyone is talking about Baroness Hale's bejewelled giant spider brooch' *Tatler* (24 September 2019).
Sandford, M, 'Directly-Elected Mayors' (House of Commons Library, 2025), https://commonslibrary.parliament.uk/research-briefings/sn05000.
Sandford, M and Dempsey, N, 'Metro-Mayors and Devolution Deals' (House of Commons Library, 2017), https://commonslibrary.parliament.uk/metro-mayors-and-devolution-deals.
Seddon, P, 'Calling us the Blob is insulting, says top civil servant' BBC News (12 July 2023).
Seymour, D, 'Whitehall, Transparency, and the Law' in D Feldman (ed), *Law in Politics, Politics in Law* (Hart Publishing, 2013).
Sharma, K, 'The Rule of Law and Racial Difference in the British Empire' in S Wheatle and E O'Loughlin (eds), *Diverse Voices in Public Law* (Bristol University Press, 2023).
Shawcross, H, 'The Office of the Attorney-General' (1953) 7 *Parliamentary Affairs* 380.
Shelchuk, T, 'The Problem of "Democratic Deficit" in the European Union' [2019] Economics. Finances. Law 11
Skovgaard-Petersen, H, 'Impeachment in Denmark: Law and Practice' in C et al (eds), *Impeachment in a Global Context: Law, Politics and Comparative Practice* (Routledge, 2024).
Smith, A, 'New Ministers and State Minister Sworn In' (Jamaica Information Service, 11 January 2022).
Stuart, G, 'The Making of Europe's Constitution | Fabian Society' (Fabian Society, 1 December 2003), https://fabians.org.uk/publication/the-making-of-europes-constitution.
Sumption, J, 'On the court' (2022) 44 *London Review of Books* (10 February 2022), www.lrb.co.uk/the-paper/v44/n03/letters.
– *The Challenges of Democracy and the Rule of Law* (Profile Books, 2025).
Sunkin, M, 'Crown Immunity from Criminal Liability in English Law' [2003] *Public Law* 716.
The Brown Report, https://labour.org.uk/wp-content/uploads/2022/12/Commission-on-the-UKs-Future.pdf.
The Burns Report, www.parliament.uk/globalassets/documents/lords-committees/size-of-house/size-of-house-report.pdf.
Thimont, JM and Pannell, J, 'Constitutional Guardians' (Bennett Institute for Public Policy and the Institute for Government, November 2022).
Thomas C, *Are Juries Fair?*, Ministry of Justice Research Series 1/10 (February 2010).
– 'The 21st century jury: contempt, bias and the impact of jury service' (2020) *Criminal Law Review* 987.
Tomkins, A, 'The Role of the Courts in the Political Constitution' (2010) 60 *University of Toronto Law Journal* 1.
Toobin, J, 'Our Broken Constitution' *The New Yorker* (1 December 2013), www.newyorker.com/magazine/2013/12/09/our-broken-constitution.
Torrance D, 'The United Kingdom constitution – a mapping exercise' Briefing Paper No CBP 9384 (House of Commons Library, 21 June 2025).
– 'The removal of titles and honours' Research Briefing (The House of Commons Library, 17 November 2025).
'Two Draft Bills Submitted for Making Jamaica a Republic' *Our Today* (26 September 2024).
UK Government, 'Police and Crime Commissioners', www.gov.uk/police-and-crime-commissioners.
– 'The Coalition Documentation' (20 May 2010), www.gov.uk/government/publications/the-coalition-documentation.

– 'English Devolution and Community Empowerment Bill: Guidance' (10 July 2025), www.gov.uk/government/publications/english-devolution-and-community-empowerment-bill-guidance/english-devolution-and-community-empowerment-bill-guidance.
UK Parliament, 'Results of Labour Hereditary Peers By-Election' Press release (27 March 2003), www.parliament.uk/mps-lords-and-offices/offices/lords/house-of-lords-external-communications/hoflpressnotice301003,
Vernon, D, 'From a Queen to a King to What? Belize Stil Waiting in 2024' *Belize Breaking News* (22 April 2024).
Waldron, J, 'Is the rule of law an essentially contested concept (in Florida)? (2002) 21 *Law and Philosophy* 137.
Wallace, E, 'The West Indies Federation: Decline and Fall' (1962) 17 *International Journal* 269.
Walker, P, 'UK Covid Response Was London-Centric, Andy Burnham Tells Inquiry' *The Guardian* (27 November 2023), www.theguardian.com/uk-news/2023/nov/27/uk-covid-response-was-london-centric-andy-burnham-tells-inquiry.
Warner S et al, 'English Devolution and the Covid-19 Pandemic: Governing Dilemmas in the Shadow of the Treasury' (2021) 92 *The Political Quarterly* 321.
Weldon, D, *Two Hundred Years of Muddling Through: The Surprising Story of Britain's Economy from Boom to Bust and Back Again* (Abacus, 2022).
Wellings, B, 'Brexit and English Identity' in P Diamond, P Nedergaard and B Rosamond (eds), *The Routledge Handbook of the Politics of Brexit* (Routledge, 2018), https://research.monash.edu/en/publications/brexit-and-english-identity.
White, H, 'What Boris Johnson taught us about the UK constitution' *Prospect* (17 August 2022).
Williams, G (ed), *The Reform of the Law* (Gollancz, 1951).
Williams, OC, *The Clerical Organisation of the House of Commons 1661-1850* (Clarendon Press, 1954).
Wilson Stark, S, *The work of the British Law Commissions. Law Reform…now?* (Hart Publishing, 2017).
Wood, M, Corbett, J and Flinders, M, 'Just like us: Everyday celebrity politicians and the pursuit of popularity in an age of anti-politics' (2016) 18 *The British Journal of Politics and International Relations* 581.
Woodhouse, D, 'Individual Ministerial Responsibility and a "Dash of Principle"' in D Butler, V Bogdanor and R Summers (eds), *The Law, Politics, and the Constitution: Essays in Honour of Geoffrey Marshall* (Oxford University Press, 1999) 102–30.
Woolf, H, 'Droit Public – English Style' [1995] *Public Law* 57.
Yong, B, *Risk Management Government Lawyers and the Provision of Legal Advice within Whitehall* (Constitution Society & UCL Constitution Unit, 2013).

INDEX

References are to page number.

www.ingramcontent.com/pod-product-compliance
Ingram Content Group UK Ltd.
Pitfield, Milton Keynes, MK11 3LW, UK
UKHW020810260926
475945UK00003B/57

9 781509 988761